Southern Legal Studies

SERIES EDITORS

Paul Finkelman, *Gustavus Adolphus College*
Timothy S. Huebner, *Rhodes College*
Charles Zelden, *Nova Southeastern University*

ADVISORY BOARD

Alfred L. Brophy, *University of North Carolina School of Law*
Lonnie T. Brown Jr., *University of Georgia School of Law*
Laura F. Edwards, *Duke University*
James W. Ely Jr., *Vanderbilt University Law School*
Sally E. Hadden, *Western Michigan University*
Charles F. Hobson, *College of William & Mary*
Steven F. Lawson, Rutgers, *The State University of New Jersey*
Sanford V. Levinson, *University of Texas at Austin, School of Law*
Peter Wallenstein, *Virginia Polytechnic Institute and State University*

A Degraded Caste of Society

A Degraded Caste of Society

UNEQUAL PROTECTION OF THE
LAW AS A BADGE OF SLAVERY

Andrew T. Fede

The University of Georgia Press
ATHENS

Published by the University of Georgia Press
Athens, Georgia 30602
www.ugapress.org
© 2024 by Andrew T. Fede
All rights reserved
Set in 10.25/13.5 Minion Pro by Kaelin Chappell Broaddus

Most University of Georgia Press titles are
available from popular e-book vendors.

Printed digitally

Library of Congress Cataloging-in-Publication Data
Names: Fede, Andrew, author.
Title: A degraded caste of society : unequal protection of the law as a badge of slavery / Andrew T. Fede.
Description: Athens : The University of Georgia Press, 2024. | Series: Southern legal studies | Includes bibliographical references and index.
Identifiers: LCCN 2024003674 | ISBN 9780820366296 (hardback) | ISBN 9780820367118 (epub) | ISBN 9780820367101 (pdf)
Subjects: LCSH: Slavery—Law and legislation—Southern States | Slavery—Law and legislation—United States. | Race discrimination—Law and legislation—Southern States. | Race discrimination—Law and legislation—United States. | African Americans—Civil rights—History. | Equality before the law—United States. | Appellate courts—United States.
Classification: LCC KF4545.S5 F423 2024 | DDC 342.7308/7—dc23/eng/20240129
LC record available at https://lccn.loc.gov/2024003674

CONTENTS

Acknowledgments   ix

Free Black Insolence Timeline   xi

INTRODUCTION   The Enslavement Law Breakout and Slavery's Badges   1

CHAPTER 1   The Antebellum Equal Protection Criminal Justice Road Not Taken   19

CHAPTER 2   Chief Justice Taylor and Unequal Criminal Law Protection for Slaves   39

CHAPTER 3   Ruffin and Gaston Extend Separate and Unequal Protection   62

CHAPTER 4   Justice O'Neall and Unequal Protection for Free Blacks   84

CHAPTER 5   Justice Pearson and Unequal Protection for Free Blacks   113

CHAPTER 6   The Louisiana and Virginia Statutes Criminalizing Insolence   141

CHAPTER 7   The Differing Texas and Georgia Legislative Responses to Insolence   159

CONCLUSION   A Violent Badge of Slavery   174

Notes   187

Index   285

ACKNOWLEDGMENTS

This is the fourth book in my continuing study of the troubling topic of enslavement law in the U.S. South. I began this effort with a paper for a fall 1980 course at Rutgers Law School–Newark on law and social change in U.S. history, which was taught by the late Professor and former Dean James C. N. Paul. With the encouragement of Professor Paul, Professor John Anthony Scott, also at Rutgers, and others, that paper evolved into my first two published articles.[1] I can trace back to this earliest research and analysis my interest in exploring the relevance of the antebellum positive law legitimizing white violence against enslaved and free Blacks to both the continuation of interracial violence after the Civil War and the interpretation and enforcement of the Thirteenth Amendment.

I revisited these questions, so many years later, while completing my most recent book, as foreshadowed in that volume's conclusion.[2] I also was encouraged to further develop my ideas after some found my work to be relevant when they interpreted the Thirteenth Amendment and applied it to twentieth- and twenty-first-century cases of interracial violence.[3]

I thank the series editors, Paul Finkelman, Timothy S. Huebner, and Charles Zelden, and Nathaniel Francis Holly from the University of Georgia Press, for their recommendations and encouragement. I also acknowledge the anonymous readers for their critiques and recommendations. I thank Jeff Strickland for his comments, Joseph Dahm for his editorial assistance, and the Harry A. Sprague Library staff at Montclair State University, where I have been an adjunct professor since 1986. As a practicing lawyer and independent scholar, I continue to benefit from internet sites and search engines, including Google Books, Google Scholar, Ancestry.com, and GenealogyBank.com, which were not available to me when I published my early articles and my first book.

Most important, I remain very thankful that my wife, Daniele Fede, continues to tolerate my books and boxes of documents for each new writing project.

FREE BLACK INSOLENCE TIMELINE

Criminalization of Insolence and the Legitimization of White Violent Responses

YEAR	JURISDICTION	DESCRIPTION
1806	Louisiana	Free Black insolence a crime by statute
1819	Virginia	Free Black insolence a crime by statute
1832	South Carolina	Modified mitigation standards permit white violence in response to insolence in *State v. Harden*
1837	Republic of Texas	Free Black insolence a crime by statute
1850	North Carolina	Modified mitigation standards permit white violence in response to insolence in *State v. Jowers*
1850s	City of Richmond	Ordinances prohibit acts viewed as insolent on sidewalks and in public places
1856	Texas	Modified mitigation standards permit white violence in response to insolence by statute
1860/1863	Georgia	Free Black insolence a crime and citizen's arrest expanded by statute

A Degraded Caste of Society

INTRODUCTION

The Enslavement Law Breakout and Slavery's Badges

Antebellum Equal and Unequal Protection of the Criminal Law

Ahmaud Arbery, a twenty-five-year-old Black man, was jogging on Sunday afternoon, February 23, 2020, in the southern Georgia residential neighborhood known as Satilla Shores when he was "trapped, shot, and killed" by three white men.[1] Located "just outside" Brunswick, "a majority-Black coastal city of about 16,000 people," Satilla Shores was an unincorporated part of the "majority-white" Glynn County, the "home to about 85,000" people. *Time* magazine described Satilla Shores as an "overwhelmingly white enclave" of single-family residences, "where private riverfront docks can be found in the backyards behind what are mostly larger homes."[2] According to the *New York Times*, it was "a mixed bag of blue- and white-collar retirees, young working-class families, lifelong residents and transplants from northern states. Some homes have weedy lawns and old vehicles and old boats in their yards. Some are pristine."[3]

The tragic chain of events began when Gregory McMichael, from his front yard, saw Arbery jogging on Satilla Drive and apparently assumed that Arbery was a suspect in several break-ins that allegedly had occurred in the area. McMichael immediately ran into his house and alerted his son, Travis McMichael. Both men grabbed guns—Gregory a .357 Magnum hand gun and Travis a pump-action shotgun. They then chased after Arbery in Travis's white Ford F-150 pickup truck.[4] A neighbor, William "Roddie" Bryan, promptly joined the pursuit in his vehicle. He was unarmed but recorded some of what occurred in a video.[5]

The chase lasted about four minutes on several of the "looping streets" of

Satilla Shores, until Arbery was cornered by the vehicles.[6] As Gregory McMichael, standing in the truck bed, yelled at Arbery to stop, "a shotgun-wielding" Travis jumped out of the truck and confronted Arbery. "When Arbery struggled to take the gun away, [Travis] shot him," apparently three times. "Arbery took a few final steps to flee his killers, staggered, and fell dying." There was evidence of the pursuers' racial animus; as Travis "stood over Arbery's dying body, he spat out the words, 'fucking nigger.' Arbery's murder is now part of the long, mournful litany of killings of unarmed Black men."[7]

More than two months elapsed without any prosecution, but after the public outcry following the May 5, 2020, disclosure of Bryan's video, all three defendants were arrested and charged with assault and murder. A Georgia state court jury of eleven white people and one Black person, on November 24, 2021, found them all guilty.[8] The McMichaels were sentenced to life in prison without the possibility of parole, and Bryan's sentence was for thirty years.[9] Arbery's mother, Wanda Cooper-Jones, declared, "It's been a long fight. It's been a hard fight. But God is good. He will now rest in peace." Arbery's father, Marcus Arbery added, "We conquered a lynch mob."[10]

These defendants were tried again in U.S. District Court, in February 2022, when another jury found them guilty of attempted kidnapping and interfering with Arbery's civil rights in violation of the federal anti-hate-crimes provisions of the Civil Rights Act of 1968.[11] Judge Lisa Godbey Wood sentenced the McMichaels to life in prison and Bryan to thirty-five years.[12] Judge Wood admonished Travis, stating, "You acted because of the color of Mr. Arbery's skin," and "I know that you received a fair trial, it is the kind of trial that Ahmaud Arbery did not receive before he was shot and killed."[13]

These convictions no doubt evidence progress when compared with the countless cases in which white killers of African Americans escaped justice. Among the most notorious are Roy Bryant and J. W. Milam, who confessed to the 1955 kidnapping and murder of Emmett Till after an all-white jury had acquitted them of murder.[14] Till's mother, Mamie Till-Mobley, never had the opportunity to witness the conviction of those who so brutally murdered her fourteen-year-old son.[15]

Arbery's murder—65 years after Till was killed and 155 years after emancipation—nevertheless exemplifies one of slavery's lingering badges. The district attorney who initially reviewed the case concluded that there was "insufficient probable cause" to arrest the defendants. He found that the defendants' actions were "'perfectly legal' because 'their intent was to stop and hold this criminal suspect until law enforcement arrived.'"[16] Among other things, he asserted that these men's actions were justified by a Georgia citizen's arrest law, which was adopted in 1863 in the state's Criminal Code. Thomas R. R. Cobb, this provision's primary drafter, also wrote the leading U.S. enslavement law treatise. This code's text and legislative history therefore establish one explicit link from antebellum southern law to twenty-first-century crimes such as Arbery's murder.[17] After Arbery's death, Georgia's lawmakers repealed this citizen's arrest law and adopted a hate crimes statute, leaving only South Carolina, Arkansas, and Wyoming as states then without hate crimes laws.[18]

This twenty-first-century legislation evidences a renewed debate concerning the curse of interracial violence in the United States, which was sparked by Arbery's murder and by the police killings later in that year of George Floyd in Minnesota and Breonna Taylor in Kentucky.[19] This book contributes to this debate in two ways: (1) by explaining how both case and statutory law extended state-legitimized violence against enslaved people to free Blacks in the antebellum South and (2) by using this legal history to demonstrate why white violence against Blacks has been a persistent badge of slavery.

Chapters 2 and 3 trace the roots of twenty-first-century racially motivated legitimized violence in the United States to southern colonial and antebellum enslavement law.[20] These chapters focus on North Carolina appellate case law, beginning with Chief Justice John Louis Taylor's 1820 opinion in *State v. Tackett*.[21] That decision, and the cases following it, created rules and doctrines—unknown to the English common law of crimes—subjecting enslaved people to "racially invidious over-enforcement of the criminal law" and "under-enforcement" that "purposefully denie[d] African-American victims of violence" the criminal law's equal protection.[22] Antebellum North Carolina offers a unique legal history laboratory, within which we can study how judges modified well-settled common-law rules and doctrines with little legislative intervention, compared to other enslavement societies.

Chapters 4 and 5 then focus on two relatively obscure appellate court decisions, from North and South Carolina, that applied these enslavement law principles of legal inequality to create a new legal privilege authorizing all whites to violently, but reasonably, respond to what were perceived to be instances of the intolerable insolence of free Blacks. The North Carolina case, *State v. Jowers*, discussed in chapter 5, began when Atlas Jowers confronted Bob Douglass and demanded to know why Douglass had called Jowers a liar.[23] When Douglass replied that he said this because Jowers had in fact told a lie, Jowers struck Douglass "and a fight ensued." Both men were indicted, tried, and convicted for participating in an affray, which is a fight between two or more persons in a public place, causing terror to members of the public.[24]

Jowers's violent behavior was typical of a man in his time and place defending his "honor." Historian John Hope Franklin concluded that antebellum southerners believed that "the concept of honor . . . was something inviolable and precious to the ego, to be protected at every cost."[25] Edward Ayers later asserted that calling a southern man a liar or a coward "was to invite attack." "All knew that the failure to respond to insult marked them as less than real men, branded them, in the most telling epithets of the time, as 'cowards' and 'liars.' A coward tolerated insult[;] a liar attacked honor unfairly."[26]

But perceptions of race added another dimension to this dispute. Douglass was a fifty-five-year-old "free person of color." Jowers was a white farmer, about thirty years of age, who owned one slave.[27]

Jowers appealed his conviction because trial judge William H. Battle instructed the jury to apply the by-then-accepted common-law rule providing that Douglass's "mere words" would not justify an assault or a battery, absent a relationship between parties such as parent and child, master and servant, teacher and student, and jailor and prisoner. Battle also distinguished Douglass's legal status from an enslaved person, when he charged the jury "that, though the Courts have held, that insulting language, used by a slave, may justify a white man in striking him, yet the principle did not apply to the case of a free negro, stricken under similar circumstances, by a white man."[28]

Justice Richmond Mumford Pearson's opinion for North Carolina's Supreme Court reversed Jowers's conviction and applied—by an alleged analogy—the then "settled" enslavement law principle "that insolent language from a slave is equivalent to a blow by a white man, in its legal effect, as an excuse for a battery." According to Pearson, "*The same reasons*, by which a blow from a white man upon a slave, is excusable on account of insolent language, apply to the case of a free negro, who is insolent." He relied on the "maxim of the common law, where there is the same reason there is the same law." Pearson declared, "Unless a white man, to whom insolence is given, has a right to put a stop to it, in an extra judicial way, there is no remedy for it. This would be insufferable."[29]

In the South Carolina case, *State v. Harden*, discussed in Chapter 4, Justice John Belton O'Neall, eighteen years earlier, had endorsed this "extra judicial remedy" while affirming the assault and battery conviction of Charles Harden, a white man who, "on some pretext," severely beat and injured Tom Archer, a free Black man.[30] Although there was no evidence that Archer was insolent, O'Neall's opinion nevertheless included extended dicta authorizing all of his state's white citizens to punish—on the spot—free Blacks who dared to confront whites with "words of impertinence, or insolence." He based this rule on the broader social and cultural principles of white supremacy and Black subordination. "Free negroes belong to a degraded *caste* of society," O'Neall declared, "they are, in no respect, on a perfect equality with the white man. According to their condition, they ought, by law, to be compelled to demean themselves as inferiors, from whom submission and respect, to the whites, in all their intercourse in society, is demanded." O'Neall's only "authority" for this "proposition" was his belief that "it is according to good public policy, and the general conduct of the people of this State towards this class of our population since they first existed among us; and this makes it the common law in relation to them."[31]

Both O'Neall and Pearson borrowed the nebulous concept of insolence from enslavement law to create vague mitigation and justification standards that vested white judges and juries with discretion to decide whether whites improperly inflicted violence on free African Americans. North Carolina justice Frederick Nash's attempt to define insolence, in his 1852 *State v. Bill, a Slave* opinion, was no more enlightening than Supreme Court justice Potter Stewart's often-quoted definition of pornography: "I know it when I see it."[32] The court affirmed a justice of the peace's conviction of an enslaved man named Bill who, it was alleged, "at a late hour of the night" was "discovered concealed under the bed of Thomas Thompson, with an intent to commit some felony or violence." In response to "being so charged, in order to avoid it," Bill "'impudently and insolently' made charges, injurious to the character of a young lady living in the house."[33]

Nash referred to James Emerson Worcester's dictionary, which defined "insolently" "to be any thing said or done rudely, and insolent, its root, to be, rude, saucy, insulting, abusive, offensive."[34] Nash admitted, "What acts in a slave towards a white person will amount to insolence, it is manifestly impossible to define—it may consist of a look, the pointing of a finger, a refusal or neglect to step out of the way when a white person is seen to approach. But each of these acts violates the rules of propriety, and, if tolerated, would destroy that subordination, upon which our system rests." Thus, anticipating Groucho Marx's refrain, "Whatever it is, I am against it," Nash concluded that this indescribable objectionable conduct "must be restrained."[35]

South Carolina Court of Appeals judge David L. Wardlaw's 1847 opinion in *Ex parte Boylston* similarly held that an enslaved man named Jim could be tried on the charge that he directed "insolent language and behavior towards Mrs. Cook."[36] Wardlaw explained, "Insolence is multiform and incapable of definition—so is official misconduct, ungentlemanly deportment, disrespect by a soldier, and every offence which consists of inconsistency between conduct and station." He trusted that his state's judges will "wisely" exercise their "discretion . . . , according to the circumstances of every case: distinguishing, for instance, between a case where a white person has, by familiarity, encouraged insolence, and a case where a rebellious temper has broken forth against one whose conduct as well as station was entitled to respect and submission."[37]

The *Jowers* and *Harden* opinions, and their progeny, when read in their social, political, and economic contexts, therefore evidence the antebellum roots of legitimized interracial violence against free Blacks. They also raise questions about the interpretations of biographers and historians feting Pearson and O'Neall as southern "moderates" or "contrarians." These judges were among their generation's most competent southern jurists, but they applied to free Blacks the logic of oppression that similarly esteemed and "moderate" jurists, including North Carolina's John Louis Taylor and William J. Gaston, had created when enslaved people were crime victims or were accused of committing crimes.[38] These decisions thus confirm the need for further study of the role that moderates played in establishing and perpetuating Jim Crow law—both before and after emancipation.[39]

Chapters 6 and 7 shift the book's focus from case law to statutory law, confirming that southern antebellum whites supported the *Harden* and *Jowers* separate and unequal protection principle. These chapters identify two strategies that were enacted to enforce the principles of white supremacy and Black subordination. The Louisiana Black Code, the Virginia and Georgia criminal codes, and the Richmond city code of ordinances all made free Black insolence a crime to be prosecuted and punished through the courts, and not by individual actors. In contrast, the Texas criminal code, consistent with the *Harden* and *Jowers* opinions, privileged all whites to inflict immediate interracial violence to punish the alleged perpetrators of free Black insolence. These chapters also include contextual sources illustrating these laws' purposes and how "they actually operated out in the world."[40]

This book thus offers a historical analysis of law that, according to Markus Dirk Dubber, explains "the emergence and development of legal practices and their legitimation."[41] Instead of a chronological survey of legal doctrines and social practices, this nonlinear structure demonstrates how enslavement law rules and doctrines began to break out of what I have called the enslavement law box and infect the law that applied to free Blacks. The separate and unequal protection doctrine is a concept that describes how antebellum southern judges and legislators enforced white-supremacist principles and confined free Blacks in what then was labeled a degraded legal caste, whose members had defined unequal rights and duties, even under the criminal law. Explicit white-supremacist attitudes formed a thread running through these judicial decisions and statutes.[42] These concepts enable us, as Elizabeth Dale suggests, to keep "the past and the present in creative tension by using the insights of the present to expand and reconfigure our inquiries into the past."[43]

Three reasons support the analytical comparison of these court sources in their differing legal and nonlegal contexts. First, Virginia, the Carolinas, and Georgia represent Old South states with long histories as British settler colonies and their own enslavement law precedents and traditions. Louisiana and Texas, in contrast, were former French and Spanish colonies. They represent the newer slave states, which were part of the expanding cotton kingdom. In the decades before the Civil War, settlers from the Old South states took more than one million enslaved people to the lands that included the Mississippi and Florida territories, the Louisiana Purchase, and the Texas Annexation, and they transplanted their enslavement law and culture of oppression.[44]

Second, the period for comparison concludes with enslavement's violent and involuntary abolition in the United States and with the end of the era of de jure criminal law discrimination against free Blacks.[45] Secession, the Civil War, Emancipation, and Reconstruction intervened before the southern courts and legislatures could further define the separate and unequal protection doctrine's nascent transmission from the incidents of enslavement law into a badge of slavery that was applied to free Black people.[46]

And third, these sources raise issues of broader significance regarding the influence of social and political change on the relative autonomy of case and statute law. They tend to refute A. E. Keir Nash's contention that southern antebellum statutes provided a more "flimsy armor" than the common law for the protection of the legal rights of Blacks.[47] They instead suggest that "both the statutory law and common law . . . proved to be equally malleable."[48] Indeed, Georgia's legislators apparently believed that their state's common-law armor was too flimsy; the conclusion will discuss how their statutory code moderated the state Supreme Court's extreme version of the separate and unequal protection under the criminal law.

The Equality of Rights Road Not Taken

The book begins nonchronologically with the hypothesis that the separate and unequal legal protection doctrine based on race can be best understood when it is considered within social, political, and legal contexts, which include *Campbell v. The People*.[49] That 1854 Illinois Supreme Court decision is offered in chapter 1 as evidence of the road not taken in the South. The court reversed the manslaughter conviction of Decator Campbell, a free nineteen-year-old African American man. Campbell and his alleged victim, Goodwin Parker, a fifty-three-year-old white man, had recently moved with their families from the Upper South to southern Illinois. On the night of December 9, 1853, Parker and three other men with southern roots went to the Campbell family's house, a few days after an altercation between Campbell and Parker, "to inflict [on Campbell] a good sound beating."[50] A melee ensued, in which Parker was killed. He and his confederates acted in accord with the widely held beliefs favoring legitimized white violence, which they and other Upland southerners had imported into Illinois and the courts in the *Harden* and *Jowers* decisions had by then legitimated.[51]

Justice John Dean Caton's opinion cited and applied well-established common-law principles to hold that the trial judge read to the jury erroneous self-defense instructions and improperly excluded evidence of Parker's threats against Campbell. Caton also ruled that the judge should have granted Campbell's lawyer's request to instruct the jury to deliberate "as if [Campbell] were a white man, for the law is the same, there being no distinction in its principles in respect of color."[52]

This was but one tentative step on the counterfactual path to the equal protection doctrine.[53] The substantive criminal law, which defines the elements of crimes and the available defenses, however, is a logical starting point for advocates of true de jure and de facto equality.[54] This decision requiring racial equality under the substantive criminal law suggests that the separate and unequal protection principle was not inevitable or universally accepted in the antebellum United States. Although Caton does not call for color-blind justice in all cases, by equating some Black rights with those granted to whites, his opinion suggests that those backing free Black citizenship and civil rights were more than just "a tiny handful of visionary radicals" among antebellum northerners.[55] This decision was one of the "few victories" in the antebellum years, which "helped to establish a discourse of rights that would flourish in Reconstruction" and "form an essential part of the background to the second founding."[56]

Full legal equality for all people without regard to perceptions of their race—or other status—has not always been experienced where the equal protection doctrine prevails.[57] Nevertheless, the goal of equal rights was impossible—and maybe even unthinkable—to the separate and unequal protection doctrine's advocates. The *Campbell* decision thus provides contextual evidence supporting the conclusion that antebellum southern judges and legislators chose to insert the rule of free Black inequality into the common law of crimes, not, as Robert Gordon suggests, "because it had to be but because the people pushing for alternatives were weaker and lost out in their struggle." This becomes clear when we look at the "counterfactual trajectories, the roads not taken," which can be found in "the experience of other societies, [and] from the hopes of those who lost the struggle."[58] Indeed, the *Campbell* decision can be understood as an example of what Alan Watson might have labeled resistance to legal change in response to social change, here the presence of free Blacks in society.[59] Russell Sandberg likely would call this analysis subversive legal history, which goes beyond describing and contextualizing legal doctrines and texts to offer a critique "showing that every legal feature and every dividing line is a human construct that has been, and therefore could, be designed differently."[60]

Racially Motivated Violence as a Badge of Slavery

The conclusion advances the book's second major purpose by demonstrating that antebellum state-sanctioned violence against both enslaved and free Blacks and post-emancipation violence against Black people is a persistent badge of slavery that has resulted in thousands of assaults, batteries, kidnappings, and murders by whites acting on their own or in lynch mobs.[61] This racially motivated violence's specter continues to cast what Robert Cottrol called a long and lingering shadow over the United States, so many years after slavery was abolished.[62]

Although the Thirteenth Amendment confirmed the immediate and uncompensated emancipation of all remaining enslaved people in the United States, it could not—by its own force—eradicate all of slavery's "modes of thought, attitudes, and practices." These slavery survivals, known as the badges of slavery, "did *not* vanish in a flash" after emancipation.[63] Accordingly, Justice Joseph P. Bradley concluded for the U.S. Supreme Court, in the *Civil Rights Cases*, that section 2 of the Thirteenth Amendment authorizes Congress to pass laws enforcing the prohibition of slavery and involuntary servitude as well as "all laws necessary and proper for abolishing all badges and incidents of slavery in the United States."[64] The essential issues, therefore, are the following: (1) How should the courts define the amendment's self-executing prohibition that the courts may enforce? And (2) may Congress make findings defining badges of slavery when adopting necessary and proper enforcement legislation, and, if so, what standard of review should the courts apply to Congress's findings?[65]

A Degraded Caste of Society contributes to the debate about the second question by offering evidence supporting Congress's 2009 finding that racially motivated violence is a badge of slavery that it could include among the hate crimes proscribed by the Matthew Shepard and James Byrd Jr. Hate Crimes

Prevention Act.[66] This enslavement badge is not a tangible physical marker like a yellow Star of David or pink triangle stitched to a person's clothing.[67] It instead is an indicator based on a person's appearance or family history, which triggers violent manifestations of the white-supremacist belief system existing in the hearts and minds of people like Goodwin Parker, Atlas Jowers, Charles Harden, Gregory and Travis McMichael, and William Bryan.[68]

The private acts of racially motivated violence perpetrated by these and other whites originated in one of slavery's principal incidents, which had a regrettably solid foundation in antebellum legal rules and doctrines. Southern jurists and legislators legitimized this incident of slavery for enslaved Blacks who were involved in cases of interracial violence, whether as the accused offenders or as the victims. This book demonstrates how, in the decades before the Civil War, some of the criminal law incidents of enslavement, including legalized race-based violence, were imposed on free Blacks. This positive written law was one crucial means by which Blacks were confined in a separate legal caste, to guarantee their permanent subordinate and degraded status in what the dominant whites thought was a white man's country.

This book therefore is an exercise in what Alfred Brophy called applied legal history, which he defined as "deeply researched, serious scholarship that is motivated by, engages with, or speaks to contemporary issues."[69] The following chapters undertake this "risky enterprise" by suggesting an essential continuity between the antebellum South's white-supremacist criminal law and its survivals in the post-emancipation law in the books and in action, while contrasting this with the discontinuity separating this explicitly white-supremacist law from the ideal of formal legal equality, at least in the substantive criminal law.[70] Decator Campbell's case exemplifies the enslavement badge's violent nature, which positive law could either permit or prohibit. The Illinois Supreme Court foreshadowed the equality ideal, which became law in the Thirteenth and Fourteenth Amendments and two of the Civil Rights Act of 1866's guarantees to all U.S. citizens. These are the rights of all citizens "to the full and equal benefit of all laws and proceedings for the security of persons and property, as is enjoyed by white citizens" and to "be subject to like punishment, pains, penalties, and to none other, any law statute, ordinance, regulation, or custom to the contrary notwithstanding."[71]

Of course, true equality has not always been achieved, even in free states like Illinois, and the *Campbell* decision did not mandate total free Black equality under law. But the court's mere articulation of the equality principle at least enabled lawyers to continue to advocate for equal justice for all, as they and their clients confronted what Eric Foner calls "the complex legacy of Reconstruction and its overthrow."[72]

Note on Legal History:
Combining the "Old" and the "New"

The slavery law box is an important concept in this book's analytical approach to legal history.[73] I have proposed this conceptual container to delimit the constitutional provisions, statutes, and court decisions and doctrines that defined and regulated the everyday interactions among masters, slaves, third parties, and the state. The *Jowers* and *Harden* opinions, and the statutes criminalizing free Black insolence, are examples in which judges and legislators reached into the slavery law box for precedents and doctrines to govern issues and cases that did not involve slaves or slavery.[74]

This slavery law box is an analytic analogy to the "law box" that Robert Gordon uses to describe "whatever appears autonomous about the legal order—courts, equitable maxims, motions for summary judgment." Gordon compares this law box's contents, which he calls the "sphere of 'legal' phenomena," with the "'society,' the wide realm of the non-legal, the political, economic, religious, social." He depicts this law box as part of a two-dimensional "crude model" of the relationship between law and society and between legal and social change. According to this model, nonlegal inputs are the "social influences upon the shape of the mass of things inside the law-box," and the outputs are "the effects, or impact, of the mass [in the law box] upon society."[75] This analysis is consistent with Lawrence M. Friedman's suggestion that we study, first, "the demands made [by persons] upon legal institutions, calling for action . . . ; second, the responses made by legal institutions; [and] third, the impact and effect of these responses on the persons making the demands, and on society as a whole."[76]

Gordon's model does not attempt to explain how the law box's contents are established or how they change over time. It instead allows for "a great range of possible theories of law." These theories are points on a continuum extending "from a theory asserting that law derives its shape almost wholly from sources within the box (i.e. that it is really autonomous as well as seeming so), to one claiming that the box is really empty, the apparent distinctiveness of its contents illusory, since they are all the product of external forces."[77] Indeed, legal historians' views range from attempts to explain the law's relative autonomy to the notion of the "plurality" of law in society and what Christopher Tomlins calls law's "totalized contingency," which, he warns, is "a deeply tragic form of subversion, for it does not discriminate in the paralysis it metes out. In undermining the authority of all narratives, it spares none, not even those that may be precious to the powerless, those whom we once desired to liberate."[78]

Gordon, and scholars following him, thus modify or even reject this law box model in favor of "the idea that law is constitutive in history and the idea that its history is contingent."[79] These historians no longer consider law and society to be "necessarily distinct anymore in a meaningful way, or at least [they] perceive the two realms as mutually constitutive of one another." In place of a "sharp demarcation" between law and society, these historians contend that "the boundary between the legal and the non-legal is porous and difficult to pinpoint with a great deal of precision."[80] Scholars employing the cultural and sociological approaches to law and legal history invoke two key concepts—"legal culture" and "legal consciousness"—to study how people experience law in their everyday lives and try to influence law. Legal culture is "the constellation of attitudes and experiences concerning law in a particular time and place—separate from formal legal institutions like statutes and court proceedings, though these institutions certainly influenced how antebellum Americans understood law and legal authority." Legal consciousness is the "individuals' view of the law, their experience of the law, and the considerations they make when approaching the legal system for assistance."[81] Sally Engle Merry explains legal consciousness as "the ways people understand the law," whether from habit or intentional choices. Different people in a society may at the same time have different understandings of the law and a person's understandings of law may change after dealing with others and with the legal system.[82]

Russell Sandberg thus concludes, "It is not a question of studying law 'and' society but law 'in' society and society 'in' law."[83] But this study need not necessarily end with "totalized contingency" and "powerlessness," as illustrated by an analysis of Melissa Milewski's use of these concepts to contrast the approaches of legal historians who have written this "newer cultural and legal history" of the southern antebellum and Jim Crow years with the work of scholars who "looked largely at the laws enacted by legislatures and at judges' decisions in appellate court cases."[84] The newer approach in part follows my suggestion that enslavement law scholars look beyond the law box to "examine both lower court records and newspapers as supplements to the reported cases and statutory provisions."[85]

The move away from the older approach should not go too far, however; enslavement law and its aftermath may best be understood from our postemancipation perspective by combining these approaches, so that we "simultaneously steep [our]selves in the legal and non-legal history of American slavery." The reported appellate court opinions and legal doctrines provide context for trial court records and other sources, which, from the bottom up, evidence the people's legal consciousness.[86] "The study of doctrine is a powerful tool in writing legal history," according to Cynthia Nicoletti, "because it can reveal a great deal about lawyers' (and non-lawyers') legal consciousness. It can provide a window onto 'how law . . . and identity . . . help construct one another.'" Although "the exploration of doctrine for its own sake may be excessively narrow, . . . so is legal history that shuns doctrine for the sake of being trendy."[87] The legal historian's task "is to try to understand how legal doctrine informed historical actors' conceptions of what 'law' was and how they understood legal doctrine to interact with the world around them." Accordingly, "if our historical subjects conceived of legal doctrine as an important part of the fabric of law (as multitextured as that might be), taking doctrine seriously allows us to reconstruct their thoughts more faithfully."[88]

In the decades before the Civil War, southern white elites appeared to take seriously the separate and unequal doctrine. They did not always agree on the details, but even those whom historians have included among the "moderates" applied to all free Blacks some of the rules and legal doctrines that had been developed for enslavement, which, in 1619, was unknown to English statutory and common law. Colonial and antebellum southern legal evolution is best understood as a continuation of the profound legal doctrinal development that began when British colonial legislators—step-by-step—accommodated slavery's oppressive and dehumanizing relationships into the written law. Customs and practices of enslavement came first; the colonial lawmakers later legalized and encouraged what the colonists were doing.[89]

Antebellum southern judges and other legal elites continued this trend and even began expanding it to include free Blacks, as documented by legal treatise writers.[90] Thomas R. R. Cobb's 1858 slavery law treatise exemplifies this trend. According to Paul Finkelman, this "is the most comprehensive antebellum restatement of the law of slavery and the only treatise on slavery written by a southerner," which also is an explicitly pro-slavery and racist defense of slavery.[91] Cobb's final chapter discusses "the effect of manumission" and "the status of free persons of color."[92] His decision to explain the law applying to free Blacks in his enslavement law treatise suggests that he believed that the slavery law box was semiporous. This is important because he was the primary drafter of criminal law sections of the Georgia Code, which enacted the separate and unequal protection doctrine for free Blacks.[93] Even treatises digesting general legal principles and authorities began increasingly to include enslavement law cases.[94] Abolitionists also published books documenting, analyzing, and evaluating this antebellum enslavement law, in the effort to hasten emancipation.[95]

Accordingly, the crude two-dimensional flat law box can be replaced with a three-dimensional law box floating within a larger three-dimensional sphere representing the society and culture. The slavery law box, in turn, can be seen as a smaller three-dimensional box floating in the law box. The walls and surfaces of these boxes are not solid, like wood or cardboard. They are instead more like semipermeable or selectively permeable cell membranes. Through a process of legal osmosis, these membranes permit some ideas, customs, norms, rules, and doctrines to pass in and out of the law boxes and the wider sphere, to influence and to be influenced by each other.[96] Legal historians and theorists can be thought of as engaging in a debate about the mechanics and degrees of this permeability, if any, in a given society or in all societies. This book's sources exhibit substantial law box permeability, but they also support Kunal Parker's contention that this positive law was "irreducible" to society and society was "irreducible" to law.[97]

The antebellum southern decisions and statutes adopting the principle of free Black inequality before the criminal law were contingent and expanding responses to social change, they did not express timeless and essential principles of a universal legal evolutionary process. The *Harden* and *Jowers* opinions are especially revealing because the judges grounded the separate and unequal criminal law doctrine upon their understanding of the white community's legal culture and legal consciousness. The novel rules these judges created were influenced by—and in turn influenced—the development of the white elites' legal consciousness, as it was experienced by all people in the society, including all Blacks. The study of how these customs and practices came to be expressed in the primary legal sources and legal treatises is essential to the most complete understanding of antebellum law and society.

I therefore continue to believe that "students of slave law should seriously compare the 'instrumentalist' theories of nineteenth century legal change and consider the parallel development of slave and non-slave law." This approach shows how "the study of slave law becomes relevant to all legal historians, as well as lawyers in general, who want to know how our courts have formulated legal rules and doctrine in the past so they can predict how lawmakers will and should act in the future."[98] It also demonstrates enslavement law's lingering impacts on current legal rules, doctrines, and results.[99] This study thus extends my earlier work explaining how freedom suits influenced the development of the hearsay rule of evidence and how slave sales cases influenced the development of the law of sales.[100] These patterns of legal change suggest that scholars should combine the *longue durée* and narrower historical perspectives to further explore the potential links between slavery law's colonial and antebellum origin and development and its influence on antebellum and post-emancipation legal history.[101]

Contextualization:
Broad and Narrow in Scope

This analysis of the *Campbell*, *Harden*, and *Jowers* opinions, and the related decisions and statutes, also illustrates how contextualization offers a conceptual bridge between the old and new legal history approaches, and how it is a necessary part of an interdisciplinary and integrative study of law and society and of jurisprudence. I discuss each of the principal court decisions and statutes on two contextual levels. One places the text within its broader multidisciplinary legal, social, political, and economic background. The other explains the text's more immediate foreground, including the biographies of the principal participants involved in the origin of the case or statute.

Some readers may think that these background discussions deliver excessive detail, but this book endeavors to demonstrate that this contextualization is an essential technique in legal history. Contextualization permits scholars to evaluate "a text, or author, or work of art . . . in part through an examination of its historical, geographical, intellectual, or artistic location."[102] It is "a means to an end" that reveals insights that were not perceived through a more truncated analysis of the contexts of primary source legal texts.[103] Contextualization thus can inform a broader integrative and interdisciplinary approach to legal history. Harold J. Berman, on the history side, and Jerome Hall, on the law and jurisprudence side, are among those who explored the relationship between change in the positive law and in the wider society. Berman suggested that scholars of jurisprudence draw on insights from the three "classical schools: legal positivism, natural-law theory, and the historical school."[104] Hall added that the integrative approach is interdisciplinary: "As one explores a social problem from the perspectives of the various disciplines, his [or her] knowledge accumulates and it fuses into a 'total' knowledge of the problem."[105] Interdisciplinary studies theorists call this total knowledge "a more comprehensive understanding," which can be achieved by deriving and then integrating insights from different academic disciplines.[106]

But Christopher Tomlins cautions that "'articulating the past *historically*' means much more than simply 'recognizing it "the way it really was."'" Historians instead actively create the contexts for the documents they find in the record of the past. Accordingly, "if we understand history as an enlivened understanding of an object of contemplation, which is to say an object rendered intelligible, we must recognize that the contemplated object is not enlivened by the relationalities within which it allegedly belongs (the relationalities of *its* time) but by the fold of time that creates it in constellation with the present."[107]

Tomlins thus suggests that legal history is not merely an effort "to recover the reality of an object situated temporally and specially in the past." Instead, he quotes Walter Benjamin's assertion that "the goal of history is to represent 'our age'—the age that examines historical events—'in the age during which they arose.'"[108] This enables us to understand the present by studying the past, because "historical inquiry could only exist in a condition of constellation with the moment—the 'now'—of its observation":

> It is said that the dialectical method consists in doing justice each time to the concrete historical situation of its object. But that is not enough. For it is just as much a matter of doing justice to the concrete historical situation of the *interest* taken in the object. And *this* situation is always so constituted that the interest is itself preformed in that object and, above all, feels this object concretized in itself and upraised from its former being into the higher concretion of now-being [*Jetztsein*].[109]

Historian Shadi Bartsch-Zimmer expressed this point plainly when she wrote, "We might wonder whether the stories we choose to recreate from the past are not always the ones that can be told but rather those that flatter our values. So has it always been with history."[110]

Legal historians can—with these cautions—create two types of contexts to make more "intelligible" the evidence of the past that they select and the present reality of their interest in the past. One context establishes the social, political, economic, religious, and ideological background that reveals the legal text's broader significance, while the other informs the reader about the text's author or authors and the principal protagonists in the social relations that gave rise to the legal text or the evidence of the law in action.[111] This interdisciplinary and integrative approach can reveal patterns of legal and social change from the different and potentially conflicting epistemological "vantage points" afforded by the relevant disciplines, including jurisprudence, the humanities, history, and the social sciences.[112] But historians should be careful not to serve up "law office history," political propaganda, or a usable past designed to advance some present interests.[113] Nor should they employ an approach "that fetishizes thick description, contingency, and complexity."[114]

Note on the Language of Enslavement

Deborah Gray White explains the prevailing preference for the word "enslaved" instead of "slavery," better to "implicate the inhumane actions" of those who enslave other people.[115] Margaret Abruzzo also notes that the words "enslaved persons" and "enslavers" remind readers that "enslavement was a process, not a natural state," and they "emphasize the human dignity of the enslaved human being." Some enslavers, however, also "disliked the term *slave*, preferring *Negroes* or *servants*." They substituted these euphemisms to soften the perceptions of slavery's everyday reality.[116] As before, I will at times, for stylistic reasons, use the terms "owner" or "enslaver" and "slave" or "enslaved," but of course this does not suggest that, during slavery's long career in human history, enslaved people were better suited for their enslavement, nor were their enslavers rightfully in their more advantageous position in life.[117]

"Enslaver" is an ambiguous word in enslavement law because it could include a person who owns or holds legal title to an enslaved person, a person who hires or rents an enslaved person from an owner, a member of an owner's or hirer's family, or an owner's or hirer's employee or agent. To accurately describe transactions involving enslaved people, we need to distinguish between buyer and seller, mortgagor and mortgagee, assignee and assignor, or bailor and bailee. The use of these legal terms now does not endorse or even normalize these relationships. I also follow scholars, such as Jamila Jefferson-Jones, who "capitalize the term 'Black' when referring to people of African descent individually or collectively because 'Blacks, like Asians, Latinos, and other "minorities," constitute a specific cultural group and, as such, require denotation as a proper noun.'"[118]

We also must remember that enslaved people's thoughts and words were most often not recorded in the archives and sources reflecting the enslavers' perspectives.[119] This caveat is important when reading legal texts referring to enslaved people as property. The legal definition of people as property was the enslaver class's conceptual response that cut off enslaved people's claims of right, other than the right to assert that they were not legally enslaved, while subjecting them to the web of rights and duties of enslavers and others, including the state. This notion of human property thus was not a legal fiction; it was a lived, everyday reality as conceptualized through the law's language and logic.[120] Wesley N. Hohfeld's insights enable us to perceive the enslaved as people without rights who were encumbered with more onerous legal duties, a double shot of oppression, unlike other forms of living property that were denied rights and duties.[121]

Enslaved people throughout recorded human history nevertheless also shaped the law when they asserted their humanity, which, in their enslavers' minds, determined their value as property, but also frustrated their enslavers' efforts to dehumanize them. The study of this conflict "suggests the limits" of the law's power to "sort[] people according to legal status," by focusing on the actions of "those people who do not accept the law's vision of them or the social order more generally."[122]

I also have retained the original archaic spellings used in the primary and secondary sources quoted, to give the reader a sense of the passage of time and to preserve the authenticity of the quoted texts. But consistent with the press's style, I do not indicate all punctuation alterations made within quotations, which I otherwise would have included according to the currently accepted legal writing style.[123]

CHAPTER 1

The Antebellum Equal Protection Criminal Justice Road Not Taken

The Illinois Supreme Court, in 1854, held that African Americans who were accused of crimes were entitled, at least during their trials, to the application of the same substantive law as if they were white, when the court reversed the manslaughter conviction of Decator Campbell, a young African American man who was accused of murdering a white man named Goodwin Parker. This decision is part of the broader context against which it is fair to evaluate the contrary *Harden/Jowers* rule of unequal caste and race under the criminal law, to avoid the alleged pitfalls of what is called the hindsight defense, by which it may be claimed that those in the present cannot fairly evaluate the decisions of past judges and legislators.[1]

We may not be accustomed to thinking of the antebellum northern and southern states as separate societies. But in the decades before the southern states' actual attempted secession, the white people in these regions held increasingly divergent views about the potential for the enforcement of legal equality for all. These divisions were increasingly evident within the state of Illinois in the decade before the Civil War.

The Social, Political, and Economic Context

In order to understand the *Campbell* decision's significance, we need to develop two levels of context. One is the broader legal, social, political, and economic background for the legal text. The other is found in its more immediate foreground, which includes the biographies of the case's principal participants.

On the first contextual level, Illinois was not necessarily the most obvious state, in the 1850s at least, to be the source of this rule of formal equality.

Indeed, Elmer Gertz calls antebellum Illinois "a southern-oriented citadel in the North."[2] The state "operated under a set of discriminatory laws known as the Black Laws. Under these laws, African Americans could not vote, serve in the militia, assemble in groups of more than three, testify in court or serve on a jury."[3] These laws illustrate how Illinois was an antebellum amalgam of the free and slave states. As Paul Finkelman explains, "From its early settlement until at least the Civil War, Illinois was in many ways as much a southern state as a northern state." Geography played a part in this, as "almost half of the state was south of the Mason-Dixon line," and "much of Illinois bordered on two southern states."[4] Indeed, Finkelman includes Illinois, along with Indiana and Oregon, in the bottom tier of the free states in his comparison of the legal status that those eighteen states in 1860 afforded to free Blacks.[5]

But maybe its location on the fault line between the free and slave states, in the American Confluence that also included Ohio, Indiana, Kentucky, and Missouri, made Illinois the state where the issue in Campbell's case was contested and decided in favor of equality. This confluence included the waters of the region's rivers and the convergence of diverse people who migrated to what became the Midwest.[6] John Craig Hammond thus argues for the significance of Illinois history because "Illinois sat at the center of an increasingly divided continental empire. Sectional divisions within Illinois mirrored larger sectional divisions in the Union."[7]

Antebellum Illinois society and politics reflected and anticipated national sectional divisions and conflicts between the northern and southern states. Residents of the northern and southern Illinois regions clashed because they were "two very different groups of people."[8] Upland southerners, primarily from Kentucky, Tennessee, Virginia, and Maryland, made up the majority of the pre-1830 migrants. They tended to settle in the state's southern third, which was known as Egypt or Little Egypt. After the mid-1830s, more settlers began to move into the northern part of the state from the by then free states north of the Mason-Dixon Line.[9]

According to John Barnhart, "Farmer emigrants from the Upland South brought with them the ideal of a white man's society, and unfriendliness to the negro and to the aristocrat."[10] These settlers also imported their culture of honor and violence, which, as Edward Ayers argues, cannot be separated from slavery's influence on southern society.[11] Nicole Etcheson thus quotes early antebellum English Illinois settler Morris Birkbeck's observation that the Kentucky migrants "were reluctant to give up 'their right of defence against every aggression, even to the laws which themselves had constituted.' This attitude encouraged taking the law into their own hands. These Kentuckians did not hesitate to commit deeds of 'ferocious violence' against someone public opinion judged guilty, regardless of the verdicts of the courts."[12]

The Illinois history of slavery and race relations also reflects these intrastate sectional divisions. Native Americans and Europeans enslaved Native Americans and Africans when the land that became the state of Illinois was in the French and British colonial empires.[13] During the American Revolution, Virginia captured from the British and claimed this territory, which became Illinois County, Virginia.[14] Virginia ceded this territory to the United States in 1784. Both the Virginia cession and article VI of the 1787 Northwest Ordinance established a general rule prohibiting slavery, but they were interpreted to preserve the preexisting property rights of the Illinois enslavers.[15]

Even article VI, section 1, of the state's first constitution, which was ratified in 1818, protected the preexisting enslavers' rights. It deviated materially from the Northwest Ordinance's antislavery provision when it declared, "Neither slavery nor involuntary servitude *shall be introduced into this state* otherwise than for the punishment of crimes whereof the party shall have been duly convicted."[16] This provision also continued, with some modifications, earlier territorial laws that were interpreted to permit African Americans to agree to "voluntary" servitude contracts. Although new contracts were not to exceed one year, except for apprentices, unlimited annual renewals were permitted.[17] New York congressman James Tallmadge offered an amendment that was defeated in the House of Representatives, objecting to this constitution because it was so inconsistent with the Northwest Ordinance.[18]

Moreover, in 1819, the Illinois legislature enacted a comprehensive statute, also called the Black Law, restricting free Black migration into the new state, while imposing restrictions on Illinois free Black residents. Black settlers were required to produce certificates of freedom and register with the county in which they were to reside. African American emigrants without these certificates were presumed to be runway slaves, and advertisements were to be published so that their owners could reclaim them. These new residents could not immediately be employed in the state as free workers; instead, they were to be hired out for one year to the highest bidder. If no alleged owner claimed them after one year, they were to be issued certificates of freedom. To discourage slave owners from taking their slaves to Illinois and freeing them, the law also required slave owners to post a thousand-dollar bond for each freed slave. Later acts reconfirmed and expanded on these provisions.[19]

The legislature, also in 1819, adopted a statute that prohibited the testimony of a "negro, mulatto, or Indian," except in a criminal prosecution against a "negro, mulatto, or Indian," or in a civil case in which these persons "alone shall be parties."[20] The legislators copied an evidence rule that the southern states, by the antebellum years, applied to enslaved and free Blacks because of their alleged mendacity as a race.[21] This rule permitted whites to get away even with murder, if the prosecution could call only Black witnesses to testify at a white defendant's trial.[22]

The state's antebellum pro-slavery Upland South population was so influential that "in 1823–1824 Illinois came within a few hundred votes of calling another constitutional convention that would have explicitly allowed slavery in the state."[23] After this pro-slavery defeat, the legislature nevertheless continued to adopt laws that obviously were intended to discourage free Black migration into the state and to assist slave owners who sought to recover fugitive slaves. For example, the 1827 criminal code included provisions declaring that anyone harboring or secreting "any negro, mulatto, or person of color" who was a "slave or servant" of another person in the state or from another state committed a misdemeanor. Convicted offenders faced fines of up to five hundred dollars and prison terms not exceeding six months.[24] And an 1829 act required free Blacks migrating to Illinois to post, in addition to their freedom certificates, thousand-dollar bonds in which two sureties agreed to guarantee that the free Blacks would not become public charges if they could not support themselves. Steven Savery notes that "the state's chronic need for money may have been a motivating factor in the size of the bond," but he also adds that it appears that the legislature's "main objective was to exclude free Negroes from the state altogether without specifically saying so."[25]

Free Blacks nevertheless migrated from the Upper South to Illinois, and some settled in Little Egypt. As Darel Dexter explains, "They were attracted to Illinois by the same factors which brought white pioneers [t]here; inexpensive farm land and forested land with game. In addition, there was probably a belief that their freedom would be greater protected in 'free' Illinois."[26]

Dexter thus labels Illinois a "quasi slave state." It combined both de facto and de jure antebellum slavery with "widespread opposition to slavery from the northern part of the state and pockets of opposition in southern Illinois."[27] But migrants from the northern states gained both in numbers and in political power; by 1850, southern state emigrants made up 16.8 percent of the Illinois population, while 16.7 percent of the state's population hailed from New England, New York, and Pennsylvania. These free state migrants brought with them different legal cultures and attitudes toward race.[28]

Conflicts in social and legal cultures among migrants from the southern slave states and northern free states therefore intensified in the years before the Civil War, and they also prefigured the legal conflicts between the states that resulted in secession and war. These conflicts emerged in the 1847 constitutional debates and in the state's new 1848 constitution. That constitution finally abolished "the remnants of indentured servitude in Illinois."[29]

But the convention delegates also hotly debated the proposal of Benjamin Bond, from the state's southern region, to bar all Black migration into Illinois. Delegates from the northern part of the state opposed this ban, and a compromise was achieved. The proposed constitution was submitted to the voters along with a separate question on this Black migration ban. The state's all white electorate approved both, thus requiring the legislature to pass laws to "effectively prohibit free persons of color from immigrating to and settling" in the state and to prevent owners from bringing enslaved people to Illinois "for the purpose of setting them free."[30]

Contrary to this clear constitutional mandate, however, there were insufficient votes in the state's General Assemblies of 1848–50 and 1850–52 in favor of a free Black exclusion law. This all changed in early 1853, when the newly elected twenty-six-year-old southern state legislator John A. Logan became this cause's champion. As a result of his efforts, "the deadlock was broken" on February 12, 1853, when the legislators approved a free Black exclusion law.[31] Kate Masur argues that a December 1852 U.S. Supreme Court decision rejecting a challenge to the state's anti-harboring law may have given this proposal a boost, by suggesting "that Logan's proposed Black exclusion measure would pass constitutional muster if challenged."[32] Illinois was not alone in its anti-Black sentiments. In 1851, an Iowa law imposed a fine of two dollars per day on any Blacks who thereafter settled in the state and failed to leave within three days of receiving notice to do so, and Indiana ratified a constitution prohibiting free Black migration into the state. Its legislature in the next year adopted a statute enforcing this provision.[33]

The Illinois statute, "An Act to Prevent the Immigration of Free Negroes into This State," included provisions making it "a high misdemeanor" and imposing a fine on "any negro or mulatto, bond or free," who entered and stayed in the state for more than ten days "with the evident intention of residing" there. It defined a "mulatto" as anyone having "one-fourth negro blood" and authorized terms of indentured servitude for those who did not pay their fines.[34] Beginning with Virginia in 1793, most slave states, including, Alabama, Arkansas, Delaware, Georgia, Kentucky, Louisiana, Maryland, Mississippi, North Carolina, South Carolina, and Tennessee, enacted similar laws.[35]

According to Masur, this "'Logan Law,' like other antiblack measures, gave white people a sense of power and impelled some to vigilantism." Although "sporadic white violence against Blacks was already commonplace in some pockets of the state," this law "surely enhanced the climate of hostility and gave ill-disposed white people a new sense of license." She cites the fall 1854 lynching of a Black man named Joseph Spencer. He was murdered in Cairo, Alexander County, at the state's southern border. This and other incidents of mob violence occurring in the following years appear to have been intended to "clear [African Americans] out of the city."[36]

As Savery notes, the "actual numbers" of free Blacks in Illinois "could hardly account for the consternation which their residence endangered among the white inhabitants." Nor could the antebellum increase in the state's free Black population explain this increased hostility. Although the Illinois free Black population "rose by over a half from 1820 to 1850, in relation to the entire population, their proportion dropped from 4.99 percent in 1810 to less than one percent in 1850."[37]

Savery suggests, instead, that sectional differences regarding race among the state's white population better explain the severity of the state's Black Laws. "In general," he argues, white "Illinoisans regarded black freemen as an inferior and hopelessly degraded class." Although the northern residents "objected to free Negroes on theoretical and abstract grounds; southern Illinoisans regarded the presence of free blacks as a direct threat to their lives and property, indeed, to the entire social order."[38]

Masur asserts, however, that Logan's free Black exclusion law "also became an organizing tool for Illinoisans who wanted to see the state move in the opposite direction—to repeal all the black laws and secure for African Americans . . . 'fair and equal treatment.'"[39] This law, she contends, "energized" Blacks and whites to advance this goal of free Black legal equality on the local, state, and national levels.[40]

Free Blacks and some whites, mostly in the state's northern counties, did indeed oppose Logan's Law, and they continued to lobby unsuccessfully for the repeal of all of the Black Laws. The Illinois Supreme Court in 1864, by a two to one vote, rejected a constitutional challenge to Logan's Law. But after the Republicans won the November 1864 legislative elections, a February 7, 1865, statute finally repealed this exclusion law, along with the other Illinois Black Laws.[41]

The Principal Participants

These broader conflicts between the state's northern and southern oriented social and legal cultures played out in the prosecution of Decator Campbell for the alleged murder of Goodwin Parker. A young free Black man like Campbell posed a perceived threat to the social order that Upland southerners like Parker imported into southern Illinois. Notwithstanding the long history of Illinois enslavement and its Black Laws, however, the state Supreme Court's November 1854 term decision confirmed the rule of free Black equality in criminal trials—if only when not contrary to the dictates of the Black Laws.

John A. Logan, the legislator who had recently pushed the free Black exclusion law, was the prosecutor who convinced a grand jury to indict Campbell for Parker's December 9, 1853, murder. Campbell was tried in the Massac County Circuit Court during the June 1854 term, a little more than a year after the free Black exclusion law was adopted.[42]

Massac County is located in Little Egypt, along the Ohio River, across from Kentucky, south of St. Louis, Louisville, and even the Confederate capital of Richmond. It was incorporated in 1843 out of neighboring Johnson and Pope counties.[43] The county's initial population was only about fifteen hundred people; it then was "composed for the most part of emigrants from the Southern States, and a few free negroes, the rest serving by indenture."[44]

According to George W. May, the county's early frontier years were marked by unrest and violence. In response, in 1849, the state legislature extended the Circuit Court's jurisdiction to the county.[45] May concludes that, by 1850, "an astonishing tranquility had fallen upon Massac County and all Southern Illinois. Disturbances died away and law assumed sway. Thus ended an eighteen-year struggle."[46] By 1860, the county's population grew to 6,213, including 49 free Black men and 63 free Black women.[47] May does not mention the interracial violence that followed the adoption of the free Black exclusion law.

Among the six principal actors in Campbell's case, the least evidence is available on Campbell, who is the most important person. The court's opinion describes him only as "a negro."[48] Prison records following his conviction state that he was about twenty years old in 1855 and was born in Tennessee.[49]

He apparently was the son of Matthew Campbell, who was reported in the 1830 and 1840 censuses as the head of a Tennessee household living first in Rutherford County and then in Williamson County. He and his family moved to Illinois in 1848 or 1849.[50] According to the 1850 census, he was a thirty-seven-year-old "mulatto" shoemaker heading a household in Metropolis, the Massac County seat. He was born in North Carolina. His wife, Jane Campbell, was thirty-four years old, had been born in South Carolina, and also is labeled as mulatto. They had five children. The oldest, also labeled a "mulatto," was listed as a laborer who was born in Tennessee. He was fifteen years old in 1850. Although he was identified as Riley D. Campbell, he fits Decator Campbell's age and description. The Campbell family's recent move to Illinois is confirmed by the children's birthplace. All of the children, three males (Riley D., Matthew D., and James K. Polk) and two females (Sarah A. E. and Nancy Jane), were born in Tennessee, including the youngest child, James, who was one year old. The household also included a forty-five-year-old "Indian" man named Spates Davis, a blacksmith.[51]

The 1855 Illinois state census also lists the Matthew Campbell family, then consisting of four males and three females, among Massac County's "negro and mulatto" residents.[52] According to the 1860 census, Matthew, now a mechanic with a hundred-dollar personal estate, was the head of the household that included Jane and three children, Matthew, James, and Nancy.[53]

Goodwin Parker, according to the 1850 census, was a forty-nine-year-old white blacksmith. He and his thirty-nine-year-old wife, Rosa Ann Parker, were born in North Carolina. Although Goodwin could neither read nor write, he owned real estate that was valued at four thousand dollars. The Parkers had six children—all born in Kentucky—ranging from seven to twenty-one years of age. Their household also included a twenty-eight-year-old man named John H. Kelly, born in Ohio, whose occupation was "river trader."[54] Like the Campbell family, the Parkers were recent migrants to Illinois. They were married in 1826 in Pulaski County, which is in south-central Kentucky, near the Tennessee border. According to the 1830 and 1840 censuses, the family lived in neighboring Casey County.[55] Goodwin Parker purchased 40 acres of Illinois land in April 1849. Two years later, he obtained a 35.75-acre land grant from the United States.[56]

The judge in Campbell's trial, William K. Parrish, in January 1854 was the newly commissioned thirty-year-old judge of the Circuit Court for the Third Circuit, which included Massac County. Since 1850, he had been the state's attorney and thus he would have been the county's prosecutor in cases such as Campbell's. Parrish's Circuit Court tenure continued until he resigned in 1859. President James Buchanan appointed Parrish to be the U.S. attorney for the Southern District of Illinois, but Parrish died in 1861.[57]

The prosecutor Logan had succeeded Parrish as state's attorney, and in March 1853 Parrish and Logan became law partners.[58] Logan was a young lawyer and rising political star from Murphysboro in Jackson County, which also is in southern Illinois. Logan started his long political career in 1849, when he was elected Jackson County clerk. Three years later, at the age of twenty-six, he was elected to the state legislature as a Jacksonian Democrat, following in the footsteps of his father, Dr. John Logan. Young John also studied law, graduated from Louisville University Law School in 1851, and was admitted to the Illinois state bar. Soon thereafter, he was elected to a four-year term as Parrish's replacement as state's attorney. He was elected to the U.S. House of Representatives in 1858 and supported Stephen A. Douglas in the 1860 presidential election. Although considered to be a southern sympathizer, in part because of his successful advocacy of the Black exclusion law, Logan later supported the Union and achieved Civil War fame as General Black Jack Logan. After the war, he resumed his political career. He was elected—now as a Republican—to seats in the House of Representatives and later the Senate. In 1884 he unsuccessfully ran for vice president on the Republican ticket with James G. Blaine. But Logan's own presidential ambitions failed when he died two years later.[59]

Logan is held in such high regard that both a college and a museum in Illinois are named for him. The museum's website refers to Logan's transformation from a pro-South Democrat, who was an "avid racist and author of Illinois Black Laws," to a Republican "advocate for African American Civil Rights and education."[60] As late as April 1864, however, it appears that Logan may not have completed this transition. Before returning to battle with a regiment of Illinois volunteers, Logan is reported to have "made an eloquent and thrilling speech" in Springfield. He denounced those in the North who claimed to be "Unionist" but "secretly" oppose the war effort. He stated, "Some cry, 'this is an abolition war and you employ "niggers" to fight.' Well, as for himself, he had rather six niggers should be killed than one of his brave boys." And referring to the Battle of Shiloh, "and a scene on that occasion, when shell and shot fell like rain, he felt then a willingness that the negro might take the job off his hands."[61]

At Campbell's request, Judge Parrish appointed Jedediah Jack as Campbell's lawyer. Parrish made this appointment upon Campbell's arraignment and not guilty plea just before the trial began. But there is evidence confirming that Jack was involved in Campbell's defense from the start; he had visited Campbell in jail on December 10, 1853, the night after the killing.[62]

Jack was a free state migrant to Illinois who was born in about 1813 in Pennsylvania. He studied law under George W. Smith in Butler County, which is in western Pennsylvania, just north of Pittsburgh.[63] Jack was admitted to the Butler County bar in 1840 and "was a well-known citizen" of the city of Butler, before moving to Illinois.[64] According to the 1850 census, Jack and his wife Elizabeth and their children lived in Vienna in Johnson County, Illinois. Their real estate was valued at $150.[65] The Jack family eventually moved to Metropolis in neighboring Massac County. Metropolis is located on the northern bank of the Ohio River, across from Paducah, Kentucky.[66]

Jack was described as a "competent attorney, . . . who often appeared as a defense attorney when Logan was serving as a prosecutor. Both Logan and Jack were capable and aggressive, and they were known as spirited contenders."[67]

Jack is reputed to have been a friend of Abraham Lincoln, and he was described as "a man resembling Lincoln in personal appearance."[68] Jack's life ended violently when he was shot and killed on December 24, 1857, in a quarrel and affray with his brother-in-law, Elijah Stauffer (Stoeffer or Stofer). Ironically and tragically, the reports of Jack's homicide suggest unresolved doubts as to whether Stauffer shot Jack in self-defense.[69]

The last principal participant in Campbell's case is Justice John Dean Caton. He wrote the Illinois Supreme Court opinion reversing Campbell's conviction. Like Jack, Caton migrated to Illinois from a free state, but he settled in the state's north. He was a Democrat who was born in 1812 in Monroe, New York. When he moved to Chicago in 1833, the city had a population of only about three hundred people. There he started his legal career. His judicial career began nine years later, when he commenced serving as both a Circuit Court judge and Illinois Supreme Court justice, after he was appointed on August 20, 1842, to fill a vacancy. After a short two-month hiatus, which began on March 6, 1843, Caton on May 2, 1843, returned to the state's Supreme Court after once again being appointed to fill a vacancy. He served on that court until retiring from the bench in 1864. From 1855, he was the chief justice.[70] H. W. Howard Knott asserted that Caton's "opinions were always logical and expressed with great common sense and vigor. He had little respect for precedent, relying more on principles."[71] The court that decided Campbell's appeal also included Chief Justice Samuel H. Treat, originally from New York, and Justice Walter B. Scates, originally from Virginia and Kentucky.[72]

The Trial, Appeal, and Decision

The procedural history and facts of the murder case against Campbell have been obscured because the official case report includes only Justice Caton's opinion for the Supreme Court. Caton in turn recites only the facts that he found were relevant to his discussion of the four meritorious grounds for the reversal of Campbell's conviction. But the Illinois Supreme Court's file includes documents that supply essential missing details that confirm the conclusion that Parker headed a three-person night-riding proto-Klan crew. These men apparently intended to enforce the white-supremacist beliefs legitimizing interracial violence, which he and many Upland southerners imported into Illinois.[73]

O. J. Page's Massac County history provides clues about events that occurred a "few days" before the killing, which support this conclusion. According to Page, a dispute arose between Campbell and Parker "at a house raising . . . in which Campbell struck Parker with a spike."[74] A house raising, or barn raising, refers to the traditional building construction method known as timber framing. Under this method, the walls of a structure—typically a house or a barn—are first framed on the ground. They then are raised and attached to form the walls of the structure by the joint efforts of a gathering of the people in the community. This type of collective effort is often cited as an example of the harmonious outpouring of solidarity among rural neighbors. In this case, however, it was a scene of acrimony and violence between Campbell and Parker.[75]

These clues suggest that Goodwin Parker's own actions set in motion the chain of events that ended in his death. Parker's resentment arising out of his dispute carried over to the night of December 9, 1853, when Parker was killed. He and three other men met at the house of Willis Gurley, who is referred to as "Gusky a German" in the transcript of the trial testimony. Gurley was a blacksmith. Like Parker, he was born in North Carolina. His house was 150 to 200 yards from the Campbell family's house.[76]

According to Caton's statement of the facts, Parker, with a hatchet in his hands, "went to the door of the [Campbell] house, leaving his companions thirty or forty yards back, to whom he was to give warning if Campbell was in the house." Parker soon "called to the others to come on, and informed them that the negro was there. They rushed up" and saw Parker and Campbell "some distance from the house, engaged together, and there [Parker] was stabbed, and died in a few minutes." Parker's hatchet "was found near the spot where he was killed." After Campbell "was committed to jail, a wound was observed upon his head which penetrated to the skull, and which appeared to have been made with a hatchet, an axe or a hammer."[77]

Caton omits many facts that were in the testimony, however, and support Page's assertion that the purpose of this raid on the Campbell house was "to inflict [on Campbell] a good sound beating."[78] For example, Caton does not state that Parker's companions on this raid were his son, James H. Parker, William Warren, and Joseph H. Dupree. James H. Parker was a common laborer about twenty years old. He was born in Kentucky. Warren also was a common laborer about twenty-three years old. Although he was born in Indiana, both of his parents were born in Kentucky. Dupree was a forty-two-year-old farmer who was born in Virginia. He lived one residence away from the Parker family. Warren's family included his wife Cynthia Ann, born in North Carolina, and six children who were two to seventeen years of age. These children were born in Tennessee, Kentucky, and Illinois, indicating the family's history of movement.[79]

The three surviving members of this crew were among the six witnesses who testified for the prosecution at Campbell's trial. The defense called four witnesses, including Willis Gurley, whose crucial testimony Parrish excluded. All of the witnesses were white men, but none of them stated that they saw who stabbed Parker or how the stabbing happened. Also present at the scene were Campbell's mother, a sister, and a brother. His mother and sister were detained after the killing, but there is no evidence whether they were charged.[80]

Logan began the prosecution's case with Dupree's testimony. He asserted that Goodwin Parker asked that he, James Parker, and Warren assist him in a mission to "have" Campbell "if he was on the top side of the Earth, and fetch him to Justice." On cross-examination, Dupree admitted "we were all excited before we started to Campbell's house and had been drinking some." He conceded that they all were armed when they left Gurley's house. Dupree carried a knife, Goodwin Parker a hatchet, and James Parker a loaded gun. They approached the Campbell house "about one and a half or two hours after night."[81]

Caton also omitted evidence that sheds light on the night raiders' motives. James Parker admitted that he "was there the night in question we started after the Nigger" and that he was carrying a loaded gun when raiding the Campbell house. It also was an undisputed fact that gunshots were heard twice, once while these men were at Gurley's house and later during the melee after James Parker learned that his father had been stabbed and Campbell was running away from the scene.[82]

Samuel Yandell, a defense witness, also offered relevant evidence on the raiders' intent. He was a neighbor of Gurley and Campbell. He testified that he walked out of his house after dark on the night in question when he heard gunfire coming from Gurley's house. He said he also heard someone twice "call these words, come on boys, come on boys, the damned Nigger has shit." Yandell then said "a crying and lamentation was made and someone said Lord Jesus how can I stand it, about this time I heard another gun fired, just after the Lamentation."[83] The jury did not, however, hear the testimony of Willis Gurley, which Judge Parrish excluded. Jack proffered that this testimony would confirm "threats made by [Goodwin Parker] during the day and other times shortly before the death of Parker," which were made by Parker "in respect of and against [Campbell]."[84]

The jury convicted Campbell of the crime of manslaughter, not murder, and they sentenced him to serve an eight-year prison sentence. This was the maximum permitted jail term for defendants convicted of manslaughter; those convicted of murder were to be punished with death.[85] Jack made a motion for a new trial, which, on June 17, 1854, Judge Parrish denied.[86]

Jack then filed a bill of exceptions and a writ of error, to appeal the judgment to the Illinois Supreme Court. That court decided the appeal during its November 1854 term.[87] It also rejected Logan's attempt to have the appeal dismissed on procedural grounds.[88]

Justice Caton's opinion begins with the conclusion that "the evidence in the case tends very strongly to show that the deceased [Parker] made an assault on the prisoner, and that the homicide was committed in necessary self-defense." After briefly summarizing some of the facts, Caton stated, moreover, that the prosecution did not establish "any sort of justification or legal cause" for Parker's gang's attempt to arrest and, at the very least, beat Campbell.[89]

Caton's opinion poses challenges because he cites no precedents, not even the homicide statute under which the case was prosecuted. At the time of Campbell's trial, the Illinois criminal statutes, consistent with the British common law, did not grant to whites any special privileges to inflict violence against nonwhites, nor did they deny to free Blacks the usual privileges of mitigation and self-defense. These laws established three classes of homicide: murder, manslaughter, and justifiable homicide, which included homicide in self-defense. Murder was the killing of another person with "malice aforethought, either express or implied." Express malice was "that deliberate intention unlawfully to take away the life of a fellow creature." Implied malice existed "when no considerable provocation appears, or when all of the circumstances of the killing show an abandoned or malignant heart." Murder was punishable by death.[90]

The statute defined manslaughter as a sudden killing without malice "and without any mixture of deliberation whatever." Voluntary manslaughter had to be based upon "a sudden heat of passion, caused by provocation apparently sufficient to make the passion irresistable [sic], or involuntary in the commission of an unlawful act, or a lawful act without due caution or circumspection." Adequate provocation did not extend to mere words or gestures; it "must be a serious and highly provoking injury inflicted upon the person killing, sufficient to excite an irresistable [sic] passion in a reasonable person, or an attempt by the person killed to commit a serious personal injury on the person killing." The penalty for manslaughter was a prison term "not exceeding eight years."[91]

The statutes also defined justifiable homicide to include "the killing of a human being in necessary self-defense." This defense required it to "appear that the danger was so urgent and pressing, that in order to save his own life, or to prevent his receiving great bodily harm, the killing of the other was absolutely necessary: and it must appear also, that the person killed was the assailant, or that the slayer had really, and in good faith, endeavor to decline any further struggle before the mortal blow was given."[92]

Caton's first ground for the reversal of Campbell's conviction confirmed Jack's argument at trial that, in response to Parker's breach of the peace, Campbell may have acted in self-defense. In support of this defense, Jack "offered to prove that on that day, and at other times shortly before his death," Parker threatened Campbell. Parrish excluded this evidence at trial. Caton's opinion held that Parrish should have admitted this evidence, which was Gurley's proffered testimony, even if Campbell did not know of Parker's threats until after the homicide.

Caton explained that if Parker "had made threats against the defendant, it would be a reasonable inference that he sought him for the purpose of executing those threats, and thus they would serve to characterize his conduct towards the prisoner at the time of their meeting, and of the affray." Moreover, if Parker "had threatened to kill, maim or dangerously beat" Campbell, "it would be a fair inference, especially so long as the evidence shows that he had a hatchet in his hands, that he had attempted to accomplish his declared purpose, and if so, then [Campbell] was justified in defending himself, even to the taking of the life of his assailant, if necessary." Caton cited the common-law rule that Parker's "threats, of themselves, could not have justified the prisoner in assailing and killing the deceased," but he added "they might have been of the utmost importance in connection with the other testimony, in making out a case of necessary self-defense." The court therefore held that the evidence of Parker's threats "was proper, and should have been admitted."[93]

Commentators cite this ruling as an important precedent permitting trial judges to admit evidence of a crime victim's threats that were not communicated to the defendant. This evidence is not admitted to prove the defendant's state of mind. The judge and jury may nevertheless consider it to determine that the victim probably was the aggressor.[94]

Caton based his second ground for reversal on Parrish's decision to read to the jury Logan's following requested instruction, which may have steered the jurors to their manslaughter verdict and Campbell's eight-year jail sentence:

> If the jury believe, from the evidence, that the defendant was pursued by the deceased, Goodwin Parker, and turned upon him and slew him with a knife, or other instrument capable of producing a like death, when it was not necessary for self-preservation, or in necessary self-defense, or to prevent his receiving great bodily harm, although they believe there was no previous malice on the part of the defendant towards the deceased, yet they are bound to find the defendant guilty of manslaughter, and fix his term of confinement in the penitentiary of the State at not more than eight years.

Caton reasoned that "this instruction, if not absolutely wrong, was at least liable to misconstruction, and to be understood by the jury as depriving the defendant of the right of self-defense, unless his danger was not only apparently imminent, but was real and positive. If so understood, the instruction was wrong."[95]

Caton instead endorsed an objectively reasonable self-defense standard. That standard required the jury to ask if "the defendant was pursued or assaulted by the deceased in such a way as to induce in him a reasonable and a well-grounded belief that he was actually in danger of losing his life, or suffering great bodily harm." A defendant "acting under the influence of such reasonable apprehension" could defend himself or herself, "whether the danger was real or only apparent." Contrary to Parrish's instruction, Caton held, "Actual and positive danger is not indispensable to justify self-defense."[96] This holding in the decision also has been cited as establishing in Illinois this "objectively reasonable" self-defense standard.[97]

Caton's third and fourth grounds for reversal were based on Parrish's refusal to read to the jury Jack's eleventh and thirteenth requested jury instructions, both of which could have led to Campbell's acquittal. The eleventh instruction asked the jurors to consider if there was reasonable doubt about the issue of whether Campbell in fact stabbed Parker. The instruction stated, "If it is uncertain, from the evidence, in the minds of the jury, which one, out of two or more persons, inflicted the stab [that killed Parker], that would operate to acquit the prisoner, unless there is proof that the prisoner aided or abetted the person ascertained to have killed him." Although Caton critiqued this instruction as being "inartificially drawn" and "liable to verbal criticism," he held, "yet it contains an important principle of law, of the benefit of which the prisoner should not have been deprived." He explained,

> There was evidence tending to show that the mother and sister of the prisoner were at or very near the place of the affray at the time the wound was inflicted, and his counsel had the right to insist before the jury, that one of them struck the blow without his knowledge or procurement, while he was simply trying to flee from his pursuer; and had the jury so far concurred in that view of the case as to entertain a reasonable doubt whether one of the others did not strike the blow without the procurement of the prisoner, he was entitled to an acquittal.

Caton thus applied the principle of law stating, "Although it may be positively proved that one of two or more persons committed a crime, yet if it is uncertain which is the guilty party, all must be acquitted. No one can be convicted till it is established that he is the party who committed the offense."[98]

Caton based the fourth ground for reversal on Parrish's refusal to read to the jury Jack's thirteenth requested instruction, which was, "It is the duty of the jury to consider the prisoner's case as if he were a white man, for the law is the same, there being no distinction in its principles in respect of color."[99] Caton noted that Logan did not pretend "that the law of this case, by which the prisoner's guilt or innocence was to be established, was not precisely the same as if he were a white man." Indeed, "it was even insisted on the argument [apparently by Logan], that the proposition is so plain and so universally understood and recognized, that it would have been an insult to the understanding of the jury for the court to have instructed them on that point." Caton nonetheless held, "The proposition is undoubtedly exceedingly plain and altogether undeniable, and I trust is universally understood and recognized, but it was still the right of the prisoner to have the law, plain as it was, declared to the jury by the court."[100]

Caton also found unpersuasive Logan's warning, apparently alluding to the state's discriminatory Black Laws, "that the instruction asserts the absolute equality, in all respects, under our law, of the black man with the white." Caton held, instead, that the jury would apply the instruction only "to the case upon trial, where the equality is admitted. With the rights of the defendant in any other regard, the jury could have nothing to do." Caton added, "Any other construction of that instruction is altogether too refined for practical justice."[101]

This holding in Jack's successful appeal of Campbell's conviction had lasting significance, at least in Illinois case law. The Illinois Supreme Court, even into the twentieth century, continued to require that trial judges grant the requests of Black defendants to instruct juries to consider the defendants' cases as if they were white.[102]

The Supreme Court remanded the case to the Circuit Court for a new trial, and according to O. J. Page, Campbell was released from prison. The retrial was to be held in Pulaski County. Campbell obtained a change of venue returning the case to Massac County, but Page reports that Campbell was not retried and later became a preacher.[103]

We therefore never will know if a Massac County jury would have convicted Campbell after hearing all the relevant evidence and the correct legal instructions.

Evaluating the Decision

The *Campbell* case nevertheless shows how attorneys who stand up for the rule of law and for equal justice under law without regard to the race of the parties, and judges who are willing to enforce these principles, can make a difference.

Both Jack, as the advocate, and Caton, as the Supreme Court justice, carved out a space for the equal application of the law in all criminal trials, if within the limits imposed by the Illinois Black Laws.

Evidence of Jack's opinions on race and slavery could not be found. But his competent trial advocacy on Campbell's behalf, his successful appeal after the conviction, and his decision to leave Pennsylvania for Illinois may have been prefigured by his involvement in the defense by his mentor, George W. Smith, of Samuel Mohawk, a Native American man who also was accused of committing an interracial murder.

According to Butler County, Pennsylvania, farmer James Wigton, Mohawk was arrested and charged with the June 30, 1843, murder of Wigton's wife and five children at their farmhouse "just south of the Town of Slippery Rock."[104] While Mohawk was being held for trial at the Butler County jail, rumors circulated that Native Americans planned to "burn the Town of Butler" and release Mohawk. Wigton admitted that, in response to these rumors, he joined a lynch mob of almost "700 armed men" who had assembled near a tavern outside of Butler. The mob planned first to attack the jail and then to capture and kill Mohawk. When the crowd was "about to start to [go] to Butler," Wigton recalled, "the Sheriff, the Judge, Lawyers and principal men of Butler came out there to persuade us to turn back, stating that they could secure the jail against an attack from the Indians." These peacemakers told the assemblage that they could "send a delegation of [their] number to see that everything was safe," while assuring the mob that the rumors of the Native American attack were false. The rule of law prevailed and the mob eventually disbursed.[105]

Jack evidently was one of the lawyers who confronted the lynch mob, and he took action to further defend the rule of law. Wigton complains that, after this confrontation, he "was arrested, together with several others, on information of Jedediah Jack, a lawyer of Butler, for inciting a riot. We gave bail, and at court was [sic] dismissed." Wigton asserts that "the indignation of the citizens at our arrest drove Jack from the County."[106]

Before leaving Butler County, Jack was one of the defense witnesses called at Mohawk's December 1843 trial. In support of Mohawk's insanity defense, Jack recounted a post-arrest interview of Mohawk, in which Mohawk admitted to the killings. But Mohawk also said that he had seen "a great many devils" who "told him to kill people." He described the devils' clothing, acknowledged that he also saw some devils in prison, and "expressed sorrow for the act." On cross-examination, Jack called Mohawk "more an object of pity than insult."[107]

The jurors were not persuaded, however, and they convicted Mohawk of first-degree murder.[108] Mohawk was hanged in March 1844. According to Wigton, if Mohawk had been cleared, "he would have been promptly lynched, such was the excitement and feeling against Mohawk."[109] Like Jack, Smith left Butler County sometime after this case was tried. He moved to Kansas, where he became a controversial 1850s free soil advocate.[110]

Jack's defense of Campbell thus is consistent with his willingness to stand up to the lynch mob and enforce the rule of law in Mohawk's case. That case may have taught Jack not to assume that jurors will share a commitment to equal justice for all, especially in cases of interracial violence.[111]

Caton's decision also may have been foreshadowed by his judicial rulings and opinions suggesting that he was not the state's most pro-slavery jurist. For example, he presided over the October 1843 Bureau County Circuit Court criminal trial of abolitionist Owen Lovejoy. Lovejoy was charged with harboring an African American woman who did not have a certificate of freedom, in violation of one of the provisions of the 1829 Illinois Black Law. According to press reports, Caton charged the jury that enslaved people who were voluntarily brought into the state by their owners became free the moment they entered Illinois. The jury acquitted Lovejoy on all charges.[112] Caton's charge was consistent with the doctrine that Lord Chief Justice Mansfield (William Murray) announced in his opinion deciding *Somerset v. Stewart*.[113] Because Illinois state (municipal) law did not explicitly legitimize slavery, those accused of being enslaved would be presumed to be free. But later that year, Caton voted with the Supreme Court majority that did not apply this freedom presumption when a slave owner allegedly brought an enslaved person into the state only for a short time.[114] He also did not dissent when the court sustained the conviction of Richard Eells for harboring an enslaved man named Chauncy Durkee.[115]

On the other hand, Caton voted with the court's majority in *Jarrot v. Jarrot*, an 1845 decision that finally "ended what was then called 'the old French slavery.'"[116] Joseph Jarrot, who also is designated in the case report as "alias Pete, and Joseph, a colored man," sued to recover a judgment for wages he alleged that he earned while working for Julia Jarrot. She was a descendent of a pre-1787 French slaveholding family, which owned Joseph's grandmother. The case was set up to try Joseph's right to freedom. An October 1843 term jury trial in the St. Clair Circuit Court ended in a judgment for Julia, pursuant to Justice James Shields's jury instructions. Joseph filed an appeal with the Illinois Supreme Court, which was argued during the December 1843 term, soon after Caton's reappointment to the court.[117]

This was one of four slavery cases that antislavery lawyer Lyman Trumbull argued during that term, at the beginning of his long legal and political career. The court did not deliver its opinion for Joseph until the December 1844 term.

Julia then filed a petition for rehearing, and when no appearance was made, the court in its December 1845 term affirmed its judgment.[118]

A divided six-to-three court held that the descendants of people who were enslaved by the French settlers and who were born after the Northwest Ordinance was adopted could no longer be enslaved in Illinois.[119] The court's membership had, in 1841, been increased from four to nine justices under a court-packing statute that Trumbull sponsored as a freshman Democrat legislator.[120]

Four of the justices in the majority wrote opinions. Justice Walter B. Scates, joined by justices Samuel D. Lockwood and Thomas C. Browne, based his opinion on the Northwest Ordinance's slavery prohibition, as confirmed by the 1818 Illinois state constitution. Justice Richard M. Young wrote a separate opinion, essentially reaching the same conclusion. Justice William C. Wilson's two-sentence opinion was based only on the Illinois state constitution.[121] Justice Caton filed an opinion stating only, "I am of the opinion that the judgment of the court below should be reversed." The three dissenters, justices Shields, Jesse B. Thomas, and Samuel H. Treat, did not publish any opinions.[122]

Although Caton wrote the opinion reversing Campbell's homicide conviction, both Jack and Campbell were, in a sense, secondary authors of this ruling. It could be seen to originate with the reactions of Campbell and his family to the pro-South legal consciousness exhibited by Parker and his night-riding crew. We do not know why Campbell struck Parker at the house raising that preceded the homicide, but Campbell apparently offended Parker's honor, and Parker believed he had to even the score. Either Campbell stood his ground on the night of the killing, or, as Jack suggested in his arguments, Campbell's mother and sister confronted and killed Parker as Campbell fled to safety. Indeed, Campbell's family may have recently moved to Illinois to escape from a society in which Parker's actions would be justified under the law.

The Illinois Supreme Court's decision thus was a victory for Campbell because the court applied the substantive law of homicide and evidence without regard to Campbell's race or the race of his alleged victim. Although Judge Caton's opinion did not guarantee "absolute equality" to all without regard to race, it nevertheless was one triumph for the legal ideology of the northern emigrants in Illinois over the state's pro-southern immigrants' legal culture, which had held the upper hand for many years, even on this ostensibly free soil.

The questions remain, however, why Jack requested that Parrish read to the jury the explicit equality under the law instruction and why the Supreme Court justices concluded that its omission was a reason to reverse the conviction. They all may have had concerns about the effects of the jurors' knowledge of the Illinois Black Laws, including the provisions that resulted in all-white juries and prohibited the testimony of a "negro, mulatto, or Indian," except in a criminal prosecution against a "negro, mulatto, or Indian," or in a civil case in which these persons "alone shall be parties."[123] This testimonial bar would not have excluded evidence in Campbell's case. But Jack and the justices likely had concerns that this rule conveyed a message about unequal justice.

Jack and Campbell also must have known that their courtroom adversary Logan was the state legislator who had recently opposed an effort to repeal this testimonial ban and, on January 29, 1853, introduced the law that was intended to stop Black migration into Illinois.[124] They also may have known that Logan argued that Blacks were "not suited to be placed upon a level with white men."[125] But they may not have known that, about two weeks before Logan introduced the exclusion bill, Parrish wrote Logan a letter supporting the idea. Parrish declared, "The move or resolution in relation to the immigration of free negroes into this state is one that will reflect credit and distinction. . . . The harder the fight on such a measure[,] the greater will be the distinction. . . . I have no fears but what we will be able to exert an influence in the political arena in Egypt sufficent [sic] for all practical purposes."[126]

Conclusion

Contrary to the assurances of Logan and Parrish, Jack and the Illinois Supreme Court believed that Massac County's Little Egypt jurors must be instructed on the requirements of the equal protection of the law to protect Campbell from the racial bias lurking in the jurors' legal consciousness and in their local legal culture, which to some extent was grounded in southern customs, statutes, and common-law doctrines. Would the all-white jury side with a mature white man who believed that an insolent young African American man like Campbell deserved a "good sound beating"? Parker's belief that he had the privilege to inflict a violent response had by then been expressly legitimated in southern law, including by the Supreme Court in Parker's birth state of North Carolina. Many Massac County residents, like Parker and his co-conspirators, were of southern birth, heritage, or leanings. They also likely brought this southern legal consciousness into the courtroom.

Decator Campbell and Jedediah Jack nevertheless won a victory for formal legal equality in the substantive criminal law.[127] This was not a novel idea. Decades before, southern trial court judges applied this rule to free Blacks in the criminal law. But even the antebellum South's most moderate appellate judges disagreed. They instead created the rule of inequality under the criminal law for enslaved people and later extended this rule to free Blacks.

CHAPTER 2

Chief Justice Taylor and Unequal Criminal Law Protection for Slaves

Jedediah Jack and the Illinois Supreme Court justices who decided Decatur Campbell's appeal apparently understood how the legal consciousness of the white members of Massac County's Upland South–oriented community was influenced by the long history of southern U.S. enslavement law. This evolving body of law discriminated against people because of their enslaved status and their perceived race.

Southern antebellum appellate court judges, including John Louis Taylor and William J. Gaston of North Carolina, were among the agents of legal innovation who established in the common law the novel doctrine of separate and unequal protection of the criminal law based on enslavement and race. These judges used this doctrine to create new rules and standards for mitigation and justification in cases of violence involving whites and slaves.

This and the following chapter explain this process of common-law legal change. They focus on North Carolina case law because this state's appellate court judges wrote this essential enslavement law doctrine with little legislative intervention, beginning with Chief Justice Taylor's seminal 1820 opinion in *State v. Tackett*.[1] This chapter and the one to follow discuss the cases following that decision in the wider contexts that show how and why these judges modified the common law to create new rules and doctrines that replaced settled judge-made criminal law precedents.

Chapters 4 and 5 will then demonstrate how justices John Belton O'Neall and Richmond Mumford Pearson later extended these novel criminal law rules and standards to cases involving violence between whites and free Blacks. All of these jurists have been included among the "moderate" southern judges, whom scholars have contrasted with others, such as Georgia's first chief justice, Joseph

Henry Lumpkin, who are included among the era's "thoroughgoing pro-slavery fire-eaters on the southern benches."[2] Nevertheless, both the moderates and the fire-eaters shared essential assumptions about the need to enforce white supremacy. Their opinions differed only on how best to implement this policy of race, caste, and legitimated violence in the law.

The Common Law of Homicide and Slavery

This enslavement law's principal underlying assumptions can be traced to the 1661 Barbados statute titled "An Act for the Better Ordering and Governing of Negroes." The act's preamble asserts two findings that allegedly justified the colonists' enslavement of Africans. The legislators declared that their enslavement practices were unknown to English law, "there being in all the body" of that law "noe track to guide us where to walke nor any rule sett us how to govern such slaves." These lawmakers also confirmed their racist conclusions that the African people they were enslaving were "an heathenish, brutish and uncertaine, dangerous kinde of people" who, among other things, were not entitled to the equal protection of the common law of crimes.[3]

The legislators in Britain's other colonies, and later in the antebellum southern states, adopted criminal law statutes based on these two assumptions. Although the details differed, these laws all included provisions decriminalizing degrees of fatal and nonfatal violence committed by whites against enslaved victims. Moreover, they created crimes that only slaves could commit, while imposing more severe penalties on enslaved people who were convicted of acts that also were crimes if committed by whites.[4]

Taylor's *Tackett* opinion was the first reported North Carolina appellate court decision establishing and explaining the unequal mitigation doctrine when whites were accused of inflicting violence against enslaved victims. The then-existing common-law homicide authorities did not mention enslavement or race at all. Therefore, there were no common-law slavery exceptions to resolve the mitigation issues that arose in slave homicide cases. Following Taylor's lead, the North Carolina antebellum appellate court decisions modified these common-law mitigation doctrines to limit the criminal liability of whites who were accused of killing enslaved victims.

The courts' application of these mitigation doctrines often meant life or death for accused killers in societies, including antebellum North Carolina, which threatened murderers with capital punishment. Although homicide is the killing of one person by another person or persons, not every homicide violates the legal norms of the society in which it occurs. Depending on the social and legal context, a homicide may be impermissible, permissible, or even required.[5]

By the eighteenth century, the British common-law judges established three classes of homicide: murder, manslaughter, and excusable homicide. Murder was the killing of another person with malice aforethought. Malice aforethought eventually came to include cold-blooded killings or killings committed while the defendant was perpetrating a felony. The common law also prohibited killings that were classified as manslaughter. These homicides were defined as sudden killings with provocation and without premeditation.[6]

The courts, by the early nineteenth century, required that defendants seeking to mitigate killings to common-law manslaughter prove that they responded to their victim's legally adequate provocation. This provocation, as a general rule, did not extend to mere words or gestures that the victim directed at the accused killer.[7] The common law recognized exceptions to this "mere words" doctrine, however, which reflected the social class structure. These exceptions granted to "superiors" in relationships such as master/servant, parent/child, and schoolmaster/student, the privilege to physically—but moderately—correct and punish misbehaving "inferiors." The homicide might be excused if this "reasonable" correction caused the "inferior" person's death. In contrast, those who imposed what were deemed to be immoderate or unlawful punishments, or who used improper instruments of correction, could be convicted of murder or manslaughter.[8] But, as Lea VanderVelde explains, nineteenth-century statutes, appellate court opinions, and legal treatises began to reject these status-based criminal law rules. She concludes that these sources, "in Hohfeldian terms," reassigned this privilege from these "superiors" to the "inferiors," who gained an expanded "right of bodily integrity from intentionally inflicted pain." Those who engaged in what previously had been privileged violence and abuse—over time in the nineteenth century—became potentially criminally and civilly liable for their actions.[9]

And by the seventeenth century, the common-law judges held that some killings were excusable. These included killings *per infortunium*, by misadventure, and homicides *excusable se defendendo*, in self-defense. Homicide by misadventure occurred when a defendant killed his or her victim while doing a lawful act without the intention to kill. But an accidental killing could have been manslaughter or murder if death occurred while the defendant was committing an unlawful act.[10] An accused killer claiming self-defense had to establish that he or she killed an aggressor who presented an imminent or immediate danger of unlawful bodily harm to the accused, and that the killer used force to the extent that it was necessary to avoid the danger the aggressor posed. The courts also required defendants to prove that they retreated to the wall, if they could do so safely, before resorting to killing their victims.[11]

Initially, those who were convicted of murder or manslaughter were punished with death, but the courts afforded the benefit of clergy to first-time offenders.[12] This, according to Lawrence M. Friedman, "was a privilege originally (as the name suggests) for clergymen only. Later it came to cover anybody who knew how to read." But even those who were illiterate could memorize a Bible verse to prove their right to the privilege. The lives of those given this benefit were spared on their first murder convictions. They were instead branded on the hand. If they committed a second offense, they would be executed.[13] Statutes adopted between 1496 and 1547 denied this benefit to those convicted of murder. All convicted murderers were to be executed, unless they were pardoned by the king or queen in England, or by the governors in the colonies and later in the United States.[14]

North Carolina's earliest colonial enslavement laws did not exempt homicides of slaves from these common-law rules and doctrines, unlike South Carolina's laws, which, until 1821, expressly superseded the common law of homicide for slave killings. Among other things, these laws imposed only fines as the punishments for those convicted of even the willful murder of slaves, as well as for those killing slaves "on a sudden heat or passion, or by undue correction."[15]

In contrast to this clarity in South Carolina law, uncertainty characterized North Carolina's slave homicide law after 1709, when Carolina was legally divided.[16] A 1774 statute declared the North Carolina legislators' intent to resolve these doubts by establishing that willful and malicious slave killings were murders. But this act imposed only a twelve-month prison term on first-time slave murderers. Death without the benefit of clergy was reserved for second-time slave murderers. This law also excused the killing of an outlawed slave or a slave who was "in the Act of Resistance to his lawful Owner or Master, or [the homicide of] any Slave dying under Moderate Correction."[17] North Carolina law declared that slaves would be outlaws if they ran away from their enslavers, concealed themselves, and killed hogs or cattle for subsistence.[18]

North Carolina's legislature later adopted statutes in 1791 and 1801 making first-time malicious slave murders capital offenses. But these acts retained the 1774 act's exemptions confirming the slave owners' privilege to discipline their slaves, thus decriminalizing homicides that would be murders under the then established common-law principles. The courts interpreted these laws to continue to decriminalize all slave killings that otherwise would have been common-law manslaughters.[19]

During the North Carolina legislature's term beginning on November 17,

1817, the lawmakers adopted "An Act to Punish the Offense of Killing a Slave," apparently—once and for all—equating slave murder, manslaughter, or excusable homicide with any other homicide. These killings, according to this act's plain language, would be "homicide, and shall partake the same degree of guilt when accompanied with like circumstances that homicide now does at common law."[20]

The Seawell/Taylor Rule of Inequality for Enslaved Crime Victims

North Carolina's newly reformed Supreme Court, in 1820, had to interpret this statute after William Tackett (also spelled Tacket) and Mason Scott were convicted for murdering enslaved men owned by others. Between 1806 and 1818, the state had a Supreme Court that, Laura Edwards concludes, "was supreme in name only." The court met twice each year in Raleigh. It was made up of two or more Superior Court judges, "to which were submitted, not appeals, but difficult or doubtful cases," which these judges heard on trial while riding on the state's judicial circuits. "Only in 1818 did the court become 'supreme' in more than name, acquiring its own panel of judges and authority over points of law and equity."[21] The state legislature selected as the court's initial members Chief Justice John Louis Taylor and justices John Hall and Leonard Henderson. The legislature elected the court's justices until 1868, when the state's constitution authorized their popular election.[22]

Harry Seawell, one of the defense lawyers for Scott and Tackett, deserves the credit—or the blame—for advancing the unequal mitigation doctrine. Seawell convinced the court to ignore the 1817 statute's plain language and interpret the act to give the court the option to create under the common law a new separate and unequal standard of provocation and mitigation when whites were prosecuted for killing slaves.[23]

Seawell was described as "one of the strongest criminal lawyers who ever appeared at the Bar in North Carolina."[24] His extensive legislative and judicial career, by 1820, was well underway. He was, in 1799–1802, 1810, and 1812, elected to North Carolina's House of Commons and Assembly, and he was elected as the state's attorney general from 1803 to 1808. His judicial career began in 1811, when he was appointed to fill a vacancy on the state's Supreme Court. He served until the end of the year, when Edward Harris defeated him in the legislature's election of a judge to complete the term. Seawell was again appointed to the court in April 1813 to fill the vacancy that occurred when Harris died. This time Seawell was elected to complete the term. He sat on the court until February 1819, when he resigned in response to the governor's change of his circuit court assignment and the legislature's failure to elect him to be one of the three justices of the new Supreme Court. He then resumed his legislative career and was elected to serve in the state Senate from 1821 to 1826 and again from 1831 to 1832. In that year, he again was elected to the Superior Court, where he served until his death in 1835.[25]

Seawell was a slave owner. According to the 1830 census, his Wake County household included forty-seven enslaved people and one "free colored" male who was between thirty-six and fifty-four years of age.[26]

Seawell's record on race relations and slavery is mixed. On the one hand, he headed a state Senate committee that drafted a statute, adopted in 1827, further restricting the rights of free Blacks.[27] This was in part a response to Governor Hutchins G. Burton's December 26, 1826, message to the legislature. Burton asked the legislators to consider responding to Vermont's expression of opposition to slavery, not with ameliorative measures, but with "increased restriction of, or at least, by a more urgent exercise of our police." He suggested a measure designed to stop free Black migration into the state.[28]

The legislators approved an act that, like an 1820 South Carolina statute, required free Blacks entering the state to leave within twenty days. If they did not, they were subject to arrest, conviction, and a fine of five hundred dollars. If they could not pay the fine, they were to be confined for up to ten years of involuntary servitude as apprentices. The statute also included racially discriminatory anti-vagrancy provisions, which authorized the arrest of a "free negro or mulatto" who was "found spending his or her time in idleness and dissipation, or who has no regular or honest employment or occupation, which he or she is accustomed to follow." If convicted by a jury, the accused was required to post a bond for one year, "conditioned on his or her good behaviour and industriousness, peaceful deportment." Failing this, the county court could hire out the offender "for a term of time to service and labor, which . . . may seem reasonable and just, calculated to reform him or her to habits of industry and morality, not exceeding three years for any one offence."[29] As John Hope Franklin explained, free Blacks "were now at the mercy of justices of the peace, and it is needless to say that at times extremely personal and petty considerations determined whether or not the free Negro was to provide a bond for his good conduct and pay the costs of the court, which he not infrequently lacked."[30]

But, on the other hand, Seawell was among the delegates to the state's 1835 constitutional convention who opposed an amendment providing "that free Negroes and Mulattoes within the four degrees, shall not be allowed to vote for the members of the Senate or House of Commons of this State."[31] North Carolina's 1776 constitution permitted "all freemen, of the age of twenty-one years" who satisfied a twelve-month residency requirement to vote for members of the state's Senate and House of Commons. But to vote for state senators residents had to own at least fifty acres of land for six months before the election, and to vote for House members, they had to have "paid public taxes."[32] Some free Black men therefore voted until 1835, when North Carolina became the last southern state to prohibit free Black voting.[33]

This amendment's supporters appealed to racism and white supremacy among the reasons favoring the total disenfranchisement of free Blacks. Jesse Wilson, for example, supported disenfranchisement even though he represented a county that was more than 40 percent Black. He expressed what others may have been thinking when he argued that no matter how "much colored persons might be elevated, their color alone would prove a barrier to keep them in a degraded state." He also warned that "the moment a free mulatto obtains a little property, and is a little favored by being admitted to vote, he will not be satisfied with a black wife. He will soon connect himself with a white woman."[34]

Disenfranchisement opponents disagreed, however, noting that free Blacks paid taxes and should have the right to vote on those who imposed those taxes. And several delegates proposed compromises that would have substituted racially discriminatory qualifications for total disenfranchisement.[35]

Seawell objected to one of these proposals, which would have continued to enfranchise only free Blacks who owned fifty acres of land because "this . . . would exclude a number of men who might be as respectable and as well qualified to exercise the privilege as those in possession of freeholds." He added that he would prefer "if the qualification had reference to four or five years of residence and the regular payment of taxes."[36] Seawell nevertheless later voted in favor of William J. Gaston's unsuccessful alternative discriminatory property ownership qualification. It would have permitted African Americans owning five hundred dollars' worth of property to continue to vote, as long as they had not been convicted of "an infamous offence."[37]

Seawell therefore brought to the Tackett and Scott defense teams a unique political and judicial insider's perspective and expertise. When he was a trial judge, he presided over the 1815 trial of John R. Cooke, John Davis, and Samuel Bailey, who were charged with murdering Bailey's slave Stephen. The jury found Cooke guilty of murder and acquitted the other two defendants. Seawell sentenced Cooke to death, but Governor William Miller later pardoned Cooke after receiving "numerous petitions" in Cooke's favor.[38]

Mason Scott was tried first under the 1817 act on the charge that he murdered an enslaved man named Caleb. Scott was described as "a handsome young man, about 18 or 19 years of age, of strong passions and intemperate habits," which apparently included excessive alcohol consumption.[39] His victim Caleb, an older man, was described as "a useful and obedient servant" who nevertheless "was addicted to intemperate drinking."[40] A Wake County grand jury, on April 23, 1820, indicted Scott for Caleb's murder, finding that, on July 16, 1819, Scott, a "labourer," killed Caleb, who was "the property of Frederick S. Marshall," by stabbing him with a dirk.[41]

Scott was tried in the Wake County Superior Court before Judge John Paxton and a jury. Seawell, Charles Manly, and Anthony G. Glynn represented Scott. The trial began on April 6, 1820, and continued until around two o'clock the following morning. Although the official report of the case does not include a statement of the facts, the state apparently proved that Scott stabbed Caleb without any provocation.[42] The trial was covered by local and out-of-state newspapers. They reported that around ten o'clock on the night of the killing, Scott and Caleb were in a Raleigh grocery store. Scott was carrying a dirk. He was "drunk with liquor, met the negro, renewed an old quarrel with him, and stabbed him to death."[43] "On a search, the bloody dagger was found in the street—and not long afterwards Scott was discovered fast asleep on one of the benches of the market house, scarce fifty yards from the store."[44]

The jury found Scott guilty of murder, and Judge Paxton denied Scott's new trial motion. Manly and Seawell unsuccessfully argued Scott's appeal during the North Carolina Supreme Court's June 1820 term. They challenged the objectivity and sanity of one of the jurors, alleged that the trial judge should have permitted the jury to hear evidence of a statement that Scott made the day after the killing, and contended that the state failed to offer evidence sufficiently identifying who was Caleb's owner. In the alternative to these arguments for a new trial, Seawell asked the court to vacate Scott's death sentence. He contended that the court should, in effect, roll the clock back to 1774 and interpret the 1817 act to once again make slave murder a crime that afforded defendants the common-law benefit of clergy on the first offense.[45]

Justice Henderson wrote the court's opinion rejecting all of these arguments. After Governor John Branch denied Scott's pardon request, on November 10, 1820, Scott became the first white North Carolinian to be executed for killing a slave.[46]

Meanwhile, also during the Superior Court's spring 1820 term, the Wake County grand jury indicted William Tackett, a "labourer," for the December 18, 1819, murder of an enslaved man named Daniel, who was identified as "the property of William Ruffin."[47] Ruffin operated a hotel in Raleigh. Upon his death in 1825, he owned approximately ten slaves.[48]

The case was scheduled for trial during the court's spring 1820 term, after Scott's case. But Judge Paxton continued the case to the court's fall term because two witnesses allegedly were not available.[49]

It may have seemed to Tackett that he too would suffer Scott's fate. This may be why, on June 25, 1820, Tackett, Scott, and three other men dug their way out of the Wake County jail. Press reports of this jailbreak describe Tackett as "22 or 23 years of age, of a low stature, square built, and is by trade a Carpenter." A fifty-dollar reward was offered for each escapee. All of the runaways were soon apprehended.[50]

Tackett's trial in Raleigh began on October 6, 1820, at the end of the Wake County Superior Court's fall term. Seawell and Glynn represented Tackett at the trial. The judge that term was Joseph J. Daniel, who was in the early part of a long judicial career.[51] He had been elected to North Carolina's legislature in 1807, 1812, and 1815. The next year he was elected to his first three-year term as a Superior Court judge. And in 1832 Daniel was elected to the North Carolina Supreme Court, where he served until his death in 1848.[52]

At the trial, Judge Daniel denied Tackett's request for more time to obtain the testimony of a witness in another county. Tackett claimed that he was not able to prepare his defense, in part because he was "a stranger in the Country without friends or connections and is extremely poor." He signed the affidavit supporting this request with his mark, suggesting that he was illiterate. He also admitted that he "escaped from prison since the last Term of the Court, yet it was with others and as proof of [his] not fleeing from justice it is known that he surrendered himself when there was every opportunity of his escaping."[53]

Tackett was described as a "journeyman" who was employed by Millington Richardson, a carpenter. Tackett was living in Richardson's house in Raleigh when the killing occurred. The evidence at trial confirmed that, on the night of December 18, 1819, Tackett shot the enslaved man Daniel with Richardson's gun. For a time before the shooting, Tackett and Daniel argued and fought because Daniel believed that Tackett "kept" Daniel's "wife" Lotty. She was described as "a free colored woman" who lived in a house that was built on a lot owned by Richardson. This lot was close to the house in which Richardson lived.[54]

North Carolina law, like that in the other southern states, declared that slave contracts, including marriage contracts, were unenforceable, thus barring the enforcement of slave marriages in the courts. Enslavers did, however, permit their slaves to have de facto marriages as one of their privileges. But of course these privileges, unlike legal rights, could be withdrawn or terminated at the will of the owner or others, including the owner's heirs or creditors.[55] Ruffin may have extended this privilege to Daniel, who was described as "a favorite servant belonging to" Ruffin.[56]

Tackett did not deny shooting Daniel. His defense instead claimed that Daniel provoked the killing. But the evidence did not rise to the level of provocation that the common law required. Tackett's lawyers, apparently confirming this, thus attempted to prove that Daniel "was a turbulent man" who "was insolent and impudent to white people." Judge Daniel refused to permit this testimony, "unless it would prove that the deceased was insolent and impudent to the prisoner in particular."[57]

Moreover, Judge Daniel's jury instructions were consistent with the principle of equality before the criminal law. He told the jury that the 1817 act required them to apply "the same rules and principles of law as if the deceased had been a white man," thus anticipating the jury charge in the *Campbell* decision. Judge Daniel also directed the jury consistent with the common law of homicide and the 1817 act's "like circumstances" directive. He told the jurors that "murder was the felonious killing of a human being, with malice aforethought, which might either be expressed, as by declarations or lying in wait, or implied, as from the instrument used." He explained "that no words would justify or extenuate homicide, and make it less than murder." And he said that the common law did not permit them to extenuate the killing to manslaughter if Daniel inflicted "a slight blow" that "did not threaten death or bodily harm," and that if Tackett in response used a deadly instrument, like a loaded gun, "it was of no consequence, at what part of the body the aim was directed, if death or great bodily harm was intended."[58]

The jury followed these instructions and found Tackett guilty of murder. Tackett's lawyers responded with a new trial motion. They alleged that "proper evidence had been rejected" and that "the Court erred in the charge to the Jury." Judge Daniel, on October 7, 1820, denied the motion and pronounced the "sentence of death ... upon the prisoner."[59] On the same day, he established October 20, 1820, as the initial date on which Mason Scott was to be executed.[60]

Tackett filed an appeal, which Seawell argued during the North Carolina Supreme Court's December 1820 term. His adversary was William Drew, the attorney general. Drew had practiced law in Halifax County, and he was elected to the state legislature in 1803, 1809, 1813, 1814, and 1816. He then served as the state's attorney general from 1816 until November 1825. Like his father, John Drew, William Drew was interested in horse breeding and racing. He never married and died in 1827, at the approximate age of fifty-seven, after filing for bankruptcy.[61] In his history of early North Carolina, John W. Moore asserted that Drew reminded him of John Dryden's suggestion that a "close alliance sometimes exists between a great wit and a madman." From his own "personal observation," however, Moore concluded that Drew's "eccentricities did not prevent him from being elected to positions of public trust."[62]

Seawell therefore may have had an edge over Drew as a Supreme Court advocate, but both the 1817 act's text and the common-law mitigation standards favored Drew and the state. Therefore, Seawell based his primary argument on a form of judicial activism. He asked the court to ignore the 1817 act's plain language and find that the legislature really intended that the act would have "no other effect than . . . to create the offence of manslaughter, as applied to the homicide of slaves." Before the legislature adopted that act, Seawell contended, slave killing "was either murder or nothing; at least such was the prevailing opinion, and great doubts existed on the Bench, as well as with the ablest lawyers at the Bar." He asserted that the legislature intended only to resolve that debate by defining slave manslaughter as a crime, and thus the act "does not pretend to define what shall constitute the slaying of a slave manslaughter." The legislature instead left it to the judges to define the standards of mitigation "under the ordinary rules of law."[63]

After creating this opening for judicial discretion, Seawell shifted to a white-supremacist public policy argument. He conceded that "the Common Law lays down general rules, by which we are to ascertain whether the killing of one man by another, between whom there is no relation, and who stand on an equality with each other, be murder or manslaughter, or neither." But he added that the law "lays down different rules to govern cases in which the deceased stand in particular relations of dependence and inferiority to the slayer, as an apprentice, servant, pupil, sailor or soldier, to his master, tutor, or officer." He asked the court to apply this general principle to enslaved people because of their inferior enslaved status and their race:

> So here, where the wide distinction exists in the grades of our society between freemen and slaves—*whites and blacks*; and where the policy of the Law as well as the inveterate habits of our population, and the best feelings of our nature enjoin it upon us to keep these classes as distinct in every respect as possible, and, to that end, to enforce the superiority of the one, and the subordination due from the other, a new rule must be laid down fitted to this state of things, and adapted to this particular relation and the exigency of our situation. A free man, who hath been taught from his infancy to look for humility and obedience in a slave, and

who feels every moment of his life the vast superiority that he has over him, early learns that tamely to submit to words of reproach from a slave is degrading to the last degree, and that a blow, even the slightest, is the greatest dishonor. At such an insult, therefore, his passions are inflamed to the utmost pitch; and if, in such a state, he slay the offender, he has a right to claim the benefit of that rule which regards mercifully the frailty and infirmity of human nature.[64]

Seawell then suggested, "If any precise rule could be laid down, I would say that a word from a slave was a provocation equal to a blow from a free man; and the most trifling assault, to a deadly stroke." He concluded, "There is, in the very nature of things, an essential difference between the cases of slaves and free men; and the Court cannot disregard it, arising as it does, out of our population, laws, education, and habits."[65]

In response to Seawell's creative advocacy, Drew asked the court to enforce the 1817 act's unambiguous language in light of the common law of homicide. He "insisted upon the words of the act of 1817, which are, 'that the killing of a slave shall partake of the same degree of guilt, when accompanied with the like circumstances, that homicide now does.'" He relied on settled precedent when he contended, "The Common Law declares what circumstances shall make one guilty of that degree of homicide called manslaughter, or of that higher degree called murder. These were well ascertained before the statute; and that statute declares, in express terms, that the same circumstances that would constitute the slaying of a white man murder, shall likewise constitute the killing of a slave murder." He thus contended that "there is no feature of manslaughter in this case; and the prisoner is guilty of murder, and may be punished therefor under the acts of 1791, and 1801, without the aid of that of 1817."[66]

Drew also urged the court to find that Judge Daniel properly applied the "mere words" doctrine to exclude evidence that "was clearly inadmissible; for no words will justify an assault, much less a deliberate striking another down." Drew cited the leading treatises written by William Blackstone, Edward East, and Michael Foster for the principle that a homicide victim's mere words are not adequate provocation to mitigate the killing to manslaughter. Drew explained that "there was no evidence that the deceased gave the prisoner any blow; but if he had given a slight blow, the [trial judge's] charge was right."[67]

Taylor's *Tackett* opinion nevertheless stated four reasons to reverse the verdict, adopting three of Seawell's arguments departing from these well-settled common-law principles. Taylor first held that Judge Daniel should have permitted Tackett to offer evidence that Daniel "was a turbulent man, and that he was insolent and impudent to white people" in general. This evidence, Taylor stated, "might have an important bearing on" the mitigation issue. He held that both Daniel's enslaved status and the races of Daniel and Tackett were relevant: "It cannot be doubted that the temper and disposition of the deceased, and his usual deportment towards white persons, might have an important bearing on this enquiry, and according to the aspect in which it was presented to the Jury, tend to direct their judgment as to the degree of provocation received by the prisoner." Taylor then illustrated this race-based view with two contrasting scenarios:

> If the general behaviour of the deceased was marked with turbulence and insolence, it might, in connexion with the threats, quarrels and existing causes of resentment he had against the prisoner, increase the probability that the latter had acted under a strong and legal provocation. If, on the contrary the behaviour of the deceased was usually mild and respectful towards white persons, nothing could be added by it to the force of the other circumstances. They must still depend upon their own weight and the probability be lessened, that the prisoner had received a provocation sufficient in point of law to extenuate the homicide.

He concluded, on this point, that "the evidence therefore ought to have been received; and this will be the more apparent when the charge to the Jury is considered."[68]

Second, Taylor held that Judge Daniel erred when he instructed the jury to apply "the same rules and principles of law as if the deceased had been a white man." Taylor instead adopted Seawell's interpretation of the 1817 statute. He held that the legislature "had no design beyond that of authorising a conviction for manslaughter, in cases where a slave was killed under a legal provocation." Before the act was approved, he contended, "a white person [who] had killed a slave under such circumstances as constituted murder, . . . might have been convicted and punished for that offence; but if the homicide was extenuated to manslaughter, no punishment was annexed to that offence, and the accused persons were uniformly acquitted." Therefore, "it seemed just to the Legislature, that the manslaughter of a slave should be punished in the same manner with that of a white person. This they have provided for, and it is all they intended to provide for."[69]

Taylor then determined that the legislators did not intend to require that slave killings "could be only extenuated by such a provocation as would have the same effect where a white person was killed." Instead, he found that the legislators left "the different degrees of homicide to be ascertained by the Common Law of the country—a system which adapts itself to the habits, institutions and actual conditions of the citizens, and which is not the result of the wisdom of any one man, or society of men, in any one age, but of the wisdom and experience of many ages of wise and discreet men." White supremacy was at the root of Taylor's decision. According to Taylor, "It exists in the nature of things, that where slavery prevails, the relation between a white man and a slave differs from that, which subsists between free persons."

Taylor thus, in effect, took judicial notice of the legal consciousness and customs of the whites of his state when he held that "every individual in the community feels and understands, that the homicide of a slave may be extenuated by acts, which would not produce a legal provocation if done by a white person." Taylor stated, however that it would be "impossible" for him "to define and limit these acts." He instead left these issues for "the sense and feelings of Jurors, and the grave discretion of Courts," to balance "the rights respectively belonging to the slave and white man—to the just claims of humanity, and to the supreme law, the safety of the citizens."[70]

Third, Taylor rejected the settled common-law "rule of law, that neither words of reproach, insulting gestures, nor a trespass against goods or land, are provocations sufficient to free the party killing from the guilt of murder, where he made use of a deadly weapon." He instead created a slavery law exception to this "mere words" rule. He held that "it can not be laid down as a rule, that some of these provocations, if offered by a slave, well known to be turbulent and disorderly, would not extenuate the killing, if it were instantly done under the heat of passion, and without circumstances of cruelty."

And fourth, Taylor disagreed with Judge Daniel's instruction that a homicide victim's slight blow did not permit the jury to mitigate the offense to manslaughter when the killer responded with deadly force. He applied race-neutral authorities.[71]

Evaluating the Seawell/Taylor Inequality Principle in *Tackett*

Seawell's race-based mitigation argument and Taylor's opinion adopting it are significant for several reasons. Seawell convinced the court to modify the common law's standards for mitigation to deny to enslaved people the law's equal protection when they were involved in violent interactions with white strangers. He did not base his argument on the perceived necessities of enslavement alone; he made race an equal reason for the rule of inequality, all to advance the well-established customs of white supremacy.

Seawell and Taylor achieved this result by interpreting the 1817 act as if it stated the legislature's intent only to permit juries to mitigate to manslaughter slave killings that were not murder, in cases in which they found that the homicides were not justifiable or excused. This would have been a more plausible interpretation if the legislature had actually used more specific language unambiguously stating that intention, instead of using the broader "like circumstances" language. The statute's text more obviously supports Judge Daniel's apparent conclusion that the legislature intended to extend the common-law mitigation standards to slave killings, to the extent that these standards had not been modified by statute.[72]

Seawell and Taylor also rejected Judge Daniel's instruction that the jury must decide the case in a race-neutral manner, as if the enslaved man Daniel were a white person. Taylor instead created the new unequal protection principle. But he did not base that doctrine on an analogy to the old common-law superior/inferior relationships that Seawell cited in his argument. Taylor instead relied on—and thus legitimized—his understanding of the legal consciousness and the customs of the state's white people. His opinion thus deviated from the common law's mitigation and justification doctrines, which made no exceptions for homicides of enslaved or free African American victims.

Judge Daniel's reading of the statute may have been based on his feeling that, as a trial judge, he should not make this "new law," which should instead be declared by the state's highest court or by the legislature. His jury charge also appears to be consistent with the relatively "moderate" views on race that are revealed by the positions he asserted as a delegate to the 1835 North Carolina constitutional convention.

He, like Seawell, unsuccessfully opposed the state constitutional amendment that disenfranchised all free African American men. Daniel instead offered a motion to impose a $250 freehold estate requirement for "free negroes or mulattoes to vote for members in the House of Commons," while continuing the fifty-acre landownership restriction on voting for state senators. He explained, "He was willing to leave the door open to all colored men of good character and industrious habits, as such would find no difficulty in obtaining the necessary qualification." He conceded "that many of this class are worthless in character," and that his proposal would deny them the vote. But he thought that it was a "good policy . . . to conciliate the most respectable portions of the coloured population," because they "might be very serviceable to us in the case of any combination for evil purposes among their brethren in bondage." Daniel acknowledged the limits of his moderate views, however, when he assured the delegates that he believed the state's "Bill of Rights did not apply to men of colour."[73] Daniel may have been motivated by his own sincere concern for free Blacks, but practical political concerns also may have influenced his thoughts. The county he represented, Halifax, had the state's greatest number of Black voters. According to Lacy Ford, "In no North Carolina county was free black voting more common or more important."[74]

Seawell and Taylor's bold deviation from the well-settled common-law precedents upon which Drew and Judge Daniel relied is especially remarkable because it is so inconsistent with the deferential jurisprudential philosophy Seawell endorsed in the 1818 opinion in *State v. Dick, a Slave*, which he wrote for the North Carolina Supreme Court.[75] The enslaved man Dick, who was identified as being "the property of Mrs. Blount," was indicted under the common law for the July 1, 1817, rape of "Judith Wilkins, a spinster." After Dick was convicted, the Supreme Court arrested the judgment, holding that the indictment was defective in form. Seawell explained that the indictment should have been written under the form of the applicable statute and not the common law. He relied on settled precedents, declaring that the common-law treatises of "Lord Coke, Lord Hale, and Hawkins, all concur in the necessity of such a conclusion." He cited Edward East's treatise for "a contrary opinion," but he declared "we cannot feel ourselves justified, in so important a case, to depart from what has been by the great men above mentioned, considered in settled law, in complaisance to the opinion of any writer however respectable: more especially, as all the precedents have such a conclusion."[76] In contrast to the judicial deference to precedent exhibited in Dick's case, Seawell the appellate court advocate convinced the Supreme Court to deviate from precedents that were uniformly established by the common law's "great men."

Why Taylor based his reasoning on both race and enslavement status became clear three years later when the court in *State v. Reed* denied the appeal of Thomas Reed, who was convicted of murdering an enslaved man named Tom.[77] The published official report of the North Carolina Supreme Court's decision states neither Reed's race nor the evidence asserted against him. But the March 1823 indictment identifies Reed as a free Black man. It alleges that, on December 10, 1822, in Hertford County, he allegedly struck Tom, who lingered until January 7, 1823, when he died. Reed pled not guilty and was tried before Judge Frederick Nash and a jury.[78]

According to the case summary in the Supreme Court's file, Reed went to Tom's house—armed with a large stick—to ask Tom if he had said that Reed "had stole [sic] his bacon." When Tom answered that he had said this, Reed hit Tom with the stick. Judge Nash read to the jury instructions based on the common-law principles that Taylor eschewed in *Tackett*, stating that "words of reproach however insulting would not extenuate a homicide from murder to manslaughter more particularly in a case like this when the prisoner had gone to the house of the deceased and brought upon himself the insulting language." The jury thus convicted Reed of murder. Reed's counsel moved to arrest the judgment, alleging that the indictment was insufficient because it was drafted under the common law and not the 1817 statute. Nash denied the motion. Reed appealed the case to the North Carolina Supreme Court.[79]

If Reed had been white, his lawyer, Gavin Hogg, could have asked the court to reverse this conviction under the *Tackett* ruling. But apparently because Reed was a free Black man, Hogg argued that the indictment was defective because it was based on the common law of crimes instead of the 1817 statute and because slave murder could not be a common-law crime, as slavery was unknown to the common law.[80]

The Supreme Court's majority rejected these arguments and affirmed the conviction. All three justices wrote opinions. Taylor's short opinion cited *Tackett* and restated his belief, which he had explained in his 1801 opinion in *State v. Boon*, that slave murder was cognizable as a common-law crime, even though no reported common-law precedents so held.[81] Justice Leonard Henderson wrote a longer opinion agreeing with Taylor's conclusion. Justice John Hall's dissent restated his conclusion, first stated in *State v. Boon*, that because slavery was unknown to the common law, slave murder could not be a common-law crime.[82]

John Hope Franklin refers to the cases of North Carolina free Blacks Trueman Goode, in 1826, and Louis Hunt, in 1851, who were prosecuted and acquitted for slave homicides.[83] These cases confirm that race had to be added to enslavement as a reason for the *Tackett* rule; only whites could assert the *Tackett* doctrine.

Taylor Extends Unequal Protection to Cases of Nonfatal Violence

Taylor's December term 1823 opinion in *State v. Hale* extended the separate and unequal protection doctrine to permit white strangers to the master-slave relationship to commit nonfatal attacks on enslaved people, which otherwise would have been criminal assaults or batteries.[84] The court limited this white privilege only to prohibit excessive violence that threatened enslaved property values and the public order.[85]

Hale was indicted for committing "an inhuman assault and battery" on another person's slave. The report of the case does not refer to Hale's first name, nor does it identify his victim or any facts supporting the indictment. A Cumberland County trial jury gave a special verdict finding that Hale struck his enslaved victim. This verdict, in effect, asked the judge to decide under the law whether Hale was guilty of a crime. The trial judge once again was Joseph J. Daniel. This time he found in favor of Hale, suggesting that he believed that, under North Carolina law, Hale committed no crime. District solicitor Alexander Troy filed an appeal on behalf of the state.[86]

The Supreme Court once again reversed Judge Daniel. John Orth notes that there appears to be no opinion of the court in which all of the justices joined without reservations. Taylor wrote the longer published opinion, in which Hall concurred. But Hall also published a concurring opinion, and Henderson concurred without any opinion.[87]

Taylor began his opinion by asserting that the appeal presented one issue: "whether a battery, committed on a slave, no justification, or circumstances attending it, being shewn, is an indictable offence."[88] He answered this question in the affirmative. But he also explained, in dictum, that the *Tackett* unequal mitigation doctrine applied to cases of nonfatal violence in which white strangers to the enslavement relationship asserted claims to justify and excuse their assaults or batteries.

Taylor stated that he could find "no positive law, decisive of the question," and therefore "a solution of it must be deduced from general principles, from reasonings founded on the common law, adapted to the existing condition and circumstances of our society, and indicating that result, which is best adapted to general expedience." He added that "presumptive evidence of what this is, arises, in some degree, from usage, of which the Legislature must have been long since apprised, by the repeated conviction and punishment of persons charged with this offence."[89]

Taylor therefore held that free people could be indicted for common-law "inhuman assault and battery" on people enslaved by others. This rule, he found, would preserve the "public peace." According to Taylor, "A wanton injury committed on a slave is a great provocation to the owner" because this "awakens his resentment, and has a direct tendency to a breach of the peace, by inciting him to seek immediate vengeance. If resented in the heat of blood, it would probably extenuate a homicide to manslaughter." But Taylor tellingly cited Sir Matthew Hale's English treatise, when he applied "the same principle with the case stated by Lord Hale," that it would be manslaughter, and not murder, "if A. riding on the road, B. had whipped his horse out of the track, and then A. had alighted and killed B."[90]

Taylor also expressed class bias when he declared, "These offences are usually committed by men of dissolute habits, hanging loose upon society, who, being repelled from association with well disposed citizens, take refuge in the company of coloured persons and slaves, whom they deprave by their example, embolden by their familiarity, and then beat, under the expectation that a slave dare not resent a blow from a white man." He concluded, "If such offences may be committed with impunity, the public peace will not only be rendered extremely insecure, but the value of slave property must be much impaired, for the offenders can seldom make any reparation in damages."[91]

Taylor added, moreover, that "a person who has received an injury, real or imaginary, from a slave," did not have to "carve out his own justice; for the law has made ample and summary provision for the punishment of all trivial offences committed by slaves, by carrying them before a justice, who is authorized to pass sentence for their being publickly whipped." This statutory summary process before a single justice of the peace, Taylor opined, "while it excludes the necessity of private vengeance, would seem to forbid its legality, since it effectually protects all persons from the insolence of slaves, even where their masters are unwilling to correct them upon complaint being made."[92]

Taylor nevertheless invoked the *Tackett* doctrine to limit even a white stranger's liability for batteries. He first noted that "the common law has often been called into efficient operation, for the punishment of public cruelty inflicted upon animals, for needless and wanton barbarity exercised even by masters upon their slaves, and for various violations of decency, morals and comfort. Reason and analogy seem to require that a human being, although the subject of property, should be so far protected as the public might be injured through him." But he also recognized the master's "complete authority" over his or her slave: "For all purposes necessary to enforce the obedience of the slave, and to render him useful as property, the law secures to the master a complete authority over him, and it will not lightly interfere with the relation thus established."[93]

Taylor also explained that he believed that the criminal law must protect the slave owner's property rights from the injuries influenced by others: "It is a more effectual guarantee of his right of property, when the slave is protected from wanton abuse from those who have no power over him; for it cannot be disputed, that a slave is rendered less capable of performing his master's service, when he finds himself exposed by the law to the capricious violence of every turbulent man in the community." Taylor could have ended his opinion here. He adequately explained why he resolved the only issue that he stated the appeal presented.

But Taylor included dictum extending the *Tackett* doctrine to legitimize some white assaults and batteries:

> Mitigated as slavery is by the humanity of our laws, the refinement of manners, and by public opinion, which revolts at every instance of cruelty towards them, it would be an anomaly in the system of police which affects them, if the offence stated in the verdict were not indictable. At the same time it is undeniable, that such offence must be considered with a view to the actual condition of society, and the difference between a white man and a slave, securing the first from injury and insult, and the other from needless violence and outrage.

"From this difference" that Taylor perceived "between a white man and a slave," he declared, as in *Tackett*, "it arises, that many circumstances which would not constitute a legal provocation for a battery committed by one white man on another, would justify it, if committed on a slave, provided the battery were not excessive."

Accordingly, Taylor's *Hale* opinion delegated wide discretion to white trial judges and juries to apply these general principles: "It is impossible to draw the line with precision, or lay down the rule in the abstract; but as was said in *Tacket's* [sic] case, the circumstances must be judged of by the Court and Jury, with a due regard to the habits and feelings of society."[94]

Hall's opinion states, "I concur in the opinion given [by Taylor]," including the dicta extending the *Tackett* doctrine:

> *I think it would be highly improper that every assault and battery upon a slave should be considered an indictable offence; because the person making it, might have matter of excuse or justification on his side, which could not be used as a defence for committing an assault and battery upon a free person.* But where an assault and battery is committed upon a slave without cause, lawful excuse, or without sufficient provocation, I think it amounts to an indictable offence. Much depends upon the circumstances of the case when it happens; these circumstances are not set forth in this case, and I think it material that they should appear. I therefore think the judgment of the Court below should be reversed, and a new trial granted for that purpose.

The italicized language suggests that the court's majority supported the unequal justification doctrine. Henderson concurred without a separate opinion. But he later did not dissent when the court expanded this doctrine to cases in which slave owners and hirers directed violence against people they enslaved.[95]

Taylor's *Hale* opinion thus evidences the white elite's concerns about the familiar and sometimes violent interactions between enslaved people and "turbulent men" in the community with "no power over" enslaved people. These "men" included poor whites, who often were disparagingly called vagabonds.[96] Taylor related these social class biases with economic concerns, when he complained about impecunious offenders who damaged slaveholders' valuable enslaved human property without having the means to "make any reparation in damages."[97]

This socioeconomic concern about poor white violence was later exemplified in the criminal law by the 1844 North Carolina Supreme Court decision in *State v. Armfield*.[98] The court affirmed the forcible trespass conviction of three "laborers" for taking away the goods of John Myers. These goods were an enslaved man named Baal. He had for seven years been in the possession of Myers, who was described as being "very old and a cripple."[99] The court approved of the conviction to protect the property rights of this "old enfeebled man" whose goods were taken at night by the defendants' misrepresentations and "superior force."[100]

Taylor the Moderate and the Unequal Protection Doctrine

Taylor's doctrinal innovations in the *Tackett* and *Hale* decisions are telling because of his reputation as a moderate southern jurist and because he rose to prominence from early misfortune. Taylor has been praised for trying to "rationalize the common law, state history, and the circumstances of a case to the benefit of both free blacks and slaves and others who were downtrodden" and because he asserted "compassionate views toward Africans and his decisions sometimes stretched the bounds of social acceptance."[101]

This compassion would be an understandable product of Taylor's unfortunate early life. He was born in 1769 in London to Irish parents. By the age of twelve he was an orphan, and he came to America to live with his older brother James Taylor. John attended the College of William and Mary, but because of his finances he did not graduate. He moved to North Carolina, and in 1788 he began a law practice and later started his political career. In the 1790s Taylor served three terms in the state legislature, where he supported laws suppressing the slave trade and favoring the owners' right to free their slaves. Taylor was elected to the state's Superior Court in 1798. Beginning in 1818, he served as the state Supreme Court's first chief justice. He died in 1829.[102]

Early in his judicial career, however, Taylor foreshadowed his race-conscious approach to enslavement law in *Gobu v. Gobu*, which is the report of Taylor's 1802 jury charge in a freedom suit.[103] The jury found for the apparently mixed-race freedom claimant. But Taylor stated that he agreed with the defense counsel's argument that the common-law presumption of freedom did not apply when the enslaved claimants appeared to be Black. Taylor instead held that the presumption of freedom applied only to those like the claimant in that case, who appeared to be white or to be "persons of mixed blood, or to those of any color between the two extremes of black and white."[104] The majority of southern courts later adopted this presumption of slavery when the freedom claimants appeared to be of African ancestry.[105]

Taylor's *Tackett* and *Hale* opinions also provide a window into his understanding of the legal consciousness of North Carolina's white population. Taylor recited and relied on these beliefs and customs when he legitimized fatal and nonfatal interracial violence to enforce white supremacy. He also delegated wide discretion to local all-white juries to use these beliefs when deciding when white defendants exceeded the limits of the racially motivated violence that was acceptable in their communities.

Taylor apparently accurately assessed the tenor of his times. North Carolina's legislators never adopted a statute ameliorating the separate and unequal mitigation doctrine, confirming their acquiescence in this doctrine and in the Seawell and Taylor interpretation of the 1817 act. Moreover, no southern appellate decision rejected the *Tackett/Hale* provocation doctrine.[106] To the contrary, Thomas R. R. Cobb's enslavement law treatise praises *Tackett* as following from "the necessarily degraded social position of the slave."[107] Other antebellum criminal law treatise writers also cited the *Tackett* decision for creating an enslavement law exception to the common-law mitigation principles.[108]

Even the Court of Appeals in the border state of Kentucky explicitly endorsed the *Tackett/Hale* doctrine in its 1860 decision in *Commonwealth v. Lee*.[109] The trial court judge dismissed an indictment charging Lee and Bledsoe with assault and battery on George, Betsy, and Tabitha, who were slaves owned by A. B. Watkins.[110] On the commonwealth's appeal, Judge Belvard J. Peters wrote the opinion reversing this dismissal. Peters acknowledged that no Kentucky statute authorized the indictment. He followed Taylor's opinion in *State v. Hale* to hold that the commonwealth could indict the defendants for common-law assault and battery because third-party attacks on enslaved victims were "a great provocation to the master," who might feel "resentment," tending to cause "breaches of the peace" that "may end in fatal conflict."[111] But Peters also endorsed Taylor's unequal mitigation rule, stating that "many circumstances which would not constitute legal provocation for one white man to commit a battery upon another, would justify it when committed upon a slave." He added that trial judges and juries must consider "these circumstances . . . , having due regard to the differences between a white man and a slave, and the habits of society."[112]

Mississippi's highest court also followed the *Tackett* rule permitting the use of evidence in court of enslaved homicide victims' usual deportment to whites—their reputation for insolent words or deeds—when it reversed a slave owner's manslaughter conviction for killing his slave.[113] The North Carolina courts later applied this rule, but only to cases involving slaves.[114]

Conclusion

The Seawell/Taylor separate and unequal mitigation doctrine inserted white-supremacist principles into the common law of crimes, thus restricting the cases in which whites could be convicted for fatal and nonfatal white violence they inflicted upon enslaved victims. Taylor's *Tackett* principle was a more moderate alternative than North Carolina's pre-1817 law, which legitimized all white slave killings that were not murders. Similarly, his *Hale* opinion is a better alternative than the South Carolina rule, which held that no white person—not even a stranger—could be indicted for an assault and battery on an enslaved person.[115]

All of these precedents nevertheless were consistent with the slave owners' right also to pursue civil suits to recover the monetary damages that they claimed when others injured or killed the people they enslaved. The legislatures and the courts in effect supplemented these civil remedies with criminal prosecutions, as limited by the separate and unequal mitigation doctrine, to balance the perceived need for public order with slave owners' economic, social, and political interests, which were embodied in the people they enslaved.[116]

Related issues arose when enslavers and hirers were charged with violence against the enslaved people under their command, and when enslaved people were charged with committing interracial violent crimes. Would the courts apply the unequal mitigation doctrine to further limit white criminal liability while expanding the criminal liability of enslaved defendants? The North Carolina courts answered this question in the decades following Taylor's *Tackett* and *Hale* opinions.

CHAPTER 3

Ruffin and Gaston Extend Separate and Unequal Protection

Chief Justice John Louis Taylor's *Tackett* and *Hale* opinions unambiguously established new limits on white criminal liability for fatal and nonfatal violence inflicted on those who were enslaved. But this separate and unequal mitigation and justification doctrine nevertheless suggested two unanswered questions.

First, Tucker's statement in *Tackett* that masters had "complete authority" over the people they enslaved signaled that the court might grant an even broader immunity to slave owners, as it balanced the white intraracial social and economic interests and conflicts that the court perceived to be relevant. These white socioeconomic class tensions explain the continuity between Taylor's *Tackett* and *Hale* opinions and Justice Thomas Ruffin's infamous 1830 opinion in *State v. Mann*, which answered this question by affording slave owners—and even hirers—complete immunity from assaults and batteries that they inflicted on the enslaved people they owned or controlled.[1] Much more has been written about Ruffin's *Mann* opinion and its author than Taylor and his *Tackett* and *Hale* opinions. Nevertheless, Taylor's opinions set the doctrinal foundation for *Mann* and for Ruffin's later *State v. Hoover* opinion, which established the limits of enslavers' homicide liability.[2]

Second, Taylor's *Tackett* and *Hale* opinions also suggested that the court may have to again weigh these white social, political, and economic interests when enslaved defendants are accused of committing violent crimes against whites. Would the court adapt the separate and unequal protection doctrine to increase the potential criminal liability of enslaved people? The slave owners' economic interests and social prestige embodied in their human property would more likely conflict with the public interest when enslaved people were prosecuted for their alleged violent crimes. Justice William J. Gaston's North

Carolina Supreme Court decisions in *State v. Will* and *State v. Jarrott* nevertheless applied the unequal mitigation doctrine when enslaved defendants were prosecuted for violent crimes.[3]

Unequal Protection, *Mann*, and Slave Owners' and Hirers' Liability

According to Sally Hadden, Ruffin's *Mann* opinion "became a *cause celebre* among northern abolitionists like Harriet Beecher Stowe."[4] Stowe's powerful critique of southern enslavement law declared that no one can read Ruffin's *Mann* opinion, which is "so fine and clear in expression, so dignified and solemn in its earnestness, and so dreadful in its results, without feeling at once deep respect for the man and horror for the system." She concluded that Ruffin "has one of that high order of minds, which looks straight through all verbiage and sophistry to the heart of every subject, which it encounters."[5] Almost eighty years later, Harvard Law School dean Roscoe Pound included Ruffin among "the ten judges who must be ranked first in American judicial history."[6]

More recently, Mark V. Tushnet placed Ruffin's *Mann* decision at the center of his 2003 enslavement law monograph, and six years later the North Carolina Law Review published a symposium dedicated to Ruffin and the *Mann* case.[7] According to Eric Muller's symposium article, then recent research "reveals that Ruffin's personal 'lamentations' about the harsh outcome of *State v. Mann* likelier reflected posturing than honest confession." He states that "the full archival record"—including evidence of Ruffin's slaveholdings, his treatment of enslaved people, and his involvement in slave trading and family separation—"shows that Thomas Ruffin was not among the better men of his time and place on matters relating to slavery and that he may have been among the worst."[8]

When compared to Taylor's immigrant orphan story, Ruffin appears to have been among the South's more fortunate sons. Ruffin was born in 1787 into a Virginia slave-owning family. Like others in his social class, he, in 1805, graduated with honors from the College of New Jersey, which became Princeton University. During his college years, New Jersey became the last state before the Civil War to adopt a gradual emancipation law. Ruffin may have, in a letter to his father, expressed doubts about slavery or the treatment of enslaved people in the South.[9] Ruffin nevertheless did not publicly critique or question enslavement. He returned to Virginia after graduation and began to read law, which he continued after he moved in 1807 to North Carolina. He was admitted to the North Carolina bar the next year and soon began his long political and legal career. He served in the state's House of Commons from 1813 to 1816, when he was elected speaker. He resigned to serve as a trial judge for two years and practiced law, until returning to the bench in 1825. Ruffin resigned to become the president of the North Carolina State Bank, until November 1829, when he was nominated and elected to fill the vacancy on North Carolina's Supreme Court, which was created upon Taylor's death.[10]

Ruffin wrote his *Mann* opinion at the start of his long and illustrious North Carolina Supreme Court tenure. He served as the chief justice from 1833 until 1852, when he retired from the court, although he returned in 1857–1859 to fill a vacancy. He later supported the Confederate government, although he believed that his state had no legal right to secede from the union.[11]

The *Mann* case arose in Edenton, then "a major port city" in Chowan County, which "lies at the end of the Albemarle Sound."[12] Sally Greene's research into the case's immediate context confirms that the defendant, John Mann, was a relatively poor white man, a mariner, and a recent widower whose social and economic "position hovered near the bottom of the ladder."[13] He, in 1828, hired as a domestic an enslaved woman named Lydia. She was owned by Elizabeth Jones—a minor and an orphan who was the ward of her guardian, Josiah Small. Small was married to Elizabeth's older sister.[14]

Small apparently permitted Mann to continue hiring Lydia into 1829.[15] On Sunday, March 1, of that year, Lydia allegedly committed "some small offense, for which the defendant [Mann] undertook to chastise her." Lydia "ran off" during this chastisement, "whereupon the defendant called upon her to stop, which being refused, he shot at and wounded her."[16] A Chowan County grand jury, during the spring 1829 term, indicted Mann for assault and battery, apparently after "Josiah Small persuaded solicitor John Lancaster Bailey to take the case to a grand jury."[17] Mann picked the wrong enslaved person to shoot; Small was a justice of the peace and person of higher standing in the community.[18]

Once again Joseph J. Daniel was the trial judge. He charged the jury "that if they believed the punishment inflicted by the Defendant was cruel and unwarrantable, and disproportionate to the offence committed by the slave, that in law the Defendant was guilty, as he had only a special property in the slave." Thus, Daniel limited his instruction to Mann's criminal liability as a slave hirer, leaving for another case the description of the liability—if any—that the court would impose on slave owners for similar nonfatal shootings of their own slaves. The jury convicted Mann.[19] He filed an appeal, although his punishment was only a five-dollar fine. Tushnet in 2003 asserted that this fine would be "about ninety dollars today. We would regard someone who was fined ninety dollars for assaulting another person as having received a slap on the wrist."[20]

Mann's appeal was argued on February 15, 1830, when Ruffin had been on the Supreme Court for a little more than a month.[21] No attorney appeared on Mann's behalf. The attorney general, Romulus M. Saunders, argued for the state. Saunders was in the midst of a long and controversial political and legal career. He was "an acid tongued partisan" in what became the John C. Calhoun pro–states' rights wing of the Democrat Party. Saunders was President James K. Polk's minister plenipotentiary to Spain who negotiated a secret agreement with Spain to sell Cuba to the United States. He was remembered as "a man of considerable ability and talent, but he was rough-hewn in his appearance and speech, often intemperate in his statements, and intensely partisan in his associations."[22]

Saunders relied on Taylor's *Hale* decision, arguing "that no difference existed between this case and that of the State v. Hall [sic] (2 Hawks, 582)." He asserted, moreover, that "in this case the weapon used was one calculated to produce death." Therefore, like his predecessor William Drew in *Tackett*, Saunders cited to the court well-established common-law principles and authorities. He "assimilated the relation between a master and a slave, to those existing between parents and children, masters and apprentices, and tutors and scholars, and upon the limitations to the right of the superiors in these relations."[23] Saunders referred to "the American edition of an influential English treatise, *Russell on Crimes*."[24]

Writing for a unanimous court, Ruffin reversed the conviction, holding that neither masters nor hirers could be indicted at common law for assaults and batteries upon slaves under their control. He thus rejected both of the premises of Saunders's argument and Daniel's jury charge as well as the common-law authorities supporting them.[25]

Ruffin acknowledged that the *Hale* decision remained the controlling law in North Carolina when the defendant was a stranger to the assaulted slave. "But the evidence makes this a different case. Here the slave has been *hired* by the Defendant" when he committed the alleged battery.[26] Ruffin then applied the same standards to slave owners and hirers. He legitimized their "uncontrolled authority over the body" of the slave.[27] Ruffin admitted that "there may be particular instances of cruelty and deliberate barbarity where, in conscience, the law might properly interfere." But he held that the courts "cannot look at the matter in that light. . . . We cannot allow the right of the master to be brought into discussion in the courts of justice. The slave, to remain a slave, must be made sensible that there is no appeal from his master."[28]

Like Taylor in *Tackett*, Ruffin "cited no legal authority for this proposition; his holding was based on [his perception of] realities of the master-slave relation that made it imperative that the master have this unlimited power" to commit assaults and batteries while correcting their slaves.[29] He found that the master-slave relationship, unlike the other common-law superior and inferior relationships to which Saunders referred, had as its "end . . . the profit of the master, his security and the public safety." Ruffin asserted that enslaved people must "toil that another may reap the fruits" of their labor, which was for their enslaver's profit alone. He then asked,

> What moral considerations shall be addressed to such a being to convince him what it is impossible but that the most stupid must feel and know can never be true—that he is thus to labor upon a principle of natural duty, or for the sake of his own personal happiness, such services can only be expected from one who has no will of his own; who surrenders his will in implicit obedience to that of another. Such obedience is the consequence only of uncontrolled authority over the body. There is nothing else which can operate to produce the effect. The power of the master must be absolute to render the submission of the slave perfect.[30]

Ruffin noted further, "There have been no prosecutions of the sort. The established habits and uniform practice of the country in this respect is the best evidence of the portion of power deemed by the whole community requisite to the preservation of the master's dominion."[31]

Ruffin also explicitly balanced what he believed were the relevant interests. To Ruffin, the enslavers' "full dominion" over the people they enslaved "is essential to the value of slaves as property, to the security of the master, and the public tranquility, greatly dependent upon their subordination; and, in fine, as most effectually securing the general protection and comfort of the slaves themselves."[32]

Evaluating Ruffin's *Mann* Opinion

Although Ruffin may have been correct when he asserted that this prosecution was unprecedented in North Carolina, Mann was not the first U.S. enslaver or hirer to be prosecuted for nonfatal slave abuse. About seven years earlier, Robert Brockett Sr. was indicted in the Circuit Court of the District of Columbia on the allegation that he assaulted and did "cruelly, inhumanly, and maliciously, cut, slash, beat, and ill-treat" his own slave, whose name was Nat, causing "other wrongs and injuries."[33] Brockett lived in Alexandria, Virginia, when it was part of the District of Columbia. According to the 1820 census, Brockett owned seven slaves. He was a native of Scotland and a real estate investor who, before his death in 1829, built several houses that still stand today.[34]

The published report of Brockett's trial during the court's November 1823 term states that his lawyer, William Taylor, argued "that if the whipping be private, there is no limit, so that it does not extend to voluntary killing or mutilation." Notwithstanding this objection to the indictment, Taylor let the charge go to the jury, guessing correctly that they would not convict Brockett. District Attorney Thomas Swann prosecuted the case. He cited in support of the indictment the Supreme Court of Pennsylvania decision in *Respublica v. Teischer* sustaining an indictment of the defendant for the malicious killing of a horse.[35]

Several similar prosecutions were pursued in the 1820s in Virginia's state courts. William Booth was indicted by a grand jury on May 10, 1821, for "unlawfully and violently" beating "a negro man slave named Bob," who was the property of Robert Fenn. The trial on this charge was held in the Superior Court of Petersburg. The jury gave a special verdict. They found Booth was guilty and assessed a sixty-dollar fine, "subject to the opinion of the Court upon these questions: Can the Defendant be indicted and punished for the excessive, cruel and inhuman infliction of stripes on the slave *Bob*, while in his possession, and under his control as a hired slave, for the space of one month, no permanent injury having resulted to the said slave from such infliction?—Can the Defendant be punished under the Indictment found in this Case?" The trial judge adjourned this case to the General Court "for its decision on the question, 'What judgment shall be rendered on the said verdict?'"[36] The General Court then was the court of last resort in criminal cases. It decided questions adjourned such as this, with the consent of the defendant, and ruled on writs of error filed by convicted defendants. The Court of Appeals did not yet have jurisdiction to hear appeals in criminal cases.[37]

The court heard the case during its June 1824 term, but it evaded the question that Ruffin later answered in *Mann*. According to Judge Richard E. Parker's opinion, the court's "majority" agreed that judgment should be entered on this special verdict in favor of Booth. Parker cited the common-law principles prohibiting masters from "ill-treating their apprentices," and he stated that the charge "of making an unlawful assault upon the slave of another person, however cruel and severe the subsequent battery, is, certainly, not the same offence with making an assault upon one's own slave." Slave-owner assaults were only "unlawful by subsequent excess and inhumanity, and, if this last is intended to be the charge against the Defendant, he ought to have clear notice of it, by the frame of the Indictment." Therefore, Booth's evidence establishing that he owned Bob when the beating occurred led Parker to hold that this "so changed the nature of the offence, as to entitle him to a judgment under this Indictment."[38] But Parker added that the court did not express an opinion on the first question raised by the verdict, which "involves a grave and serious, as well as delicate enquiry into the rights and duties of slave-holders, and the condition of their slaves, which we shall be prepared to enter upon with a due sense of its importance, whenever a proper occasion arises." The court's decision thus was made "without reference to this more interesting question, and is not intended, in any manner, to affect it."[39]

Three years later, the court answered this question in favor of enslavers in *Commonwealth v. Turner*, over the dissenting opinion written by Ruffin's cousin.[40] Richard Turner was indicted during the October 1826 Superior Court term in King George County. The indictment alleges that Turner assaulted his slave named Emanuel "with certain rods, whips and sticks," and that he did "willfully and maliciously, violently, cruelly, immoderately, and excessively beat, scourge, and whip" Emanuel "against the peace and dignity of the Commonwealth." Turner apparently was in a higher social and economic stratum than John Mann. Turner inherited from his father a King George County plantation, which was known as Walsingham. His slaveholding increased from thirty in 1810 to seventy in 1820. He died in 1829, at the age of fifty-one.[41]

Turner pled not guilty and "demurred to the Indictment." The commonwealth joined in the demurrer. The Superior Court judge thus was asked to decide whether Turner could be so charged. But "because of the novelty and difficulty of the questions arising on the demurrer," the judge adjourned the issue to the General Court.[42]

The General Court, in its November 1827 term, held that Turner could not be criminally liable for the alleged assault and excessive battery, with Ruffin's cousin Judge William Brockenbrough as the only dissenter.[43] Judge William Dade's long majority opinion denied Emanuel the personal right to even the unequal protection of the law of assault and battery. He instead explained that the court could sustain the indictment only by criminalizing cruel slave battery because this behavior by a master "disturbed the harmony of society, was offensive to public decency, and directly tended to a breach of the peace." He reasoned by analogy to common-law precedents that applied to other personal property, stating, "The same would be the law, if a horse had been so beaten. And yet it would not be pretended, that it was in respect to the rights of the horse, or the feelings of humanity, that this interposition would take place."[44]

Dade thus held that the court would be creating a new common-law crime *contra bonos mores* if it were to approve the indictment. Judges in England and the United States used this doctrine to prohibit acts that they believed were immoral or that tended to disturb the peace. Dade disclaimed the court's power to do so in Turner's case. Only the legislature could declare an enslaver's cruel slave battery to be a crime, according to Dade, because slavery was "a wholly new condition," and "the common law could not operate on it." A judicial decision creating this crime would be a legal change that he believed was too swift and severe for the courts, which should declare only "silent, and almost imperceptible changes," so that "society [could] easily conform itself to the law."[45]

Ruffin's cousin Brockenbrough's dissenting opinion confirms that another result was indeed conceivable; Brockenbrough even conceded that "on one occasion within a few years past, in one of the Courts of my circuit, I sustained an Indictment of this character, and pronounced judgment against the defendant."[46] He agreed that slavery was unknown to the common law of England, but he found analogies in the violent privileges that the courts granted in the relationships between masters and servants, parents and children, and tutors and pupils. But he also explained the fundamental differences between the master-slave relationship and these other relationships:

> The moment either of these persons transcended the bounds of due moderation, he was amenable to the law of the land, and might be prosecuted for the abuse of his authority, for his cruelty and inhumanity. When slaves were introduced, although the power conferred on the master by that relation, was much greater than that conferred by either of the others, yet the common law would easily adapt itself to this new relation. The slave was the *property* of his master, and every power which was necessary to enable the master to use his property, was conferred on him. He might correct him for disobedience; he might sell him to another master; and he would be liable for the payment of his debts. If he was merely property, and nothing else, he might be destroyed by his master. But, to this extent the common law would not allow his power to reach, because it was unnecessary for his full enjoyment of the right of property. The slave was not only a *thing*, but a *person*, and this well-known distinction would extend its protection to the slave as a person, except so far as the application of it conflicted with the enjoyment of the slave as a thing.[47]

He concluded that a rule of law protecting slaves "from all unnecessary, cruel, and inhuman punishments" had "no incompatibility" with the master's "full enjoyment of the right of property." He cited in support of this line of reasoning the 1788 Pennsylvania decision sustaining the indictment for malicious horse killing.[48]

Although Brockenbrough did not think "it necessary to say any thing on the subject of the consequences of the doctrine which I have supported," he nevertheless explained his belief that this slave master criminal liability would not be "injurious to the peace of society." His state's courts and juries "are composed of men who, for the most part, are masters," and thus he could not "conceive that any injury can accrue to the rights and interests of that class of the community." He added that "with respect to the slaves, whilst kindness and humane treatment are calculated to render them contented and happy, is there no danger that oppression and tyranny, against which there is no redress, may drive them to despair?"[49]

Accordingly, unlike Brockenbrough, both Dade and Ruffin found that these prosecutions were based on a "new idea" whose time had not yet come. Unlike Dade, however, Ruffin was forced, by Taylor's *Hale* holding, to explain his understanding of the oppressive and violent foundations of the master-slave relationship, in order to distinguish *Hale* and the common-law authorities that permitted "superiors" to correct their children, pupils, and apprentices without liability for simple battery, while at the same time limiting the extent of this legalized battery.[50]

It may appear, on an initial reading, that the *Mann* decision is, at least in part, a retreat from *Hale*, but the *Hale* and *Mann* decisions are consistent when they are read together. Ruffin's *Mann* opinion did indeed declare a new absolute immunity when it held that slave owners and hirers could not, under any circumstances, be indicted for assaults and batteries on enslaved people under their command. But Ruffin derived this immunity from Taylor's separate and unequal protection doctrine as well as his understanding of the enslavement relationship and the white community's beliefs regarding race and caste. Taylor's *Tackett* and *Hale* opinions thus formed the conceptual doctrinal basis for Ruffin's *Mann* decision.

The absence of dissenting or concurring opinions in *Mann* from John Hall, the new chief justice, and Leonard Henderson supports this conclusion. Their silence confirms that they agreed that Ruffin's *Mann* opinion was consistent with *Hale*. It is not known if Taylor would have agreed with Ruffin's *Mann* opinion. But Hall and Henderson may have believed that Ruffin followed Taylor's suggestion that the court create an explicit exception to the *Hale* rule in favor of slave owners and hirers to protect the enslavers' "complete authority," which Taylor stated they held over the people they enslaved. Moreover, the North Carolina legislature also apparently concurred with this decision. It, like Virginia's legislature, failed to "take up Ruffin's invitation" in his *Mann* opinion "to regulate the master's power of correction, thus implicitly endorsing the standard set forth in *State v. Mann*."[51]

Both Dade in *Turner* and Ruffin in *Mann* acknowledged the harsh nature of the new enslavement law rule that they engrafted upon the common law of crimes. Dade "deplored that an offense so odious and revolting . . . should exist to the reproach of humanity."[52] And Ruffin could not "but lament when such cases as the present are brought into judgment."[53] I still maintain that these lamentations, "whether sincere or not, did not square with the results reached by both courts, which vindicated the 'absolute despotism' that was at the heart of American southern slavery."[54]

Unequal Protection and Slave Owner Homicides

Ruffin's *Mann* opinion, of course, did not decide whether the masters' absolute despotism and uncontrolled authority over their slaves extended to homicide. North Carolina's later slave-owner homicide decisions are consistent with Taylor's unequal protection doctrine, including Ruffin's 1840 opinion in *State v. Hoover*.[55] The court affirmed John Hoover's conviction for the brutal murder of Mira, a pregnant woman he enslaved. I have elsewhere summarized at length the horrible evidence of Hoover's sadistic brutality, which was elicited from the testimony of the twelve white witnesses at Hoover's trial.[56]

Ruffin thought Hoover's appeal lacked any merit, but he nevertheless explained at length why some slave master killings should be murders. He began by citing the rule he established in *State v. Mann*: "A master may lawfully punish his slave, and the degree must, in general, be left to his own judgment and humanity, and cannot be judicially questioned." Ruffin then distinguished Mann's case, because "the master's authority is not altogether unlimited. He must not kill. There is, at least, this restriction upon his power: he must stop short of taking life." North Carolina's homicide statutes by then made that proposition unassailable, but Ruffin also noted that the courts had held, "independent of the act of 1791," that slave killing may be murder, whether committed by a master or a stranger to the slave.[57]

Ruffin did not, however, even mention the 1817 act's requirement that slave homicide should "partake the same degree of guilt when accompanied with the like circumstances that homicide now does at common law."[58] Instead, he extended Taylor's *Tackett* doctrine, asserting, "It must indeed be true, in the nature of things, that a killing by the owner may be extenuated by many circumstances, from which no palliation could be derived in favor of a stranger."

Ruffin explained the limits on the master's liability for slave killing as a matter of the common law of slavery: "If death unhappily ensue from the master's chastisement of his slave, inflicted apparently with a good intent, for reformation or example, and with no purpose to take life, or to put it in jeopardy, the law would doubtless tenderly regard every circumstance which, judging from the conduct generally of masters towards slaves, might reasonably be supposed to have hurried the party into excess." But, in contrast, he declared that "the acts imputed to this unhappy man [Hoover] do not belong to a state of civilization. They are barbarities which could only be prompted by a heart in which every humane feeling had long been stifled; and indeed there can scarcely be a savage of the wilderness so ferocious as not to shudder at the recital of them." Ruffin thus concluded that Hoover's heinous "acts cannot be fairly attributed to an intention to correct or to chastise. They cannot, therefore, have allowance, as being the exercise of an authority conferred by the law for the purposes of the correction of the slave, or of keeping the slave in due subjection."[59]

Ruffin also criticized the trial judge John M. Dick's jury instructions. Judge Dick heard this case at the start of his long career as a Superior Court judge, which began in November 1835 and continued until his death in October 1861. Timothy Huebner called Dick "[a] gentleman planter of moderate wealth" from Guilford County. Some of his contemporaries critiqued his election to the court by the legislature, which was said to be "more for political reasons than because of his legal expertise. At least a few observers within the North Carolina legal community severely criticized him for his 'muddy and halting' knowledge of the law."[60]

Judge Dick suggested that because Hoover offered no evidence of legal provocation, the jury could mitigate the homicide to manslaughter. Ruffin disagreed, stating that Hoover's crime "must have flowed from a settled and malignant pleasure in inflicting pain, or a settled and malignant insensibility to human suffering. There was none of that *brief fury* to which the law has regard, as an infirmity of our nature." Ruffin then reasoned,

> On the contrary, without any consideration for the sex, health or strength of the deceased, through a period of four months, including the latter stages of pregnancy, delivery, and recent recovery therefrom, by a series of cruelties and privations in their nature unusual, and in degree excessive beyond the capacity of a stout frame to sustain, the prisoner employed himself from day to day in practising grievous tortures upon an enfeebled female, which finally wore out the energies of nature and destroyed life. He beat her with clubs, iron chains, and other deadly weapons, time after time; burnt her; inflicted stripes over and often, with scourges, which literally excoriated her whole body; forced her out to work in inclement seasons, without being duly clad; provided for her insufficient food; exacted labour beyond her strength, and wantonly beat her because she could not comply with his requisitions. These enormities, besides others too disgusting to be particularly designated, the prisoner, without his heart once relenting or softening, practised from the first of December until the latter end of the ensuing

March; and he did not relax even up to the last hours of his victim's existence. In such a case, surely, we do not speak of provocation; for nothing could palliate such a course of conduct.

Ruffin concluded, "Punishment thus immoderate and unreasonable in the measure, the continuance, and the instruments, accompanied by other hard usage and painful privations of food, clothing and rest, loses all character of correction *in foro domestico*, and denotes plainly that the prisoner must have contemplated the fatal termination, which was the natural consequence of such barbarous cruelties."[61]

Accordingly, on an appeal that revealed no evidence of provocation by Myra and extensive evidence of Hoover's prolonged history of sadistic brutalities, Ruffin's opinion included extensive dicta confirming that North Carolina's slave owners continued to enjoy a broader exemption than strangers for slave killings that may have resulted from moderate correction. Taylor's narrow reading in *Tackett* of the 1817 slave homicide act's "like circumstances" requirement provided the conceptual basis for this decision and for the slave master and hirer prosecutions that followed.[62]

Ruffin's *Mann* and *Hoover* opinions therefore are not inconsistent or incoherent, as scholars have suggested.[63] Nor is *Mann* inconsistent with Taylor's opinion in *Hale*. All of these decisions can be reconciled as applications of the separate and unequal protection principle to the different balance of the perceived relevant interests that these cases presented. I have elsewhere contended that the complex and shifting structure of slavery law in the antebellum South can best be understood as a process by which the judges and legislators accommodated slavery's essential social elements into the common law, for which slavery was a long-forgotten institution. They achieved this by balancing what they perceived to be the salient interests implicated in the issues presented. These interests included the slave master class's perceived need (1) to foster slave control, obedience, and submissiveness; (2) to perpetuate the plantation economy and preserve slave property values; (3) to regulate the behavior of overseers and slave hirers; and (4) to control poor white violence and slave abuse, while co-opting poor whites into becoming supporters of the slave economy.[64]

Judges did not always agree on what was the "right" balance of these interests, as confirmed by the different opinions of Dade, Ruffin, and Brockenbrough. But this analysis provides a means to better understand Taylor's separate and unequal protection principle as the common thread that runs through decisions such as *Tackett*, *Hale*, *Turner*, *Mann*, and *Hoover*. These opinions, on a superficial reading, may appear to be conflicting or even incoherent. But when read in their social and legal contexts, they reveal how enslavement law's "terrible texture" came to be accommodated into the common law.[65] These insights, as Anthony V. Baker explained, can be derived from a study of these decisions not as "history in pure form," but instead as "an interesting view of jurisprudence 'on the ground'—the process by which law may come to catalyze a culture in measurable and particular ways."[66]

Criminal Procedures in Trials of Enslaved Defendants

Enslaved defendants usually faced the death penalty when they were charged with inflicting fatal and often even nonfatal violence on whites. The enslaved defendant's owner's social prestige and economic investments in his or her enslaved property thus were aligned with the enslaved defendant's interests in escaping execution. Even when enslaved people were accused of killing their owners, the heirs of the deceased slave owner had property interests to protect, especially if they believed that their enslaved defendants were wrongfully accused.[67] Chief Justice Roger B. Taney thus considered—but rejected—an enslaver's claim that the prosecution by the United States of alleged enslaved criminals implicated potential governmental takings of the slave owners' interest in their enslaved persons' life or labor.[68]

Slave owners in many of these cases therefore hired high-priced lawyers to defend their slaves.[69] Would these lawyers convince the courts not to apply the Seawell/Taylor unequal mitigation doctrine because it would increase the liability of enslaved defendants, especially when their lives were at stake? Or would the public interests in slave control and punishment prevail?

The North Carolina Supreme Court conclusively answered this question twenty years after *Tackett* in an opinion written by Taylor's brother-in-law, Justice William J. Gaston. Like Taylor, Gaston has been labeled a moderate and even a progressive southern jurist, in contrast to Ruffin. But Gaston's 1840 opinion in *State v. Jarrott* extended Taylor's separate and unequal mitigation doctrine to cases in which enslaved defendants were accused of directing fatal violence against whites.[70] He held that the trial judge correctly rejected the request of Jarrott's lawyer that the jury be instructed that "in trials affecting life, a negro slave should not be convicted of murder, unless a white man would be convicted on the same evidence."[71] He instead relegated enslaved defendants to the same second class status that Taylor created for enslaved crime victims.

North Carolina's statutes establishing the criminal procedures when enslaved people were accused of capital crimes required the state's highest court to resolve this mitigation issue in Jarrott's case. Lawmakers in the colonial and antebellum South were divided on the issue of whether to deny to enslaved defendants one or more of the common and statutory law's usual criminal procedural rights and protections from unjust or unlawful convictions. On one end of the continuum, North Carolina's 1715 colonial law declared that enslaved defendants who were accused of "any Crime or Offense whatsoever" were to be tried before courts composed of three justices of the peace and three slave-owning freeholders. A majority vote in these courts—not a unanimous verdict—was sufficient to convict enslaved defendants even of capital crimes. Over time, North Carolina law evolved to require that the courts enforce most of the usual criminal procedures in the prosecutions of enslaved defendants. These procedures included the rights to grand jury review of the charge, a trial by jury in the regular courts, and an appeal to the state's highest court.[72]

North Carolina's substantive criminal law, like the law in the other southern jurisdictions, nevertheless discriminated against enslaved people. Its statutes prohibited acts that were not crimes if committed by whites, while providing enhanced penalties for some acts that were crimes for both whites and slaves.[73] George Stroud, in 1856, therefore found that North Carolina's criminal statutes imposed thirty-four capital crimes on whites, while including forty for the enslaved.[74]

Gaston's Extends the *Tackett* Rule to Enslaved Defendants

William J. Gaston wrote two Supreme Court opinions that extended both the *Tackett/Hale* "mere words" doctrine exception and the rule denying the common law's standards of mitigation to enslaved defendants who were tried for killing whites. The court had to address these issues because North Carolina's statutes did not preclude manslaughter verdicts mitigating killings by slaves that were not murders, nor did they explicitly codify the separate and unequal mitigation rules when enslaved people were accused of committing violent crimes against whites.[75]

Gaston first confirmed this extension in his 1834 opinion in *State v. Will*.[76] The court, which then included Gaston, Chief Justice Thomas Ruffin, and Justice Joseph J. Daniel, reversed an enslaved man named Will's conviction for the murder of Richard Baxter, who was the overseer employed by Will's owner James S. Battle. Battle paid a thousand dollars to hire two top lawyers, George Washington Mordecai and Bartholomew Figures Moore, to defend Will.[77]

After Will's trial in Edgecombe County, the jury announced a special verdict. They found the facts and left it to the trial judge, John Robert Donnell, to decide whether, under the law, the killing was murder or manslaughter. This verdict stated that, on January 22, 1834, Will stabbed and killed Baxter after a dispute arose between Will and an enslaved foreman named Allen. This dispute centered on the "ownership" of a hoe, which Allen directed another slave to use. Will claimed the hoe because he helved on his own time. Will and Allen exchanged "some angry words." Will then broke the helve of the hoe and went to work in a cotton screw about a quarter mile away.

Baxter, in response, went to his house, grabbed his gun, and rode on horseback to the location where Will was working. Baxter also ordered Allen to take a whip and follow him at a short distance. Gun in hand, Baxter ordered Will to come down from packing cotton. As Baxter approached, Will "took off his hat in a humble manner and came down." Baxter then said something to Will, who "made off." After Will had taken ten or fifteen steps, Baxter shot Will in the back. Will's flight nevertheless continued, with Baxter and two other slaves in pursuit. Baxter eventually overtook Will. In a scuffle that followed, Will stabbed Baxter, who by then was no longer armed. Will again fled. Baxter died that evening because of blood loss. On the same day, Will surrendered to Battle. The next day, Will was arrested. When he was told of Baxter's death, Will "exclaimed, '*Is it possible!*' and appeared so much affected that he came near falling, and was obliged to be supported." On these facts, Judge Donnell found Will guilty of murder.[78]

The appellate case report includes long summaries of the lawyers' arguments. Mordecai and Moore asserted that, on the facts found by the jury, Will was guilty of manslaughter, while Attorney General John R. J. Daniel contended that Will had no right to resist Baxter, and Judge Donnell therefore correctly found that Will was guilty of murder.[79] They all agreed, however, on what Moore conceded was "the inexorable necessity of keeping our slaves in a state of dependence and subservience to their masters."[80] And both Mordecai and Moore conceded that the *Tackett* rule would determine the standards of mitigation if the court adopted their contention that Will's killing could be mitigated to manslaughter.[81]

Gaston's opinion reversing the judgment held that Will's conviction should be mitigated from murder to manslaughter.[82] Gaston found that the appeal presented a single issue of law: "Whether upon the facts found the law adjudges that the killing was committed with malice aforethought."[83] He stated that had Will and Baxter both been white, the killing would have been manslaughter.[84]

Thus, the issue narrowed to whether the same result applied to Will. Gaston conceded that Will's enslaved status was indeed relevant. He acknowledged both the masters' and overseers' right to punish slaves short of taking life and limb, as well as their legal authority to reduce resisting slaves to submission.[85]

But Gaston concluded that Will was not in a state of resistance when Baxter shot him and that Baxter's actions therefore were not justified. The dispositive issue was "if the passions of the slave be excited into unlawful violence by the inhumanity of his master, [hirer, or overseer], is it a *conclusion of law* that such passion must spring from diabolical malice?" Gaston found that this rule was too "repugnant" for "the law of a civilized people and of a Christian land."[86] He concluded, "The prisoner is a human being, degraded indeed by slavery, but yet having 'organs, dimensions, senses, affections, passions,' like our own. The unfortunate man slain was for the time, indeed, his master, this dominion was not like that of a sovereign who can do no wrong."[87] Gaston also harmonized this decision determining the standards to establish an enslaved person's criminal liability with Judge Ruffin's holding for the court in *State v. Mann*, which decriminalized batteries committed by masters, hirers, and overseers. Ruffin, the author of the *Mann* opinion, apparently agreed because he did not file a dissenting opinion.[88]

Gaston's opinion in *State v. Jarrott*, six years later, extended this rule to a case involving a stranger to the enslaved defendant, when the court ordered a new trial for a man named Jarrott, after a jury found him guilty of the murder of Thomas Chatham. Chatham was a white man, about eighteen or nineteen years old.[89] The killing occurred following an altercation between Jarrott and a free Black man named Jack Hughes. Their dispute arose out of a late Saturday night card game. Jarrott's owner was Thomas Trotter, a planter who owned twenty-six slaves. He hired William A. Graham, a prominent politician and lawyer, to defend Jarrott.[90]

The appeal focused on the four requests to charge the jury that Jarrott's counsel made at trial. Although the Supreme Court reversed the conviction, it also affirmed trial judge John M. Dick's ruling denying Jarrott's first requested jury charge. Jarrott's lawyer asked Judge Dick to advise the jury that "in trials affecting life, a negro slave should not be convicted of murder, unless a white man would be convicted on the same evidence."[91]

Gaston rejected this principle of equal protection of the criminal law. He instead held that although Jarrott was entitled to seek to mitigate his charge from murder to manslaughter, it did not follow that "the same matters which would be deemed in law a *sufficient provocation* to free a white man, who had committed a homicide, in a moment of passion, from the guilt of murder, will have the same effect, when the party slain is a white man, and the offender a slave." Gaston cited Taylor's *Tackett* opinion as authority for the rule that

> the killing of a slave by a white man may be reduced from murder to manslaughter, by acts, which, proceeding from a white man, would not in law constitute a sufficient provocation. Among equals, the general rule is, that words are not, but blows are, a sufficient provocation; while in Tackett's case, it was declared that there *might be* words of reproach, so aggravating when uttered by a slave, as to excite the temporary fury which negatives the charge of malice. *Tackett's case*, 1 Hawks 210, 217, 218. This difference in the application of the same principle, arises from the *vast* difference which exists, under our institutions, between the social condition of the white man and of the slave; in consequence of which difference, what might be felt by one as the grossest degradation, is considered by the other as but a slight injury. And from the same cause, it must necessarily follow, that some acts, which between white persons are grievous provocations, when proceeding from a white person to a slave—whose passions are, or ought to be tamed down to his lowly condition—will not, and cannot be so regarded.

Gaston, like Taylor, thus held that both Jarrott's enslaved status and his race were relevant. He explained that "the degrees of homicide are indeed to be ascertained by common law principles," which "are necessarily, in their application, accommodated to the actual conditions of human beings in our society."[92]

Gaston further confirmed the principle of white supremacy when he affirmed Judge Dick's ruling refusing Jarrott's second request to charge the jury that Jarrott's insulting language did not give an apparently low status white man like Chatham the right to whip Jarrott, "and in that aspect of the case, [Jarrott] was entitled to be regarded as a white man on this trial." Gaston instead held that Chatham's race—and not his inferior social standing—was the critical fact. "It is the difference of condition between the white man and the slave—as recognized by our legal institutions—and not the difference between personal merit and demerit—which creates a legal distinction between the sufficiency and insufficiency of the alleged provocation." Race-based distinctions, Gaston explained, applied even to Chapman, a young white man "who debases himself by a familiar association with a slave, and, in the course of that association, is guilty of acts of meanness like that attributed—whether justly or unjustly—to the unfortunate deceased." Gaston concluded that "the distinction of castes yet remains, and with it remain all the passions, infirmities, and habits, which grow out of this distinction."[93]

The Supreme Court nevertheless reversed the conviction and remanded Jarrott's case for a new trial, finding that Judge Dick erred when his jury instructions suggested that Chapman had the right to respond to Jarrott's alleged insolence with an attempt to commit an "excessive battery" using "a sharp pointed knife, three inches long, and a piece of a fence rail of the length of one's arm," which "are not lawful instruments wherewith to check or to correct insolence." Gaston's opinion cited *State v. Hale* for the proposition that a battery committed by one person on another person's slave "might be justified, if not excessive, by circumstances which would form no justification for the battery of a white man." Although recognizing that these circumstances cannot be described "with precision," Gaston nevertheless held that Judge Dick should have read to the jury the defense's fourth instruction, which asserted that Chapman "had no right to correct the prisoner, with the piece of rail or the knife, for insolent language; but ought to have applied to his master, or to a justice of the peace for redress."[94]

A key disputed fact, Gaston wrote, was whether Chapman responded immediately to Jarrott's alleged insolence, or whether Jarrott's insolence was "clearly discontinued, then the attack of the deceased upon the prisoner was for vengeance on account of past insolence, and not in order to stop continuing abuse." Gaston suggested that "on this point, we are instructed by our predecessors that it is not necessary, in any case, that a person who has received an injury, real or imaginary, from a slave, should carve out his own justice; for the law has made ample and summary provision for the punishment of all trivial offences committed by slaves, by carrying them before a Justice, who is authorised to pass sentence for their being publicly whipped." According to Gaston, this statute's summary procedure for whipping of slaves "while it excludes the necessity of private vengeance, would seem to forbid its legality, since it effectually protects all persons from the insolence of slaves, even where their masters are unwilling to correct them upon complaint being made."[95]

After the remand, the trial's venue was transferred from Person County to Orange County, where, in March 1841, Jarrott was tried for murder before Judge Richmond M. Pearson and a jury, but this time his life was spared. The jury found Jarrott guilty of manslaughter—not murder. Jarrott was sentenced to appear in open court to be branded by a hot iron with the letter "M" on his left hand.[96]

Evaluating Gaston's Opinions and His Views on Slavery

Carl Degler called Gaston "one of those rare antislavery Southerners—or Northerners for that matter—who carried his attack on slavery's degradation to a realistic appreciation of the effect of the institution on free Negroes."[97] John

Orth credits Gaston with "supporting certain rights for blacks," although he notes that Gaston was a slave owner.[98] And Alfred Brophy asserts that Gaston was "different from the usual justice of his era."[99]

Gaston's views on race and enslavement may have been influenced by his early life misfortune. Born on September 19, 1778, his father, Alexander, was a doctor from Ireland. His mother, Margaret Sharpe, was from England. Her family was Catholic, and she was educated at a convent in France. During the Revolutionary War, Alexander fought on the patriot side and was killed in August 1781 by loyalists. Margaret persevered and encouraged William's Catholic education. At the age of thirteen, he began his studies in November 1791 at Georgetown, where he was celebrated as the school's first matriculating student. But in the spring of 1793, he left school because of ill health and returned home to North Carolina.[100] Nevertheless, Gaston Hall, a 728-seat hall and theater, which is called "a crown jewel" of the Georgetown campus, was named in his honor.[101]

Gaston later resumed his college career at Princeton, graduating in 1796 with honors. He returned to North Carolina and studied law under François-Xavier Martin, who later was chief justice of Louisiana's Supreme Court. Gaston was admitted to the bar in 1798. His luck soon improved when he continued the law practice of his brother-in-law, John Louis Taylor, who was elevated to the state's Superior Court. Gaston also began his political career as a Federalist, although he later became a Whig. He served in North Carolina's Senate and House of Commons, where he became speaker. He also served two terms in the U.S. Congress. His legal clients included Quakers who sought to free their own slaves. He was elected to the North Carolina Supreme Court in 1832, and he served on the court until he died in 1844.[102]

Gaston's estate upon his death included more than two hundred enslaved people.[103] During his lifetime, Gaston freed one enslaved young man named Augustus. According to a September 1, 1824, letter, Gaston placed "my boy Augustus under the charge of the Rev'd Joseph Carburry to receive moral and religious instructions, to be taught a useful trade, and, when qualified to make a fit use of his freedom to be emancipated."[104]

Moreover, Gaston, in 1832, delivered a graduation speech at the University of North Carolina calling for "the mitigation, and (is it too much to hope for in North Carolina?) the ultimate extirpation" of slavery, which he disparaged as "the worst evil that afflicts the Southern part of our Confederacy." Gaston offered a Whig critique of slavery, however, not because of the injustice it inflicted on the enslaved but because it, "more than any other cause, keeps us back in the career of improvement. It stifles industry and represses enterprize—it is fatal to economy and providence—it discourages skill—impairs our strength as a community, and poisons morals at the fountain head."[105]

Gaston also was one of the delegates to the 1835 state constitutional convention who unsuccessfully opposed a proposed constitutional amendment that disenfranchised all free Blacks.[106] Gaston argued that this amendment was unfair because it would take away a right that free Blacks had long exercised, but he was not opposed to a race-based restriction of Black voting rights. He explained that "a person of that class who possessed a freehold, was an honest man, and perhaps a [C]hristian, ... should not be politically excommunicated, and have an additional mark of degradation fixed upon him, solely on accounts of his color. Let them know they are part of the body politic, and they will feel an attachment to the form of Government, and have a fixed interest in the prosperity of the community, and will exercise an important influence over the slaves."[107]

Gaston thus asked the delegates to modify the disenfranchisement amendment to permit voting by free Blacks, as defined in the amendment, who "for one year next preceding any election, have owned and possessed property, real or personal or both, of the clear value of five hundred dollars over and above all incumbrances, charges and debts," provided they have not "been convicted of an infamous offence." Gaston argued that, in the colonial period, the majority of free Blacks were the children of white mothers who were "entitled to all the rights of free men." He added that those who had been freed for "meritorious services" under a 1777 act were "entitled to all the rights and privileges of colored freemen." He feared that the disenfranchisement proposal would "force" free Blacks "down yet lower in the scale of degradation, encouraging ill disposed white men to trample upon and abuse them as beings without a political existence, and scarcely different from slaves."[108] The convention delegates defeated Gaston's proposal by a relatively close 64–55 vote.[109] His opposition to total free Black disenfranchisement thus was not unique; local newspapers published opinions opposing the amendment.[110]

According to Brophy, Gaston "was perhaps best known in his time" for his 1834 opinion in *State v. Will*.[111] Historians offer different interpretations of Gaston's opinion. Patrick Brady, for example, noted, "Cheers for *Will* have been as numerous as jeers for *Mann*." He quoted writers who concluded that Gaston's *Will* opinion was inconsistent with Ruffin's *Mann* opinion, with some contending that it qualified or even overruled *Mann*.[112] According to Herman Schauinger, the *Will* opinion resolved "uncertainty in regard to the protection of slaves from masters," and it "became a landmark in a more liberal and humane attitude."[113] Nevertheless, I continue to believe that *Will* is one of "the most misunderstood case[s] in the Southern case law." Abolitionist slave law treatise writers George Stroud and William Goodell contributed to the confusion when they failed even to mention Gaston's opinion, leaving others a clear field "to each take their turn[s] praising the opinion" and its author.[114]

But Gaston's *Will* opinion must be read together with *Jarrott*, which Barbara Jackson states "sustains [Gaston's] reputation for progressive thought in protecting the civil rights of slaves in criminal trials."[115] Jackson admits that the *Jarrott* opinion is contrary to Gaston's "usually progressive philosophy," and demonstrates that he simply "could not view" enslaved Blacks and whites "as equals under the law."[116] Indeed, Gaston's *Jarrott* opinion confirms that his views on race were limited by his support for the white-supremacist principles that are assumed even in his opinion in *State v. Will*.[117] Thomas Cobb thus commented favorably upon Gaston's *Will* and *Jarrott* opinions in his proslavery enslavement law treatise; their extension of the *Tackett/Hale* separate unequal mitigation rule was in the mainstream of antebellum enslavement jurisprudence.[118] The outliers included Georgia's chief justice, Joseph Henry Lumpkin, and the other justices of that court who, in 1854, denied to enslaved defendants the right to mitigate the alleged killings of any whites from murder to manslaughter. That rule, which is discussed in chapter 7, would have increased the number of homicides committed by slaves that would be defined as murders. To this extent, Taylor's *Tackett* doctrine could be viewed as the more "moderate" alternative.[119]

Nevertheless, both of these approaches were based on the separate and unequal protection for enslaved people under the state's criminal law. Indeed, Taylor's opinions creating new enslavement law exceptions to the common-law rules established the doctrinal basis for the Georgia judges to expand this inequality principle according to their own views about the violence that was necessary in their slave societies.

Conclusion

North Carolina's Supreme Court was the leader in establishing, in the common law of enslavement, Harry Seawell's separate and unequal mitigation doctrine, beginning with Chief Justice Taylor's *Tackett* opinion vesting white strangers to the enslavement relationship with enhanced rights to reduce slave murders to manslaughter. These killers were not among the "superiors" to whom the common-law authorities had conferred violent privileges and immunities. Taylor's *Hale* opinion later extended this doctrine to permit white strangers to commit what otherwise would have been assaults and batteries against victims who were enslaved by others.

Justices Ruffin and Gaston soon extended this doctrine in opinions that they built on Taylor's doctrinal foundation. Ruffin's notorious *Mann* decision decriminalized all assaults and batteries committed by masters and hirers upon the people they enslaved or controlled, while his *Hoover* decision limited the master's murder liability to the most wanton and sadistic killings. And Gaston's *Will* and *Jarrott* opinions restricted the right of enslaved defendants to mitigate homicides of white overseers and strangers to the master-slave relationship.

Moreover, because Taylor based the unequal mitigation rules on the dual pillars of enslavement and race, the courts later extended the principles of white supremacy and separate and unequal protection of the law to free Blacks. This substantive enslavement law's survivals persisted long after emancipation. For example, it was not until 1975 that North Carolina's Supreme Court expressly overruled the *Tackett* and *Jarrott* decisions, while affirming the conviction of Rufus Coley Watson Jr., a Black prisoner, for the murder of Roger Dale Samples, a white prisoner. Watson's lawyer, Wright T. Dixon Jr., conceded that North Carolina law did not generally permit a defendant to use the mere words spoken by a homicide victim to mitigate a murder charge to manslaughter. He nevertheless relied on *Tackett* and *Jarrott* to argue that Samples used racist words that were so provocative that the jury could consider them to mitigate the homicide to manslaughter.[120] Justice James W. Copeland noted that the *Tackett* and *Jarrott* opinions "contain language that tends to support defendant's contention." But he held that "the exceptions to the 'mere words' doctrine recognized in both cases are totally without relevance today."[121] Copeland did not explain why these cases were irrelevant, nor did he acknowledge that they were important enslavement law precedents.[122]

CHAPTER 4

Justice O'Neall and Unequal Protection for Free Blacks

Justices John Belton O'Neall of South Carolina and Richmond M. Pearson of North Carolina extended the *Tackett/Jarrott* unequal protection doctrine to permit whites to commit what otherwise would have been extralegal assaults on "insolent" free Blacks. The legislatures in these states, unlike those discussed in chapters 6 and 7, did not define free Black insolence as a crime to be punished by the state. Therefore, the courts in the *Jowers* and *Harden* cases, and the decisions following them, presumptively would apply the well-established common-law rule to not permit justification of nonfatal violence based on "mere words," in the exercise of autonomous legal reasoning. O'Neall and Pearson instead extended this new separate and unequal protection doctrine for free Blacks before the Civil War and Reconstruction intervened to stop the process.

These decisions are significant for reasons including what they tell us about O'Neall and Pearson as jurists. Joseph Ranney recently lauded both as important members of the "legal world," which "they shared with most other American judges." The judges in this "World of Legal Order," according to Ranney, "emphasized order and procedural fairness" and were thus able to "withstand political opposition and adjust to the tides of social change." Nevertheless, in their *Jowers* and *Harden* decisions these judges legitimized what they recognized were politically popular views about the need for a white privilege to respond to free Black insolence with what otherwise would have been extralegal racially motivated violence that was prohibited by the common-law rules of "order and procedural fairness."[1] These decisions also are important because these "two judges shaped Southern life and law in important ways both before and after slavery. Traces of their work remain visible in American law and inform dilemmas of race the nation faces today."[2]

O'Neall's 1832 South Carolina Court Appeals opinion in *State v. Harden* first announced this separate and unequal protection principle confining all of South Carolina's free Blacks to what he called their "degraded caste," thus advancing the cause of white supremacy.[3] Howell Meadoes Henry described O'Neall's *Harden* opinion as "the best authoritative statement of the legal status, rights and privileges of the free negro."[4] Historians Michael Johnson and James Roark summarized this decision's impact on South Carolina's African Americans: "In the daily round of life, every free person of color had to be constantly on guard against committing some act that a white person might consider an act of insolence: a sharp word, a careless boast, failure to remove one's hat, or neglecting to give a passing white man proper deference on the street. Any of these and dozens of other acts might be interpreted as insolence and [would] justify a white man in 'correcting' a free person of color." Not all interracial encounters resulted in violence that this doctrine would immunize. Nevertheless, "in every encounter with a white person, the person of color had to exercise restraint." Free Blacks always had "to discipline spontaneity, to scrutinize each statement and every gesture for anything potentially offensive" because "the legal definition of insolence was intentionally vague."[5]

O'Neall's endorsement of the separate and unequal protection principle for free Blacks is significant. During his forty-nine-year career as a lawyer, author, state legislator, and trial and appellate court judge, O'Neall wrote in favor of temperance, female education, and enslavement law amelioration. Scholars thus have included him among the southern antebellum jurists who were most concerned about the welfare of slaves and free Blacks.[6] South Carolina's lawyers and judges continued to hold him in such high regard that—in 1986—they named their state's first inn of court for him.[7] Two years later, O'Neall's portrait was hung near the South Carolina Court of Appeals courtroom in the then newly restored John C. Calhoun State Office Building.[8]

But the *Harden* opinion calls for a nuanced analysis of O'Neall's contributions to the separate and unequal protection doctrine for free Blacks as well as his defense of slavery and white supremacy. This effort is rooted in the *Harden* decision's social context and South Carolina's oppressive statutes regarding its enslaved and free Black people.[9]

The Social and Legal Context

It at first may seem unclear why South Carolina's small free Black population percentage would have raised much concern among the state's dominant white people. Historians have identified several reasons for the whites' racial fears and laws, including South Carolina's unique Black-majority demographic profile and its early settlement by slaveholders from Barbados.[10]

As to demographics, between 1790 and 1860, the state's free nonwhite population steadily increased, but from only about 0.7 percent to a mere 1.4 percent of the total population. According to the 1830 census, the state's 7,921 free Black people made up only 1.36 percent of its total population of 581,185. They were by far outnumbered by the state's 257,863 whites. But the state's 315,401 enslaved people formed the largest population segment.[11] It is not surprising, then, that those in the white minority, including the moderate O'Neall, felt threatened by the large numbers of African Americans, whether enslaved or free. This was especially so in the state's Atlantic coastal low country. This region's residents dominated South Carolina politics and its legislature. Beginning in the colonial era and continuing into the nineteenth century, the low country's population was concentrated in the Charleston District, which was made up of the two parishes that composed the City of Charleston and the surrounding rural and agricultural parishes.[12]

This low country region also had the state's largest concentration of enslaved and free Black populations. Almost 72 percent of the Charleston District's population in 1830 was enslaved. These enslaved Charlestonians by far outnumbered those labeled as white, who were only 24 percent of the population. The District's 3,627 free Blacks made up the other 4.2 percent of the total, but they were almost 46 percent of the state's total free African American population.[13] Charleston's free Black population in 1830 was 6.95 percent of the city's total population, which was 50.69 percent enslaved.[14] "During the two decades preceding the Civil War," the city's free Black population increased at a greater rate than the state's free Black population as a whole, suggesting to historian Jeff Strickland that "free blacks were migrating to the city."[15]

Among Britain's North American colonies, South Carolina had the most significant linkages with Barbados, prompting Peter Wood to label South Carolina a colony of the Barbados colony because emigrants from Barbados contributed to South Carolina's early settlement and lawmaking.[16] Jack Greene described South Carolina as "a successful extension of the Barbados culture hearth." This was the large cash crop plantation colonization pattern of development, which included an enslaved population majority. Similar mixtures of climate, soils, and cash crops enabled this cultural system to spread to other British Atlantic island colonies, including Jamaica, as well as the South Carolina coast, the Cape Fear region in North Carolina, Georgia, and Florida.[17]

South Carolina's Caribbean connections influenced its history of law and race relations. Historians suggest that this Barbados influence explains why, unlike the upper southern states, South Carolina's colonial and antebellum legislators never prohibited interracial sex or marriage. Nor did they adopt the one-drop rule, by which a person with any African heritage was conclusively considered to be Black. They also failed to institute a fixed rule establishing who was defined as white and who was Black. Instead, white families and local communities were free to treat some mixed-race people as white. The courts and local juries resolved any disputes on a case-by-case basis.[18] South Carolina, unlike the other southern states, thus included what Carl Degler called a "mulatto escape hatch," which, similar to the law in Jamaica and Brazil, permitted "an escape from the disabilities of blackness for some colored people."[19]

Justice William Harper's 1835 opinion in *State v. Cantey* explained how the South Carolina courts decided who was included in the white caste:

> We cannot say what admixture of negro blood will make a coloured person, and, by a jury, one may be found a coloured person, while another of the same degree of blood may be declared a white man. In general it is very desirable that rules of law should be certain and precise. But it is not always practicable, nor is it practicable in this instance. Nor do I know that it is desirable. The condition of the individual is not to be determined solely by the distinct and visible mixture of negro blood, but by reputation, by his reception into society, and his having commonly exercised the privileges of a white man. But his admission to these privileges, regulated by the public opinion of the community in which he lives, will very much depend on his own character and conduct; and it may be well and proper, that a man of worth, honesty, industry and respectability, should have the rank of a white man, while a vagabond of the same degree of blood should be confined to the inferior caste. It will be a stimulus to the good conduct of these persons, and security for their fidelity as citizens.

He concluded, "It is hardly necessary to say that a slave cannot be a white man."[20] Thus, according to Ariela Gross, "To be white was to act white: to associate with whites, to dance gracefully, to vote. Blood may have been the signified, but the signifiers were social acts. More than that, the signifiers of race were not only social and political but also prescriptive and legal." A white man could be "a citizen, a civic being, someone who could do certain kinds of things." But "judges gave greater weight to particular kinds of racial performance. At the appellate level, when courts referred to performances of whiteness, it was civic performances they found determinative."[21]

It also was "hardly necessary" to note that, unlike a "white man," people with some African heritage could be treated in law as if they were white only if they earned the approval of the white people in their community. In contrast, the state's white people did not need to conduct themselves in a way that was sufficient to earn and retain the legal rights and privileges of whiteness. "Respectable" whites did indeed hold in low social regard some whites, whom they disparaged as vagabonds or poor white trash. But these disadvantaged whites always retained their racially privileged legal position. They never were threatened with the legal disabilities and political, social, and economic inequities that routinely were inflicted on free Blacks.[22]

These free Black disabilities, according to a writer identified only as "A Carolinian," advanced two policies: "to preserve such a system of discipline in relation to them as will effectually mark their *distinctive* condition in society, and regulate their *degree*, when placed in oppositions to that of our own."[23] Thus, the colonial assembly adopted acts as early as 1716 and 1717 declaring that only white men could vote. And to reduce the "degree" of free Blacks, a 1717 statute stated that "any white woman, whether free or a servant, that shall suffer herself to be got with child by a negro or other slave or free negro, . . . shall become a servant for . . . seven years." Free Blacks or white fathers of mixed-race children were subject to the same penalty. Moreover, the male and female children "of this unnatural and inordinate copulation" were to serve as involuntary servants for twenty-one or eighteen years, respectively. The law was repealed in 1744.[24] The 1722 slave code also required owners freeing slaves to "make provision for" the formerly enslaved persons' "departure out of this Province" within twelve months. Anyone failing to so depart "shall lose the benefit of such manumission, and continue to be a slave," unless the "manumission shall be approved of and confirmed by an order of both Houses of Assembly."[25]

South Carolina's criminal law imposed unique disadvantages upon "negroes" or upon mixed-race people, including those labeled as "mulattoes." Slave control was always a concern of the South Carolina's white minority. According to Sally Hadden, South Carolina established the first mainland "official slave patrols in 1704."[26] And Elizabeth Dale credits Charleston with, in 1783, establishing the first urban police force in the United States.[27] The state's enslaved and free African American majority may have presented one reason why it became the last state to make the murder of an enslaved person a capital offense.[28]

South Carolina's colonial slave codes reflected these concerns about security, when they denied the common law's procedural rights to enslaved and free Blacks who were accused of crimes. The 1690/1691, 1696, 1712, and 1722 laws authorized justices of the peace to try criminal charges asserted against slaves, either on their own or with another justice of the peace and three freeholders, depending on the severity of the crime.[29] These provisions were similar to the Barbados enslavement laws dating back to its 1661 slave code.[30]

The legislature in 1735 extended to free Blacks a provision in the 1690/1691 law that made it a crime for "any negro or Indian slave" to "offer any violence, by striking or the like, . . . any white person," unless the enslaved persons acted "by command of or in lawful defense of their owner's persons."[31] The 1735 law stated that "any negro or slave" who "shall strike a white person" was to be tried by "any two justices of the peace." A first-time offender was to be "severely whipped, and have his or her right ear cut off." Second-time offenders were to be tried before two justices of the peace and three freeholders, "or a quorum of them," who had the discretion to impose any punishment other than death. These courts also were to try "any negro or slave" who dared to "wound, maim, bruise or disable any white person," unless the defendant acted "by command, or in the defense of, his or her owner or manager, or their family or goods." Death was the penalty for those convicted of this offense.[32]

The legislature expanded upon this separate and unequal principle of criminal procedure in the comprehensive 1740 enslavement law, which, Christopher Tomlins notes, was "the tenth return to the basic law of slavery since 1690/1."[33] This act, which was a response to the 1739 Stono slave rebellion, remained in effect for the next 125 years. Although the legislature included "new polite language of legality and humanity," it "reenacted all of the familiar features" of the colony's earlier laws.[34]

This law included a provision vesting inferior courts consisting of two magistrates and three or five freeholders with the jurisdiction to try capital charges asserted against slaves. Courts made up of one magistrate and three freeholders had jurisdiction to try noncapital charges.[35]

This statute also expanded the jurisdiction of these inferior courts to include "all crimes and offences committed by free negroes, Indians . . . , mulattoes or mustizoes," which were to "be proceeded in, heard, tried, adjudged and determined by the justices and freeholders appointed by this Act for the trial of slaves, in like manner, order and form, as is hereby directed and appointed for the proceedings and trial of crimes and offences committed by slaves; any law, statute, usage or custom to the contrary notwithstanding." These defendants were denied the right to a grand jury review of the charges against them before their trials. They were instead to be tried quickly, not more than six days after their arrests, in these courts of magistrates and freeholders. The only exception was for "free Indians in amity with this government."[36]

Because the 1740 act did not define the terms "negroes, Indians . . . , mulattoes or mustizoes," judges and juries decided whether to include defendants or witnesses—with at least one drop of African or native American blood—in these disadvantageous categories.[37] These racially segregated court proceedings legitimized the notion that nonwhite defendants were so inferior that they were not entitled to trials in the regular courts, which heard similar cases in which white defendants were accused of wrongdoing.[38]

As in the other southern colonies and states, free Blacks—like enslaved people—also were denied the rights that whites enjoyed to serve on juries and testify in the regular courts. They could testify in the magistrates and freeholders courts, but not under oath, and only when nonwhite defendants were tried for criminal offenses.[39]

Moreover, South Carolina's nonwhite defendants had no right to appeal to the state's highest appellate court the judgments of the inferior magistrate and freeholder courts. Before 1833, the regular trial courts instead exercised jurisdiction to grant common-law writs of prohibition at the request of defendants who challenged the magistrates and freeholders court's jurisdiction or composition, or who alleged legal jurisdictional errors by magistrates.[40] This writ's "great object . . . is to restrain all inferior jurisdictions from proceeding without due authority, and to keep them within their appropriate limits." The writ, however, did not permit courts to "correct errors in the proceedings, or to set aside the sentences or decrees pronounced by them, which are supposed to be irregular." Only the appellate courts were authorized "to correct errors in cases of erroneous proceedings. It is not the province of the writ of prohibition to correct such abuses."[41]

Therefore, the state's highest court could not correct errors of law or fact made by the magistrates and freeholders. Nor did that court have jurisdiction to issue precedents establishing rules of law that it could ensure would be followed by the magistrates and freeholders. This was a significant detriment to free Blacks. They could not challenge in the state's highest court the magistrates' substantive or procedural legal rulings or the verdicts of the freeholder juries. This race-based procedural disadvantage continued even after the legislature, in 1833, approved an act permitting new trial applications by those who were convicted of capital offenses by the magistrates and freeholders courts. Defendants could make these applications to any single trial-level Circuit Court judge or Court of Appeals judge. A judge who believed "that the conviction has been erroneous" could order a new trial before a court composed of different magistrates and freeholders.[42] This statute was designed to "avoid the technicalities of prohibition"; it permitted the reviewing judges to order new trials on legal or factual grounds.[43] But the state's Court of Appeals held that this act did not expand the court's jurisdiction to permit it to decide appeals from judicial orders granting or denying these new trial applications.[44] The courts of magistrates and freeholders, on more than one occasion, convicted defendants on charges that did not allege crimes under any state statute.[45]

These procedural innovations are examples of how South Carolina's free Black laws were among the most oppressive that were adopted in the slave states, which to different degrees extended their state's enslavement criminal law norms and principles to free Blacks. In part, this was because South Carolina's laws also denied to free Blacks the right to vote and thus participate directly in the legislative process.[46] The state's free Blacks "were subject to the community in general." The "legal power over free people of color was decentralized to each courthouse," and "the administration of justice for free Afro-Americans, like that for slaves, was firmly in the hands of local whites."[47]

Like the legislatures in the other southern states, South Carolina's white lawmakers also subjected free Blacks to the separate and unequal protection principle in the substantive criminal law. The state's legislators adopted criminal laws that applied only to free Blacks, and they subjected free Blacks to more severe punishments than those inflicted on white criminals for some acts that were crimes if committed by those in both of these racial categories.[48] For example, an 1843 act states that "any slave or free person of color, who shall commit an assault on a white woman with intent to commit a rape, on being thereof convicted, shall suffer death without benefit of clergy."[49] Local governments also enacted racially discriminatory ordinances, such as an 1819 Charleston City ordinance stating "that it shall not be lawful for any colored person or negro, whether free or slave," to play games of chance, including those with cards and dice. Those violating the act could be punished with any number of lashes, not exceeding twenty, which could be commuted for a fine not exceeding fifty dollars.[50]

Moreover, the state's legislature adopted statutes in 1820 and 1822 responding to South Carolina's whites' increased fears of free Blacks and servile insurrection. The preamble to the 1820 law, titled "An ACT to Restrain the Emancipation of Slaves, and to Prevent Free Persons of Color from Entering into This State, and for Other Purposes," proclaims the legislative finding that "the great and rapid increase of free negroes and mulattoes in this state, by migration and emancipation, renders it expedient and necessary for the Legislature to restrain the emancipation of slaves, and to prevent free persons of color from entering this State."[51]

The statute's four-part approach to these perceived threats began with section 1, requiring that slave owners obtain acts of the state legislature approving slave manumissions. The second through fourth sections sought to stop "free negro or mulatto" migration into the state. People entering the state in violation of this act could be arrested and brought before a justice of the peace, who was to order the accused to leave the state. Those failing to leave as ordered could be fined twenty dollars. If they did not pay their fines, they were to be sold into involuntary servitude for terms not exceeding five years. The law included exceptions, however, for free Blacks brought into the state as servants for white persons, who were permitted to remain up to six months, and for free Black sailors, who were to depart with their vessels. The fifth section was designed to stop kidnapping. It prohibited bringing free Blacks into the state to be enslaved. And the sixth section fixed penalties for those disseminating literature with an intent to disturb the state's "peace and security."[52]

White South Carolinians' fears of the state's free Blacks intensified after the 1822 trials concerning the rebellion alleged to have been incited by Denmark Vesey, a free Black man.[53] In that controversy's wake, citizens of Charleston filed a memorial with the state legislature. It expressed the petitioners' fears of the city's free Black population, both at that time, as a bad influence on the enslaved population, and in the future, with the potential to one day outnumber the city's whites. The petitioners therefore asked the legislature to adopt a law expelling from the state "all free persons of color." They also called for laws better regulating the hiring out of Blacks and the clothing they could wear and recommended that "a regular, efficient military force" replace the then current City Guard. They requested laws prohibiting free-Black real-property ownership, prohibiting Blacks from living "upon a premises where no white persons reside," and "prohibiting under severe penalties, all persons from teaching negroes to read and write." Finally, they believed that the legislature should impose the death penalty on whites who aid "actual or projected" slave insurrections.[54]

The legislature responded with an 1822 law adopting some of these proposals.[55] The statute included the first version of the antebellum laws that have been called the Negro Seamen Acts. It in effect created an irrebuttable presumption of criminality based on race, when it declared that all free Black sailors "shall be liable to be seized and confined in jail" while their ships were docked in South Carolina's harbors. The law obviously did not apply to white seamen. It also stated that enslaved who left the state could not return. And it further regulated the lives of free Blacks who were permitted to live in the state. It imposed a tax on free Black males who were not South Carolina natives or who had not lived in the state for five years when the act went into effect. It prohibited the hiring out of enslaved males other than by their owners. It required free Black males to have legal guardians. And it also made it a capital crime for any person to "counsel, aid or hire any slave or slaves, free negroes or persons of color, to raise a rebellion or insurrection within this State," whether the rebellion or insurrection took place or not.[56]

These anti–free Black laws apparently achieved their desired effect, at least in part. South Carolina's free Black population between 1810 and 1820 increased by 49.9 percent, while the white population increased by only 10.9 percent. In the next four decades, the population percentage increases for free Blacks were 16.0, 4.5. 8.3, and 10.7 percent, while for whites the increases were 8.1, 0.5, 6.0, and 6.1 percent, respectively.[57] Marina Wikramanayake concludes that, after 1840, the state's free Black population increase "came completely from within the free black community, which in turn became a more restricted and more exclusive group."[58]

Hostility to free Blacks, or at least the majority of the nonelite free Blacks, intensified in the 1850s. Governor Whitemarsh Benjamin Seabrook in 1849 and 1850 proposed a bill that would require the removal from South Carolina of free Blacks who did not own property. Although this bill failed, between 1856 and 1859, seventeen grand jury presentments "called to the attention of the legislature the dangers existing within the free colored population." These presentments "demanded the removal or enslavement of the state's free blacks."[59] Free Black removal and voluntary enslavement bills were introduced in the legislature, in 1859 and 1860, but they were not adopted.[60]

Notwithstanding these anti-Black laws and public sentiments, some free Blacks achieved a measure of economic success, especially those living in Charleston and Columbia, the state's two largest cities. According to Jeff Strickland, the principal free Black male occupations in antebellum Charleston included skilled worker categories such as "bricklayers, boot- and shoemakers, tailors, carpenters, painters, fishermen, cooks, ships carpenters, and barbers; they rarely worked as laborers." Most of the women, in contrast, were employed as "domestic servants, mantua makers, seamstresses, tailors, and laundresses, although some worked as pastry cooks, nurses, and house servants."[61] David O. Stowell found similar occupations among Columbia's free Blacks.[62]

Some of these economically successful free African American people became property owners, according to census and tax records.[63] On the eve of the Civil War in 1860, moreover, 137 of Charleston's free Blacks were listed as the enslavers of a total of 544 people. Statewide, 171 free Blacks owned 766 slaves.[64] But the wealth discrepancy between whites and free Blacks was extreme. Stowell's analysis of the Columbia data from 1860 reveals that the mean personal estate of whites was $11,687 and for free Blacks it was $310.[65] Wikramanayake also found that, although "a comparatively large number" of Charleston's free Black's owned real estate, this wealth was "concentrated in the hands of a few." She found that a similar concentration of wealth existed among free Black enslavers.[66]

Robert L. Harris's study of Charleston's free Black elite associations, however, concludes that even that city's most prosperous free mixed-race residents did not occupy "a safe position between whites on the top and blacks at the bottom." Although the state's wealthiest elite free Blacks continuously sought to secure a legal and social status between whites and the majority of free Blacks, Harris contends that, both under the law and according to the evidence he cites of their social status and conditions, "Charleston's free Afro-Americans compare unfavorably with freedmen in Brazil, the Caribbean, and even in New Orleans."[67]

According to David Dangerfield, some free Black yeoman farmers achieved levels of success in the 1850s in the Charleston District's agricultural low country parishes and in the state's upcountry region.[68] He implies that this evidence may support a "new paradigm" to understand the status of free Blacks in the antebellum South, which Kirt von Daacke had suggested in his study of free Blacks in antebellum Virginia.[69] But even the state's most elite free persons of color's economic prosperity did not guarantee their total legal or social equality, as illustrated by the ever-expanding scope of the separate and unequal protection doctrine for free Blacks.[70]

O'Neall Extends the *Tackett* Unequal Protection Rule to Free Blacks

When considered against the background of this social and legal context, O'Neall's decision in *State v. Harden* relegating South Carolina's free Blacks to second-class inferior and degraded protection under the state's judge-made substantive criminal law is predictable. It nevertheless was extraordinary because it was unprecedented under the generally applicable rules and doctrines of the common law of crimes.[71]

O'Neall signaled this new doctrine's jurisprudential foundation in an 1831 Court of Appeals of Law and Equity opinion confirming that the *Tackett* doctrine applied to criminal cases involving South Carolina's enslaved population. The court affirmed Thomas Crank's conviction for murdering his father, Stephen Crank. In the alternative, the state alleged that Thomas was an accessory before or after the fact of the murder that was committed by his wife, Mary Crank, or by an enslaved man named Jack, who was the property of Stephen. A court of magistrates and freeholders had previously convicted Jack of Stephen's murder.[72]

Thomas's arguments on appeal included the contention that different mitigation standards applied to a homicide committed by an enslaved person such as Jack and Thomas, as a white person. Judge O'Neall's opinion agreed with this contention. O'Neall defined manslaughter as "an unlawful killing of a human being, upon sudden heat and passion, arising from reasonable provocation. Reasonable provocation being proven reduces a killing, upon a consequent sudden heat of passion to manslaughter." But O'Neall recognized that under the common law of crimes not all people were equal, when he asked,

> What is reasonable provocation? It is as various as the different stations and relations of man. Two freemen are equal, the slightest touching of the person of one by the other in a rude, insolent, or angry manner *might* reduce a killing to manslaughter. Parent and child, master and apprentice, stand in a different relation to each other: obedience is due from the child, or apprentice to the parent or master, and to enforce it, they have the right to use moderate correction; if in the exercise of this right, the child or apprentice was to kill the parent or master, it would be murder.

Although not citing any authority, this summary is consistent with the then prevailing doctrines of the common law of crimes.

O'Neall acknowledged, however, that when an enslaved person was accused of murdering his or her owner, South Carolina's courts modified these legal principles: "To a master, *by the common law of this State*, a slave owes passive obedience; to enforce it the master has the right of correction, and if while exercising this right the slave should kill his master, he would be guilty of murder at common law, and not by statute." Notwithstanding this difference, the court affirmed Thomas's murder conviction on the facts of his case, and he was executed for his crime.[73]

One year later, O'Neall wrote his *Harden* opinion extending this unequal protection enslavement law principle to a case of nonfatal violence involving "two freemen" who he found were not "equal" in society and under the state's own common law. A grand jury had indicted Charles Harden for inflicting an assault and battery on Tom Archer, "a free negro." Harden's case went to trial during the spring term 1832 in the Chester District before Judge Baylis J. Earle and a jury.[74] Chester District (now Chester County) is in north-central South Carolina. It is separated by one county from the North Carolina state line. No evidence could be found about Harden. But "T. Archer" is listed in the 1830

Chester District U.S. census records as a "free colored" person between the ages of twenty-four and thirty-five. He was living in a household with a "free colored" woman between the same ages. They were among the district's 94 "free colored" people, who made up only 0.006 percent of the district's 17,182 free and enslaved residents.[75]

The case report recites no evidence explaining why Harden assaulted Archer. But the altercation occurred in the aftermath of the 1831 Nat Turner insurrection. Those events caused heightened interracial tensions in the South, including in South Carolina and neighboring North Carolina. These tensions may have had an influence in the community and on the case.[76]

The prosecution proved at the trial that Harden, "on some pretext, (for no provocation was proved,) first beat [Archer] in the street, giving fifty or sixty blows with his fist, and a stick or cowhide." Harden "then deliberately tied [Archer], carried him out into the woods, near the village, stripped him, and gave him, on the bare back, ninety-three lashes." Archer "was much abused, his back was severely cut, and the blood flowed freely. He fainted, or fell down under the infliction." Only white men were called to testify at Harden's trial. Archer could not testify about the beatings he endured.

Harden's trial counsel, whose name is not mentioned in the case report, asked the trial judge to quash the indictment, arguing that a white person cannot be indicted for assault and battery on a free African American. Judge Earle denied this motion. Harden's lawyer also contended that no "deed of manumission" was produced proving that Archer was free, "and that no other evidence was admissible." Judge Earle again disagreed, finding that Archer "was known throughout the country as free Tom Archer, and had been for ten years and upward." Earle found no evidence proving that Archer was enslaved or was freed by a manumission deed. He suggested that Archer "may have descended, for aught that appeared, from ancestors who were free."[77]

The jury convicted Harden. He filed an appeal to the Court of Appeals seeking a new trial. His appellate lawyer, N. R. Eaves, argued, (1) "That an indictment will not lie for an assault and battery committed on a free negro" and (2) "That the evidence to establish the freedom of the negro was insufficient."[78]

Justice O'Neall's opinion for the court denied both of these contentions and affirmed Harden's conviction. Most relevant here is O'Neall's holding on the first issue, that "for upwards of thirty years" it has been "well settled" that the state could prosecute whites who committed assaults and batteries on free Blacks. This precedent, he wrote, would "constitute a conclusive reason" for his decision. But he chose to explain at some length why both "principle, as well as precedent" supported the indictment.[79]

O'Neall began this line of reasoning with the premise that "an assault and battery may be defined to be, 'any touching of the *person of an individual*, in a rude or angry manner, without justification.'" He held that free Blacks were entitled to the criminal law's protection against assault and battery, even if they were denied the political and other rights of citizens. "To be an assault and battery, it is not necessary that the person who sustains it, should be a citizen of the government. All natural persons who, by law, are entitled to protection, may be the subject of assault and battery." He nevertheless excluded enslaved people because they "are chattels, and their right to protection belongs to the master; and is, therefore, not cast, so far as regards them personally, upon society." But free Blacks, "without any of the political rights which belong to a citizen, are still, to some extent, regarded by the law as possessing both natural and civil rights. The rights of life, liberty and property, belong to them, and must be protected by the community in which they are suffered to live. They are regarded, in law, as persons capable of committing and receiving an injury; and for the one, they are liable to punishment, and for the other, they are entitled to redress." Free Blacks thus could sue to recover monetary damages if they were assault and battery victims.[80]

O'Neall then concluded that the criminal law therefore also protected free Blacks from assaults and batteries:

> In an indictment, the defendant is proceeded against for doing an act unlawful in itself, and which has disturbed the peace of society. The unlawfulness of an assault and battery upon a free negro, without *reasonable provocation*, cannot be doubted. For to no white man does the right belong of correcting, at pleasure, a free negro. The peace of society is as much broken by an assault and battery upon him, as it is upon a white man. Like the latter, he has his passions, and with the means of attack and defence in his possession, if the law refused to protect him, he too, at last, might be driven to repel force by force.[81]

O'Neall's opinion could have ended here. He adequately explained why the court affirmed Harden's conviction for his unprovoked assault and battery.

O'Neall wrote on, however, with dicta extending discriminatory standards of justification to cases in which free Blacks were the victims of white violence. O'Neall did not cite the *Tackett* decision. But, like Taylor, he asserted that the "only difference in the law" between "indictments for assaults and batteries on free white men and free negroes, seems to me to consist in the different justifications which would excuse an assault and battery on the one or the other." This was not a trivial difference. According to O'Neall, free Blacks, who were denied political rights, also "belong to a degraded *caste* of society; they are, in no respect, on a perfect equality with the white man." He explained the legal and social significance of this racial caste system: "According to their condition, [free Blacks] ought, by law, to be compelled to demean themselves as inferiors, from whom submission and respect, to the whites, in all their intercourse in society, is demanded." O'Neall then deviated from the common-law "mere words" doctrine when he admitted that "I have always thought, and while on the circuit ruled, that words of impertinence, or insolence, addressed by a free negro, to a white man, would justify an assault and battery." O'Neall also delegated wide discretion to local juries, stating, "As a general rule, I should say, that whatever, in the opinion of the jury, would induce them, as reasonable men, to strike a free negro, should, in all cases, be regarded as a legal justification in an indictment."

O'Neall apparently realized that this white-supremacist doctrine was both controversial and unprecedented in the common law. He thus felt compelled to explain, "If, for this position, I am asked for authority, I answer, it is according to good public policy, and the general conduct of the people of this State towards this class of our population since they first existed among us; and this makes it the common law in relation to them."[82]

On the second issue, O'Neall held that Archer lived as a free person for a sufficient period to no longer be enslaved under the doctrine of implied manumission by prescription.[83] Justices David Johnson and William Harper concurred.[84]

Of course, O'Neall could cite no statute, case law, or legal treatise supporting his race-based assertion "that words of impertinence, or insolence, addressed by a free negro, to a white man, would justify an assault and battery." This rule was contrary to the well-settled common-law rule providing that "mere words" inflicted by one stranger or unrelated person on another person never justified an assault or battery. John Fauchereaud Grimké's 1810 edition of his manual for South Carolina justices of the peace confirms the general rule that "no words whatsoever can amount to an assault."[85] Grimké also cites the report of a 1794 South Carolina Courts of Common Pleas and General Sessions of the Peace case in which three of four judges similarly ruled "that no words would justify an assault."[86]

Grimké also explains the common-law exceptions to this rule that permitted a person to "justify an assault, in defense of his person, or of his wife, or master, or parent, or child within age; and even a wounding may be justified in defence of his person, but not of his possessions."[87] And an assault, he contends, is justified "if an officer having a lawful warrant, lay hands on another to arrest him, or if a parent in a reasonable manner chastise a child, a master his servant, a schoolmaster his scholar, a gaoler his prisoner, and even a husband his wife, as some say; or if one confine a friend who is mad, and bind and beat him in such a manner as is proper in his circumstances; or if a man force a sword from one who offers to kill another therewith."[88] Twenty-nine years later, John Bouvier's legal dictionary similarly did not list insulting, impertinent, or insolent words among the grounds that would justify a battery, while excluding husband and wife from the list of privileged relationships.[89]

Because these common-law authorities did not mention slavery, O'Neall, like Taylor in *Tackett*, relied on his own notions of justice, good public policy, and the accepted customs and conduct of the people whose views he thought were relevant while creating a new rule that is contrary to well-settled common-law authorities. Johnson and Roark state that O'Neall, who "was a moderate man in such matters," announced a doctrine guaranteeing that any white person who "corrected" an insolent free Black person "had no other person to account to, unless, as in the case of Tom Archer, the correction was so outrageous that it aroused whites' sympathy." This rule imposed on free African Americans the duty "to convince the whites they saw that they were sufficiently inferior. Each day they had to be prepared to act instinctively toward whites as if they were as subordinate as slaves."[90]

O'Neall readily entrusted his state's all-white juries with the discretion to apply his rule of unequal mitigation and justification to enforce their own views on proper racial subordination. His opinion did not order a new trial. It is likely that the appellate court found that Judge Earle included this rule of unequal protection in his charge to the jury, or that if Earle omitted this jury instruction this was harmless error because the white witnesses who testified at trial confirmed that Archer was not insolent.[91]

O'Neall apparently believed strongly in this rule of unequal criminal law protection for free Blacks. His *State v. Harden* opinion was not published until 1843, when, at his request, it was included in full as a note to his Court of Appeals opinion in *State v. Hill*.[92] In that case, the court affirmed William Hill's conviction for assault and battery and for the false imprisonment of Judah Bowser, who was described as an "old woman," and her daughters Malinda, Tabitha, and Lizzy. Hill, with the aid of two other men, captured his victims as part of a plan to take them to Georgia and enslave them or sell them into slavery. Judah or her daughters must have somehow made their plight known because several men pursued them and stymied Hill's scheme.[93]

O'Neall's Court of Appeals opinion rejected all of Hill's arguments on appeal, including his contention that he could commit common-law assault and battery and false imprisonment with impunity against his free Black victims.

O'Neall was the judge at the trial. This occurred because Court of Appeals judges, between 1824 and 1859, also rode circuit and presided over cases as trial judges. They even at times wrote appellate decisions affirming their own trial court rulings.[94]

O'Neall's appellate opinion explained, "Free negroes, as the law of South Carolina has been repeatedly ruled, have all the rights of property and protection, which white persons possess, with the exception that they cannot, with force, repel force, exhibited by a white man, and a less provocation might excuse a white man, in an assault and battery upon a free negro, than would in the case of a white person." He cited his unpublished *Harden* opinion as authority for these propositions. "If ever any such doubt existed, it ought to have been removed by the case of the *State* vs. *Harden*, decided by the Court of Appeals, in 1832 (and which, I hope, will be appended in a note to the report of this case)."[95]

O'Neall, and the other Court of Appeals justices, may have looked favorably on the plight of Judah Bowser and her daughters because the court's decision vindicated the obvious intention of Judah's onetime owner, Mrs. Funderburk, to free Judah. William Hill's kidnapping plot was part of an intrafamily dispute that his father, Richard Hill, also had pursued. Mrs. Funderburk was William's maternal great-grandmother. In 1809, she obtained approval of a deed freeing Judah, apparently in substantial compliance with the requirements of the 1800 manumission law that then was in effect. William's defense counsel raised hypertechnical objections about the deed's validity. The evidence also suggests that William may have found a way to "remove" the manumission deed from the county clerk's office, where it was required to be on file. O'Neall's opinion sustains both the deed and Mrs. Funderburk's manumission of Judah. He also suggests that, even if they were not valid, Bowser had lived free for a sufficient time to invoke the doctrine of implied manumission by prescription. Moreover, the trial evidence included an 1826 freedom judgment that was obtained against Richard and others in favor of Judah's children.[96]

Two years after deciding *Harden*, O'Neall wrote the Court of Appeals opinion in *State v. Maner*, which demonstrates the difference between the limited assault and battery protections afforded to South Carolina's free Blacks and the absence of rights of slaves.[97] Jonathan Maner "was indicted for an assault and battery with an intent to murder a slave named Phil." Maner and Phil "were on terms of intimacy." They "got into a quarrel and a fight ensued, after which [Maner] shot [Phil]." The trial judge charged the jury that they should find Maner guilty as charged if they believed that he would have been guilty of murder if Phil had died. The jury convicted Maner. He filed an appeal, arguing that "an indictment for an assault with an intent to murder a slave, will not lie."[98]

The Court of Appeals rejected this argument and affirmed Maner's attempted murder conviction. But O'Neall's opinion also confirmed that, under South Carolina law, "the *criminal* offence of assault and battery cannot be committed on the person of a slave." He explained that "notwithstanding for some purposes a slave is regarded in law as a person, yet generally he is a mere chattel personal, and his right of personal protection belongs to his master, who can maintain an action of trespass for the battery of his slave."[99] Thus, contrary to Taylor's opinion in *State v. Hale*, no one in South Carolina could be indicted for "a mere beating of a slave, unaccompanied by any circumstances of cruelty or attempt to kill and murder. The peace of the State is not thereby broken; for a slave is not generally regarded as legally capable of being within the peace of the State. He is not a citizen, and is not in that character entitled to her protection."[100]

Although he did not believe it was relevant to the decision, O'Neall also quoted—with added emphasis—a provision in the state's 1740 slave code, which stated, "In case any persons shall wilfully cut out the tongue, put out the eye, castrate or cruelly scald, burn, or deprive any slave of any limb or member, or *shall inflict any other cruel punishment*, other than by whipping or beating with a horsewhip, cowskin, switch, or small stick, or by putting irons on, or confining or imprisoning such slave, every person shall, for every such offence, forfeit the sum of one hundred pounds current money."[101] O'Neall reasoned that "under this act," a person "shooting a slave might be indicted [for] . . . cruel punishment." But after making this suggestion, he explained, "Be this as it may, (for it is wholly unimportant on this occasion,) this act shews, that for injuries done to the person of a slave short of the destruction of life, a white man might be charged criminally and punished."[102]

O'Neall also could have cited another section of this statute, which authorized a forty-shilling fine if any person beat, bruised, maimed, or disabled an enslaved person without "sufficient cause or lawful authority for doing so," provided that the slave was "employed in the lawful business or service of his master, overseer, or other person having charge of such slave." In addition, this law permitted enslavers to receive compensation for slave labor lost and medical expenses incurred if a stranger unlawfully whipped the master's slave who was "maimed or disabled by such beating."[103]

These statutes afforded O'Neall the option of crafting a more limited decision. The first part of the statutory section O'Neall quoted preempted the common-law crime of mayhem. English statutes adopted in the fifteenth through seventeenth centuries expanded upon this crime to include the dismemberment, disablement, or disfigurement of another person. Among these was a statute that is known as the Coventry Act. According to Sir William Blackstone, this 1670 law provided "that if any person shall of malice aforethought and by lying in wait unlawfully cut out or disable the tongue, put out an eye, slit the nose, cut off a nose or lip, or cut off or disable any limb or member, of any other person, with intent to maim or disfigure him, such person, his counsellors, aiders, and abettors, shall be guilty of felony without benefit of clergy." This act "did not displace the English common law of mayhem," but it instead added to the existing prohibition of malicious dismemberment and imposed the death penalty.[104]

South Carolina's enslavement law adopted seventy years later included only some of these extended mayhem prohibitions when slaves were the victims, and it reduced the penalty to a fine. It also prohibited certain types of cruel punishment, but when doing so it authorized the enumerated actions that were deemed to not be cruel, all in derogation of the common law of battery. O'Neall thus could have stated that these statutory provisions established the substantive rules, standards, and punishments for nonfatal violence inflicted on slaves. They granted an immunity authorizing any person to commit common-law simple assault or battery on any slave, as well as some acts that would have been mayhem under the prevailing law.[105]

O'Neall instead based his reasoning on the broader principle of enslavement law, which defined enslaved people as human property—and thus as people without legal rights. He went even further than did North Carolina chief justice Thomas Ruffin in his infamous 1829 opinion in *State v. Mann*.[106] That decision, like the less well-known 1827 Virginia opinion in *Commonwealth v. Turner*, excluded enslaved people from the state's peace and protection from all assaults and batteries perpetrated by slave owners and hirers.[107] O'Neall confirmed that South Carolina's criminal law would extend this assault and battery privilege to all whites, even if the legislature had not adopted the statute O'Neall cited in his opinion.[108]

Three years after his decision in *Maner*, O'Neall tellingly explained why this criminal law immunity did not extend to civil suits, which enslavers were permitted to file against others who injured their slaves. The Court of Appeals, in *Tennent v. Dendy*, affirmed Martha Tennent's right to sue Charles Dendy, a patrol captain, for beating her slave, even though Tenant did not suffer any lost enslaved labor because she had hired the enslaved victim to a third person.[109] O'Neall reasoned that an enslaved victim's common-law rights to sue for damages were vested in his or her owner. Although slaves were "chattels personal," he reasoned that

> slaves . . . cannot in every respect be treated by the rules which apply to and govern personal estate. They are human beings, with passions and feelings like our own, and with the same capability of right and wrong action. They, if in a state of nature, would have the right of self-protection, which is given by the great Creator to every human being. Their transfer from a state of nature to a state of slavery in society, has not destroyed the right of personal protection; it has taken it from the slave and given it to the master.[110]

This rule, he contended, was "consistent with good policy."

> Slaves are our most valuable property. For its preservation, too many guards cannot be interposed between it and violent unprincipled men. In the relation of master and servant, the dependence of the latter on the former alone for protection, cannot be too much encouraged. The slave ought to be fully aware that his master is to him what the best administered government is to the good citizen, a perfect security from injury. When this is the case, the relation of master and servant becomes little short of that of parent and child—it commences in the weakness of the one and the strength of the other. Its benefits produce the corresponding consequence of deep and abiding grateful attachment from the slave to the master—and hence result those striking instances of devotion, which, at least on one occasion in this State, induced a slave to peril his life to save that of his master, and failing in the attempt, nobly to perish with him.[111]

O'Neall addressed a letter to the editor of the *New-York Tribune* in 1853 confirming that the state's General Assembly adopted an 1841 law that he declared was "intended to remedy the defect in our jurisprudence."[112] According to that statute, any person who "shall unlawfully whip, or beat any slave, not under his or her charge, without sufficient provocation, by word or act" would be subject to a fine not to exceed five hundred dollars and a prison term not exceeding six months.[113] Thus, the legislature confirmed that all white persons continued to have a privilege under the common law to beat and whip slaves belonging to others. The state's all-white juries would decide if a defendant charged under this act inflicted the beating or whipping without sufficient provocation, in words or acts. This law also confirmed that the common-law "mere words" rule did not apply in these cases.[114]

O'Neall's *Harden* and *Hill* opinions therefore held that South Carolina's free African Americans, unlike those who were enslaved, were protected from assaults, batteries, and false imprisonment. But he also confirmed that these decisions and *Maner* are variations on the same principle of separate and unequal protection of the law. He included dicta in both of his opinions applying the unequal provocation doctrine when free Blacks were the victims of white violence, even though both cases lacked any evidence of resistance or insolence.

As noted above, South Carolina law denied free Blacks the right to file appeals if they were convicted in the magistrates and freeholders courts. Therefore, no appellate court opinions decided whether to apply O'Neall's separate and unequal protection doctrine when free Blacks were accused of committing crimes against whites.

Evaluating O'Neall as the Quintessential Moderate Southern Jurist

How, then, can O'Neall's reputation for the amelioration of enslavement be squared with his explicitly racially discriminatory jurisprudence? A review of his biography provides a good starting point. O'Neall was born on April 10, 1793, in Newberry County, South Carolina, into an Irish American Quaker family. He in 1812 graduated second in his class from South Carolina College (later the University of South Carolina). The next year he joined the state militia. By 1827, he had risen to the rank of major general.[115]

Meanwhile, O'Neall started his legal career. After reading law, he, in 1814, was admitted to the state bar. Two years later, he was elected to represent the Newberry District in the South Carolina General Assembly. He was defeated in 1818 and 1820, but he was the winner in the 1822, 1824, and 1826 elections. Assembly members elected O'Neall as the house's speaker from 1824 until 1828, when he once again lost a bid for reelection, thus ending his legislative tenure.[116]

O'Neall's long and at times controversial judicial career began in 1828, when the South Carolina General Assembly elected him to serve as a Court of Common Pleas and General Sessions judge. Two years later, the legislature elected him to the three-judge Court of Appeals, which the legislature created in 1824. He served on that court along with William Harper and David Johnson until 1835, when the legislature abolished this court in the midst of the tariff nullification debate. This was a form of court packing by the legislature, in response to O'Neall's and Johnson's decision in *State ex rel. McCready v. Hunt*.[117] Over Harper's dissent, the court's majority decision, in a ruling favored by the Unionists, invalidated the state's oath of allegiance, which had been adopted with the support of those favoring nullification. But this legislative retaliation did not end O'Neall's appellate judicial career. In the next year, the legislature created new separate Courts of Appeal for cases in law and in equity, and it elected O'Neall to be a justice of the Court of Appeals at Law. In 1850, he became that court's president, a position that he held until 1859. In that year, the legislature created a new Court of Appeals, made up of a chief justice and two associate justices. O'Neall was selected to be that court's first chief justice, an office he held until he died on December 27, 1863.[118]

O'Neall was a farmer who by 1860 owned two plantations and more than a hundred slaves. He also was successful in business, became a leading Baptist, and pursued other interests and causes. Although he was a Unionist during the nullification and succession controversies, after his state seceded he continued to serve as chief justice until his death during the Civil War.[119]

O'Neall was a jurist who often declared his own policy views in his judicial opinions. For example, he explained in an 1842 opinion that "kindness to slaves" was "the true policy of slave owners," and "its spirit should go (as it generally has) into the making of the law, and ought to be a ruling principle of its construction. *Nothing will more assuredly defeat our institution of slavery, than harsh legislation rigorously enforced.*" He also confidently contended that, as in the past, "with all the protections of law and money around it, [slavery] has nothing to fear from *fanaticism abroad or examination at home.*"[120]

O'Neall elaborated on his benign vision of slavery and slave law in an 1848 monograph, *Negro Law of South Carolina*, which he prepared as authorized by his state's Agricultural Society.[121] O'Neall wrote a summary of South Carolina's slavery law. But he also called for ameliorative measures, including criminal law reforms and new laws to better protect enslaved families and to permit masters to free their slaves.[122] A South Carolina Senate Judiciary Committee report, signed by Senator Wilmot G. DeSaussure, criticized O'Neall's proposed reforms, but not his slave law summary. Although O'Neall's publication prompted a public debate on the merits of his suggested reforms, South Carolina's legislature did not enact O'Neall's slave law reform proposals.[123] "Celebrated as an educator, a judge, and as a temperance advocate, his ideas on slavery did not appear to be the focus of discussion during his lifetime or upon his death."[124]

O'Neall also confirmed his continuing commitment to his *Harden* decision in his monograph *Negro Law of South Carolina*. On the one hand, O'Neall wrote, "Free negroes, mulattoes, and mestizos, are entitled to all of the rights of property, and protection in their persons and property, by action or indictment, which white inhabitants of this State are entitled to."[125] But on the other hand, he asserted that free Blacks "cannot repel force by force; that is, they cannot strike a white man, who may strike any of them." He referred to an unreported Court of Appeals decision holding that "insolence on the part of a free negro, would not excuse an Assault and Battery." O'Neall asserted that he dissented from that ruling, apparently based on his *Harden* decision. But he did not provide the defendant's name, and the court's decision has not been found.[126]

O'Neall's 1853 Court of Appeals opinion in *State v. Young* reaffirmed his support for the unequal provocation doctrine.[127] The appeals court reversed a trial court order dismissing an assault and battery indictment against Allen Young. Young proved at trial that his alleged victim, Mark Johnson, was "a colored person." Young therefore argued that Johnson could not testify because of his race and that the indictment was defective because it did not mention Johnson's race. O'Neall held that the indictment was not defective because the allegation of Johnson's race was immaterial in the indictment. Johnson's race was relevant at trial, however, according to O'Neall, who noted, "The only shades of difference are in justification or mitigation. These do not depend on the pleading, but on the proof." O'Neall cited his *Hill* and *Harden* opinions for this caveat. He also failed to note, however, that the rule barring Johnson's testimony at trial posed another potentially important "shade of difference" if, unlike in the *Harden* and *Hill* cases, white witnesses were not willing or able to testify in support of the state's case against Young.[128]

It may not be fair to evaluate O'Neall's racially motivated exception to the common-law "mere words" doctrine against modern equal protection principles, which nevertheless have recently been criticized for still falling short of the ideal of truly equal justice for all.[129] And it may also be unfair to measure O'Neall's unequal protection doctrine against the *Campbell* decision because it was issued by the highest court of an antebellum "free" state. But it may indeed be fair to note that O'Neall's opinions compare unfavorably against the common-law authorities that he acknowledged contained no race-based exceptions in cases of violence between "two freemen."

Moreover, the Supreme Court of the civil law slave state of Louisiana, in *The State v. Jose Fuentes*, decided in 1850, rejected an invitation to make new law creating this unequal protection doctrine in an interracial homicide case.[130] The court affirmed the murder conviction of Jose Fuentes, who was described in Justice Isaac Preston's opinion as "a foreigner, and subject of the Queen of Spain."[131] A New Orleans jury in 1849 found that Fuentes murdered a free person of color, whose name is not mentioned in the decision. Justice Preston's opinion also does not recite any of the facts of the crime. But according to a press report, Fuentes killed his victim, Manuel Ducre, in the fish market.[132]

Preston states that the lawyer for Fuentes requested that the trial judge "charge the jury 'that the use of grossly insulting and indecent language by a free man of color to a white man, naturally must excite the passions of a white man, and if immediately succeeded by a mortal stab, it may well be imputed to the weakness and infirmity of human nature, and a jury may render a verdict of manslaughter if they so find the fact.'" Preston held that the trial judge "declined so to charge the jury, and we think properly."[133]

Preston applied the generally applicable "mere words" principles, citing *Blackstone's Commentaries*, a leading English common-law treatise, for "one of the first and most familiar principles in trials for homicide 'that no affront by words or gestures only is a sufficient provocation so as to excuse or extenuate such acts of violence, as manifestly endanger the life of another.' 4 Black Com. 200." Moreover, Preston explained,

> The law has made no distinction whether the affront proceeds from a white, or a free man of color. Indeed, as was well observed by the attorney general, since the law makes a distinction between white and free colored men, as to their condition, and punishes free persons of color, who, even by words, insult white persons, their situation imposes upon us, perhaps, a higher obligation to suppress our passions, and resort to the laws to punish their insolence, than in the case of white persons, against whose insolence and verbal outrage there is no redress by prosecution.[134]

He was referring to the Louisiana Code, which since 1806 stated, "Free people of color ought never to insult or strike white people, nor presume to conceive themselves equal to whites; but on the contrary that they ought to yield to them in every occasion, and never speak or answer to them but with respect, under the penalty of imprisonment according to the nature of the offense."[135] Louisiana free Blacks thus were prosecuted and punished for uttering insolent words insulting to whites, but Preston did not feel free to make new law permitting these mere words to mitigate a white person's interracial murder to manslaughter.[136]

Scholars have nevertheless praised O'Neall because he did not entirely exclude free Blacks from the criminal law's protection against white assaults, batteries, and false imprisonment. For example, A. E. Keir Nash enthusiastically celebrated O'Neall's opinions, including *Harden*, in one of several articles that he published between 1969 and 1979. Nash derived these articles in part from his unpublished Harvard doctoral dissertation. In the article featuring O'Neall, Nash declared, "On balance, one is well-nigh forced to conclude that the South Carolina court's record in protecting slaves and free Negroes was marked by a persistent demand that the lower castes—though lower—be accorded, not 'equal protection' but, and still remarkable, what may be best summed up as 'due protection and ordered process.'"[137]

Nash's euphemistic turn of the phrase "due protection and ordered process" implicitly concedes, however, that O'Neall denied to free Blacks the standards of due process of law and the law's equal protection, which the common law of crimes guaranteed to whites. Thus, stated more plainly and in O'Neall's own words, he extended to free Black lives and personal integrity only the degree of the criminal law's unequal protection that he thought was rightly due to them as members of a "degraded *caste* of society," which was "in no respect, on a perfect equality with the white man."[138]

Similarly, Alexander Sanders's O'Neall biographies cite with approval O'Neall's dissenting opinion in *State v. Nathan*.[139] That appeal followed after a court of magistrates and freeholders convicted an enslaved man named Nathan of the capital crime of robbery. This conviction followed another trial that had been based on the same accusation and incident, in which Nathan was found guilty of the noncapital crime of assault and battery, and not guilty on a charge of the capital crime of attempted rape. According to Sanders, O'Neall "asked pointedly, 'If the prisoner was a white man and not a negro, could such a course receive the countenance of anyone?'" Sanders then suggests, "If the principle of law implicit in O'Neall's rhetorical question—that the law should make no distinction between a white man and an African American—had been adopted generally, the 14th Amendment would not have been needed." And he concludes, even further, "Nor, for that matter would the 13th Amendment abolishing slavery. A major cause of the Civil War would have been eliminated—not that it might have been fought anyway."[140]

O'Neall did indeed ask this abstract rhetorical question in his opinion, but he never endorsed the principle of equal protection of the criminal law for all without regard to race or color. He instead opposed abolition while endorsing and enforcing the doctrine of free Black legal inequality.

W. Caleb McDaniel correctly includes O'Neall among the white southerners who, in the 1840s, began to respond to the increasingly aggressive abolitionist critiques of their enslavement practices and laws with "a more assertive defense of the peculiar institution." He contrasts this "active engagement" strategy with the "defensive offensive" approach that is epitomized by the "gag rule," which sought to stop or censor debate about slavery.[141]

McDaniel cites O'Neall's extrajudicial publications forcefully defending the death sentence that he imposed on John L. Brown. Brown was convicted in November 1843 before Judge O'Neall and a jury for aiding an enslaved woman named Hetty's escape from John Taylor. Taylor had hired Hetty from her owner, Charlotte Hinton, who was Taylor's sister. The jury found that Brown violated a 1754 South Carolina law that made slave stealing a capital offense. This law was enacted sixty-seven years before the legislature included the murder of slaves among the state's capital crimes.[142]

Brown filed an appeal with the Court of Appeals, which affirmed the judgment.[143] O'Neall later, while imposing the death penalty, "melodramatically addressed Brown as 'the vilest sinner' ... with words that soon echoed across the Atlantic." O'Neall declared that Brown was "to die! 'Die a shameful ignominious death, the death upon the gallows.'"[144] Reports condemning the death sentence and O'Neall's statements soon were published in the abolitionist press in England and in the United States, before it was known that Governor John Henry Hammond first commuted the death sentence to a public whipping and then granted Brown a full pardon.[145]

O'Neall wrote two letters responding to his critics, which were published in the local press, defending his sentence while expressing his contempt for Brown. In a March 27, 1844, letter, O'Neall stated, "It astonishes me beyond measure at the interest which John L. Brown's case has excited among the Abolitionists." He asserted that the jury's verdict and his sentence were consistent with a duly adopted statute and that the governor spared Brown any penalty. But he also condemned Brown: "He is no abolitionist. He did not seek, by aiding the woman to run away, to enable her to go to a free State, and there be free; but his object was either to prolong an adulterous intercourse with the woman, or taking advantage of the power which he thus had, to carry her off and sell her. What difference there is between this and stealing, it is difficult to perceive."[146] And O'Neall's May 1, 1844, letter to the chairman of the Anti-Slavery Meeting in Glasgow, Scotland, declared that O'Neall was "astonished" that "a name so utterly infamous as John L. Brown" was given "pre-eminence ... by your community." In addition to again defending the verdict and death sentence, O'Neall branded Brown "an idle dissipated young man. He kept the mulatto woman whom he aided to run away as his mistress." And he also asserted his belief that Brown intended "to conceal her in South Carolina, and still keep her as his mistress, or to carry her to some of the other slave States, and then, after his lust was satiated, to sell her."[147]

O'Neall's letter expressed his unyielding support for enslavement, when he asked, "Is Scotland free from the sin of slavery—white slavery? Are there no taskmasters in England, Scotland, and Ireland, who can vie with the very worst amongst us? Compare our slaves, negroes though they be, with your white servants, your starving laborers, your suffering peasantry, and if they have not more comfort, more happiness, South Carolinians will be content to be branded as merciless tyrants." O'Neall concluded this line of argument with the admonition, "But until that condemnation is brought about, we say to your censors, 'Physician heal thyself.'"[148]

According to McDaniel, "The abolitionist attack had mainly led O'Neall to make explicit and more public some charges that had earlier been swaddled in euphemism and allusion."[149] About ten years later, O'Neall once again publicly challenged the abolitionists in a letter objecting to some of Harriet Beecher Stowe's assertions in *The Key to Uncle Tom's Cabin*, a book Stowe wrote answering her novel's critics with evidence of antebellum southern enslavement law on the books and in practice.[150] O'Neall critiqued Stowe's legal analysis. But he also repeated a positive good pro-slavery argument when he claimed, "Generally, slaves in the South, are treated with more kindness, have more comforts, and more money of their own, than free servants at the North, or in Europe." He even suggested that Stowe come to South Carolina and see all of this for herself.[151]

O'Neall's comparison of the horrors of freedom and the benefits of enslavement thus is consistent with the positive good literature that was published in the years before succession by enslavement advocates including John C. Calhoun, George Fitzhugh, Thomas R. Dew, George Frederick Holmes, James Henry Hammond, Henry Hughes, William Harper, and Thomas R. R. Cobb. Fitzhugh, in 1854, for example, echoed O'Neall's words when he compared the lot of free laborers, who must earn wages to support their families and pay for their housing and other expenses, with those whom he asserted benefited from their enslavement, because he believed that it "relieves our slaves of these cares altogether." He even boasted that enslavement was "the very best form . . . of socialism."[152]

O'Neall was singular, however, as an ardent supporter of enslavement law amelioration, which he declared was the best way to defend slavery against its enemies—both foreign and domestic. For example, O'Neall criticized his state's criminal trial and appellate procedures for enslaved and free Blacks for creating "the worst system which could be devised." He explained "that the passions and prejudices of the neighborhood, arising from the recent offence, enter into the trial, and often lend to the condemnation of the innocent." He recommended reforms, including provisions permitting defendants the right to file appeals "in cases not capital" and allowing "sufficient time in such cases, for an application for a pardon." He also called for a new "tribunal to consist of one judicial Magistrate, to be appointed by the Legislature, to try all criminal cases against free negroes, mulattoes, mestizos and slaves." This magistrate would hear these cases with juries made up of twelve freeholders or slaveholders. Those convicted by this court would have the right to file appeals with the state's Court of Appeals.[153]

O'Neall's reforms would, however, have continued his state's racially segregated criminal court system. As limited as they were, these suggestions may have been the product of his own benevolent feelings toward enslaved and free Blacks, "negroes though they be." Or maybe he thought these measures would be the best way to buttress slavery against the abolitionists' mounting critiques. His reformist views also may, at least in part, have been colored by his own experiences as an enslaver. Several years before he published his enslavement law monograph, one of his slaves was executed for murder, no doubt after a trial before a court of local magistrates and freeholders. O'Neall then filed an 1844 petition with the state legislature seeking indemnification from the state for his financial loss pursuant to an 1843 statute permitting slave owners to obtain compensation if their slaves were executed after they were convicted of capital offenses by the magistrates and freeholder courts. The legislators denied O'Neall's claim for compensation. His slave's conviction predated the statute's four-year retroactive compensation period.[154]

Conclusion

O'Neall is both a complex and a consequential southern antebellum jurist whose views on white supremacy and legitimized white interracial violence continued to have deleterious effects long after emancipation. His writings, both on and off the bench, confirm that he should be remembered as a unionist who was possibly the South's preeminent judicial moderate on enslavement law. But in his *Harden*, *Hill*, and *Young* decisions and in his treatise *Negro Law of South Carolina*, O'Neall repeatedly rejected the principle of equal protection of the criminal law for free African Americans. He instead created the new principle of separate and unequal protection based on race.

According to Gary B. Mills, in his *Harden* opinion, O'Neall's "prejudice ... carried out nuances that sketch out the narrow trough within which free nonwhites were expected to channel their lives." Mills also correctly noted that race prejudice was not confined to the antebellum South; bias against free Blacks was expressed in the northern states, including Pennsylvania, New York, and Rhode Island, in the "ideological battle over universal manhood suffrage."[155] O'Neall's opinions prove, however, that the stakes for southern free Blacks were much higher; he put at risk their personal safety—and even potentially their very lives. The positive law, including this novel southern common law of crimes and criminal procedure, explicitly legitimized what would have been extralegal interracial violence.

Accordingly, the Civil War Amendments, and the war itself, were necessary to overcome O'Neall's moderate and contrarian views on both enslavement and unequal protection under the law. His publications, moreover, raise the broader question about what it means to assert that one was a contrarian or moderate in the antebellum South.[156] O'Neall grounded his unionism and his ameliorative enslavement law proposals on his belief that his was the best way to defend South Carolina's slave society against *"fanaticism abroad or examination at home."*[157]

This focus on the positive law and legal treatises may seem archaic to some readers. It is warranted here, however, because O'Neall did not base his separate and unequal protection doctrine on legal precedents or reasoning from legal principles. He instead ignored the common-law decisions and treatises confirming the well-settled "mere words" doctrine, while creating new standards based on his understanding of the dominant white legal consciousness in his community. His legal doctrinal innovations thus confined free African Americans to the "degraded *caste* of society," which was "in no respect, on a perfect equality with the white man."[158]

O'Neall in two ways incorporated these community standards into South Carolina's common law. First, he established an explicitly race based de jure exception to the "mere words" doctrine. He required trial judges to tell juries that the law legitimized white violent rebukes to what the white perpetrator— in the heat of the moment—perceived to be free Black insolence. And second, he granted to local white juries the discretion to apply their own community standards when deciding whether white persons had gone too far in exercising their newly minted legal privileges and immunities. O'Neall did indeed limit this new white immunity, when he disapproved of both Harden's wanton and excessive abuse of Archer and Hill's kidnapping scheme, which was designed to defeat Mrs. Funderburk's intention to free Judah and her children. But he also empowered the state's all-white jurors to draw the line between white liability and white privilege, based upon their own views of the circumstances and the participants in each case.

O'Neall's separate and unequal protection doctrine for free Blacks is important because it was not unique to South Carolina law; other judges and legislators adopted it, thus evidencing the dominant white southern legal consciousness. North Carolina's appellate court decisions in the decade before succession and Civil War, especially those of O'Neall's fellow contrarian Richmond Pearson, exemplify this emerging legal trend.

CHAPTER 5

Justice Pearson and Unequal Protection for Free Blacks

Other southern whites outside of South Carolina shared John Belton O'Neall's beliefs about the need to modify their state's criminal law to authorize what otherwise would have been extralegal white violence to enforce white supremacy and to confirm the free Blacks' second-class caste status. This trend was confirmed, in the decade before the Civil War, by North Carolina's appellate court decisions and by statutes adopted in other southern states. These positive law sources are consistent with O'Neall's underlying free Black separate and unequal protection principle.

Justice Richmond M. Pearson wrote opinions for the North Carolina Supreme Court adopting this doctrine, although Pearson did not refer to O'Neall's *Harden* and *Hill* opinions or his enslavement law monograph. Pearson first applied this doctrine in his 1850 opinion in *State v. Jowers* to legitimize white nonfatal violence directed at free Blacks.[1] Nine years later, in *State v. Davis*, he extended this inequality principle to free Black nonfatal violence directed against whites.[2]

The great historian John Hope Franklin, citing decisions including *Jowers* and *Davis*, praised Pearson's jurisprudence and commended the North Carolina Supreme Court as the state's "greatest protector of the rights of free Negroes," which "can be seen by the decision it made in several important cases."[3] Although the court confirmed that North Carolina's free Blacks were not enslaved, it also held that they were not citizens who were entitled to the equal protection of the state's criminal laws.

The court unambiguously declared this general rule of unequal nonwhite citizenship in the reputedly moderate Justice William J. Gaston's 1838 opinion in *State v. Manuel*.[4] Pearson extended this inequality principle when free Blacks were involved in interracial violence—either as the alleged criminals or as the victims of crime. These decisions suggest a less sanguine interpretation of the role of the North Carolina Supreme Court—and of the legal status of the state's free Blacks—than has been suggested by Franklin and other scholars.[5]

Pearson's authorship of these opinions tacitly endorsing O'Neall's separate and unequal protection principle in the criminal law is significant. "He was the only Southern Superior Court Judge who served continuously through the changing currents of the antebellum, Civil War, Restoration, Congressional Reconstruction, and late-Reconstruction eras."[6] Secession followed soon after Pearson wrote his *Jowers* and *Davis* decisions, thus stopping the de jure version of this doctrine's development soon after it started. But the separate and unequal protection principle's de facto afterlife demonstrates the importance of Pearson's decisions.

The Social and Legal Contexts

As in South Carolina, free Blacks made up a relatively small percentage of North Carolina's total antebellum population, but the state's free Black population percentage increased steadily from about 1.27 percent in 1790 to 2.61 percent in 1830. The rate of this population segment's increase slowed after 1830. The free Black population percentage was 3.01 percent in 1840 and 3.16 percent in 1850, but it fell to 3.07 percent in 1860. Most of the state's free Blacks lived in the coastal or piedmont counties. Unlike in South Carolina, whites by far outnumbered nonwhites, whether enslaved or free. But the white population percentage gradually declined during this period from 73.19 percent in 1790 to 61.33 percent in 1850, and then back up slightly to 63.58 percent in 1860.[7]

Franklin discusses several reasons for these free Black population growth trends: enslavers freeing their slaves, as approved by the courts or the legislature; miscegenation among Blacks and whites; and runaway slaves and free Blacks moving to North Carolina. But he also explains that the state's free Black growth rate slowed after 1830 due, in part, to the adoption of laws limiting these paths to freedom.[8]

Also as in South Carolina, beginning in the colonial period, some free Blacks achieved economic success. According to Warren Milteer, the state's "free people of color were vital to local economies."[9] Following in Franklin's footsteps, Milteer cites examples of free Blacks who worked both as skilled laborers and as low-wage workers, as well as those employed in fishing and agriculture. Free Blacks also were consumers of goods and services sold by whites.[10] Both

Franklin and Milteer also document free Black ownership of real and personal property, including slaves.[11]

Milteer concludes, from this and other evidence, that scholars, including William S. Powell and Ira Berlin, "have overstated the importance of racial hierarchy in the lives of colonial North Carolinians." He instead states, "North Carolina law, like the laws of many other colonies, erratically interjected racial categorization into the lives of North Carolinians. It failed to place racial categorization solidly above distinctions between free persons and enslaved persons or even beyond the legal differences between servants and slaves."[12]

Nevertheless, Milteer, again following Franklin, cites evidence tracing North Carolina's free Blacks' separate and unequal legal status back to 1715, only six years after North Carolina was established as a separate colony, when its lawmakers began enacting one after another racially discriminatory provisions. A statute adopted in that year included a provision requiring enslaved people who were freed by their enslavers to leave the colony in six months. The General Assembly also imposed a fine on "White women, whether Bond or Free," who have "a Bastard child by a Negro, Mulatto or Indyan [sic]." Women who did not pay the fine were to be sold into two years of involuntary servitude. Their multiracial children also were required to be involuntary servants until they were thirty-one years of age.[13] Another 1715 act provided that "no Negroes, Mulattoes, Mustees or Indians shall be capable of voting for members of the Assembly," but the law later was disallowed by the Crown and was not reenacted.[14] Eight years later, the legislators adopted a statute imposing a discriminatory tax on free Blacks. They also required freed slaves who left the state and then returned to endure seven years of involuntary servitude.[15]

Unlike their South Carolina counterparts, however, North Carolina's lawmakers never consigned free Blacks who were accused of crimes to trials in inferior segregated courts. But a 1754 act declared "that all Negroes and Mulattoes, bond or free, to the Third Generation, and Indian Servants and Slaves, shall be deemed and taken as incapable in Law to be Witnesses, in any Cause whatsoever, except against each other."[16]

North Carolina's legislators continued to adopt discriminatory laws after independence, including race-based criminal statutes. For example, an 1823 act declared that "any person of colour" who was convicted of "an assault with intent to commit a rape upon the body of a white female, shall suffer death without benefit of clergy."[17] This law's references to the races of both the perpetrators and the victims of this capital crime reinforced the de jure principle of separate and unequal protection; it was not "merely a reinforcement of the general law against rape that had been always on the statute books."[18]

Moreover, the legislature, in its 1830–1831 session, adopted a dozen laws imposing more restrictions on the state's enslaved and free Blacks, apparently responding to the September 1829 publication of Wilmington, North Carolina, native David Walker's influential *Walker's Appeal in Four Articles*.[19] These included statutes regulating manumission; prohibiting marriages between free Blacks, whites, and slaves; regulating free Black "peddling and hawking"; and prohibiting free Blacks and whites from gambling with slaves.[20] They also included a version of the South Carolina Negro Seaman's Act, which quarantined for thirty days all free Black passengers and crew members arriving on ships docked in the state's harbors, to prevent them "from coming into this State, or from communicating with the coloured people of this State."[21] And in 1835, all free Black men were disenfranchised, thus denying them any direct involvement in the election of the representatives who would enact future laws.[22]

This anti-Black trend intensified in the 1850s, which Franklin labeled a hard decade for North Carolina's free Black people.

> Having already been disfranchised in 1835, the free Negro saw the gradual diminution of his liberties to an almost negligible level. Not only were freedom of speech, assembly, movement, and other vestiges of liberty denied him, but what was equally as devastating, the hostility to him reached a high peak in the decade of the fifties that what the law had not taken from him was denied him by the growing body of extra-legal restrictions imposed on him by the larger community. The expressions of hatred for the free Negro and the policy of completely isolating him from the political, economic, and social life of the state reached a new high by 1858; and it became more and more difficult to distinguish North Carolina from her neighbors as far as the policy toward free Negroes was concerned.[23]

Franklin quotes the 1858 petition of fifty-eight citizens of Onslow County. They called the state's free Blacks an "intolerable nuisance," because "as a general thing the free Negro is an indolent lazy thievish drunken individual, working only when he cannot steal, or induce the slave to steal for him."[24]

Franklin also cites several anti–free Black laws, which the legislature considered but did not enact, to exemplify the temper of the times. One bill, requiring free Blacks to leave the state within two years or be sold into slavery, was based on an Arkansas law. Another bill required free Blacks to register each year with their county clerks or be sold into slavery; it was similar to a Virginia law and the Illinois Black Acts. Moreover, bills proposed an expeditious procedure by which free Blacks could petition the courts for "voluntary" self-enslavement.[25] Six other states adopted self-enslavement laws, following the lead of Virginia's 1856 act.[26] Franklin documents the plight of free Blacks who, even without this streamlined "voluntary enslavement" procedure, asked the legislature to approve individual private enslavement laws "at almost every session of the General Assembly from 1858 to the end of 1863." These "petitions of the destitute free Negroes and the proposed laws for their enslavement," Franklin asserts, "are an excellent mirror of certain phases of life in North Carolina at the end of the period and the attitudes of whites toward freedom for Negroes."[27]

More recently, Warren Milteer, citing Melvin P. Ely's study of free Black life in Prince Edward County, Virginia, calls for a more benign understanding of free Black life in North Carolina.[28] He relies on the legislature's rejection of the most extreme examples of radically racist legislation—even in the tumultuous years before succession—and on Ely's vision of "wide webs of social entanglement among free people of color, whites and slaves." Milteer concludes, "Even during the most contentious moments, people of color maintained important rights, privileges, and relationships that placed them distinctly beyond the toils of human bondage."[29]

Similarly, Richard C. Rohrs asserts that, in antebellum Wilmington, North Carolina, "as elsewhere in the South, enforcement of state laws and local regulations was often lax."[30] He suggests that this may explain the relative economic prosperity of some of Wilmington's free Blacks, who achieved successes as business owners, as skilled or semiskilled laborers, and even as slave owners.[31]

Nevertheless, North Carolina positive law continued to place all of the state's free African Americans—including those who were themselves enslavers—in a lower and degraded legal caste. Unlike slaves, who were denied all legal rights, free Blacks were entitled to legal rights that always were inferior to those guaranteed to even the poorest whites.[32]

Justice William J. Gaston's 1838 North Carolina Supreme Court opinion in *State v. Manuel* articulated the state constitutional law doctrinal foundation for this racial caste law, including Pearson's de jure rule of free Black inequality under the criminal law.[33] That case began when William Manuel, a free Black man, was convicted of committing assault and battery. The court imposed a fine, which Manuel did not pay. Manuel filed an appeal with North Carolina's Supreme Court. His appeal included a state constitutional challenge to an 1831 law stating that a free Black person convicted of a criminal offense who did not pay a court-imposed fine would be hired out for the shortest term, not exceeding five years, offered by any person who was willing to pay the fine in return for the defendant's services.[34]

The legislators adopted this law imposing involuntary servitude on only free Blacks in response, at least in part, to a petition signed by seventy-four Guilford County residents. These petitioners asserted their belief that free Blacks "are generally thievish, drunken, Idle, disorderly people, committing riots, affrays, Sabbath breaking, and committing all manner of illegal and immoral acts." They asserted, moreover, that because free Blacks "are generally poor and Insolvent," they "go often unprosecuted for fear of incurring expense to the County." Accordingly, the petitioners called for special legislation applying to their county, which the legislature voted to enact statewide.[35]

Because this statute did not apply to impecunious white convicts who did not pay their fines, Manuel claimed on appeal that this explicit race-based discrimination against free Blacks was "arbitrary, repugnant to the principles of free government, at variance with the spirit of the [state constitution's] 3d section of the bill of rights denouncing exclusive privileges, and not of the character properly embraced within the term 'law of the land.'"[36] This contention was based on the third section of the North Carolina constitution's Declaration of Rights. It stated, "That no man or set of men are entitled to exclusive or separate emoluments or privileges from the community, but in consideration of public services."[37]

Gaston rejected "the validity" of Manuel's "objection" that, by exempting all whites from this statute, the legislature created for them an "exclusive or separate" privilege, which was not in consideration of their public service. Instead, he approved this racially discriminatory criminal law, when he declared, "Whatever might be thought of a penal Statute which in its enactments makes distinctions between one part of the community and another capriciously and by way of favoritism, it cannot be denied that in the exercise of the great powers confided to the legislature for the suppression and punishment of crime, they may rightfully so apportion punishments according to the condition, temptations to crime, and ability to suffer, of those who are likely to offend." This de jure legal inequality, Gaston reasoned, would "produce in effect that reasonable and practical equality in the administration of justice which it is the object of all free governments to accomplish."

Gaston then explained his Orwellian theory that this inequality advanced equality, based on his understanding of human psychology and racial differences: "What would be cruelty if inflicted on a woman or a child, may be moderate punishment to a man. What might not be felt by a man of fortune, would be oppression to a poor man. What would be a slight inconvenience to a free negro, might fall upon a white man as intolerable degradation." Gaston concluded that "the legislature must have a discretion over this subject, and that once admitted, [Manuel's] objection must fail for the reasons already assigned in examining the objections as to the exercise of the powers admitted to be discretionary."[38]

Gaston therefore confirms that the state's constitution permitted the legislature and the courts to deny to all Blacks—enslaved and free—substantive and procedural equality with white citizens. Instead, he applied a deferential standard of review—a rational basis test—permitting the legislature to adopt different criminal laws for whites and for Blacks. He thus vindicated the Guilford County petitioners' overtly racist biases, which also may have convinced some legislators to vote for their suggested legislation.[39]

The legislature in 1841 applied this separate and unequal protection principle when it repealed as to "free Negroes and free Persons of Colour" an 1839 law that limited to twenty days the prison terms that could be imposed on insolvent persons convicted of crimes.[40] And on the same day, the legislators adopted a racially discriminatory gun control law, apparently in response to a petition of fifty-one Halifax County residents, who called for a law prohibiting "Free Negroes and Mulattoes from carrying or using fire arms under any circumstances what ever."[41] This act made it a "misdemeanor" for "any free Negro, Mulatto, or free Person of Colour," to "wear or carry about his or her person, or keep in his or her house, any Shot-gun, Musket, Rifle, Pistol, Sword, Dagger or Bowie-knife," without having "obtained a license therefor from the Court of Pleas and Quarter Sessions of his or her County, within one year preceding the wearing, keeping or carrying thereof."[42] According to Antwain Hunter, "There were virtually no limitations on free people of color's firearm use prior to 1840, except for their militia service."[43]

Three years later, the Supreme Court, in *State v. Newsom*, rejected a constitutional law challenge to this statute.[44] Elijah Newsom, a free Black man, was indicted and convicted by a jury for carrying a shotgun without having first obtaining the required license. The trial judge, John L. Bailey, granted Newsom's motion to arrest the judgment. The state appealed to the North Carolina Supreme Court, which reversed this order and remanded the case to the trial court for the entry of a judgment against Newsom.[45]

Justice Frederick Nash wrote the court's opinion rejecting Newsom's federal and state constitutional right to bear arms claims. Following *Manuel*, Nash affirmed the legislature's right to adopt this discriminatory gun control law and thus denied to free Blacks the state constitutional rights that white citizens enjoyed: "We *must*, therefore, regard it as a principle, settled by the highest authority, the organic law of the country, that the free people of color cannot be considered as citizens, in the largest sense of the term, or, if they are, they occupy such a position in society, as justifies the legislature in adopting a course of policy in its acts peculiar to them; so that they do not violate those great principles of justice, which ought to lie at the foundation of all laws."[46]

The court, four years later, again applied these principles, in *State v. Lane*, to affirm a not guilty special verdict in favor of Ephraim Lane.[47] Lane was described as "a free man of colour" who was indicted for carrying a "pistol and other articles" without having a license.[48] But he did this while working for a man named Barker "as a hireling" who "was engaged in *his* [Barker's] business." Justice Nash's opinion explained, "It is not pretended, that this employment was simulated, and intended or used as a cloak to avoid the law. We must presume therefore that the contract was made in good faith between Barker and the defendant, and that the latter in good faith was executing it."

Nash concluded that the legislators adopted this discriminatory act

> to prevent the owning or possessing, by this class of persons, of the offensive weapons enumerated, as dangerous to the peace of the community and the safety of individuals. But that they did not intend, that they should not be owned or possessed by any person of colour, is evident from the fact, that they have rendered the possession lawful in one contingency. Degraded as are these individuals, as a class, by their social position, it is certain, that among them are many, worthy of all confidence, and into whose hands these weapons can be safely trusted, either for their own protection, or for the protection of the property of others confided to them.

Nash noted that the statute granted to the county courts the power to issue licenses to the "worthy" among what he called the "degraded" persons in this regulated class. He cited "an old maxim in the construction of statutes, that he who sticks to the letter, adheres to the bark." He instead applied "a reasonable construction" to carry out his view of "the legislative will."[49]

When Lane carried Barker's pistol, he did not offend the legislative will, according to Nash, because Lane did not own the gun. Instead, he "was complying with a contract, he had a right to make."[50] Nash therefore held that the legislature could deny free Blacks the right to carry arms, unless either the county courts, or individual white employers, thought members of the "degraded class" were "worthy" of white "confidence." The legislature three years later abolished even this limited right, however, with an act imposing a fifty-dollar fine on any "free negro" wearing or carrying a gun or other weapon and declaring that free Blacks could no longer be granted licenses for these purposes.[51]

Pearson Applies the Unequal Protection Rule to Free Black Victims

The North Carolina legislature did not in these statutes modify the common-law standards of mitigation and justification when whites were accused of violence against free Blacks or when free Blacks were accused of violence against whites. Nevertheless, the state's Supreme Court, in Pearson's 1850 opinion in *State v. Jowers*, extended to free Blacks Taylor's *Tackett* doctrine of separate and unequal protection.[52] An Anson County grand jury, in the spring term 1850, indicted Atlas Jowers, a white man, and Bob Douglass, "a free person of color," for having an affray on January 1, 1850.[53] An affray is a fight between two or more persons in a public place that causes terror to members of the public.[54]

Jowers and Douglass were tried in the Superior Court of Law in Anson County, which is in south-central North Carolina on the South Carolina border, during the fall term 1850, before Judge William H. Battle and a jury. According to the evidence presented at trial, Jowers and Douglass "got into a quarrel" when Jowers asked Douglass "why he had reported at a certain place that [Jowers], had told a lie, to which [Douglass] replied, because [Jowers] had told one." Jowers then struck Douglass "and a fight ensued." Douglass hit Jowers with "the butt end of a wagon whip," and Jowers "knocked [Douglass] down with the broken limb of a tree."[55]

The fight between Jowers and Douglass was a mismatch, at least if measured by their ages. Jowers, according to the 1850 census, was a farmer who was about thirty years old. He owned one fifteen-year-old male slave, but he did not own any real estate.[56] Douglass was listed in both the 1830 and 1840 Anson County censuses as a "free colored" man who was older than fifty-five years of age. He was not reported to be the owner of any real or personal property and could not be found in the county's 1850 census.[57]

Jowers's trial lawyer, whose name was not mentioned in the report of the case or in the documents in the Supreme Court's file, "contended, that the insulting language, used by the free negro, justified the blow which the defendant gave him, and that he afterwards used no more violence, than was necessary to protect him in the fight." Judge Battle disagreed. He instead charged the jury "that, though the Courts have held, that insulting language, used by a slave, may justify a white man in striking him, yet the principle did not apply to the case of a free negro, stricken under similar circumstances, by a white man." The jury convicted both Jowers and Douglass. They each were fined ten dollars plus court costs.[58]

Jowers filed an appeal with North Carolina's Supreme Court, which included Pearson, Chief Justice Thomas Ruffin, and Justice Frederick Nash. The court reversed the judgment and ordered a new trial, although no counsel appeared for Jowers on the appeal. The case report states that the attorney general, who was Bartholomew Figures Moore, argued for the state. No transcript or summary of his arguments is published or contained in the Supreme Court's file. Moore had a long career in North Carolina politics and law. For example, he argued successfully on behalf of the enslaved man named Will, in *State v. Will*, Gaston's decision permitting enslaved defendants to attempt to mitigate at least some murder charges to manslaughter.[59]

Pearson's *Jowers* opinion asserts that "it is settled, that insolent language from a slave is equivalent to a blow by a white man, in its legal effect, as an excuse for a battery." But he added, "The question presented to this case is, does the principle apply to free negroes? His Honor was of opinion that it did not. In this a majority of this Court believe there is error."[60]

Like O'Neall, Pearson cited no judicial decision or statute as authority for this rule or to support his assertion that Judge Battle committed a legal error. He instead relied on his own views of public policy, stating, "The same reasons, by which a blow from a white man upon a slave, is excusable on account of insolent language, apply to the case of a free negro, who is insolent." He cited the "maxim of the common law, where there is the same reason there is the same law." Pearson held "that free negroes differ from slaves in this, they have a right to own property, and to make contracts, which necessarily must frequently give rise to a difference of opinion, and if a free negro disputes the accounts of a white man, it is insolence, and will excuse a battery."[61]

Pearson then explained his views of the low status of free Blacks in his state:

> It is unfortunate, that *this third class* exists in our society. All we can do is to make it accommodate itself to the permanent rights of free white men. What amounts to insolence is a question for the Court, and is the subject of review in the Court of supreme jurisdiction; this is some protection. But as compared with a slave how stands the case? If a slave is insolent, he may be whipped by his master, or by order of a justice of the peace; but a free negro has no master to correct him, a justice of the peace cannot have him punished for insolence, it is not an indictable offence, and unless a white man, to whom insolence is given, has a right to put a stop to it, in an extra judicial way, there is no remedy for it. This would be insufferable.

Thus, Pearson held "we infer from the principles of the common law, that this extra judicial remedy is excusable, provided the words or acts of a free negro be in law insolent."[62]

Pearson implicitly acknowledged that this holding was contrary to the common-law rule providing that a victim's mere words do not constitute justification for a battery. He, like O'Neall, nevertheless avoided these precedents by equating free Blacks with enslaved people. He wrote, "Such a being as a slave or a free negro, did not exist when the ancient common law was in force." He found that the "excellence" of the common law's "'perfection of reason' consists" in its flexibility. This flexibility, Pearson reasoned, permits "its principles [to] expand, so as to accommodate it to any new exigence or condition of society, like the bark of a tree, which opens and enlarges itself, according to the growth thereof, always maintaining its own uniformity and consistency."[63]

No statute or constitutional provision required Pearson and the other justices to devise this unequal protection rule. But "new exigencies," Pearson believed, permitted him to create a race-based exception to the common-law "mere words" rule, thus legitimating white violence. Like O'Neall, Pearson vested local all-white juries with wide discretion to decide when those who attacked free Blacks abused this newly legitimated white privilege to commit assaults and batteries.

Pearson's decision legitimizing what he termed "extra judicial" violence thus brought within the law individual and potentially even multiparty private incidents of white violence, which in his mind were understandable responses to "insufferable" free Black insolence. John Hope Franklin discussed a notorious case of mob violence in Raleigh, which illustrates the legal consciousness that Pearson legitimized. Franklin quotes the *Raleigh Register*'s October 1842 report of a mob's nighttime proto-Klan attack on Allen Jones, a free Black blacksmith. Jones was "dragged from his home" in Raleigh "and was 'shockingly whipped.'" The *Register*'s report states, "No cause is assigned for the act, but if we recollect aright, it was this Allen Jones, who, with his wife and several children whom he had purchased and emancipated, some months ago appeared before the Anti-Slavery Convention of New York and made a speech, in which he spoke of a coat of tar and feathers he had received from a certain class of persons in Raleigh. Having imprudently returned to Raleigh, we suppose these persons have thus revenged themselves on him." According to Franklin, "Raleigh was aflame over the beating of Allen Jones." Residents at a large town meeting, including T. P. Devereux, one of the state's largest slaveholders, condemned the mob's actions. The editor of the *Register* also commented on the breakdown in the rule of law evidenced by the incident: "We hope that the good people of Raleigh will not stop short of the most condign punishment of this outrage, not because of the individual against whom it was perpetrated (for we suspect that he is deserving no sympathy) but for the sake of LAW, which we desire to be upheld against all infractions."[64] Pearson's *Jowers* doctrine most likely would not have legalized this lynch mob's actions. But it would have brought within the rule of law the violent actions of whites who were permitted to act out their frustrations when they were confronted with mere words that they believed to be insolent.

Pearson Extends the Inequality Rule to Free Blacks Accused of Crimes

Because North Carolina's free Blacks were prosecuted and tried on criminal charges in the regular courts, the state's Supreme Court soon had to decide whether to extend the race-based unequal protection doctrine to free Blacks who were accused of crimes. Pearson's 1859 opinion in *State v. Davis* answered this question, while reversing the assault and battery conviction of Lawrence Davis, a free Black man.[65] By then, Judge Battle, who, like Pearson, had a long career in law and politics, had been appointed to North Carolina's Supreme Court. He filled the vacancy in the seat that had been held by Frederick Nash.[66]

Davis was indicted by a grand jury and was tried in the Superior Court, Craven County, during the fall 1859 term, for committing a battery on Edward H. Hart.[67] The trial was held before Judge Romulus M. Saunders and a jury. Saunders was nearing the end of his long but controversial political and legal career. Among many other things of note, he was the North Carolina attorney general who unsuccessfully argued to sustain the conviction of John Mann in the infamous case *State v. Mann*.[68]

Davis lived in the Town of New Bern. His case originated in the enforcement of a racially discriminatory local taxation ordinance. The ordinance, which was adopted on July 18, 1859, required that "all free negroes, who have not paid their taxes, shall be made to work on the streets two days for each and every dollar of tax due the town by them." The ordinance did not apply to whites who did not pay their taxes. Anyone refusing to comply "upon due notice being given him," was to "pay a fine, at the discretion of the Mayor, not exceeding $10." Hart was a New Bern Town constable. He was given a notice, which was issued on September 1, 1859, directing Davis "to show cause why he should not work on the streets as the penalty for not having paid his taxes." Hart arrested Davis "and attempted to tie him, when the latter struck him."[69]

Davis's trial counsel was Duncan Kirkland McRae. He had a long career as a lawyer and a politician and was a Confederate Army colonel. He was praised as the "greatest criminal lawyer the state has produced."[70] McRae contended that on these facts Davis "was, in law, not guilty, and asked his Honor so to charge." But Judge Saunders "refused, and gave his opinion that, in law, [Davis] was guilty." Davis appealed from this verdict and judgment.[71]

Attorney General William A. Jenkins's arguments in favor of the judgment are not preserved in the official case report or the Supreme Court's file. But Pearson, who by then was the state's chief justice, rejected two arguments that he believed may have been thought to support the decision attributed to Judge

Saunders. Pearson first stated that the conviction "may involve the proposition that a free negro is not justified, under any circumstances, in striking a white man. To this, we cannot yield our assent." He explained that "self-defense is a *natural* right, and, although the social relation of this *third class* of our population, and a regard for its proper subordination requires that the right should be restricted, yet, nothing short of manifest public necessity can furnish a ground for taking it away absolutely." This was "because a free negro, however lowly his condition, is in the 'peace of the State,' and to deprive him of this right, would be to put him on the footing of an outlaw." Although "the law will not allow a free negro to return blow for blow, and engage in a fight with a white man, under ordinary circumstances, as one white man may do with another, or one free negro with another, he is not deprived, absolutely, of the right of self-defense." Pearson thus believed that he was charting "a middle course . . . , by which, in order to make out a justification for a battery on a white man, the free negro is required to allege and prove that it became necessary for him to strike, in order to protect himself from great bodily harm or grievous oppression."[72]

Pearson added that this limited self-defense privilege for free Blacks was supported by "the adjudications of our courts, and considerations growing out of the abnormal state of society, caused by the existence of free negroes in our midst." This "abnormal" free Black population called "for a new application" of the common law, "the excellence of which consists in the fact that it is flexible, and expands so as to embrace any new exigence or condition of society." Accordingly, "while on the principle of self-protection, the paramount rights of the white population are secured, the rights of this inferior race are made to give place, as far, but no farther, than is necessary for that purpose."[73] Pearson cited his opinion in *State v. Jowers* and Chief Justice Thomas Ruffin's dissenting opinion in the slavery law decision *State v. Caesar* as support for his rule of separate and unequal protection for the free people of this "inferior race."[74]

Pearson then explained this limited protection afforded to free Blacks from cruel and unusual white "oppression": "Without undertaking to decide that a free negro stands precisely on the same footing with a slave who strikes a white man, other than his master, or one having authority over him, we think it follows from the principles established by these cases, that, although a free negro, upon receiving an ordinary blow, is not allowed to strike back, and get into a fight with a white man, yet, if there be cruelty, or unusual circumstances of oppression, a blow is excusable." Pearson reached this conclusion "because, in such a case, a resort to the natural right of self-protection is not inconsistent with that feeling of submission to white men which his lowly condition imposes, and public policy requires should be exacted."[75]

Pearson next held that if Judge Saunders instead intended to apply the principle that Pearson announced in *Jowers* to the facts proven at the trial, "we differ from his Honor in respect to its application." Pearson explained, "An officer of the town having a *notice to serve on the defendant*, without any authority whatever, *arrests him and attempts to tie him*. Is not this gross oppression? For what purpose was he to be tied? What degree of cruelty might not the defendant reasonably apprehend after he should be entirely in the power of one who had set upon him in so high-handed and lawless a manner? Was he to submit tamely?—Or, was he not excusable for resorting to the natural right of self-defense?" Therefore, Pearson concluded, "upon the facts stated, we think his Honor ought to have instructed the jury to find the defendant not guilty." The court ordered a new trial.[76]

Pearson's opinion is consistent with the antebellum cases suggesting that executive officials or officers, like Hart, could be held liable for common-law torts if their actions are "actuated by malice, cruelty, or willful oppression."[77] But Pearson held that these standards applied differently depending on the race of the victim.

The court applied this rule during its December 1860 term in its *State v. Norman* opinion, after Nehemiah Norman, a white man, was indicted for assault and battery on a "a free man of color" named Richard Fisher.[78] This case illustrates the separate and unequal protection doctrine's impact on free Black lives on the eve of the Civil War. The case arose out of the racially discriminatory state law that the court sustained in *State v. Manuel*.[79] Fisher was arrested for the murder of Elijah Hassell and was tried and convicted during the spring 1859 term in Washington County Superior Court before Judge Saunders and a jury. The Supreme Court affirmed the conviction during its June 1859 term in *State v. Fisher*.[80]

Fisher had previously been convicted of larceny in the county court in Washington County, but he could not pay his fine and was sold to a man named Peacock for a five-year term of involuntary servitude. Fisher was legally married to a woman whose name is not mentioned in the case reports. They had been living with Hassell, but before Hassell's killing Fisher was living with a neighbor. On the morning of February 24, 1859, Hassell's body was found near his crib. He was shot dead. There were no witnesses.

Fisher's attorney objected to the prosecution's proffer at the trial of a witness named Johnson to testify that Fisher admitted to the killing. Fisher's lawyer responded by calling Nehemiah Norman. He testified that he arrested Fisher on the day Hassell's body was discovered, and he then essentially beat and tricked a confession out of Fisher. Norman admitted that he "ironed" Fisher and took him to Hassell's body. With several others present, Norman admitted accusing Fisher of committing Hassell's murder. He "called upon" Fisher "to tell them where he had hid a gun which they alleged he had used in perpetrating the crime—that they were satisfied of the fact, and wanted him to tell where the gun was."[81] They "immediately took [Fisher] a short distance off, and tied him up to a tree and told him they intended to whip him until he would agree to show them the gun—that they were not going to whip him to make him confess the murder." Norman asserted "that they then struck him five or six licks with a whip on his bare back, when he agreed to show the gun, and they went, under his direction, and found the gun." On the way to find the gun, Norman "said to the prisoner he did not see how he could have the boldness to shoot a white man, and asked how he came to do it; to which he replied, because he had taken away his wife—that he had kept her for some time, and he had warned them, and did not regret what he had done."[82]

"Notwithstanding this statement," Saunders permitted Johnson to testify on behalf of the state that, the day after Fisher's arrest, he went to the jail and called to the window of Fisher's cell, "'Dick, you have played hell now.' To which the prisoner replied, 'yes master Johnson, they have got me now, but I didn't intend to kill Hassell; it was dark, and the shot went higher than I intended.'" Fisher's counsel of course objected to this testimony. The state also proved Fisher's hiring out, the discovery of the body, Fisher's objection to his wife living with Hassell, and that he "had desired her to come home."

Fisher's lawyer essentially admitted his client's guilt, but he argued that the proof of adultery was sufficient provocation to reduce the crime from murder to manslaughter, therefore invoking "what has been called the 'unwritten law.'" Nineteenth-century lawyers hoped that, according to this principle, a jury would not convict a man for killing another man who had sexual relations with his wife, no matter what the written law stated.[83] Judge Saunders disagreed and instructed the jury that adultery would mitigate the killing only if Fisher discovered Hassell with his wife, "and that he slew the adulterer at the moment, under the excitement produced by the discovery." The jury convicted Fisher of murder, and Fisher appealed.[84]

Justice Battle's opinion affirming the conviction found that Fisher's second confession to Johnson was sufficiently removed in time and place from the coerced confession. He also rejected Fisher's argument "that the second confession ought to be excluded upon the ground of public policy, for the purpose of discountenancing, and thus putting an end to such gross violation of law as the officer and his party, who made the arrest, were guilty of, in their treatment of the prisoner." Battle answered, "We think the purposes of justice will be best accomplished by having the officer indicted and punished for his unlawful and tyrannical abuse of his official power."

Battle also found that the adultery defense was not relevant. He explained, "If the prisoner killed the deceased at all, it was an act of assassination and not a killing upon provocation, and the Court ought to have instructed the jury, that the testimony did not present any view in which the question of provocation could be raised. We will not, therefore, express any opinion upon what we consider a purely hypothetical case."[85]

Norman then was prosecuted for his actions, as the Supreme Court suggested. He was tried in Washington County Superior Court during the spring 1860 term before Judge John M. Dick and a jury. The jury entered a special verdict, which was substantially consistent with the facts proven in Fisher's trial, accepting Norman's defense that Peacock consented to the whipping inflicted on Fisher. Judge Dick concluded that Norman was not guilty, and the state appealed.[86]

Justice Matthias Evans Manly, who, in December 1859, had been elected to the Supreme Court, wrote the court's opinion reversing this judgment and ordering that a verdict be entered against Norman. The court held that Peacock's alleged consent provided Norman no excuse for the assault and battery.[87] Manly acknowledged that the statute authorized masters to legally correct their "free" Black apprentices, who "may be whipped for such an object." But he also limited this privilege to "lawful objects." He explained that "if, under pretense of correction, the master whipped of malice, or, which we regard as equivalent, for an illegal object, it would be a violation of law." In comparison,

> Where one has a discretionary power of whipping for correction, and resorts to it in good faith, the law will not hold him to an account for any error of judgment in respect to the need for it, or in respect to the amount, unless it be grossly excessive. But it is different where the whipping is inflicted for an unlawful object, or of malice. In such cases, every blow is an unlawful battery. It has been thought proper, by the Legislature, to place the negro convict, who is sold for the pecuniary penalty annexed to his offense, in the condition of an apprentice. This relation we find regulated by general principles, and to the benefit of them the man is entitled in this case.[88]

Manly downplayed the harm to Fisher, however, when he concluded, "The five blows inflicted under the circumstances, make it a case of minor importance; but nevertheless, we think, for the reasons given, that it is technically an indictable battery."[89]

The court therefore did not approve of Norman's attempt to beat a murder confession out of Fisher with the "five blows" inflicted. But Manly's assertion about the "minor importance" of the beating suggests that the court would excuse an ordinary whipping inflicted to correct a disobedient Black apprentice. This moderate correction would be within the privilege that the law created when it imposed involuntary servitude upon free Black people and not upon similarly situated whites who could not be sold as apprentices for not paying their fines.

Evaluating Pearson as a Southern Moderate

Pearson's *Jowers* and *Davis* opinions employed the separate and unequal criminal law mitigation doctrine to confirm and advance the legal culture and legal consciousness legitimizing and encouraging what otherwise would have been extralegal white violence toward free Blacks. Pearson nevertheless has been included among southern antebellum moderates by scholars, including John Hope Franklin, who celebrated the North Carolina Supreme Court as "the greatest protector of the rights of free Negroes," citing decisions, including *Jowers* and *Davis*, that shielded free Blacks from "lawless violence."[90]

Writing toward the end of the turbulent decade of the 1960s, A. E. Keir Nash showered more effusive praise on moderate antebellum southern jurists—including Pearson. He favorably contrasted Pearson's decision in *Davis* with the Jim Crow–era state court decisions that resulted in the leading U.S. Supreme Court decisions in *Moore v. Dempsey* and *Brown v. Mississippi*.[91] According to Nash, the Arkansas Supreme Court in *Moore* "found nothing fundamentally unfair about passing a death sentence upon a black whose trial for murder had been conducted with an angry mob assembled outside the courtroom." And he condemned the Mississippi Supreme Court's majority in *Brown* for having "discerned nothing shocking to the conscience in a capital conviction based on a confession procured by whipping the black defendant over a three-day period." In contrast, Nash lauded the *Davis* decision both as a potentially "representative" example of southern antebellum jurisprudence and as proof of the discontinuity between the Jim Crow–era criminal law and this pre-emancipation law, which he labeled "an overlooked antebellum tradition of solicitude for the black defendant."[92] Indeed, he asserted, "Few judges appear to have been eager to find loopholes to excuse white attacks on blacks."[93]

Nash also frankly acknowledged the political implications of this interpretation of antebellum law, as the 1960s came to an end. He recommended that, in the "future quest for justice in the South," civil rights lawyers and federal appellate court judges seek "to reawaken a regionally-indigenous behavior once genuinely inclined to greater fairness."[94] He also suggested that these decisions were inconsistent with Ulrich B. Phillips's thesis that "the central theme of southern history has been the maintenance of white supremacy."[95]

Nash failed to fully appreciate the symbolic and practical import of the opinions of O'Neall and Pearson casting aside settled common-law rules and doctrines to eagerly create "loopholes to excuse white attacks" on all Blacks.[96] These jurists readily consigned free Blacks to a race-based separate and unequal criminal law caste, which came dangerously close to that of the enslaved. Pearson's *Jowers* and *Davis* opinions, when read together, are significant because they both defined and justified the newly minted "certain limits" of free Black rights to personal safety and the privileges of self-defense by a direct and explicit analogy to the separate and unequal protection analysis that the court applied to slaves. Of course, this analogy held true only in part; Pearson's doctrine protected the persons and lives of free African Americans to a greater extent than those who were enslaved. But he did this only "to a certain extent." His perceived need to vindicate "public justice" while preventing Black "insolence" and "public wrongs" set the limits of that "certain extent."[97]

Some later scholars have tended to fit within what Michael Hindus calls "the Nash mold,"[98] although they may not necessarily agree with Nash's suggested contemporary constitutional and policy prescriptions, by downplaying the importance of the *Jowers* opinion and emphasizing *Davis*. For example, Reuel E. Schiller commends Pearson's *Davis* opinion: "By recognizing that blacks had a certain natural right at all, Pearson granted them a measure of humanity no other southern court did." He notes further that in the *Davis* case, "there was no property right at issue because Davis was a free black. By allowing him to defend himself against a sheriff's assault, even though Davis was breaking the law by not working on the roads, the court clearly undermined its interests in safeguarding society from just the type of resistance that Davis was offering."[99] This undermining is not necessarily so sweeping. Pearson's *Davis* opinion creates a limited right of self-defense for free Blacks, while not questioning the racially discriminatory tax law, which was the root cause of the case.

More recently, Joseph A. Ranney praised Pearson as a jurist who "generally emphasized humanity over economic interest in slave cases."[100] Pearson's experiences as a "small-farm" slave owner, according to Ranney, "enabled Pearson to carve out a place for slaves' humanity in his decisions while defending slavery as an institution," and these experiences "made it easier for him to accept and accommodate the legal changes that followed the Confederacy's defeat and emancipation."[101]

Warren E. Milteer Jr. also extoled Pearson's *Davis* decision as "one of the biggest blows to the radical proslavery agenda." He conceded that Pearson "evidently did not believe whites and people of color were equal." But Milteer declared, "Yet the court left room for free people of color to protect themselves from physical violence by white people who believed they had the right to dominate free people of color."[102] He thus favorably contrasted Pearson's *Davis* opinion with Chief Justice Roger Brooke Taney's infamous declaration, asserted in his *Scott v. Sandford* opinion, that free Blacks "had no rights which the white man was bound to respect."[103] In contrast, according to Milteer, "Justice Pearson's words suggest that North Carolina law required white men to respect the rights of free people of color within certain limits, including the right of free persons of color to defend themselves."[104]

Wilson Angley aptly cautioned, in contrast, that Pearson's "views on slavery and on the relationship between the races were not noticeably in advance of his time."[105] Pearson is an important jurist because he was among those whom Cody Marrs calls "transbellum" authors, whose opinions span the years before, during, and after the Civil War.[106] He had a ten-year career as a lawyer and legislator before his 1836 election to the Superior Court. Twelve years later, he was elected to the state's Supreme Court. He was the court's chief justice from 1859 until his death in 1878. He also was a law teacher and owned a Yadkin County plantation, known as Richmond Hill.[107] Pearson owned eighteen slaves in 1850. By 1860, his slaveholding had doubled to thirty-seven people.[108]

Pearson was a Whig who in the 1830s opposed nullification. He also opposed succession before the Civil War. But he remained loyal to his state during the war. He was one of only two southern justices who served on their state's highest courts during both the Civil War and Reconstruction, but he also issued Civil War draft exemption and habeas corpus decisions that defied the Confederate government's policies. Indeed, in 1864, he in effect ignored the Confederate government's suspension of the writ of habeas corpus. After the war, President Andrew Johnson pardoned Pearson, who then reinvented himself as a Republican who supported Ulysses S. Grant for president in 1868. But Pearson nevertheless "appealed to conservative friends to exploit reconstructed politics to their advantage."[109]

Pearson explained his "conservative" and complex racial views in a July 20, 1868, letter urging his fellow white North Carolinians to "concede to freedmen political equality" because white resistance to Black voting "makes them 'pull together.'" Without this "pressure," he thought that the Black "vote will be neutralized." He also expressed his belief that "the power and effect of the superiority of the white man, aided as he is by education, and the possession of the wealth of the country, in a few years" would cause Blacks "to vote as before 1835," when the state constitution first denied all free Blacks the right to vote.[110]

Unlike O'Neall, Pearson did not advocate slavery law reforms, but he was an important antebellum slavery law jurist. He captured slavery law's essence in his 1858 opinion in *Howard v. Howard*.[111] The court held that enslaved people who had lived as husband and wife—according to custom—were not legally married, even after they were freed by their owner and continued to live as if they were married. Pearson explained the enslaved person's legal status: "A slave, being property, has not the legal capacity to make a contract, and is not entitled to the rights or subjected to the liabilities incident thereto. He is amendable to the criminal law, and his person (to a certain extent) and his life are protected." Pearson nevertheless made it plain that he viewed the enslaved as people without rights when he added the caveat, "This, however, is not a concession to him of civil rights, but is a vindication of public justice, and for the prevention of public wrongs."[112]

Two years later, Pearson, in *Lea v. Brown*, explained why masters violated the state's public policy when they permitted their slaves to work and earn substantial sums of money—$1,200 plus interest in that case—or acquire property such as mules, hogs, and cattle.[113] These privileges, he declared, were "certainly calculated to make other slaves dissatisfied, because they are not allowed the same degree of freedom and privilege."[114] He distinguished this extravagance from the more benign practices of slave owners, noting that the court had "not only recognized the right of a master, but treated it as commendable, to adopt a system of rewards, by which a slave is allowed a half, or a whole day, every time 'the crop is gone over,' to work a *patch of cotton, corn or watermelons* and the like, and to sell the proceeds, so as to make a little money with which to buy small amounts of luxuries—sugar, coffee, tobacco, &c., and to indulge a fancy for 'finery in dress,' for which the African race is remarkable." Pearson thus recognized an enslaver's right to bestow these "commendable" privileges aimed at what he perceived to be the "African race['s]" alleged fondness for watermelons and fashionable clothing. But, he declared, "when it comes to an accumulation of $1500, the question is a very different one, and other considerations are suggested."[115]

The opinion most often cited as an example of Pearson's humanity to enslaved people is *State v. Caesar*.[116] Pearson voted with Justice Frederick Nash to reverse an enslaved man named Caesar's murder conviction, over Chief Justice Thomas Ruffin's dissent. Caesar killed one of two white strangers who participated in an unprovoked attack on Caesar and another slave named Dick.

Pearson held that the trial judge should have permitted the jury to mitigate the homicide from murder to manslaughter. Although he found that the white attackers' unprovoked battery was excessive, he tellingly called these white assailants "two drunken ruffians." He reversed Caesar's conviction "to protect slave property from wanton outrages, while, at the same time, due subordination is preserved."[117] Pearson also wrote opinions holding that enslaved people could not be convicted of murder based on their coerced confessions and permitting slave owners to testify in court in favor of their slaves who were accused of crimes.[118]

But, according to Daniel Flanigan, Pearson evidenced "obvious delight in reducing the rights of free blacks."[119] He cited the *Jowers* opinion and another 1850 Pearson opinion, *State v. Haithcock*, to support his interpretation.[120] The court in *Haithcock* affirmed Judge Battle's Superior Court order denying Williamson Haithcock's motion to dismiss a paternity action that an unnamed white woman filed against him under the state's laws on the paternity and support of "bastard children." Haithcock claimed that these laws did not apply to him because he was a free Black man. Pearson first explained the status of free Blacks, who "are capable of holding property, they can sue and be sued, and are bound to support their bastard children, whether begotten upon a free white woman or free black woman. They can set up no 'exclusive privilege' in this behalf." He added the public policy favoring his interpretation: "The counties ought not to be charged with the support of these bastards, until it is judicially ascertained, by exhausting the legal remedy, that the putative father is unable to do so."[121]

Pearson's record as a trial court judge also is mixed. Early in his judicial career, in April 1839, Pearson rebuked in court the jury and defense counsel for Nicholas C. Robinson, a white man who was tried for the murder of a free Black man named "Fellow or Othello Merrick." According to the *Wilmington Advertiser*, the killing occurred on Saturday night, January 26, 1839. A coroner's inquest found that Robinson, "with a knife or dirk, did give Fellow Merrick a negro man, one mortal wound on the right side of the neck, just above the collar bone, of which wound he instantly died."[122]

The trial was held in Wilmington, beginning on April 26, 1839. Three leading local lawyers, Robert Strange, D. B. Baker, and Owen Holmes, defended Robinson. The *Wilmington Advertiser* reported, "The evidence detailed by the witnesses established clearly and unquestionably the guilt of the prisoner, as charged in the bill of indictment—the jury however, thought otherwise, notwithstanding the charge of [Pearson], who remarked that if they believed the witnesses, they must bring the verdict of *murder*." The jury deliberated "from ten o'clock at night until six in the morning," when contrary to Pearson's view of the case, "they rendered a verdict of manslaughter."

Later that day, Pearson sentenced Robinson, whom he called "a lawless and dangerous man." Pearson found that "the circumstances on the trial [were] of a highly aggravated character, amounting in the opinion of the Court to murder." Pearson imposed a six-month jail term, ordered the branding of Robinson's left thumb with the letter "M," and required Robinson to post a five-year bond of five hundred dollars to guaranty his good behavior. The *Wilmington Advertiser* article also reported a concern about undisclosed comments made by Robinson's counsel, while approving of Pearson's response:

> We cannot close our notice of this case, without most solemnly protesting, in behalf of the community, against the dissemination of some of the sentiments expressed by one of the counsel who conducted the defence. They are unfounded in truth, and are highly calculated to inflame the popular mind; to array one class of society against another; to endanger the public peace; to shake society to its centre; to substitute anarchy, bloodshed, and barbarism, for good government, happiness, and civilization. The ardour of debate cannot justify, scarcely extenuate, words of such dangerous import, and we are happy to see his Honour object to them in this case as irrelevant and exceptionable.[123]

It is not clear if the lawyer's comments were racially charged. But even if they were not, Pearson publicly admonished the jury for its refusal to convict Robinson of what Pearson believed was a clear case of interracial murder.

Also as a trial court judge, Pearson, in 1843, instructed a jury in a civil trial that an overseer, John F. Parker, had "no right" to shoot an escaping enslaved person in the back and thigh, in a case with facts similar to those of *State v. Mann*.[124] The plaintiff, Martha Copeland, in 1840, had hired her twenty-year-old slave Gilbert "to certain gentlemen, who were opening a turnpike in Gates county." John F. Parker was Gilbert's overseer. On the day before he was shot, Gilbert had left his work "without leave," but he returned to work the next morning. At about ten o'clock that morning, a trial witness, whose name was not reported, testified that, while he was passing by, Parker asked him "to stop and help him whip Gilbert for having run away. As the witness was getting off his horse, Gilbert stuck his spade in the ground and started off in a walk." Parker then ordered Gilbert to stop, but Gilbert instead "continued to walk and rather quickened his pace, and [Parker] then fired and brought him to the ground. This was done at a place in the swamp, where, at the distance of some twenty or thirty paces, the bushes and water rendered it difficult to get along."

Pearson rejected Parker's lawyer's request to charge the jury that Parker's shooting "was fully justified." Pearson instead instructed the jury "that a gun was not a fit instrument for chastisement, and that an overseer had no right to shoot a negro down, who refused to stop, when ordered, and was in the act of making off. If he did so, it was a wrongful act, and he was responsible to the owner for any loss sustained by reason thereof."[125] The North Carolina Supreme Court, in a brief opinion by Justice Daniel, affirmed Pearson's instruction and the judgment in favor of Copeland.[126]

In contrast, Pearson, in an 1847 trial, extended to a hirer the slave owners' privilege to kill with impunity rebellious or resisting slaves. Ira Westbrook, a hirer, allegedly killed a slave named Lot during the term of hiring. Westbrook was indicted and tried in the Jones County Superior Court. He is described as "an illiterate whom the 1850 census lists as owning no real estate. He was a poor man in a rich neighborhood."[127] Lot was "insolent and impudent in his language toward" Westbrook, who "took down a cowhide to whip him." Lot told Westbrook "that he would not be whipped by any such man, and began to move off. Westbrook then took down his gun, upon which the negro in an impudent manner told him to shoot—repeating it three times." Westbrook shot Lot, "and lodged the contents of gun" in one of Lot's calves. Lot fell, but soon crawled back to the door of Westbrook's house "and told him in an impudent manner, to shoot the other barrel of the gun into his head, which the prisoner did not do." Lot died of his wounds three days later.[128]

James W. Bryan defended Westbrook, arguing that Lot "was in a state of rebellion and resistance" to Westbrook, "who for the time being was [Lot's] owner, and had all the rights of [Lot's] actual master. That but for this resistance and rebellion, it would be at most a case of manslaughter." Pearson agreed, holding that Westbrook had the same enslaver's privilege to kill Lot as if he were Lot's owner. Pearson "charged the jury that if they believed Westbrook killed Lot upon the provocation of impudence and insolence, it was in the eye of the law but a case of manslaughter." But he added, "If the deceased was in an actual state of rebellion, and resistance to the prisoner, then he would have a right to kill him, and would not be liable criminally for the act, but would be justified in law for so doing." Pearson then defined "what he deemed rebellion and resistance, on the part of a slave toward his master." The jurors apparently believed that Lot's conduct was rebellious or resistant; they found that Westbrook was not guilty.[129]

This case was reported in northern abolitionist newspapers as an example of slavery's inherently evil essence. But this trial was viewed differently in the local press. The *Raleigh Star and North Carolina Gazette* declared, "We regard this as a very important case, it having called forth as we believe, the first decision upon these principles of law, that has been made in the State."[130]

Pearson, as a trial judge, in 1838, ruled in favor of a free Black man's interests in *State v. Bennett*.[131] John H. Bennett and three other men were indicted for "unlawfully, riotously, and routously," trespassing on the real property of Benjamin Curry, in order to take possession of Curry's farm of twelve years and his personal property, including his five slaves, who were his wife Phillis and their children. Pursuant to Pearson's instructions, the jury convicted these defendants. Pearson imposed a hundred-dollar fine on Bennett and ten-dollar fines on the others. He also sentenced Bennett to a six-month prison term. But he ordered that the incarceration "be remitted" if Bennett surrendered possession and ownership of all of the property at issue—including Curry's family members.[132] Justice Gaston wrote the Supreme Court's opinion affirming the conviction and, in part, the sentence. He vacated Pearson's order of remission of Bennett's prison sentence, with instructions that the court below may instead suspend the sentence to give Bennett the opportunity to "make restitution to the person peculiarly aggrieved by this offence, or to redress its mischievous public consequences."[133]

Nineteen years later, Pearson decided a habeas corpus petition in favor Elizabeth Post, "a free woman of color." It was alleged that she was hired out for a term of years by the Cumberland County court, most likely for not paying a court-imposed fine. The original purchaser later sold the remainder of her time in involuntary service to James Bryant, of the neighboring Bladen County. Bryant brought Post "down to Wilmington on board of one of the steamboats, on the Cape Fear [River]." While on the boat, Post "overheard some conversation leading her to believe that it was designed to carry her out of the State with the supposed intention of holding her as a slave." Judge Pearson issued the writ requiring that Post be produced in court. Upon hearing the facts, "it appeared beyond question that she was a free woman, and she was consequently set at liberty." No one appeared to contest Post's claim. She may nevertheless still have been obligated to serve Bryant for the reminder of her court-ordered term, but the press reported that she later "was found on board the Manchester [Cumberland County] cars."[134]

These trial rulings are consistent with Pearson's decisions holding that free Blacks were—to some lesser degree than whites—under the criminal law's protection. They could defend themselves against a white person's violence, but only "within certain limits" that Pearson created to cut down the ordinary common-law self-defense privilege for free Blacks. They could defend themselves against whites only who inflicted "great bodily harm" or "unusual," "grievous," or "gross" oppression. This privilege did not apply to the "ordinary" oppression that Pearson and the white population perceived to be necessary in order to guarantee white supremacy and to deter insolence. All whites could legally punish what they perceived to be insolence in their everyday interactions with free Blacks. And, moreover, all-white juries and judiciaries would decide if these white responses to insolence rose to the level of unusual, outrageous, or gross oppression.

All southern whites therefore were soldiers in the war against Black insolence. Pearson's opinions were parts of the positive law that empowered this de jure army to enforce the dominant norms of white supremacy. Pearson's reference in the *Davis* opinion to its "middle course" also suggests that he considered and consciously refused to embrace the rule guaranteeing equally to free Black people to benefit from all of the common law of crime's protections. This equality was not a novel legal notion. To the contrary, the middle-ground approach that Pearson and O'Neall selected was the judicial innovation. Justice (then judge) Battle had applied the common law's equal protection principles at trial in *State v. Jowers*, and the Illinois Supreme Court in 1854 enforced them in *Campbell v. The People*.[135]

The Unresolved Issue: Free Black Criminal Defendants

The North Carolina Supreme Court did not decide whether it would extend to free Black criminal defendants the separate and unequal mitigation and extenuation rules that the court created in *State v. Jarrott* for enslaved criminal defendants. It nevertheless appears almost certain that, if the Civil War and emancipation had not intervened, the court would have applied these enslavement law rules to free Blacks by analogy, just as it did when whites were on trial for violent crimes directed against free Blacks victims.

The South's white-supremacist policies and separate and unequal protection principles applied with equal force in these cases. Indeed, these North Carolina decisions, when read together, are inconsistent with Christopher Waldrep's assertion that "the logic of the common law resisted formation of a distinct 'Negro law.'" Waldrep advanced this interpretation while focusing on what he believed were fair criminal procedures in the trials of enslaved people who were accused of capital crimes.[136] Antebellum southern statutes and court decisions did indeed endorse several different models for slave trials, ranging from near procedural equality with whites in North Carolina to South Carolina's separate and unequal courts and procedures for the trials of enslaved and free Blacks.[137] But, as Melvin Ely acknowledges, to the extent that these procedures may now appear to protect enslaved people from "unwarranted conviction[s]," they also protected the enslavers' private property interests and their "personal interest in vindicating one who they believed had been wrongly accused."[138]

Even if some antebellum enslavers were motivated by paternalistic concerns for the welfare of the people they enslaved, both the slave owners' economic interests and their perceptions of their honor and standing in the community were embodied in the people they enslaved. These considerations also may have motivated enslavers to hire expensive and skilled lawyers to defend in the courts their slaves who were charged with crimes. Fair criminal procedures in the trials of enslaved defendants also advanced the master class's collective interests by securing their property rights from arbitrary state interference and by perpetuating the existing social order and the enslavers' place at the top.[139] These pragmatic interests and class biases were always in the background of appearances of benevolence toward those who were enslaved. But the legislators also authorized exceptions to these rules, which further truncated the procedural rights guaranteed in slave trials when the slave owners' collective real or imagined fears of insurrection overshadowed all other interests. These procedures channeled into the legal system cases that might otherwise have been "adjudicated" by lynch mobs.[140]

In contrast, antebellum southern free Blacks who were accused of committing crimes, like those who were the victims of crimes and mob violence, did not benefit from this same convergence of their interests in their right to personal safety with the enslaver class's interests.[141] This analysis is consistent with Derrick Bell's "interest-convergence" theory, which asserts the general principle that "the interest of blacks in achieving racial equality will be accommodated only when it converges with the interests of whites."[142] This is not to suggest that free African Americans lacked either agency or the will to exert their equal rights to personal security, integrity, and respect, as well as their right to contest the white privilege permitting nonstate actor violence.[143] To the contrary, the *Harden* and *Jowers* opinions confirm that free Blacks contested both of these rules of inequality before the criminal law and the underlying white-supremacist legal culture and legal consciousness.[144] Others instead thought it best to protect "themselves against legal and extralegal violence by building friendships with powerful whites."[145] Free African Americans each day had to live with "the threat of persecution that always loomed over" them, while living "in a society in which blackness denoted slavery, and in which the law could only offer partial protection."[146]

Conclusion

Pearson, like O'Neall, enforced his perceptions of the prevailing local customs and public policies when he decided to modify the common law of crimes in his state to consign free Blacks to a degraded, second-class legal caste. This result was not compelled by any statute or common-law authority. Nor did these judges defer to their state legislatures, based on the belief that legislators—and not judges—should make this radical legal change in the common law of crimes. Instead, they exhibited an approach to adjudication that rightly can be seen as judicial activism. They balanced what they perceived to be the relevant social interests and policies to extend to free Blacks their state's enslavement law rules and doctrines—by analogy—to create in their states' common law a new separate and unequal criminal law category for free Blacks.

This judicial activism unambiguously incorporated within the common law the local customs and public policy preferences that legitimized violence based on an alleged criminal's or victim's race—and not his or her enslaved or free status. The judges who extended to free Blacks the principle of separate and unequal criminal law protection that was created for the enslaved people reflected, preserved, and promoted the prevailing overtly white-supremacist social order. Pearson's opinion in *State v. Caesar* discouraged wanton outrages by lower-class white "drunken ruffians," and his *State v. Davis* decision condemned white violence that rose to the level of "malice, cruelty, or willful oppression." But these opinions reveal the underlying white-supremacist policy that Pearson advanced because they empowered all whites with the positive law privilege to use regular, ordinary, and necessary violent means to keep enslaved and free African Americans in their legally separate and degraded place and caste.

This new common law decriminalizing white violence while criminalizing Black insolence is relevant to Laura Edwards's interpretation of the movement of the antebellum law's center of gravity from "localized law," which she states was designed to protect the "peace" through the discretionary decision making of local officials, magistrates, and juries, to "a more centralized legal system and a systemized version of 'the law.'"[147] She defines the peace as "an open-ended concept that could turn virtually any act by anyone against anyone into a public offense." She quotes John Haywood's 1808 definition of the peace as "a quiet and harmless behavior towards government, and all the citizens under its protection."[148] State law never "completely displaced" local law, although the more centralized regime's importance increased as the two coexisted.[149]

Edwards identifies O'Neall and Pearson among those who advanced these antebellum legal centralization reforms.¹⁵⁰ But these jurists decriminalized white interracial violence by incorporating the "open-ended" concept of insolence within this "systemized" and "more centralized" body of the common law. They permitted local courts and juries to turn "virtually any act" by a free African American into an offense that warranted a legitimized immediate violent rebuke, which otherwise would have been a crime or a breach of the peace if the parties were of the same race.¹⁵¹

It is not clear if O'Neall and Pearson thought that their *Harden* and *Jowers* opinions truly were legal innovations establishing new criminal law norms for cases of violence between whites and free Blacks, or that they were merely extending to racial status established common-law principles of criminal law inequality based on social status. In either event, however, these jurists legitimated the prevailing white elites' customs and attitudes, which they asserted compelled them to use the criminal law to prevent and punish free Black insolence and promote white supremacy.¹⁵²

CHAPTER 6

The Louisiana and Virginia Statutes Criminalizing Insolence

Antebellum statutes—including the 1806 Louisiana Black Code, the 1819 and 1849 Virginia Codes, the 1856 Texas Criminal Code, and the 1860 Georgia Code, as well as the 1850s Richmond city ordinances—evidence public support among white southerners for the *Harden* and *Jowers* separate and unequal criminal law principle. These enactments either criminalized free Black insolence or decriminalized white violent responses to this insolence, as permitted by the *Harden/Jowers* doctrine, by analogy to the means that were used to control enslaved people.[1]

This chapter analyzes the Louisiana and Virginia statutes that made free Black insolence a crime to be prosecuted and punished in the courts, within contexts including evidence of the enactments' legislative history and their enforcement. Judge A. Leon Higginbotham labeled Virginia "The Leader" in the creation of colonial British North American enslavement law.[2] Virginia law did impose on free Blacks enhanced taxes, legal duties, and other restrictions, while denying them many legal rights that whites enjoyed.[3] But Louisiana, in 1806, first criminalized free Black insolence. Virginia's legislators later enacted this strategy as the preferred way to enforce white supremacy and Black subordination.

The Louisiana Codes' Context

The land that became the state of Louisiana was part of the territory that was controlled by France from 1712 to 1763, and then by Spain from 1763 until 1803, when France regained and sold it to the United States. These shifts in colonial administration influenced Louisiana's unique social and legal history.[4]

The colony's enslaved population grew slowly when it first was under French control. But enslaved workers later turned Louisiana's wetlands into vast rice and sugar fields, creating an economy and society analogous to the Caribbean model of large-scale plantation agriculture.[5] Consequently, the colony's enslaved population, in 1763 and 1785, grew to about 51 percent of the total, and between 1810 and 1860, it was between 45 and 47 percent. Louisiana also was the state with the largest median slave holdings of 38.9 and 49.3 in 1850 and 1860, respectively.[6]

In contrast, Louisiana's free people of color, as they were called, were not "a distinct and sizable class until the late 18th century." But, between 1803 and 1806, Louisiana's free persons of color population doubled in size, "and by 1810 it doubled again." Moreover, by 1810, in New Orleans, free persons of color made up 27.7 percent of the city's total population, which was only 36.7 percent white.[7] These patterns of population growth, along with the reports of the Haitian Revolution, created a climate of "distrust and fears" among the colony's whites. This was the social context for the adoption of the 1806 Black Code.[8]

Louisiana's French and Spanish colonial heritage also influenced its antebellum positive written law and its legal culture. The lawmakers in both of these empires enacted enslavement law codes for their colonies. The Spanish laws were based on provisions in the thirteenth-century Castilian legal code *Las Siete Partidas de Rey don Alfonso el Sabio*, which was promulgated by Alfonso X (Alfonso the Wise). It was cited as a source of law even after Louisiana became a state in 1812.[9] French colonial enslavement law originated with Louis XIV's March 1685 statute that later became known as the *Code Noir*. This was "the first integrated slave code written specifically for the Americas." Its provisions were "derived from customary practices already developed in the colonies since the 1630s," and it was the product of "a collaborative effort by colonial officials and Catholic missionaries, modified by input from royal officials in Versailles."[10] A revised *Code Noir* for Louisiana followed in 1724 under Louis XV, as "the Crown looked to the islands to determine how to govern Louisiana."[11] After Louisiana became a Spanish colony in 1760 and a U.S. territory in 1803, its white legislators adopted modified versions of the Spanish and French slave codes, later with "massive amounts of American slave law . . . directly introduced."[12]

Criminalizing Black Insolence

Evidence that whites in French colonial Louisiana perceived insolence from nonwhites to be a problem requiring a legislative response dates back to 1745, when Charles Lemoine, a cabinetmaker, instituted a complaint "against a negro named Raphael and his wife Fanchon." Lemoine alleged that the defendants "attacked him and insulted him without cause, and had him followed and pelted by their children." He asked "for interposition" of the attorney general because Lemoine "often has to work near them on a conveyance."[13] Two years later, Etienne La Rue, a "free mulatto" ship captain, while walking in New Orleans "on the levee in the region of Dumaine Street," met three soldiers, one of whom addressed La Rue "bonsoir seigneur negritte," which was translated as "good night Lord Little Negro." The soldiers alleged that La Rue responded "Goodnight, Lord Jean foutre," which was translated, "Good evening, Mr. Jack Fool," an allegation that La Rue denied. After the exchange of more words, one of the soldiers felt free to strike La Rue. Nevertheless, La Rue was arrested, when it was discovered that he was carrying two pistols. La Rue was convicted for illegally carrying these weapons. It is not reported whether the soldier was charged for striking La Rue.[14]

Likely in response to cases like these, Governor Pierre François de Rigaud, Marquis de Vaudreuil, and the King's Counselor, Michel de la Rouvillière, made Black insolence a crime, according to article 28 of the February 18, 1751, "Regulation of Police."[15] That article states, "Any negro or other slave, either in town or in the country, who shall fail in the respect and submission which he owes to white people—that is to say, who may be so insolent as to elbow them on the high roads and public ways, and who, finally, forgetting that he is a slave, shall offend them in any way whatsoever, shall be punished with fifty lashes, and shall be branded with the flower de Luce on his back (sur la fesse), in order to make known, in case of need, the nature of his crime."[16] This article appears to be limited to "Negro or other" enslaved people. But article 23 unambiguously seeks to disarm free Blacks as well, when it states, "Any Negro who shall be met in the streets or public road, carrying a cane, a rod, or a stick, shall be chastised by the first white man who shall meet him, with the very same instrument found in the possession of said Negro; and should said Negro be daring enough to defend himself or run away, it shall be the duty of the white man to denounce the fact, in order that the black man be punished according to the exigencies of the case."[17] This provision therefore enacts what became the *Harden/Jowers* principle authorizing immediate white violent responses to Black insolence.

The Louisiana Territory's three laws that are known as the Black Code, enacted in 1806 and 1807, endorsed a different approach that extended to free Blacks the crime of insolence. Section 40 of "An Act Prescribing the Rules and Conduct to Be Observed with Respect to Negroes and Other Slaves of This Territory, Approved, June 7, 1806," states, "Free people of color ought never to insult or strike white people, nor presume to conceive themselves equal to whites; but on the contrary that they ought to yield to them in every occasion, and never speak or answer to them but with respect, under the penalty of imprisonment according to the nature of the offense."[18] Vernon Valentine Palmer concludes that, with this and other provisions, the Territorial Legislature "effectively recognized a three-caste society and targeted free persons of color in new discriminatory ways."[19] This legal order was intended to declare "that free persons of color were legally inferior and subordinate to whites."[20]

Other discriminatory laws, which became more restrictive during the antebellum era, required free persons of color to carry certificates evidencing their freedom, increased the number of capital crimes for free Blacks, prohibited the immigration of free Blacks, prohibited interracial marriage, and required that legal documents refer to free persons of color as "f.m.c." or "f.w.c." To limit the number of free Blacks, the legislature adopted laws regulating manumission, and in 1857, it prohibited all in-state manumissions.[21] And an 1859 law, following the trend set three years earlier by Virginia, established a procedure for free Blacks to "voluntarily" enter into self-enslavement.[22]

Historian Judith Schafer found evidence that the crime of insolent insulting was enforced in New Orleans, where the "First District Court heard dozens of 'insulting' cases between 1846 and 1862, and the recorders' courts heard even more." In these cases, "the usual penalty for conviction of 'insulting' involved a week or so in parish prison or the workhouse and the payment of court costs."[23] She cited two sample prosecutions from 1847. Julia Black, who was labeled a prostitute, allegedly "called a white woman a 'Huzzy [sic] and old whore & a bitch.'" And Maurice Charles, during a ten-day period, allegedly insulted two men in French and English, "calling one a '*fils de putain*' and an '*enfant de garce*' (a son of a whore and a child of a naughty woman) and another a 'son of a bitch.'"[24]

Nevertheless, these prosecutions "did little to dissuade those who wished to insult white persons."[25] For example, the *Daily Picayune* reported, on October 29, 1852, that "two free negro women, named Eudoxia and Annetta, were charged before recorder Genoia with having uttered the most gross and filthy abuse against and in the presence of Auguste Sylvain and his wife, who reside in Barrick street." The newspaper commented, "There is a stringent law on this subject, which would be well suited to some of these cases of insult." The paper prefaced its story with the following editorial: "This practice has become quite too common in almost all parts of the city. Negroes have been allowed so many liberties that in many cases they now take advantage of it, and frequently vent their dirty abuse on white persons, that they imagine are helpless. Most of the cases which have come to our knowledge lately have been those where white ladies of respectability have been grossly abused at their residences, while the male portion of the family were [away] from home."[26] And it was reported on September 8, 1855, that "Mary Douglas, f.w.c., was arraigned before Recorder Bright . . . on a charge of incessantly and outrageously abusing Mrs. Mercie Gonzales, her daughter, and their servants, at No. 109 Carondelet street." The recorder required Douglas to furnish four hundred dollars' bail.[27] The *Daily Picayune* added that, four days later, Douglas, "whose impertinence to her white neighbors . . . has recently become utterly unbearable, was fined no less than $25."[28]

These public expressions of white frustration with the perceived ineffectiveness of these repressive measures suggest that some whites may have favored the O'Neall and Pearson model that bypassed the courts and legitimized individual white violent responses to alleged insolence. But Louisiana's insolence laws remained unchanged.

The Virginia Codes' Context

Virginia's colonial and antebellum laws are consistent with the Louisiana approach criminalizing insolence. According to Ellen Eslinger, "No part of the United States exhibited a greater interest in regulating free people of color than did the state of Virginia."[29] Virginia, in 1790, was the state with the largest Black population, but for the colonial period this population total can only be estimated. It was about 1,800 in 1782, and by 1790 it had increased to 12,766, in part because the legislature adopted a 1782 act removing the restrictions that it, in 1723, had placed on the enslavers' right to free their slaves. Virginia's free Black population continued to grow to more than 58,000 in 1860. Nevertheless, free Blacks in 1790 were only 1.7 percent of the state's total population, while the enslaved population percentage was 39.1. The free Black percentage rose to 2.3 in 1800, to 3.1 in 1810, to 3.7 in 1820, to 3.9 in 1830, and to 4.0 in 1840, but it fell to 3.8 in 1850 and then to 3.6 in 1860.[30]

These population trends influenced and were influenced by Virginia's laws that sought to limit the number of free Blacks, including a 1793 provision prohibiting free Black migration into the state and requiring free Blacks to register in the municipality where they worked or resided.[31] The legislature, in 1806, rejected proposals to ban all manumissions, but it required freed slaves to leave the state within twelve months or risk the possibility of re-enslavement. In the following decades, laws permitted various exceptions to this exclusion.[32]

The legislature also imposed racially discriminatory rules and restrictions on free Blacks, including provisions regulating their use of guns. Historians have traced this trend to a January 1639/1640 "Act for Arming Persons," which states, "All persons except negroes to be provided with arms and ammunition or be fined at the pleasure of the Governor and Council."[33] Paul Finkelman explains that this act "required all white males, including servants, be provided with arms for militia service. However, the law exempted 'negroes' from this mandatory rule." He thus concludes, "The law did not preclude arming blacks to help defend against Indian attacks, but simply did not require it. This law may have reflected the fear of arming Africans, who were in Virginia against their will, and presumptively hostile to those who controlled their labor."[34]

A racially discriminatory 1723 gun control provision also evidenced these white fears. It stated that "no negro, mulatto, or Indian whatsoever; (except as is hereafter excepted,) shall hereafter presume to keep, or carry any gun, powder, shot, or any club, or other weapon whatsoever, offensive or defensive." The statute exempted a person who was "a house-keeper, or listed in the militia," who "may be permitted to keep one gun, powder, and shot," and a person "living at any frontier plantation," who was "permitted to keep and use guns, powder, and shot, or other weapons, offensive or defensive"; but only after "having first obtained a licence for the same, from some justice of the peace of the county wherein such plantations lie." Violators were subject to confiscation of their weapons and "any number of lashes, not exceeding thirty-nine, well laid on, on his or her bare back, for every such offence."[35] A March 15, 1832, act likewise declared, "No free negro or mulatto shall be suffered to keep or carry any firelock of any kind, any military weapon, or any powder or lead." But this act also divested the court's jurisdiction to grant licenses to free Blacks, although the legislature at times later adopted special legislation authorizing licenses.[36] Even the acts that allowed some free Blacks to obtain white permission to bear arms continued to "impose 'a perpetual brand' on blacks as different and inferior to whites."[37]

Other colonial and antebellum laws further imposed this brand of inferiority. Free Blacks were denied political rights after the adoption of a 1723 law providing that "no negro, mullatto [sic], or indian [sic] whatsoever" could vote in any elections.[38] An 1823 law even authorized that free Blacks who were convicted of crimes that were to be punished by jail terms of more than two years instead be sold into enslavement and transported out of the United States. The Virginia General Court, in 1824, rejected a constitutional challenge to this law. According to Daniel Flanigan, forty-four free Blacks were sentenced to slavery in the four years before the statute was repealed.[39] And a year after the 1831 Nat

Turner Rebellion, Virginia followed South Carolina's example and extended the jurisdiction of its inferior oyer and terminer courts to try free Black defendants, except for those who were accused of homicide or other crimes punishable by death.[40]

Virginia's 1819 and 1849 Codes and Insolence

Virginia's anti-insolence laws also evidence this anti–free Black legal trend. These laws' origins can be traced back to one of the provisions enacted in a 1680 statute titled "An Act for Preventing Negroes Insurrections." The act begins with the legislative finding that "the frequent meeting of considerable numbers of negroe slaves under pretence of feasts and burialls is judged of dangerous consequence." One provision states "that if any negroe or other slave shall presume to lift up his hand in opposition against any christian, [he] shall for every such offence, upon due proofe made thereof by the oath of the party before a magistrate, have and receive thirty lashes on his bare back well laid on."[41] The act's mention of "negroes or other slaves" apparently refers to native American slavery, which then was still authorized by Virginia's statutes.[42]

In addition to denying enslaved people the privilege of self-defense in response to the violence of any Christian, this act disarmed and restricted the mobility rights of "any negroe or other slave." According to Judge Higginbotham, this law "would become the model of repression throughout the South for the next 180 years." He contended that it illustrates the "codification of prejudice and the degree to which the statute attempted to make sure that the blacks would be recognized as legally inferior." Higginbotham concluded that, with enactment of these provisions, "the dehumanization process was complete because blacks were legally precluded from responding in a manner thought normal for whites or most human beings."[43]

The statute does not, however, expressly deny the self-defense privilege to free Blacks. The legislators cured that ambiguity in the more comprehensive 1705 law titled "An Act Concerning Servants and Slaves." According to the last sentence in that act's section 34, "any negro, mulatto, or Indian, *bond or free*, [who] shall at any time, lift his or her hand, in opposition against any Christian, not being negro, mulatto . . . shall, for every such offence, proved by the oath of the party, receive on his or her bare back, thirty lashes, well laid on." These charges were "cognizable by a justice of the peace for that county wherein such offence shall be committed."[44] The statute therefore prohibited any lifting of the hand that might even suggest that a free Black person was asserting the self-defense privilege against a white Christian; to that extent it denied to free

Blacks "the right to defend themselves in the streets."[45] Even "white strangers were immune from criminal prosecution for merely striking" free and enslaved Blacks.[46]

This act also required the justice of the peace to convict the defendant on only the oath of the complaining witness.[47] The Kentucky Court of Appeals, in 1820, found that a similar provision in a Kentucky act violated the state's constitution. Justice Benjamin Mills reasoned that the statute impermissibly "subjects free persons of color to punishment, on the oath of the party, without trial, and without the possibility of contradicting and disproving [that party's] statements."[48]

Almost ninety years passed before Virginia's legislature extended a limited self-defense privilege to Blacks. A December 17, 1792, statute excluded from the mandatory whipping any "negro or mulatto, bond or free" who lifted a hand in "his or her defence [sic]" after being "wantonly assaulted" by "any person not being a negro or mulatto." This act would most likely have been of limited effect, however, because free and enslaved Blacks could not testify against the oath of the complaining white person.[49] This revision may have been occasioned by cases in which enslaved people fought off the wanton attacks of third parties to the enslaver and enslaved relationship, including overseers. In one of these cases, an enslaved man named Moses was acquitted at a January 1791 trial on the charge that he murdered his enslaver's overseer.[50]

The Richmond, Virginia, prosecution of Albert Brown demonstrates the limits of the self-defense privilege. Brown worked as a "lump maker" in a tobacco factory. Richmond's longtime mayor Joseph C. Mayo convicted Brown in the Mayor's Court on the charge that Brown assaulted and beat William M. Read, an overseer. Brown had hired "as the stemmer, a small boy," who "frequently" violated the factory's timeliness rules. On April 11, 1857, Reed declared that he was going to "chastise" the boy for his tardiness. Brown "stepped forward to protect the boy." Reed ordered Brown "to go about his business and by main force [Brown] took" the boy from Reed. Reed then retrieved "a stick to punish Brown, when Brown ran up behind, seized him by the arms, gave him a violent blow to the side of the head with a stick or his flat fist, thew him on the floor, and then ran off." Mayor Mayo found Brown guilty and ordered that he be punished with thirty-nine stripes to teach "him his proper place, as well as to let him know that no negro would be allowed to lay his hands, in violence, upon a white man, unless to save his own life." Brown appealed this conviction to the Hustings Court, which ordered him to post bail of $150 to guarantee his later appearance. No further reports of the case could be found.[51]

It was not until March 12, 1819, however, that the legislature adopted another amendment to this law criminalizing a form of verbal free Black insolence. That amendment was included in the Revised Code of the Laws of Virginia. Benjamin Watkins Leigh, one of five judges and lawyers whom the legislature authorized to prepare the code, stated that it, for the most part, compiled the state's existing laws.[52] But the revisors and the legislature inserted text into this code prohibiting the "use of abusive and provoking language" by "any negro or mulatto bond or free," before the existing text banning hand lifting. This revision thus added the utterance of insolent words to the types of cases in which justices of the peace could inflict on free Blacks "such punishment as the justice shall think proper, not to exceed thirty lashes, on his or her bare back, well laid on."[53] Substantially similar provisions were adopted in 1822 in Mississippi and in 1828 in Florida.[54]

The Virginia legislature modified this crime of insolence in a comprehensive March 14, 1848, criminal law revision titled "An Act to Reduce into One the Several Acts Concerning Crimes and Punishments and Proceedings in Criminal Cases." That law's chapter 13, titled "Of Certain Offences by Free Negroes and Mulattoes," listed the use by a "free negro or mulatto" of "provoking language or menacing gestures to a white person" among the offences for which the offender "shall be punished with stripes not exceeding thirty-nine."[55] The Virginia Codes of 1849 and 1860, in chapter 200, reenacted this prohibition, while permitting the judges or justices hearing these cases to determine the number of stripes "not to exceed thirty-nine at one time."[56]

White antipathy to free Blacks intensified by the 1850s, culminating with 1856 and 1861 laws establishing streamlined procedures for free Blacks to request court approved self-enslavement. And an 1860 law once again included "sale into absolute slavery" as a punishment that the courts could impose, instead of a term in the penitentiary, after free Blacks were convicted of crimes.[57]

Enforcing the Prohibition of Insolence

As in Louisiana, these statutes were enforced against enslaved and free Black men and women. In the decade before the Civil War, Richmond's *Daily Dispatch* newspaper routinely published reports of prosecutions, while using biased, derogatory, or condescending language. For example, a September 1854 report stated that "Catharine Scott, a free negress," was charged with "using provoking language to Jane Perkins, a white woman, and threatening to kill her." Scott was convicted and sentenced to "the application of a cow-hide to the prisoner's back fifteen times, by way of teaching her better manners."[58] And in April 1857, it was gleefully reported, in a story titled "Northern Ebo [sic] with Southern Stripes," that "[a] free negro from New York calling himself Hutchinson Allen" was convicted on the "charge of using insolent and provoking language to Captain William Ruhl, on whose vessel [Allen] was employed. The evidence was so conclusive that the prisoner was sent below for a striped jacket, which was made to fit him in short order."[59] The usual reported result was a whipping of the accused.[60] But on occasion, either the complaining party withdrew the charges or the case was dismissed.[61]

According to Ervin Jordan, prosecutions continued even during the Civil War. For example, in November 1864, "a Richmond judge" imposed a sentence of "thirty lashes" on Lizzie Burns, of Charlottesville, a free Black "waiting maid for the Virginia Central Railroad." Her crime was directing "uncomplimentary remarks at one of the male passengers." And in 1865 in Richmond, Allen Tyree, "a free black, earned the usual number of stripes for impudence." Jordan also cites the 1863 Richmond arrest of James Roberts "for using threatening and abusive language to a white man, Timothy Callahan. Callahan testified that a drunken Roberts appeared before his home 'ripping and cutting up.'" Roberts responded to an order to leave by cursing Callahan "as 'a damned white livered son of a bitch,' and declared that he was not afraid of any 'damned white man.'" Roberts defended himself by stating that he was employed by Talbott's Foundry and "was not to blame because white coworkers had gotten him drunk."[62]

The Richmond Context and Ordinances

These statewide anti-insolence laws were not thought to be sufficient by the white leaders of Richmond, which was Virginia's largest antebellum city. According to Joshua Rothman, Richmond became the state's capital in 1779, and this designation "brought both people and business to the city, which was just over a square mile in size and housed around 1,000 people in 1782. By 1790 roughly 3,700 people lived in Richmond. Half the population was black, and over 90 percent of the black population was enslaved. By 1810 Richmond had expanded to 2.4 square miles—a size the city would remain until after the Civil War—and had seen its population explode to nearly 10,000."[63] Free Blacks seeking employment opportunities relocated to Richmond from the state's rural areas. Women found work in the laundry business and as domestics, and men, along with hired male slaves, worked in the city's tobacco factories, iron foundries, and flour mills, as well as in other trades and occupations. The city's economy stagnated after the Panic of 1819, but it rebounded in the 1840s and

1850s. The free Black population therefore increased from 1,235 in 1820, to 2,369 in 1850, and to 2,756 in 1860, but its growth rate was slower than that of the city's white and enslaved populations. Accordingly, the city's percentage of free Blacks fell from about 10 percent of the total in 1820, to 8.59 percent in 1850, and to 6.79 percent in 1860. The enslaved population, in contrast, remained at about 36 percent of the totals in 1820 and 1850, but it also declined in 1860 to about 30 percent of the total population.[64]

In response to the effects of this population growth, the city's Common Council, in May 1830, reorganized the city's police force and created a new court, called the Mayor's Court or the sunrise court. It served "as a filter for the Hustings Court." The mayor held hearings each morning for defendants who were arrested the night before or earlier that morning. He adjudicated cases involving minor offenses and referred the more serious matters to the Hustings Court for further proceedings. Mayor Joseph Tate presided over this court for thirteen years. According to Rothman, court records from this period do not exist, except for the years 1836 to 1839. He found that Mayor Tate resolved many cases in an informal manner, especially for white defendants who could pay fines "on the spot." In contrast, the "standard punishment for both slaves and free blacks consisted of lashes, meaning that in most cases when they were caught committing a crime they were held over to appear before the mayor in the morning." Although the court's proceedings reflect "its race and class biases," Rothman concludes that its "docket nonetheless offers a vivid sense of the rough and often riotous texture of Richmond's interracial streets, and indicates how deeply sex and sexual tensions across racial lines were interwoven with everyday life in Virginia's capital."[65]

Rothman cites several cases from these records in which enslaved and free Blacks were prosecuted for uttering mere words that whites found to be insolent. For example, Mary Fulcher, a white woman, alleged that an enslaved woman named Betsy Randal directed "violent and insolent" language at her on Independence Day 1838. According to Fulcher, "much of Randal's language was too vulgar to repeat to Mayor Tate, but [she] did mention that Randal called her a 'liar whore.'" Although Ann Thomas testified that she did not ever hear Randal call Fulcher names, Tate found that Randal was guilty. He imposed a sentence of ten lashes.[66] Tate also sentenced to ten lashes an enslaved woman named Betsey, on the complaint of a white man named Christian Freyfoyle. He alleged that Betsey used "abusive and provoking language" as he walked in the street with his young adopted daughter, whom Betsey called "a bastard."[67]

In May of the same year, a white woman named Nancy Abrahams alleged that Letty Hamilton, "a free woman of color," called her "a nasty poor bitch."

Abrahams claimed that Hamilton also said that she "had a white man for her husband which was more than she (Mrs. A.) had." Rothman concludes that this suggestion, which "impugned the racial purity of Nancy Abraham's husband," may have been true. She refused to appear in court and testify, stating this "twas the last thing she would like to do, and that if the woman conducted herself properly in [the] future she would not press her complaint." Rothman explained, "When parties to a conflict appeared before Mayor Tate, he often questioned them in an effort to determine the cause of the dispute. In this case, he surely would have probed into Nancy Abrahams's life and the racial background of her husband, which might have forced Mrs. Abrahams to admit embarrassing racial facts publicly."[68] In contrast, in July 1838, Tate found that he did not have jurisdiction to hear slander cases, when a white cotton factory worker named Mary Ann Ferris and her mother alleged that Mary Smith, another worker in the factory, "told many men and woman that Ferris was hermaphroditic." It also was alleged that "Smith and three other factory girls threw [Ferris] on her back in the bathroom to inspect her genitalia."[69]

Suzanne Lebsock includes evidence of similar anti-insolence enforcement proceedings in her study of antebellum Petersburg, which, in 1860, was Virginia's second-largest city.[70] For example, in September 10, 1856, the *South-Side Democrat* reported the prosecution of Esther Fells. She allegedly "made the mistake of talking back to a white neighbor named Thomas Tucker, who had been disturbed by the noise coming from Fell's house. Tucker took it upon himself to give Fells 'three cuts with a cowhide' and then had her taken to jail." The city's mayor ordered that Fells receive "fifteen lashes more 'for being insolent to a white person.'"[71] Two months later, the *Daily Express* reported that two free "negresses," Polly Hill and Athele Brander, were "arraigned for abusing Mrs. Jacob Crowder." Crowder claimed that Brander "spoke disrespectfully of her, and she threatened to crack her head." Brander "then grew very wroth," and said, among other things, that she would not accept this physical abuse, "especially [from] such 'poor white folks' as Mrs. C." Crowther also alleged that "both of the accused had often abused her, and she wished to put a stop to it. The mayor ordered the two girls down for ten stripes each."[72]

Anti-insolence enforcement intensified in the 1850s in Richmond, when the city's first penny newspaper, the *Daily Dispatch*, began regular local news reporting.[73] Its pages reflect the views of many of the city's whites, who began showing "much less tolerance for urban disorder."[74] Moreover, in 1853 Joseph C. Mayo began his long tenure as mayor, which included terms before, during, and after the Civil War. "Mayo adopted far more aggressive strategies than Joseph Tate ever had."[75]

Consistent with this trend, the Richmond City Council, in the 1850s, began adopting ordinances prohibiting various forms of free Black conduct, which were even more restrictive than the state's laws. These provisions were codified in 1857 and 1859.[76] Among these was a provision that prohibited what were perceived examples of insolence:

> If any negro use provoking language, or use or make insolent or menacing gestures to a white person, or speak aloud any blasphemous or indecent word, or make any loud or offensive noise by conversation or otherwise, in any street or other public place, or shall indecently expose his person, or any part thereof, to public view in this city, he shall, if a slave, be punished by stripes, or if a free negro, either by stripes, or be fined not less than one nor more than twenty dollars, at the discretion of the justice trying the offence.[77]

Rothman explains that this was among the provisions addressing

> long-standing concerns about slaves without passes, walking on any public grounds (such as Capitol Square), and purchasing and consuming liquor, while other sections dealt with the illegality of slaves hiring themselves out, boarding, and possessing cash. The ordinance also reaffirmed a set of restrictions designed to keep free people of color and slaves from associating with one another in public or private places, and to remind both groups of their inferiority relative to whites. Blacks were not only forbidden from gathering together in groups larger than five (except for church services), but they could not ride in a carriage or public hack, smoke tobacco in public, carry a cane, or maintain a cookshop of any sort.[78]

According to Richard Wade, these ordinances are a "convenient model" of the types of enslavement law regulations enacted in the more urban environments.[79]

The *Daily Dispatch*, using racist and derogatory language, repeatedly reported on prosecutions enforcing these ordinances.[80] Examples of these reports include a February 27, 1856, story asserting that "Frances Ann Rowlett, a good for nothing free negro, was ordered by the Mayor yesterday, a small taste of what Paddy gave the drum, for threatening personal violence and using insolent language towards Elizabeth F. Adams, a white woman, on Monday last."[81] On October 5, 1856, the paper stated that "Lucy Tyree, a foul-mouthed free negress, was convicted before the Mayor last Saturday of using dirty, abusive and threatening language to Mary Lewis and besides getting a dose of stripes to the number fifteen, was held to bail for her good behavior."[82] A November 25, 1857, item reported that "Mary Maxfield, a free woman, was ordered fifteen stripes, for being insolent to Mrs. Kenny."[83] And, according to a January 18, 1858, story,

Jane Goings, "a free woman," failed to appear and forfeited her bail in response to the charge that she was "insolent to Thos. Brooks. . . . Jane, it is said, left her home at an early hour on Friday morning, telling her friends that she would rather throw her carcass into the river and become food for the fish, than to suffer the flagellation which she deserves for her impudent language."[84] Goings was eventually brought to court by her bond surety, but the complaining witness evidently did not appear in court to testify.[85]

The everyday patterns of interracial encounters on Richmond's sidewalks offered free African Americans a potential for relative freedom and integration. But this prospect prompted the City Council, in the 1850s, to adopt ordinances prohibiting specific acts that whites considered to be Black insolence, which was encouraged by interracial contact or mixing in the public rights of way.[86] One Richmond ordinance provision regulating the use of the public sidewalks stated, "Not more than five negroes shall at any one time stand together on a side-walk at or near the corner of a street or public alley. And negroes shall not at any time stand on a side-walk to the inconvenience of persons passing by. A negro meeting or overtaking, or being overtaken by a white person on a side-walk, shall pass on the outside; and if it be necessary to enable such white person to pass, shall immediately get off the side-walk." The ordinance also declared that free Blacks violating this provision "may be punished with stripes."[87] According to Ira Berlin, this type of regulation was consistent with a late antebellum trend, by which "new legislation gnawed at the freedman's already limited liberty."[88] It also is a racially discriminatory example of the trend that William Novak explained, in which "expanding public powers over public ways involved the regulation of an increased range of social and economic activities deemed hostile to the people's welfare, including public morality and public health."[89]

The *Dispatch* often reported on Mayor Mayo's efforts to enforce the sidewalk use ordinance provisions, and it called for more rigorous enforcement by the city's officials. Some of the complaints objected to groups of free or enslaved Blacks congregating on the sidewalks.[90] Many others cited the apparent refusal of free Blacks to step to the outside of or off the sidewalks when they approached or were approached by whites.[91] For example, a May 25, 1859, story titled "Protecting Ladies" stated that the mayor

> directed his officers to arrest and bring before him all women of color found in the public streets refusing to give the sidewalk to ladies, when meeting or passing them. He has declared his determination to punish all negresses, however finely dressed, who offend against the ordinances of this city, and to let them know their

proper places. Complaints had been made to him of rudeness to ladies on Main and Broad streets, by certain mulattoes, and he is bent on finding them out and giving them a few lessons in good manners."[92]

A similar September 24, 1857, item titled "Warning to Negroes" reported of the mayor's complaint that "ladies were frequently elbowed out of the way by well dressed mulatto women," and that he "directed the officers to bring all such before him to, to get the lash." Furthermore, the article called on "private citizens" to help the police so that "negroes would soon learn their duty and perform it."[93] The paper also published the sidewalk ordinance, along with warnings to free Blacks, and called for enforcement.[94]

Moreover, the *Dispatch* began to complain that city officials were failing to adequately enforce the sidewalk ordinances. Accordingly, a November 17, 1857, item, titled "Not Enforced," lamented that "ladies continue to be elbowed from the walkways by both sexes of the ebo [sic] tribe." The piece reported, "Two ladies were forced from the sidewalks on Governor street yesterday morning by a negro fellow, who became very insolent to a gentleman that saw the occurrence." The public was assured that "steps will be taken to get him before the Mayor."[95]

These assurances were beginning to be seen as inadequate to the *Dispatch*'s editors and by some in the city's white community, who took the law into their own hands. A January 24, 1860, article reflected this frustration. It reprinted the relevant sidewalk ordinance provisions and noted, "The difficulty in enforcing the ordinance . . . arises from the fact that ladies are always averse to appearing as witnesses in a court of justice." The author suggests that this "may readily be obviated by calling the attention of some gentleman to the rudeness offered them, and let them make the complaint."[96]

The Virginia courts never decided whether white strangers should be afforded the common-law privilege to commit simple assaults and batteries against people enslaved by others. The General Court evaded the issue in its 1841 decision in *Commonwealth v. Howard*.[97] The court sustained the indictment of the defendant Howard for "violently and inhumanely assaulting and beating" an unnamed enslaved woman who was "the property of John Hill." But according to Judge Abel P. Upshur's opinion, the court did not need to address the unsettled common-law assault and battery issue because the indictment was based upon an 1823 statute that protected real and personal property rights.[98] That act included a section that added the following offenses to the misdemeanors that "may be prosecuted and punished as in other cases of misdemeanor at the common law": "That any person who shall knowingly and wilfully, without lawful authority, cut down any tree growing on the land of another, or destroy or injure any such tree, or any building, fence or other improvement, or the soil or growing crop on the land of another; or shall knowingly and wilfully, without lawful authority, but not feloniously, take and carry away, or destroy or injure, any tree already cut, or any other timber, or property, real or personal, belonging to another."[99] Upshur cited with approval an 1834 opinion suggesting that this statute applied to a defendant who shot and killed hogs belonging to another person.[100]

Therefore, the May 28, 1857, *Dispatch* reported on a case of what would have been a battery if it had committed on a white man. The victim was an enslaved man named David Frazier, who was accused of "using insolent and provoking language to N. B. Dickenson." Dickenson asserted what he apparently thought was his white privilege to commit common-law assault and battery, when he freely admitted "that he gave the boy a blow over the head with a stick, and an examination showed that he had punished him severely." Mayor Mayo "discharged the accused, on the ground that the complainant had taken the law into his own hands and inflicted punishment." He is not reported to have condemned Dickenson's action. He instead "remarked that he was at all times ready to have servants corrected for insolence to white persons," but held that he would not order the whipping of "a prisoner after the complainant had taken the punishment into his own hands."[101]

Some of the city's whites thus apparently began to support the *Harden/Jowers* approach granting individual whites the privilege to respond immediately and violently to Black insolence. The *Dispatch* reported, on December 12, 1856, that as "two ladies were passing down the North sidewalk of Broad street, near the creek, they were met by a negro fellow, who wilfully jostled one of them from the pavement, and then became very impudent on being complained of. A gentleman who happened to be passing at the time, went to the protection of the ladies, and gave the fellow a severe beating for his conduct, cutting his head badly in several places, and otherwise bruising his person." The article did not condemn the "gentleman" for inflicting this battery, although it did suggest that "enforcement of the ordinance would prevent such difficulties."[102] Almost three years later, the *Dispatch* again reported that "ladies are very much annoyed in the streets by well dressed negresses, so far from giving a portion of the sidewalk, when met, take all, rudely forcing their neighbors in the streets." The paper warned that if the ordinance were not enforced, "gentlemen, whose wives and daughters are continually insulted in the streets, will take the law into their own hands, and teach the offenders better manners."[103]

Ordinances like the Richmond Code, Richard Wade notes, "might provide a legal blueprint for the numberless encounters and the courts punish[ed] any transgressions; yet the functioning of daily affairs rested on the broader subjugation of the Negro to the white, and observance of the smallest matters seemed almost as crucial as the acceptance of slavery itself." Both enslaved and free Blacks were "never allowed to forget [their] servitude whenever a white man was near."[104] Despite the best efforts of the City Council and Mayor Mayo, however, the *Dispatch*'s pages confirmed that Richmond's free Blacks did not all accept these white norms of subjugation; to the contrary, some acted as if they had the same rights as whites. Ira Berlin explains that in the cities "whites and blacks lived in close proximity, often with little to distinguish their styles of life. Urban conditions simultaneously eroded much of the physical distinction between the way whites and blacks lived and shrank the social distance between the races."[105]

Although not expressly endorsing lynch law or vigilante justice, the *Dispatch* reported—with evident understanding—why Richmond's white residents took matters into their own hands when they were confronted with insolence. Joshua Rothman cites a September 1856 report of a white mob's raid on "a house kept by a white and black fellow," which was the site of "frequent assemblages of negroes and white men." The vigilantes believed "that the morals of their servants were suffering from the contaminating influences exerted upon them by designing persons, and that their hen roosts, larders and cellars were heavily taxed to pay liquor bills." Residents of the affected Church Hill neighborhood allegedly complained to the police. But after receiving no relief, a mob surrounded the house, "captured the negroes present, subjected them to a course of sprouts, and gave the white man moving orders." If he did not vacate the premises, as directed, "he is to be paid another visit, and will then fare no better than his dark associates have already done." The *Dispatch* warned of the dangers of vigilante justice, but added the caveat, "If any people in the world are justifiable in resorting to it, they are those whose slaves are being corrupted and ruined by cross road groggeries, where stolen goods are paid for in bad whiskey, and where the negro is taught to believe that to rob his owner is a virtue."[106]

Ira Berlin also notes that, two years later, the *Dispatch* reported on the arrest of a "notorious free negro, Clinton James, the keeper of a vile den in Pink Alley." He was charged with "keeping a cook shop or eating house," and "for permitting an unlawful assembly of negroes in his house on Saturday night." James, in 1853, also had been convicted on a similar charge of "keeping a cook shop," and he ultimately was unsuccessful on an appeal before the Court of Appeals. The *Dispatch* article suggests that it was "well known" that James was "was one of the agents of the underground railroad," which was why the mayor was "anxious to get rid of this fellow by some legal means." If this could not be accomplished, the editors warned, "no one need be surprised if the citizens themselves should take the matter in their own hands, and break up the vile nest in which has been hatched vice and villainy of almost every hue."[107]

Conclusion

Louisiana and Virginia legislators led the way in the quest for white supremacy with their laws criminalizing free Black insolence, a tactic that was copied in Mississippi and Florida. All of these laws can be interpreted in light of Markus Dirk Dubber's conceptual comparison of the law and the police.[108] Dubber does not limit his definition of police to modern law enforcement agencies. He instead understands the police as an expansive power of government, similar to the discretionary authority historically exercised by heads of households dating back to Ancient Greece.[109] He states that ill-defined legal concepts such as vagrancy have been used to restrain people and things that are perceived to pose threats of harm to the public health, safety, and welfare. Dubber contrasts this vagueness with the more well-defined rules and standards of social control and punishment found in the procedural and substantive criminal law.[110]

Dubber tellingly refers to American colonial enslavement law as "the most clear-cut illustration of police power before the invention of [post-independence] American 'police power,'" citing colonial plantation manuals and slave codes as enforcing the police in individual households and in the society.[111] The separate and unequal protection doctrine could be understood, in part, as a transfer of this police power from the heads of households to state actors who were authorized by law, under the vague crime of insolence, to control the perceived threats posed by enslaved and free Blacks.[112]

This police concept has an advantage in interpretation because it was a term used in the colonial and antebellum years. Nevertheless, the separate and unequal protection doctrine is a concept that better suggests how the law also decriminalized what otherwise would have been extralegal violent responses by white nonstate actors who were confronted with what they perceived to be insolence.

The sources discussed in this chapter also suggest that some whites were frustrated by free Black noncompliance with and resistance to the laws criminalizing insolence. This frustration may, in the future, have led other slave states to adopt the *Harden/Jowers* privilege. They may have found it to be more effective to explicitly legitimize the violent reactions of individual "gentlemen," who could not be expected to wait for the completion of the process ordinarily required by the rule of law.

CHAPTER 7

The Differing Texas and Georgia Legislative Responses to Insolence

Late antebellum Texas and Georgia statutory codes suggest that there was a debate among southerners about how best to use the criminal law to promote the policy of white supremacy by preventing the perceived threat of free Black insolence. The Texas Code of 1856 replaced the criminalization of insolence approach of an 1837 Republic of Texas law with the *Harden/Jowers* rule legitimizing individual acts of white violence in response to free Black insolence. But the Georgia Code, adopted seven years later, reverted back to the Louisiana and Virginia criminalization of insolence strategy. These codes are variations on the same theme, however; they both codified separate and unequal protection criminal law norms for enslaved and free Blacks.

The Texas Code's Context

Historian Randolph Campbell, more than thirty years ago, debunked the misunderstandings perpetuated in popular culture and history regarding the part that enslavement and large-scale cotton plantation agriculture played in the origins and early development of the state of Texas.[1] According to Annette Gordon-Reed, "'The father of Texas,' Stephen F. Austin," who was born in Virginia and raised in Missouri, "came to Texas not to create cattle ranches and hire cowboys, but to turn huge swaths of the Mexican province Coahuika y Tejas into a western version of the cotton fields of Mississippi that had produced such great wealth for plantation owners."[2] This territory's southeastern portion was "the perfect place" to transplant the plantation system; "the soil was amazingly fertile, the growing season was long, and there was access to the Gulf of Mexico for shipping harvested crops."[3]

The territory that became the slave state of Texas previously was included in Spain's vast colonial empire, where enslavement had long been permitted by law. After 1821, this land became a part of newly independent Mexico. Thanks in large part to the efforts of Moses Austin, and after his death his son Stephen F. Austin, Texas was increasingly populated by Anglo-American migrants from the southern United States. These immigrants imported enslaved people to raise and pick cotton, even after Mexico abolished slavery.[4]

Texas gained its independence from Mexico in 1836 and was an enslavers' republic until 1845, when it entered the Union as a slave state.[5] White immigrants from the southern United States continued to import more enslaved people to Texas. They also "brought with them a thorough familiarity with every aspect of the South's peculiar institution, including its legal framework."[6] With this legal framework in place, the Texas enslaved population grew from 58,161 in 1850, about 27 percent of the total population, to 182,566 in 1860, about 30 percent of the total. As in other slave states, the Texas enslaved population was not evenly distributed. Enslaved people, in 1850, were more than 50 percent of the total population in six eastern counties, and by 1860, thirteen eastern counties had more than 50 percent of the state's enslaved population. But in both years, some counties in western Texas had fewer than 25 percent enslaved inhabitants. The state's recorded free Black population was very small, however, and it declined from 397 in 1850 to 355 in 1860.[7]

This free Black population was depressed, at least in part, because the Texas constitution and its statutes protected slavery and enslavers' rights, while restricting free Black migration and legal rights.[8] The original March 1836 draft of the Texas Republic's constitution, following the example of the southern states, barred free Black migration into the new republic. But, as Jason Gillmer notes, the Texas founders "then took the additional step of forcing those already in Texas to leave." They proposed that the constitution state, "No free person of African descent, either in whole or in part, shall be permitted to reside permanently in the republic, without consent of congress."[9] The voters approved the constitutional text containing this mandate. Nevertheless, this exclusion was effectively amended after the Texas Republic's first congress, in June 1837, permitted free persons of color residing in Texas on the date of its Declaration of Independence to remain, while otherwise retaining the immigration ban.[10]

Nevertheless, another 1837 Republic of Texas law, titled "An Act to Provide for the Punishment of Crimes and Misdemeanors Committed by Slaves and Free Persons of Color," evidences the "disdain and distrust" that white Texans harbored for free Blacks.[11] This law's title and content also confirm that

Texas—from the start—afforded free and enslaved Blacks the separate and unequal protection of the criminal law. For example, this act criminalized insolence, in a provision stating "that if any slave or free person of color shall use insulting or abusive language to, or threaten any free white person, upon complaint thereof before any justice of the peace, such justice shall cause such negro to be arrested, and upon conviction, the slave or free person of color, shall be punished by stripes not exceeding one hundred or less than twenty-five."[12] The legislators also "grouped free people of color with slaves when they outlined the crimes worthy of capital punishment, including murder and the rape and attempted rape of a white woman." They even "threatened free people of color with slavery if they encouraged people held in bondage to rebel or escape."[13]

The legislature later responded to intensified white hostility to free Blacks with statutes limiting free Black migration and, for a time, even requiring that free Blacks be expelled from Texas.[14] In 1858, Texas joined the slave states that established a streamlined statutory process for free Blacks to enter into "voluntary" self-enslavement.[15] And the state's 1861 constitution prohibited Texas enslavers from freeing their slaves, both inside and outside of the state.[16]

Historian Kenneth Stampp cites an Austin, Texas, *State Gazette* September 1857 opinion piece as evidence of the then prevailing white bias against free Blacks.[17] The editor declared, "The existence of free negroes in any community has always been found a nuisance, even among the free soilers of the North; the complaints are loud against them." After reciting evidence allegedly supporting this perceived "nuisance," it was suggested, "The time is near at hand for determined action. The free negro in the South is evidently destined to be remitted back into slavery, which is his true condition. It is now fully realized that emancipation for services rendered is an injury to society, and of but little benefit to the slave." The conclusion asserts that the "negro . . . never does become an equal in any society in the South or North, where the whites prevail, nor will he ever become so."[18]

The legal and social context for the 1856 Texas Code also includes early Texas Supreme Court decisions that were published after 1845, when the first Texas state constitution established this court. These decisions, in dictum, repeatedly acknowledged that "the legislation of this country makes certain distinctions between slaves and freemen, respecting particular crimes and offenses," and that these "distinctions" were permitted "where the relations arising out of the institution of slavery, . . . necessarily [so] imply."[19] Although this court did not explicitly accept or reject the criminal law unequal mitigation and justification doctrine, it nevertheless suggested a doctrinal basis permitting the legislature, and possibly even the courts, to modify the criminal law's general rules when these white elites believed their emerging enslavement society "necessarily" required the separate and unequal treatment of all Blacks.[20]

The Texas Code

The 1856 Texas Code originated with an 1854 act that required the governor to appoint a commission to codify the state's civil and criminal laws. Governor Elisha M. Pease appointed John W. Harris, Oliver Cromwell Hartley, and James Willie. They prepared four codes and, in 1856, submitted them to the legislature. On August 28 of that year, the legislature adopted only the Code of Criminal Procedure, and, "with very material amendments," the Penal Code.[21]

Willie is generally credited with preparing these two criminal law codes, and his Old South origins track that of many of the new state's white elites. Born on January 5, 1823, in Wilkes County, Georgia, Willie as a youth was "thrown an orphan upon his own resources." Willie moved west to Washington County, Texas, where his uncle, Dr. Asa Hoxie, was "an eminent and affluent citizen of that county." Although he had only the education that "the common schools of his nativity afforded," Willie soon began a successful legal career. He was elected to the first Texas state legislature in 1846. After serving a second legislative term, Willie decided to spend his time developing his legal practice. He returned to public office in 1856, however, when he was elected as the Democrat candidate to serve as the state's attorney general. This was his last public role before his death in 1863, other than his work on the state's criminal codes.[22]

A. E. Wilkinson praised Willie and his codes in a 1922 article appearing in the first edition of the *Texas Law Review*. According to Wilkinson, although Willie lacked "the collegiate training of his associates, he became a man of culture and a lawyer of learning."[23] Wilkinson asserted, "No more beautiful piece of codification had been previously accomplished, and they have compelled and still compel general admiration."[24] It later was noted that these codes proved to be "quite durable"; the procedural code "was not fundamentally revised until 1965," and the penal code was not so revised "until 1973." Nevertheless, it also was conceded that these codes contained "some provisions that were peculiar to their time."[25]

Indeed, this code's explicitly race-based procedural and substantive criminal provisions restated the southern criminal law's role in controlling enslaved people and "free persons of color," whom the code defined as those with "one-fourth African blood" or more.[26] The Penal Code's three parts illustrate this legalized discrimination and segregation; they are part I, "General Provisions

Relating to the Whole Code"; part II, "Of Offences and Punishments"; and part III, "Of Offences Committed by Slaves and Free Persons of Color." The first two parts applied to all cases, unless otherwise stated in part III.[27] The code thus defined some acts as offenses only when committed by enslaved persons or free persons of color, while it imposed on them more severe penalties for other acts that were offenses when committed by all persons.[28]

The code's anti-insolence provision also permitted whites to commit what otherwise would be assaults and batteries in part III, article 802, section 4, which stated, "The insolence of a slave will justify a white man in inflicting moderate chastisement, with an ordinary instrument of correction, if done at the time when the insolent language is used, or within a reasonable time after, but it will not authorize an excessive battery, as with a dangerous weapon."[29] The legislators expressed their intent that this provision would apply to free persons of color in article 805, which asserted that the "general principles" enumerated in article 802 "with respect to the conduct of slaves under particular circumstances, are also applicable to the case of free persons of color residing in this state, whether with or without authority of law, except so much of said Article as refers particularly to the relationship of master and slave."[30] The code further confirmed this conclusion in article 481, which stated, "Assaults and assaults and batteries, as here spoken of, have reference to such offences when committed against a free white person."[31]

The code's article 802, section 9, moreover, stated that it was "lawful for a free white person to inflict chastisement upon a slave by moderate whipping":

1. If a slave, without the consent of the white person, be found upon his premises at night;
2. If the slave, against the orders of the white person, be found on his premises at any time;
3. If a slave be found using improper language, or guilty of indecent or turbulent conduct in the presence of white persons;
4. If the slave be guilty of rude or unbecoming conduct in the presence of a free white female;
5. If a slave use insulting language or gestures towards a white person;
6. If a slave commit any willful act injurious to the property or person of a free white person, or any member of his family;
7. If a slave be found drunk and making a disturbance in any public place, or upon the premises of a free white person.[32]

All whites thus had the privilege of chastising insolent free persons of color, when these sections are read along with the code's articles 481 and 805.

The code's part III expressly incorporated the separate and unequal protection doctrine for enslaved people and free persons of color who were accused of committing violent crimes against whites in the second title I: "Rules Applicable to Offences Against the Person, When Committed by Slaves or Free Persons of Color." Article 802 declared that different mitigation and justification rules applied when "slaves or free persons of color" committed violent crimes—including homicide, rape, and assault and battery—against "a free white person."[33]

The courts thus were to apply racially discriminatory "general principles" of mitigation according to article 802, section 5, which declared that the "rules of manslaughter . . . apply only to equals, and not to the case of offences by slaves, or free persons of color, against free white persons."[34] Section 6 added, "An assault and battery, not inflicting great injury, committed by a free white person upon a slave, will not be a sufficient provocation to mitigate a homicide of the former by the latter, from murder to manslaughter, although it be in a case where the law does not expressly justify such assault and battery." Accordingly, section 7 permitted judges and juries to evaluate "the amount of personal injury" constituting a "legal provocation" mitigating a homicide to manslaughter "having due regard to the relative condition of the white man and slave, and the obligation of the latter to confirm his passions to his condition of inferiority." And section 8 stated, "If a slave, by insolence, provoke chastisement, and then slay the person chastising him, it will be murder; but if the chastisement be unreasonable and excessive the killing will be manslaughter."[35]

This article's section 8 was among the code's provisions that the legislature amended with a February 12, 1858, statute that deleted from this section the phrase "but if the chastisement be unreasonable and excessive the killing will be manslaughter."[36] Thus, the legislature reverted back to the Georgia courts' "no manslaughter" rule for insolent enslaved people who were charged with murder, even if their alleged insolence was provoked by unreasonable or excessive chastisement.[37]

Furthermore, article 808 added a class-based exception to this rule of racial inequality. It stated that if a slave or free person of color was on trial for killing a white person who was "in the habit of association with slaves or free negroes, and by his general conduct placed himself upon an equality with these classes of persons, the rights of the slave or person of color are to be governed by the same rules which would apply if the offence had been committed upon a person of a slave or free person of color," unless the white person was younger than eighteen years of age. But this exception did not apply if the violence was inflicted on "the master of the slave, or any other member of the family of the master."[38] In cases of violence between enslaved defendants and people of color, however, article 807 stated that "the parties are deemed to stand upon terms of equality." And article 806 declared, "A free person of color residing in the State in violation of law, is, in all respects, upon a footing of equality, as to personal rights, with a slave."[39]

The code's provisions listing the punishments that could be inflicted on offenders also illustrate substantive racial discrimination. The general provision lists death, imprisonment in the "Penitentiary" or "County jail," forfeiture or suspension of civil or political rights, and fines as the only permitted punishments for offenses defined by the code.[40] But for enslaved persons, the code's permitted punishments were death, branding, "Standing in the Pillory," and whipping.[41] It combined these punishments for free persons of color, who could be subjected to death, branding, "Imprisonment to labor in the Penitentiary," "Whipping or standing in the Pillory," and "Labor upon any public works of a county."[42]

Accordingly, the Texas Code represents a different form of Texas exceptionalism. Unlike the Virginia and Louisiana legislators, and their Republic of Texas forbearers, the late antebellum Texans followed the *Harden/Jowers* approach privileging individual acts of white violence, pursuant to the opening that the state's Supreme Court justices created permitting statutes confirming this de jure racial discrimination.[43]

The Georgia Code's Context

According to historian Watson W. Jennison, "Georgia's founders established the colony as a haven for the common man, but within a generation their vision had evaporated."[44] Georgia's trustees initially prohibited enslavement in the colony pursuant to the 1732 charter expressing an intent to establish "a common man's utopia" of "small-scale agriculture and limited landholdings."[45] But, in 1750, the governing trustees responded to the settlers' demands and permitted enslavement, effective January 1, 1751. Within twenty years, the colony evolved into a "mature planation society," which became "a hierarchical society stratified by race and class."[46] Also in 1750, the Georgia trustees adopted the first of the colony's enslavement laws. This act, and those enacted in 1755, 1765, and 1770, after Georgia became a royal colony, legitimized enslavement and included separate and unequal criminal law provisions for enslaved Blacks.[47]

Georgia's antebellum legislators later adopted "a large number of laws which singled out" free Blacks "to curtail [their] freedom and limit considerably [their] civil rights."[48] These laws were deemed to be necessary even though, in

1820, there were only 1,763 (0.05 percent) free Blacks in the state's total population of 340,983. By 1860, Georgia's free Black population had doubled to about 3,500, but it made up an even smaller percentage (0.033 percent) of the state's total population, which had increased to 1,057,248.[49]

Like the other southern slave states, Georgia's statutes evidence a two-part strategy that was intended to limit the number of the state's free Blacks while confirming in the positive law their unequal and degraded status in society. The free Black population was suppressed by an 1801 statute that required the state legislature to approve all manumissions. The legislators also foreshadowed what became an anti-manumission southern legal trend when they adopted an 1818 act stating that masters could not directly or indirectly free their slaves by wills, by deeds, or by parol evidence.[50] Moreover, an 1859 law closed a loophole through which the Georgia courts had permitted out-of-state manumissions by will. It declared that, "after the passage of this act, any and every clause in any deed, will, or other instrument made for the purpose of conferring freedom on slaves, directly or indirectly, within or without the State, to take effect after the death of the owner, shall be absolutely null and void."[51]

The free Black population also was intended to be suppressed by statutes dating back to 1793, which taxed, regulated, and eventually prohibited free Black migration from other states into Georgia.[52] An 1859 law even imposed a penalty of enslavement on any free Black person entering the state. But the legislature, in 1861, enacted a Civil War–related exception. It permitted free Blacks to return if they left the state "in service of any person, or in connection with the military service."[53]

Georgia's antebellum statutes confirmed the state's free Blacks' separate and unequal legal rights. Georgia's ardent pro-slavery chief justice Joseph H. Lumpkin, in an 1853 opinion, explained these laws' philosophies and purposes: "The [free] black man in this State, may have the power of volition. He may go and come, without a domestic master to control his movements; but to be civilly and politically free, to be the peer and equal of the white man—to enjoy the offices, trusts and privileges our institutions confer on the white man, is not now, never has been, and never will be, the condition of this degraded race."[54] Lumpkin then, while expressing his "hearty and cordial approval," declared that a free Black person

> has neither vote nor voice in forming the laws by which he is governed. He is not allowed to keep or carry fire-arms. He cannot preach or exhort without a special license [if more than seven "persons of colour" were present], on pain of imprisonment, fine and corporeal punishment. He cannot be employed in mixing or

vending drugs or medicines of any description. A white man is liable to a fine of five hundred dollars and imprisonment in the common jail, at the discretion of the Court, for teaching a *free* negro to read and write; and if one *free* negro teach another, he is punishable by fine and whipping, or fine or whipping, at the discretion of the Court. To employ a free person of color to set up type in a printing office, or any other labor requiring a knowledge of reading or writing, subjects the offender to a fine not exceeding one hundred dollars.[55]

Other laws stated that free Blacks could not "dispense medicines" or make contracts for constructing or repairing buildings.[56]

An 1818 act also prohibited free Black ownership of enslaved people or real estate.[57] A year later the legislature ameliorated this law. It no longer applied retroactively to property that free Blacks owned when the act was passed, and its ban of real estate ownership applied only in the cities of Savannah, Augusta, and Darien.[58] Moreover, an 1859 act declared a vagrant to be "any free person of color wandering or strolling about, or leading an idle, immoral or profligate course of life." On a first conviction a violator was to be sold into slavery for a term not to exceed two years. A second offender was to be "sold into perpetual slavery."[59]

Georgia's statutes also began to equate enslaved and free Blacks under the criminal law.[60] An 1815 act required that free Blacks be tried for all crimes in the inferior courts of justices of the peace and freeholders in which accused enslaved defendants were tried.[61] The 1755 enslavement statute authorized what Betty Wood called "essentially ad hoc courts for the trial of slaves." She explained that "for capital and non-capital offenses alike, the order of the day was the speedy dispensation of justice as well as the selection of punishments which, it was anticipated, would not only fit the crime but also deter other slaves."[62] It was not until 1850 that the legislature vested the Superior Court with jurisdiction over trials of enslaved and free Blacks in capital prosecutions, with appeals to the state's Supreme Court.[63] Equal justice always was hampered because, "like the slave, the *free* person of color [was] incompetent to testify against a free white citizen."[64] Concern about unequal justice for free Blacks apparently prompted Joseph Gabriel Posner, a Polish Jewish businessman of Louisville, Georgia, to successfully petition the General Assembly in 1799 for a private law freeing his enslaved wife Sylvia and her son David, who were to have all legal rights as if they "had been born free." If either of them was charged with a crime, they would be "tried for such offence in the same manner, and be entitled to the same defence in the courts of this state, as allowed to free white persons in like cases."[65]

Georgia's Supreme Court also endorsed the common-law rule of separate and unequal mitigation for enslaved criminal defendants soon after the court was created and was granted jurisdiction to hear appeals in these cases.[66] The court's 1854 decision in *Jim v. State* held that slaves who were accused of killing their masters or overseers could not at trial mitigate their offenses from murder to manslaughter, even if the enslaved defendants reacted to their masters' and overseers' excessive violence.[67] Justice Ebenezer Starnes explained that enslaved people may not judge "the reasonableness or unreasonableness of the extent and degree" of the "patriarchal discipline which the master is permitted to exercise." This rule was necessary, he held, to discourage "insubordination, . . . servile insurrection and bloodshed." Accordingly, "the homicide of his master, overseer, or employee . . . by a slave, in resistance to an assault made upon him by that master, overseer, or employer, must, in all cases, be either justifiable homicide or murder."[68]

The court extended this rule when an enslaved defendant killed a white person who was not the slave's owner or overseer. Chief Justice Lumpkin's opinion in *John v. State* declared that every slave's homicide of "a free white person . . . is murder, or justifiable homicide."[69] He also expressed his own doubts, in dicta, whether enslaved people could ever justify homicides based on self-defense. He admitted, "It is supposed, that where a slave is under an absolute and inexorable necessity, to take the life of a white man to save his own, who has no right to punish him or control him in any manner whatever, that such killing will be excusable. And it may be so." But he added, "For myself, I have formed no very definite opinion upon this subject." Lumpkin nevertheless justified the no manslaughter rule: "But a stern and unbending necessity forbids that any such allowance should be made for the infirmity of temper or passion on the part of a slave, as to reduce or mitigate his crime from murder to manslaughter."[70]

The court never decided whether it would apply these principles to cases involving free Blacks. But these decisions did not persuade Lumpkin's own son-in-law Thomas Cobb, who expressed his dissent in his enslavement law treatise. After stating Lumpkin's rule of "stern and unbending necessity," Cobb asserted that he "cannot yield [his] assent fully to this proposition as being well-founded in law. The duty of the slave to obey, and his habit of subordination, would require a greater provocation to justify an 'infirmity of passion'; but still there are circumstances, where provocation might be given, especially by others than the master, as to reduce the offence by the slave from murder to manslaughter."[71]

Georgia's legislature sided with Cobb. It adopted a code in 1863 that, in effect, overruled the *John* and *Jim* decisions. But this code also endorsed the separate and unequal protection norm by criminalizing free and enslaved Black insolence.[72]

The Georgia Code

The Georgia Code's origin can be traced to the proposal of George Gordon, of Chatham County, calling for better organization of the state's laws. A December 1858 act authorized both houses of the legislature to elect three commissioners to prepare a code condensing all of Georgia's law "whether derived from the Common Law, the Constitution of the State, the Statutes of the State, the Decisions of the Supreme Court, or the Statutes of England of force in this State," to be "modeled, if practicable," upon the 1852 Code of Alabama. The commissioners were allowed twenty months to complete this arduous task, so that the legislature could adopt the code in 1860. This code was to "supercede [sic] all other laws and decisions."[73]

David Irwin, Richard H. Clark, and Thomas R. R. Cobb were the commissioners who prepared the code. They agreed that Cobb would draft the civil and criminal law provisions, while Irwin prepared the code of practice and Clark prepared the sections relating to the state's political and public sectors. The commissioners met in August 1860 in the state capital and revised and completed the code. Then, in October 1860, they met with a legislative committee, which ultimately recommended that the legislature adopt the code, with some changes. The legislature promptly adopted the code, which the governor signed on December 19, 1860. Its effective date was January 1, 1862. But because of Georgia's secession, the code was amended to "conform to the laws and constitution of the Confederacy." Its effective date was postponed until January 1, 1863, which, was twenty days after Cobb was killed in the Battle of Fredericksburg.[74]

Thomas Cobb was an obvious choice to be one of the code's drafters. A lifelong Georgian who was born on April 10, 1823, into a prominent Georgia family, he made the most of his abilities and familial connections. He graduated from Georgia's Franklin College first in the class of 1841, and the next year he was admitted to the Georgia bar. He then began his successful legal career in Athens, Georgia, and started securing government positions, which included clerk of the Georgia Senate and reporter to Georgia's Supreme Court. He achieved these positions thanks in part to the bipartisan support of his older brother, Howell Cobb, a Democrat whose offices included congressperson (one year as speaker of the House), governor of Georgia, and U.S. secretary of state, and his father-in-law, Joseph Henry Lumpkin, a Whig, who was Georgia's first chief justice.[75]

Thomas Cobb, in 1851, published a two-volume digest of Georgia's statutes, and, seven years later, he published the first volume of an enslavement law treatise.[76] According to Paul Finkelman, this treatise was "a self-consciously political work," which Cobb hoped would be "a practical manual for lawyers and judges," as well as "a moral tome directed at proslavery legislators, and a defense of southern interests."[77] Cobb's politics also shifted over time; he was a pro-slavery unionist who became a supporter of secession. He was elected to the Provincial Congress of the Confederate States of America, in January 1861, and was a member of the committee that drafted the Confederate Constitution. He then fought in the Civil War, achieving the rank of brigadier general in October 1862, shortly before his death in battle.[78]

The code listed four classifications of persons: citizens, resident aliens, slaves and free persons of color, and corporations. It defined "person" to include corporations, but it excluded from this definition "slaves or free persons of color, unless named."[79] Free persons of color were defined as emancipated slaves and their descendants, or others with "at least one eighth of negro blood in their veins."[80] Therefore, this definition included any freed enslaved person or descendent of a freed slave, no matter what percentage of "negro blood" was in his or her veins. Free persons of color were "entitled to no right of citizenship except such as are specifically given by law." The code explained a free person of color's degraded status: "No master having dominion over him he is entitled to the free use of his liberty, labor and property, except so far as he is restrained by law."[81]

Cobb's Criminal Code confirmed this inequality in section 4715, which included among the offenses that could be committed "by slaves or free persons of color" the directing of both "indecent or disorderly conduct in the presence and to the annoyance of a free white person" and "insolent or improper language to a white person." This offense was among those listed in section 4718, which could be punished "in the discretion of the court" trying the case. The punishment was not to "extend to life, limb or health, nor be cruel in its nature, but shall be proportioned to the offence, keeping in view the principles of humanity." The code reminded judges that the punishment was to "have for its chief object the deterring of the offender and all others from a repetition of the offence." Judges could, however, "order free persons of color hired to the highest bidder in order to raise money to pay any fine (not exceeding three hundred dollars,) which may be imposed by the court."[82]

These crimes, pursuant to a procedure dating back to 1815, were among the noncapital offenses for which enslaved or free Blacks were to continue to be tried in the local inferior justice of the peace, mayor's, or recorder's courts, instead of in a trial by jury in the Superior Court.[83] The Superior Court's trial-level jurisdiction extended only to capital cases involving these classes of defendants. A defendant disputing the lower court's decision could apply to a Superior Court judge for a writ of certiorari directed at the lower court, either ordering a new trial or entering a judgment or sentence "as, in the view of the whole case, is consistent with justice and the principles of this Code."[84]

The criminalization of insolence also should be read in connection with the code's citizen's arrest provision, section 4604, which permitted a "private person" to "arrest an offender, if the offence is committed in his presence or within his immediate knowledge." Moreover, "if the offence is a felony, and the offender is escaping or attempting to escape, a private person may arrest him upon reasonable and probable grounds of suspicion." Citizens making these arrests, according to section 4605, were to "without delay convey the offender before the most convent officer authorized to receive an affidavit and issue a warrant."[85] These provisions modified the common-law citizen's arrest doctrine by extending the arrest privilege to all offenses in the code, and not only to felonies and other offenses that involved a breach of the peace.[86] The code's definition of "person" also excluded free Blacks from those who could make citizen's arrests.[87]

The code therefore authorized any white person to arrest and promptly bring an insolent Black person to an officer for redress through the courts, but it did not authorize whites to respond violently. This may have been one of the provisions that prompted Linton Stephens to critique Cobb and the code in a January 4, 1863, letter to his brother, Confederate vice president Alexander Stephens. Linton complained that the code "'is pretty full of . . . Tom Cobb's characteristics,' especially his 'propensity to regulate everything in the world (and in the next too) by rules of his own fabrication.'" But Linton "was forced to admit that the Code was 'not . . . as bad as I expected.'"[88]

The Georgia Code further confirmed the free Blacks' separate second-class caste when it declared, "All laws enacted in reference to slaves, and in their nature applicable to free persons of color, shall be construed to include them, unless specifically excepted."[89] This presumption extended to free Blacks the Criminal Code provision permitting enslaved defendants charged with murder to seek to mitigate their offenses to manslaughter. The code thus moderated the extreme "no manslaughter" rule that Georgia's Supreme Court had in 1854 announced for enslaved defendants by enacting the critique of this rule, which Cobb had expressed in his treatise. But the legislators also codified the *Tack-*

ett/Jarrott rule, which required all Black defendants to establish "much greater provocation" than the code required in cases of killings involving whites, in view of the enslaved person's duty of "obedience and submission."[90] Juries were to decide "whether the provocation was such as to justify uncontrollable passion in one accustomed to obedience and submission."[91] The code also resolved Lumpkin's doubts about an enslaved person's privilege to kill a white person in self-defense, but it added that "it must clearly appear that the act done was in defence of his life and not in a spirit of revenge. Self defence, or defence of his master or family, is the only justification of a homicide by a slave."[92] No reported Georgia cases applied these separate and unequal protection rules in cases involving free Blacks before or after this code was adopted. This may be because Georgia did not have a Supreme Court until 1846.[93]

Conclusion

According to Watson Jennison, Thomas Cobb incorporated the views of his father-in-law, Chief Justice Joseph Lumpkin, into the Georgia Code, which "reflected the racial ideology at the core of the new Confederate nation, a rigid and absolute notion of white supremacy." He concluded, "As a result, Georgia became a white man's republic."[94] Indeed, Lumpkin explicitly linked his "hearty and cordial approval" of Georgia's separate and unequal laws for free Blacks with his devotion to slavery:

> In no part of this country, whether North or South, East or West, does the free negro stand erect and on a platform of equality with the white man. He does, and must necessarily feel this degradation. To him there is but little in prospect, but a life of poverty, of depression, of ignorance, and of decay. He lives amongst us without motive and without hope. His fancied freedom is all a delusion. All practical men must admit, that the slave who receives the care and protection of a tolerable master, is superior in comfort to the free negro. . . . Civil freedom among the whites, he can never enjoy. To this isolated class, it will ever be but a name.[95]

But this code also modified some of Lumpkin's extreme criminal law views, as Cobb previously proposed in his slavery law treatise, which William McCash called "an encyclopedia of proslavery argumentation."[96]

Indeed, the Georgia and Texas codes, when read in their social and legal contexts, suggest that, in the decade before secession, southern legal elites agreed that legitimized governmental or private individual white violence was the necessary response to what they perceived to be insolent free Black acts or words, although they preferred different means. The Texas Code permitted individual whites to respond to insolence with what otherwise would have been extralegal violence, and Georgia's Code made this insolence a crime to be prosecuted and punished through the courts.

Alabama's law and social practices present an interesting contrast to these two approaches. The Alabama Code of 1852, which was to be the Georgia Code's model, did not enact either of these responses to Black insolence. According to Richard Wade, Blacks nevertheless were prosecuted for insolence in 1850s Mobile. In 1851, "a negro girl was sentenced to twenty-five lashes for using insulting language to a white lady and otherwise acting disorderly." Six years later, "John, a mulatto," was sentenced to twenty stripes for being "disorderly and saucy in the market," and for showing "a large amount of independence." And two years after that, Ben, a drayman, was sentenced to thirty-nine lashes "for not remembering the courtesy due a white man both in words and deed."[97]

These Alabama prosecutions confirm just how pervasive were the South's white-supremacist legal customs and legal consciousnesses, which were epitomized by the appellate decisions and statutes that legitimized these customs with the separate and unequal protection doctrine.

CONCLUSION

A Violent Badge of Slavery

Antebellum appellate case law provides evidence of two incipient and fundamentally inconsistent criminal law doctrines—de jure separate and unequal protection based on perceptions of race and de jure formal equal protection. South and North Carolina jurists John Belton O'Neall and Richmond Mumford Pearson advanced the separate and unequal protection principle in their *State v. Harden* and *State v. Jowers* opinions.[1] These judges extended to free Blacks the modified mitigation and justification rules and standards that judges John Louis Taylor and William J. Gaston fashioned in enslavement law decisions. This new doctrine modified the common law of crimes by legitimizing what otherwise would have been acts of extralegal violence based upon perceptions of race—not social status or gender. Moreover, Louisiana, Virginia, Texas, Georgia, Mississippi, and Florida statutes, and City of Richmond ordinances, suggest that the antebellum South's white public supported the notion that the law should confine free Blacks to what O'Neall so candidly called their "degraded *caste* of society," in which they were "in no respect, on a perfect equality with the white man."[2]

Separate and unequal protection is a concept that expresses the essential components of O'Neall's notion of this "degraded caste of society." "Caste" confirms that the positive law confined free Blacks to a separate legal category. This reflected and reinforced their separate place in the society. "Degraded" confirms that this separation was intended to enforce—on the legal, social, and psychological levels—the inequality of all Blacks and the concomitant superiority of all whites. O'Neall was not the only antebellum jurist to refer to this free Black "degraded caste of society." Chancellor James Kent used this phrase in the second edition of his *Commentaries on American Law*, which was published in

1832, the same year that *Harden* was decided. Kent mentioned the legal disabilities that Blacks endured after slavery was abolished in New York. In a footnote, he explained, "In most of the United States, there is a distinction in respect to political privileges, between free white persons and coloured persons of African blood; and in no part of the country do the latter, in point of fact, participate equally with whites, in the exercise of civil and political rights. The African race are essentially a degraded caste, of inferior rank and condition in society." He also referred to anti-miscegenation laws as evidence of this degradation.[3]

O'Neall, Pearson, and southern legislators in two different ways further extended this degradation into the substantive criminal law. They either criminalized what were perceived to be free Black insolent acts and words or created a new legal privilege authorizing all whites to violently, but reasonably, respond to what were perceived to be instances of intolerable insolence. This privilege of course had its limits, but they were enforced by local white judges and juries, who determined whether their white neighbors acted reasonably, thus reinforcing the pro-slavery white-supremacist values of these states' white citizens.[4] This new privilege of whiteness also is significant because it was inconsistent with an emerging nineteenth-century trend evidenced by statutes, appellate court opinions, and legal treatises that led to the abolition of common-law social status and gender privileges that permitted elites, such as employers or masters, to reasonably correct misbehaving employees or servants.[5]

The separate and unequal doctrine enables us to compare and contrast the southern law it epitomized with the law that should follow under the equal protection doctrine. The Illinois Supreme Court's 1854 decision in *Campbell v. The People* foreshadowed this prohibition of legal, social, and psychological inequality based on a person's perceived race or other irrelevant status, at least in the substantive criminal law.[6] The court held that Decator Campbell, a nineteen-year-old Black man accused of murdering a white man, was to be tried under the generally applicable mitigation and justification rules and standards without reference to his race and that, upon Campbell's request, the trial judge should have instructed the jury to apply the law as if Campbell were a white person.

Justice John Marshall Harlan later expressed this ideal of substantive legal equality for all in his *Plessy v. Ferguson* dissent: "In view of the constitution, in the eye of the law, there is in this country no superior, dominant, ruling class of citizens. There is no caste here."[7] But Daniel Kiel correctly cautions that Harlan articulated "an aspiration rather than a reality."[8] The *Plessy* majority instead adopted the separate but equal doctrine, which "ensured that a comprehensive racial caste system would be maintained in the post-slavery era."[9]

A Degraded Caste of Society also suggests that Justice Harlan might have more decisively defined the issue if he declared that the Civil War Amendments were intended to guarantee that *there no longer would be any caste here*. These amendments "decreed universal civil freedom in this country" by abolishing the antebellum law of separate and unequal protection and replacing it with the equal protection of the law—not the separate but equal protection of the law.[10]

This reformulation of the doctrinal issue leads to a better repudiation of Justice Henry Billings Brown's infamous social psychological finding in *Plessy* that "the underlying fallacy of the plaintiff's argument" was "the assumption that the enforced separation of the two races stamps the colored race with a badge of inferiority. If this be so, it is not by reason of anything found in the act, but solely because the colored race chooses to put that construction upon it."[11] The positive law sources discussed in this book confirm that the differential treatment of the free members of the races originated in the perceived need to confirm and communicate to all that those who were perceived to be Black were thought to be so inferior that they must always be governed by separate and unequal laws.[12]

This study of the enslavement law origins of these racially discriminatory criminal law rules and doctrines thus provides an essential context for two overlapping contemporary issues. The first relates to the important debate about how we can best understand the nature of free Black southern antebellum life and the scope of the racist consensus interpretation of American history. The second issue is one of constitutional law and legal doctrine. When informed by the first historical inquiry, it can shed light on the meaning of the important term "badges and incidents of slavery," as well as the constitutionality of federal hate crimes laws.[13]

On the first issue, the statutes and cases discussed in the preceding chapters support Ira Berlin's conclusion that, although free Black life experiences varied over time and place, in the antebellum upper and lower southern states "extralegal terror was an integral part of the system" that white elites created to enforce their notions of the rules of propriety, racial hierarchy, and social control. Berlin referred to southern opinion leaders who ignored—and even encouraged—extralegal "vigilante action against free Negroes when officials seemed unable or unwilling" to enforce the South's "code of chivalry." But he also cited the *Harden* and *Jowers* decisions as examples of how "these extralegal punishments found sanction in the courts as well as the press."[14] These legal sources offer less support for the more recently proposed relatively benign paradigm, which is based on Melvin P. Ely's vision of "wide webs of social entanglement among free people of color, whites and slaves."[15] Antebellum southern law placed all free Blacks—including those who were relatively prosperous—in a separate "degraded" legal caste affording them inferior protection under the substantive criminal law.[16]

These legal sources also lend support to the interpretations of historians, including Richard C. Wade, Joel Williamson, and Roger A. Fischer, who disputed C. Vann Woodward's contention that the South's Jim Crow segregation laws "were a lamentable innovation of the late nineteenth century."[17] The particular legal manifestations of Black legal inequality and segregation that Woodward studied may have originated in the 1890s.[18] But according to Williamson, "The real color line lived in the minds of the individuals of each race, and it had achieved full growth even before" emancipation.[19]

Indeed, the pro-slavery lost cause historian Ulrich B. Phillips, with pride and admiration, admitted the perceived need among whites to maintain a strict color line was southern history's "central theme"—both before emancipation and into the Jim Crow era. He celebrated, in 1928, how "the white folk" had "a common resolve indomitably maintained—that it shall be and remain a white man's country."[20] William A. Dunning's pro-South critique of Reconstruction similarly concluded that enslavement was not "the ultimate root of the trouble in the South." Instead, he argued that the essence of this "trouble" was "the coexistence in one society of two races so distinct in characteristics as to render coalescence impossible." Slavery to him was "a *modus vivendi* through which social life was possible; and that after its disappearance, its place must be taken by some set of conditions which, if more humane and beneficent in accidents, must in essence express the same fact of racial inequality."[21] From a perspective rejecting this lost cause interpretation, George M. Fredrickson similarly contended that the antebellum South was a Herrenvolk democracy, not unlike apartheid South Africa. In both societies, white voters and lawmakers established and enforced de jure white supremacy over the nonwhite population.[22] Historian Edmund S. Morgan, moreover, concluded that "in Virginia (and probably in other southern colonies)," the "belief in republican equality" rested on race and slavery.[23]

Although southern whites—before and after emancipation—agreed on the imperative of their perceived social and legal supremacy, they at times used different means to achieve and maintain this end, and they even clashed on the question of "*which whites* should be supreme."[24] Their prevailing agreement on the underlying racist principles endured, however, although southern law and society, as Woodward asserts, lacked "the tradition of historical continuity" that the southerner's "fellow countrymen" experienced. The South—if only as a result of its defeat in war—did, as Woodward notes, evolve from a slave society to a free society. But this region's "tradition of historical continuity" endured in the principle of white supremacy, which white Democrats revived when they regained control of southern law and politics.[25] These race-based status norms prevailed even as the white community members' goals shifted from "how to maintain the institution of chattel slavery" to how "to maintain the social, industrial, and civic inferiority of the descendants of chattel slaves." In both of these eras, "the people of one race [were] minded to adopt and act upon some policy more or less oppressive or repressive in dealing with the people of another race."[26]

The law of race-based inequality consistently reinforced the essential connection between white supremacy and legalized state or privately administered violence directed at all insolent free Blacks.[27] According to Leon Litwack, the Jim Crow–era lawmakers "made no exceptions based on class or education; indeed, the laws functioned on one level to remind African Americans that no matter how educated, wealthy, or respectable they might be, it did nothing to entitle them to equal treatment with the poorest and most degraded whites." The "white South," he continued, "insisted upon not so much separation of the races as subordination, a system of controls in which whites prescribed the rules of racial conduct and contact and meted out the punishments."[28] Litwack was referring to the years during which most historians contend that "white supremacy became the cornerstone of the New South," but Litwack also quoted Alexander H. Stephens's 1861 Cornerstone Speech, in which Stephens explained the political philosophy of the founders of the Confederate States of America.[29] This new government, Stephens tellingly admitted, "rests upon the great truth, that the negro is not equal to the white man. That slavery—subordination to the superior race—is his natural and moral condition."[30]

In the *longue durée* view of history, however, it is a different question to ask whether the quest for white supremacy is a paradigm that helps us to comprehensively understand U.S. legal history. Historians, including Litwack, Woodward, and Paul D. Escott, advance what James Oakes calls a "racial consensus" interpretation. It emphasizes evidence of white racist beliefs and actions in the northern and western states, with dissent expressed by only "a tiny handful of visionary radicals."[31] In contrast, other historians, including Oakes, Eric Foner, Paul Finkelman, Paul Polgar, Timothy Huebner, Martha Jones, and Kate Masur, contend that, outside of the southern states, evidence of "sustained conflict" over slavery, abolition, and equal rights for free Blacks raises doubts over the national scope of this racist consensus.[32] Edward J. Larson thus concluded, "The long shadow of slavery continued to undermine declarations of liberty and equality through the twentieth century and into our own. Liberty and slavery remain our conflicted American inheritance."[33]

The antebellum legal sources discussed in this book suggest that the more helpful interpretative paradigm acknowledges that both conflict and consensus characterized the views and actions of whites on the salience of race in U.S. law, but in the pre- and post–Civil War South, the racist consensus plainly prevailed. This racism was not confined to the minds of those who committed individual acts of violence or those who joined or supported murderous lynch mobs. It was instead established in the pre–Civil War positive law, and it later was advanced by some of the Jim Crow era's most influential white scholars and opinion leaders, including Phillips, Dunning, and Woodrow Wilson. They whitewashed the inherent oppression of antebellum southern enslavement laws and customs, condemned the multiracial governments elected during Reconstruction, and offered academic and intellectual support for their own times' racially discriminatory laws and customs.[34]

This lost cause interpretation's long-term toxic effects implicate the second series of issues relating this legal history to Thirteenth Amendment legal doctrine and the constitutionality of federal hate crime laws. Racially motivated legitimized violence was a badge of slavery that reemerged—if in modified form—in the South's post-emancipation law in action and law in the books, even after the ratification of the Fourteenth Amendment and the adoption of laws, including the Civil Rights Act of 1866, guaranteeing equal protection of the law. Congress first approved that act soon after the Thirteenth Amendment was ratified in December 1865 to enforce that amendment's abolition of "slavery and involuntary servitude . . . within the United States," and in "any place subject to their jurisdiction." The 1866 act was authorized by section 2 of the amendment, which states, "The Congress shall have the power to enforce this Article by appropriate legislation."[35]

The Thirteenth Amendment commanded the immediate, unconditional, and uncompensated emancipation of people who still were enslaved or were held in involuntary servitude, but it alone could not erase underlying racial prejudices and social customs from the hearts and minds of the members of the previously slaveholding communities.[36] This should have been evident to all when the antebellum separate and unequal protection and white-supremacist norms reemerged in the Black Codes that southern states enacted in late 1865 and 1866, following the lead of Mississippi, ostensibly to regulate the labor and general conduct of the newly freed slaves.[37] These laws were based on the constitutional theory that, after slavery was abolished, the states retained the right to again adopt laws denying equal rights under law to nonwhites.[38]

Congress responded with the Civil Rights Act of 1866, which guarantees to all U.S. citizens the enumerated civil rights that whites had enjoyed throughout the colonial and antebellum years, and which, in whole or in part, were denied to enslaved and free Blacks. The act provides that citizens

> of every race and color, without regard to any previous condition of slavery or involuntary servitude, except as a punishment for crime whereof the party shall have been duly convicted, shall have the same right, in every State and Territory in the United States, to make and enforce contracts, to sue, be parties, and give evidence, to inherit, purchase, lease, sell, hold, and convey real and personal property, and to the full and equal benefit of all laws and proceedings for the security of persons and property, as is enjoyed by white citizens.

The act's protections also extended to the criminal law. It states that all citizens "shall be subject to like punishment, pains, penalties, and to none other, any law statute, ordinance, regulation, or custom to the contrary notwithstanding."[39] Whiteness thus serves as the baseline for the rights of all, evoking John Rawls's first principle of justice: "Each person is to have an equal right to the most extensive total system of equal basic liberties compatible with a similar system of liberty for all."[40]

Although the Civil Rights Act of 1866 barred the separate and unequal protection of the procedural and substantive criminal law, both the Congress and the Supreme Court enabled the resurgence of racially motivated violence in post-emancipation America, necessitating twentieth-century civil rights and criminal procedure law reforms.[41] Congress—for more than 140 years—did not adopt a hate crimes statute outlawing all private racially motivated attacks.[42] Congress also repeatedly failed to adopt anti-lynching bills, despite mounting evidence of the deaths of thousands of victims of racially motivated lynch mob murders.[43] Indeed, it was not until March 2022 that Congress enacted the Emmett Till Antilynching Act.[44]

The Supreme Court, for almost a hundred years, also contributed to the perpetuation of this interracial violence. It failed to clearly define the universal right to freedom that the Thirteenth Amendment guaranteed. It narrowly construed the judicial power to enforce the Amendment under section 1. And it limited Congress's power to prohibit badges of slavery under section 2.[45] For example, decisions including *United States v. Cruickshank* and *Hodges v. United States* limited the right of all people to be free from racially motivated violence, even though this violence was a crucial incident of enslavement.[46] "Rampant private violence tolerated by public authorities," therefore, "effectively put an end to efforts to reconstruct the southern state governments."[47]

Justice Joseph P. Bradley's 1883 *Civil Rights Cases* majority opinion epitomized this failure of Reconstruction when it invalidated provisions of the Civil Rights Act of 1875 that outlawed private discrimination in modes of transportation and places of amusement and public accommodation. Bradley conceded that the Thirteenth Amendment "clothes Congress with power to pass all laws necessary and proper for abolishing all badges and incidents of slavery in the United States,"[48] but he also both established a narrow definition of slavery's badges and authorized a searching standard of judicial review of the statutes that Congress enacted to prohibit these enslavement badges.[49]

This legal doctrine prevailed until 1968, a year in which both the Supreme Court and Congress endeavored to better enforce the ideal of universal freedom. Justice Potter Stewart's opinion in *Jones v. Alfred H. Mayer Co.* sustained a housing discrimination provision, which was originally enacted in the 1866 Civil Rights Act, pursuant to a deferential standard of judicial review that he held the courts must apply to statutes intended to eliminate what Congress found were slavery's badges and incidents.[50] Congress also responded with the Civil Rights Act of 1968, which, in title I, included anti–hate crime provisions.[51] This act made it a crime for any person, "whether or not acting under color of law, by force or threat of force" to—"because of his race, color, religion or national origin"—willfully injure, intimidate, or interfere with another person in the exercise of a list of protected activities and programs.[52] Although the law thus does not prohibit hate crimes in all places and for all purposes, the courts interpreted it to prohibit violence interfering with a person's use of streets and parks provided or administrated by state or local governments.[53]

Forty-one years passed, however, before Congress—after many unsuccessful attempts—criminalized individual racially motivated hate crimes committed anywhere. The Matthew Shepard and James Byrd Jr. Hate Crimes Prevention Act (HCPA), adopted in 2009, was, in part, Congress's response almost ten years after the brutal murders of Matthew Shepard, a gay college student, and of James Byrd Jr., a Black man who was killed by three white men.[54] This law authorizes fines and prison terms of not more than ten years for those convicted of willfully inflicting or attempting to inflict bodily injury with a weapon, "because of a person's actual or perceived race, color, religion, or natural origin." The permitted term of imprisonment may be increased to any number of years, or for life, "if death results from the offense," or if "the offense includes kidnapping or an attempt to kidnap, aggravated sexual abuse or an attempt to commit aggravated sexual abuse, or an attempt to kill."[55]

"Congress explicitly justified [this] racial violence provision under its Thirteenth Amendment badges-and-incidents authority,"[56] with the following relevant findings: "For generations, the institutions of slavery and involuntary servitude were defined by the race, color, and ancestry of those held in bondage. Slavery and involuntary servitude were enforced, both prior to and after the adoption of the 13th amendment to the Constitution of the United States, through widespread public and private violence directed at persons because of their race, color, or ancestry, or perceived race, color, or ancestry." Congress therefore concluded that "eliminating racially motivated violence is an important means of eliminating, to the extent possible, the badges, incidents, and relics of slavery and involuntary servitude."[57]

The U.S. Courts of Appeals and District Court decisions to this date all have rejected constitutional challenges to this law.[58] For example, the Fifth and Tenth Circuit Courts have held that Congress "could conceive that modern racially motivated violence communicates to the victim that he or she must remain in a subservient position, unworthy of the decency afforded to other races."[59]

The antebellum cases and statutes discussed in this book confirm that Congress could rationally conclude that legitimized racially motivated violence was an incident of slavery, which continued to function as a badge of slavery so many decades after emancipation. Professor Jennifer Mason McAward restates the accepted definition of an incident of slavery as "a term of art used by Congress and the Supreme Court" to describe the Thirteenth Amendment's effect. It is "any legal right or restriction that necessarily accompanied the institution of slavery. Most often, 'incident' was used to refer to the aspects of property law that applied to the ownership and transfer of slaves. It also was used to refer to the civil disabilities imposed on slaves by virtue of their status as property." This phrase "has clear, finite, historically determined meaning. It refers to a closed set of public laws that applied in the antebellum slaveholding states. Identifying an 'incident of slavery', then, is an exercise in historical inquiry."[60]

Scholars and judges have not reached a consensus, however, on how to define the badges of slavery or the extent of Congress's power to prohibit them under the Thirteenth Amendment. McAward identified "three possible approaches": "(1) that Congress can pass only 'pure' enforcement legislation; (2) that Congress can both define and eradicate the badges and incidents of slavery (i.e., the *Jones* Court's view); and (3) that Congress can address the badges and incidents of slavery, understood as a term of art with a fixed range of meaning, as a prophylactic exercise." "Drawing from the original understanding of Section 2, as well as its structural implications," she "concluded that the final conception was the most appropriate."[61]

McAward also found that the definition of the phrase "badge of slavery" evolved "from the antebellum to post bellum eras," and "in its most general sense," it "refers to indicators, physical or otherwise, of African-Americans' slave or subordinate status."[62] But she nevertheless is among those advocating for what Nicholas Serafin calls a restrictive interpretation of this term.[63] McAward would limit badges of slavery to laws or customs seeking "to reimpose the incidents of slavery by restricting freed slaves' fundamental civil liberties."[64]

Accordingly, McAward, and U.S. Court of Appeals judge Jennifer Walker Elrod, contend that the courts should interpret the Thirteenth Amendment to deny Congress the power to criminalize all nonstate actor racially motivated violence. Even the Court of Appeals decisions sustaining the HCPA suggest that the Supreme Court may need to consider modifying or even overruling its holding in *Jones*.[65] These contentions are based on the doctrine requiring "congruence and proportionality" between the substantive injury Congress intended to prevent under its constitutional power to enforce the Fourteenth Amendment, and the remedy chosen as a means to achieve that end. The court announced this test in *City of Boerne v. Flores*, when it invalidated the Religious Freedom Restoration Act of 1993, thereby subjecting enforcement statutes to more exacting judicial scrutiny.[66]

This "restrictive interpretation," in essence, thus calls for a revival of the "'discontinuity' thesis," which John Anthony Scott attributed to C. Vann Woodward's interpretation of the origin of southern Jim Crow laws. Woodward, according to Scott, "reformulated for a modern audience" Justice Bradley's majority opinion in the *Civil Rights Cases* narrowly construing Congress's authority to define the badges of slavery, supposedly to avoid "running the slavery argument into the ground."[67] With this dismissive phrase, Bradley read the Thirteenth Amendment to do little more than void the warranties of title in human flesh that enslavement law previously enforced in favor of enslavers, while prohibiting only labor relations that very closely resembled or threatened reenslavement, thus permitting Congress to enforce only minimal civil rights, such as those listed in the Civil Rights Act of 1866.[68]

Serafin recently summarized an alternative definition "referring to state actions or social custom that stigmatized subordinate social groups."[69] This book does not propose to reconcile this debate or offer a comprehensive interpretation of the badges of slavery, to remedy what one commentator called the "lack of a coherent [Thirteenth Amendment] jurisprudence."[70] It suggests, however, that the badges of slavery—under any doctrinal formulation—must at the very least include nongovernmental actor violence occasioned because of the perpetrator's perceptions of the victim's race.[71]

This conclusion follows from the antebellum appellate court decisions and statutes that used the separate and unequal protection doctrine to legitimize racially motivated violence as a badge of slavery, which they derived from an incident of enslavement that was extended to free Blacks. Orlando Patterson and other scholars who have studied enslavement throughout human history agree that the enslavers' legal privilege to use violence was one of slavery's three constituent elements, which, in their extremes, distinguished enslavement from other forms of oppressive human relationships.[72] Enslavement law thus legitimized what contemporary scholars would recognize as hate crimes. According to Barbara Perry, a hate crime is "[a] mechanism of power intended to sustain somewhat precarious hierarchies, through violence and threats of violence (verbal or physical)." This crime "generally" is directed against "those whom [a] society has traditionally stigmatized and marginalized."[73] It is "a way in which people of color and other ethnic minorities are reminded of their place."[74] "Oftentimes, the specific [hate crime] victim is almost immaterial. The victims are interchangeable. The target audience is not so much the victim as it is others like him or her."[75]

Only the Civil War Amendments and the Civil Rights Act of 1866 stopped the further development of this legitimized violence in the South's written criminal law. But racially motivated violence morphed into "extralegal violence targeting African Americans, alongside the state's unwillingness to seek redress for Black victims." This deadly combination "'symbolize[d] and enforce[d] the second-class status of African Americans.'"[76] The Jim Crow regime's proponents revived antebellum customs, and—to the extent they could get away with it—written laws, thereby ending the post–Civil War interlude of interracial democracy, which at least some had intended to afford liberty and true equality for all.[77]

Fundamental continuities therefore link the customs, legal culture, and legal consciousness that fueled the de jure discrimination of antebellum southern law with the post-emancipation southern Black Codes.[78] This link then extended from the antebellum racially motivated legitimized violence of people like Goodwin Parker, Atlas Jowers, and Charles Harden, to the Jim Crow–era individual violent actors and lynch mobs, and ultimately to today's racially motivated violent actors, including Gregory and Travis McMichael and William Bryan. They all used violence in their attempts "to return African-Americans to a position of de facto enslavement."[79]

This history of recurring white on Black violence is one example of how Reconstruction fell short of Thaddeus Stevens's goal of "a total overhaul of the 'fabric of Southern society.'"[80] W. E. B. Du Bois correctly concluded that the effective abolition of slavery had to be more than the mere invalidation of the legal title in enslaved people, "it meant the uplift of slaves and their eventual incorporation into the body civil, politic, and social, of the United States."[81] This uplift had to address three levels. First, the legal culture had to be changed so that the courts and Congress would interpret and apply the Civil War Amendments to justify federal intervention "in the face of violence or other expressions of racial inequality."[82] Second, the South's legal consciousness, as epitomized by the separate and unequal doctrine, had to be reformed to eradicate all of slavery's "modes of thought, attitudes, and practices," which simply "did *not* vanish in a flash" after emancipation.[83] And third, remedial measures were needed to address the physical, emotional and psychological, and economic harm that, for generations, had been inflicted on the formerly enslaved people. That harm too did not vanish upon emancipation.[84]

The antebellum white-supremacist legal culture and legal consciousness instead was revived in the South, as the newly emancipated and the previously free Blacks ultimately were subjected to the control of the Jim Crow era's white supremacists.[85] No nation-building effort eradicated the South's white-supremacist politics, law, and culture, unlike the post–World War II programs in Germany, Austria, and Japan.[86] Antebellum enslavement law's survivals might not have persisted so long if the will and adequate resources had been dedicated to a comprehensive post-slavery truth, reconciliation, and sociolegal reconstruction of the defeated southern states.[87]

Instead, slavery's badges and incidents continued to taint the South's written law, legal culture, and legal consciousness, as confirmed by the deaths of thousands of victims of interracial violence, including Ahmaud Arbery. His killers in 2020 almost successfully evaded prosecution because of an enslavement-era citizen's arrest statute. Although that law's arrest privilege was no longer limited to whites, it otherwise remained essentially unchanged until May 2021, when it was repealed in response to Arbery's murder.[88] Time will tell if this and other legal reforms finally will abolish the relics of the racially motivated public and private violence that antebellum southern statutes and appellate judicial decisions legitimized.[89] Only then might the Civil War Amendments be experienced as "a fundamentally new [constitution] with a new definition of both the status of blacks and the rights of all Americans."[90]

NOTES

ACKNOWLEDGMENTS

1. Andrew Fede, "Legitimized Violent Slave Abuse in the American South, 1619–1865: A Case Study of Law and Social Change in Six Southern States," *American Journal of Legal History* 29, no. 2 (April 1985): 95–150; Andrew Fede, "Toward a Solution of the Slave Law Dilemma: A Critique of Tushnet's American Law of Slavery," *Law and History Review* 2, no. 2 (Fall 1984): 301–20.

2. Andrew T. Fede, *Homicide Justified: The Legality of Killing Slaves in the United States and the Atlantic World* (Athens: University of Georgia Press, 2017), 224.

3. See *United States v. Nelson*, 277 F. 3d 164, 189–90 (2d Cir.) (sustaining hate crimes provisions of the Civil Rights Act of 1968 under the Thirteenth Amendment and citing Fede, "Legitimized Violent Slave Abuse," 95), cert. denied, *Nelson v. United States*, 537 U.S. 835, 123 S. Ct. 145, 154 L. Ed. 2d 54 (2002); *United States v. Beebe*, 807 F. Supp. 2d 1045, 1052 (D. N.M. 2011) (sustaining Matthew Shepard and James Byrd Jr. Hate Crimes Prevention Act under the Thirteenth Amendment and citing Fede, "Legitimized Violent Slave Abuse," 132, 141–42), aff'd, *United States v. Hatch*, 722 F. 3d 1193 (10th Cir. 2013), cert. denied, 572 U.S. 1018, 134 S. Ct. 1538, 188 L. Ed. 2d 561 (2014).

INTRODUCTION. The Enslavement Law Breakout and Slavery's Badges

1. See Ekow N. Yankah, "Ahmaud Arbery, Reckless Racism and Hate Crimes: Recklessness as Hate Crime Enhancement," *Arizona State Law Journal* 53, no. 2 (Summer 2021): 681; see also Richard Fausset, "What We Know about the Shooting Death of Ahmaud Arbery," *New York Times*, August 8, 2022, https://www.nytimes.com/article/ahmaud-arbery-shooting-georgia.html; Nicquel Terry Ellis, "What We Know about Community Where Ahmaud Arbery Was Shot: 911 Caller Reported 'Black Guy' on Property," *USA Today*, May 8, 2020, https://www.usatoday.com/story/news/2020/05/08/ahmaud-arbery-shooting-what-we-know-satilla-shores-community/3096389001/.

2. See Janell Ross, "What Ahmaud Arbery's Death Has Meant for the Place Where He Lived," *Time*, November 24, 2021, https://time.com/6121300/ahmaud-arbery-brunswick-georgia/; see also "Where Is Satilla Shores? Neighborhood at Center of a Death Trial," *11Alive*, https://www.11alive.com/article/news/crime/ahmaud-arbery/satilla-shores-brunswick-georgia-glynn-county-map/85-74af3568-f2c9-4dc8-ac13-184ce8d2bd64. In the 2016 and 2020 presidential elections, 62.47 percent and 61 percent, respectively, of the county's voters supported Donald Trump. See ibid.; Dave Leip's Atlas of U.S. Elections, "2020 Presidential Election Results—Georgia," https://uselectionatlas.org/RESULTS/states. Herschel Walker also won the county in his unsuccessful 2022 run for the U.S. Senate. But Glynn was one of the counties that swung in favor of Senator Raphael Warnock, by 2.4 percent between the general election and runoff in December. See "Large Red Counties Fell Flat in Herschel Walker's Bid for Georgia's U.S. Senate Seat," *11Alive*,

December 7, 2022, https://www.11alive.com/article/news/politics/herschel-walker-georgia-senate-loss-red-counties/85-00ce50d6-0b78-4cc7-a97e-47fc23f43eb5.

3. See Richard Fausset and Rick Rojas, "Where Ahmaud Arbery Ran, Neighbors Cast Wary Eyes," *New York Times*, May 22, 2020, https://www.nytimes.com/article/satilla-shores-ahmaud-arbery-killing.html.

4. See Glynn County Police Department, "Public Release Incident Report for G 20-11303," February 23, 2020; Fausset, "What We Know"; see also Ciji Dodds, "The Rule of Black Capture and the Ahmaud Arbery Case," *Georgetown Journal of Law and Modern Race Perspectives* 14, no. 1 (Winter 2022): 31–83, 73–79; Yankah, "Ahmaud Arbery, Reckless Racism," 681–82 (noting that the three men "pursued Arbery because they suspected him—with no evidence whatsoever—of being behind a string of (unreported) neighborhood robberies. Arbery's killers had never seen any suspect in those robberies"). For the events before the date of the murder, see Dodds, "Rule of Black Capture," 69.

5. See David Nakamura and Margaret Coker, "Greg and Travis McMichael, William Bryan Guilty of Hate Crimes in Ahmaud Arbery, Killing," *Washington Post*, February 22, 2022, https://www.washingtonpost.com/national-security/2022/02/22/arbery-verdict-hate-crimes/; Fausset, "What We Know"; Jonathan Allen and Rich Mckay, "Georgia Jury Convicts Three White Men of Arbury Murder," Reuters, November 24, 2021, https://www.reuters.com/world/us/georgia-jury-resume-deliberations-arbery-murder-trial-2021-11-24/.

6. See Allen and Mckay, "Georgia Jury Convicts Three White Men."

7. See Yankah, "Ahmaud Arbery, Reckless Racism," 681–82 (quoting Russ Bynum, "Testimony: Shooter Used Racist Slur as Arbery Lay Dying," Associated Press, June 4, 2020, https://apnews.com/article/american-protests-us-news-ap-top-news-shootings-virus-outbreak-7122aaf2c54ed22590a5b8d32565a58f); see also Dodds, "Rule of Black Capture," 78–79. Tariro Mzezewa and Richard Fausset, "Prosecutors Show Voluminous Evidence of Racism by Arbery Murderers," *New York Times*, February 22, 2022, https://www.nytimes.com/2022/02/16/us/ahmaud-arbery-mcmichael-racism.html; Hannah Knowles, David Nakamura, and Margaret Coker, "Racist Slurs, Violent Texts: How Arbery's Killers Talked about Black People," *Washington Post*, February 16, 2022, https://www.washingtonpost.com/national-security/2022/02/16/arbery-trial-racist-texts/.

8. See Dodds, "Rule of Black Capture," 68–69; Roger M. Stevens, "A Legacy of Slavery: The Citizen's Arrest Laws of Georgia and South Carolina," *South Carolina Law Review* 72, no. 4 (Summer 2021): 1006–7; "Ahmaud Arbery: What You Need to Know about the Case," BBC, November 22, 2021, https://www.bbc.com/news/world-us-canada-52623151.

9. See Jonathan Allen, "Three Georgia Men Sentenced to Life in Prison for 'Chilling' Arbery Murder," Reuters, January 7, 2022, https://www.reuters.com/world/us/three-men-be-sentenced-life-prison-ahmaud-arbery-murder-2022-01-07/; Nicquel Terry Ellis, "Why It Took More Than 2 Months for Murder Charges and Arrests in the Death of Ahmaud Arbery," *USA Today*, May 7, 2020, https://www.usatoday.com/story/news/2020/05/07/ahmaud-arbery-shooting-video-prosecutor-arrest-mcmichael/3089040001/; see also Allen and Mckay, "Georgia Jury Convicts Three White Men"; Dodds, "Rule of Black Capture," 80–81.

10. See Allen and Mckay, "Georgia Jury Convicts Three White Men."

11. See 18 U.S.C. § 245; Nakamura and Coker, "Greg and Travis McMichael"; N'dea

Yancey-Bragg and Raisa Habersham, "Ahmaud Arbery's Killers Found Guilty of Federal Hate Crimes, May Face Additional Life Sentence," *USA Today*, February 22, 2022, https://www.usatoday.com/story/news/nation/2022/02/22/verdict-ahmaud-arbery-killers-hate-crimes-trial/6890909001/; Nyamekye Daniel, "'No Evidence' of 'Racist Attitudes': Travis and Gregory McMichael Appeal Federal Case on Grounds That Ahmaud Arbery's Killing Didn't Happen in Public Streets," *Atlanta Black Star*, March 12, 2022, https://atlantablackstar.com/2022/03/12/no-evidence-of-racist-attitudes-travis-and-gregory-mcmichael-appeal-federal-case-on-grounds-that-ahmaud-arberys-killing-didnt-happen-in-p/; see also Dodds, "Rule of Black Capture," 81–82. This murder "brought to the fore a unique anxiety that has long troubled countless runners—running while black." See Matthew Futterman and Talya Minsberg, "After a Killing, 'Running While Black' Stirs Even More Anxiety," *New York Times*, May 26, 2020, https://www.nytimes.com/2020/05/08/sports/Ahmaud-Arbery-running.html. This is a variation on living while Black, which refers to limits imposed on Blacks who whites believe are in spaces they should not occupy—see Taja-Nia Y. Henderson and Jamila Jefferson-Jones, "#LivingWhileBlack: Blackness as Nuisance," *American University Law Review* 69, no. 3 (February 2020): 863–914—and driving while Black, "which refers to the challenges Black people in the United States continue to face when attempting to establish and protect their right to freedom of movement, a right exercised through their use and enjoyment of the 'open roads.'" See Jamila Jefferson-Jones, "'Driving While Black' as 'Living While Black,'" *Iowa Law Review* 106, no. 5 (July 2021): 2282; Gretchen Sorin, *Driving While Black: African American Travel and the Road to Civil Rights* (New York: Liveright, 2020), 1–17, 119–49.

 12. See Rich Mckay, "Ahmaud Arbery's Murderers Sentenced to Life, 35 Years on Hate Crimes Charges," Reuters, August 8, 2022, https://www.reuters.com/world/us/ahmaud-arbery-killers-could-face-life-prison-federal-hate-crimes-charges-2022-08-08/. Judge Wood also sentenced Travis McMichael to ten additional years for using a firearm in the commission of the murder and Gregory McMichael to seven more years for brandishing a gun. See ibid.; see also Richard Fausset, "Two in Arbery Case Sentenced Again to Life in Prison; Third Man Gets 35 Years," *New York Times*, August 9, 2022, https://www.nytimes.com/2022/08/08/us/arbery-killer-sentencing.html.

 13. See Mckay, "Ahmaud Arbery's Murderers Sentenced." The defendants were tried after Judge Wood rejected a proposed guilty plea offered by Travis McMichael. He would have admitted to the "charge of using a gun in his attempt to apprehend Arbery because of his 'race and color,' resulting in Arbery's death." See Jonathan Allen, "In Rare Move, U.S. Judge Rejects Plea Agreement by Ahmaud Arbery's Murderers," Reuters, January 31, 2022, https://www.reuters.com/world/us/us-prosecutors-reach-hate-crime-plea-deals-ahmaud-arbery-murder-court-filings-2022-01-31/.

 14. See, e.g., Margaret A. Burnham, *By Hands Known: Jim Crow's Legal Executioners* (New York: Norton, 2022); Elliot J. Gorn, *Let the People See: The Story of Emmett Till* (New York: Oxford University Press, 2018), 235–48; Timothy B. Tyson, *The Blood of Emmett Till* (New York: Simon & Schuster, 2017), 144–80, 195–97; Devery S. Anderson, *Emmett Till: The Murder That Shocked the World and Propelled the Civil Rights Movement* (Jackson: University Press of Mississippi, 2015), 85–165, 224–51; Philip Dray, *At the Hands of Persons Unknown: The Lynching of Black America* (New York: Random House, 2002), 422–25.

15. See Ellen Wexler, "How Emmett Till's Mother Galvanized the Civil Rights Movement," *Smithsonian Magazine*, October 13, 2022, https://www.smithsonianmag.com/history/emmett-till-mother-galvanized-civil-rights-movement-180980925/.

16. See Stevens, "Legacy of Slavery," 1006 (quoting letter from George E. Barnhill, District Attorney, Office of District Attorney Waycross Judicial Circuit, to Tom Jump, Captain, Glynn County Police Department [February 23, 2020]).

17. See Fausset, "What We Know"; see also Courtnee Green, "Citizen's Arrest Doctrine: Enabling the Modern-Day Vigilante," *LSU Journal for Social Justice and Policy* 7, no. 3 (2023): 45–47, 54–55, 59–60; Dodds, "Rule of Black Capture," 68; Stevens, "Legacy of Slavery," 1009, 1023–26.

18. See *Georgia Code Annotated*, secs. 17-4-60 and -61; *Graham v. State*, 143 Ga. 440, 85 S.E. 328 (1915); Marty Johnson, "Kemp Signs Bill Repealing Citizen's Arrest Law after Ahmaud Arbery Shooting," *The Hill*, May 10, 2021, https://thehill.com/homenews/state-watch/552737-kemp-signs-bill-repealing-citizens-arrest-law-after-ahmaud-arbery/; Jeff Amy, "Gov. Kemp Signs Bill Repealing Georgia's 1863 Citizen's Arrest Law," News4Jax, May 10, 2021, https://www.news4jax.com/news/georgia/2021/05/10/gov-kemp-signs-bill-repealing-georgias-1863-citizens-arrest-law/; see also Frances Robles, "The Citizen's Arrest Law Cited in Arbery's Killing Dates Back to the Civil War," *New York Times*, May 13, 2020, https://www.nytimes.com/article/ahmaud-arbery-citizen-arrest-law-georgia.html. On the hate crimes law, see Yankah, "Ahmaud Arbery, Reckless Racism," 682; Grace Hauck, "Georgia Governor Signs Hate Crime Law in Wake of Ahmaud Arbery Shooting," *USA Today*, June 26, 2020, https://www.usatoday.com/story/news/nation/2020/06/26/georgia-governor-signs-hate-crime-law-following-ahmaud-arbery-shooting/3266901001/; Rachel Sandler, "Georgia Passes Hate Crime Law, Leaving Only Three States without One," *Forbes*, June 26, 2020, https://www.forbes.com/sites/rachelsandler/2020/06/26/georgia-passes-hate-crime-law-leaving-only-three-states-without-one/?sh=4c43d3864909. The Georgia Supreme Court had previously invalidated as unconstitutionally vague a previous bias-motivated crime-penalty enhancement statute. See *Botts v. State*, 278 Ga. 538, 604 S. E. 2d 512 (2004).

19. See, e.g., Yankah, "Ahmaud Arbery, Reckless Racism," 682.

20. "Southern law" may refer to different geographic areas in different times. See Sally E. Hadden and Charles L. Zelden, "Race, Power, and the Law: Southern Legal and Constitutional History," in *Reinterpreting Southern Histories: Essays in Historiography*, ed. Craig Thompson and Lorri Glover (Baton Rouge: Louisiana State University Press, 2020), 473–76; Paul Finkelman, "Exploring Southern Legal History," *North Carolina Law Review* 64, no. 1 (November 1985): 85–87. In this book, it includes, in the colonial period, the six colonies south of Pennsylvania, and, in the antebellum years, the fifteen states that had not taken steps to abolish slavery. Ibid., 86.

21. *State v. Tackett*, 8 N.C. (1 Hawks) 210 (1820).

22. See Randall Kennedy, "The State, Criminal Law, and Racial Discrimination: A Comment," *Harvard Law Review* 107, no. 6 (April 1994): 1267; see also Randall Kennedy, *Race, Crime, and the Law* (New York: Pantheon Books, 1997), 29–36, 76–80; Andrew Fede, *People without Rights: An Interpretation of the Fundamentals of the Law of Slavery in the U.S. South* (New York: Garland, 1992; repr., New York: Routledge, 2011), 61–130; Andrew Fede, "Legitimized Violent Slave Abuse in the American South, 1619–1865: A Case Study of Law and Social Change in Six Southern States," *American Journal of Legal His-*

tory 29, no. 2 (April 1985): 93–150; see generally Andrew T. Fede, *Homicide Justified: The Legality of Killing Slaves in the United States and the Atlantic World* (Athens: University of Georgia Press, 2017).

23. *State v. Jowers*, 33 N.C. (11 Ired. Law) 555 (1850).

24. See ibid., 555–56; *The State v. Atlas Jowers*, Indictment, North Carolina State Archives, Supreme Court, 1800–1909, case no. 6717; see also *In re May*, 357 N.C. 423, 425–28, 584 S.E. 2d 271, 273–75 (2003); *State v. Huntly*, 25 N.C. (3 Ired.) 418, 420–22 (1843).

25. See John Hope Franklin, *The Militant South: 1800–1861* (Cambridge, Mass.: Harvard University Press, 1956), 34.

26. See Edward L. Ayers, *Vengeance and Justice: Crime and Punishment in the 19th-Century American South* (New York: Oxford University Press, 1984), 13.

27. See text and notes in chapter 5 at notes 55 to 57.

28. *State v. Jowers*, 33 N.C. (11 Ired. Law), 555.

29. Ibid., 556–57 (emphasis added).

30. *State v. Harden*, 29 S.C.L. (2 Speers) 152 (Ct. App. Law 1832).

31. Ibid., 155.

32. *State v. Bill, a Slave*, 35 N.C. (13 Ired.) 373 (1852). See *Jacobellis v. Ohio*, 378 U.S. 184, 197 (1964) (Stewart J., concurring) ("I shall not today attempt further to define the kinds of material I understand to be embraced within that shorthand description [hard-core pornography], and perhaps I could never succeed in intelligibly doing so. But I know it when I see it, and the motion picture involved in this case is not that."); see also Paul Gerwitz, "On 'I Know It When I See It,'" *Yale Law Journal* 105, no. 4 (January 1996): 1023–47.

33. See *State v. Bill, a Slave*, 377. The North Carolina statutes made it a crime "for any slave to be insolent to a free white person," or "to utter mischievous and slanderous reports about any free white person." See *Revised Code of North Carolina, Enacted by the General Assembly at the Session of 1854*, ed. Bartholomew F. Moore and Asa Biggs (Boston: Little, Brown, 1855), 570. The court confirmed the power of a single justice of the peace to define insolence, under the procedural statutes governing the trials of enslaved defendants. See *State v. Bill, a Slave*, 377–78; John Phillip Reid, "Beneath the Titans," *New York University Law Review* 70, no. 3 (June 1995): 674n138.

34. See *State v. Bill, a Slave*, 377; Joseph E. Worcester, "Insolent" and "Insolently," in *Dictionary of the English Language* (Boston: Hickling, Swan, and Brewer, 1860), 761.

35. *State v. Bill, a Slave*, 377; see Groucho Marx, "I'm Against It," Genius.com (n.d.), https://genius.com/Groucho-marx-im-against-it-lyrics; see also, discussing this decision, e.g., Thomas D. Morris, *Southern Slavery and the Law, 1619–1860* (Chapel Hill: University of North Carolina Press, 1996), 502n27; Kenneth M. Stampp, *The Peculiar Institution: Slavery in the Ante-Bellum South* (New York: Vintage, 1956), 205–6, 209.

36. See *Ex parte Boylston*, 33 S.C.L. (2 Strob.) 41 (Court of Appeals of Law 1847). Although no statute made insolence a crime, the majority confirmed that Jim could be tried under the statutes establishing the procedures in the trials of enslaved defendants. See ibid., 41–46. Justice O'Neall dissented, but he declared that "insolence beyond all doubt is a violation of duty, which the social condition of the slave imposes on him." See ibid., 46–47 (O'Neall, J., dissenting).

37. See ibid., 46. For examples of Black conduct that was punished for being "out of place," see Richard C. Wade, *Slavery in the Cities: The South 1820–1860* (New York: Oxford University Press, 1964), 181–82.

38. I use the term "moderate" because others have so categorized these judges' views on slavery, race, and succession, when compared with those who have been included among the "fire-eating" pro-slavery successionists. See, e.g., A. E. Keir Nash, "Reason of Slavery: Understanding the Judicial Role in the Peculiar Institution," *Vanderbilt Law Review* 32, no. 1 (January 1979): 104–23. Joseph Ranney more recently described Pearson's and O'Neall's views as "contrarian." See Joseph A. Ranney, *Bridging Revolutions: The Lives of Chief Justices Richmond Pearson and John Belton O'Neall* (Athens: University of Georgia Press, 2023), 2. Nevertheless, all of these antebellum jurists shared essentially similar beliefs in white supremacist principles, although they at times disagreed on how best to implement those principles.

39. See Anders Walker, "The New Jim Crow? Recovering the Progressive Origins of Mass Incarceration," *Hastings Constitutional Law Quarterly* 41, no. 4 (Summer 2014): 848–55; see also Anders Walker, *The Ghost of Jim Crow: How Southern Moderates Used Brown v. Board of Education to Stall Civil Rights* (New York: Oxford University Press, 2009) (southern "moderate" governors sought to sustain segregation after *Brown v. Board of Education*); Howard N. Rabinowitz, *Race Relations in the Urban South, 1865–1890* (New York: Oxford University Press, 1978), 182–97, 329–39 (asserting that segregation was less onerous than total exclusion of free Blacks from public spaces); Daniel J. Sharfstein, "*Brown*, Massive Resistance, and the Lawyer's View: A Nashville Story," *Vanderbilt Law Review* 75, no. 5 (October 2021): 1435–65 (evaluating Cecil Sims as a "moderate" opponent of integration).

40. See Karen M. Tani, *States of Dependency: Welfare, Rights, and American Governance, 1935–1972* (New York: Cambridge University Press, 2016), 20; see also Lawrence M. Friedman, *Impact: How Law Affects Behavior* (Cambridge, Mass.: Harvard University Press, 2016), 44–138. Indeed, the *Harden* and *Jowers* decisions were apparently perceived to be necessary because the North and South Carolina legislatures had not defined free Black insolence as a crime.

41. See Markus Dirk Dubber, "Historical Analysis of Law," *Law and History Review* 16, no. 1 (1998): 159.

42. The terms "degraded caste" and "white supremacist" capture the essence of the legal categories and public policies that were incorporated into antebellum southern law. For a comparative study of the concept of caste in societies including the antebellum and Jim Crow South, see Isabel Wilkerson, *Caste: The Origins of Our Discontents* (New York: Random House, 2020). On the nonlinear approach in legal history, see Anat Rosenberg, "What Do Contracts Histories Tell Us about Capitalism? From Origins and Distribution to the Body of the Nation," in *The Oxford Handbook of Legal History*, ed. Markus D. Dubber and Christopher Tomlins (Oxford: Oxford University Press, 2018), 946–52.

43. See Elizabeth Dale, "Spelunking, or, Some Meditations on the New Presentism," in Dubber and Tomlins, *Oxford Handbook of Legal History*, 314 (citing Lynn Hunt, "Against Presentism," *Magazine of the American Historical Association Perspectives on History*, May 1, 2002, https://www.historians.org/publications-and-directories/perspectives-on-history/may-2002/against-presentism). I, of course, do not claim to have originated the phrase "separate and unequal"; see, e.g., Harvey Fireside, *Separate and Unequal: Homer Plessy and the Supreme Court Decision That Legalized Racism* (New York: Carroll and Graf, 2004).

44. See generally, e.g., Fede, *Homicide Justified*, 40–42, 192; Edward E. Baptist, *The Half Has Never Been Told: Slavery and the Making of American Capitalism* (New York: Basic Books, 2014), xxi, 2–3; Sven Beckert, *Empire of Cotton: A Global History* (New York: Knopf, 2014), 100–122; Walter Johnson, *River of Dark Dreams: Slavery and Empire in the Cotton Kingdom* (Cambridge: Belknap, 2013), 3–17; John Craig Hammond, *Slavery, Freedom, and Expansion in the Early American West* (Charlottesville: University of Virginia Press, 2007), 1–75; Adam Rothman, *Slave Country: American Expansion and the Origins of the Deep South* (Cambridge, Mass.: Harvard University Press, 2005), ix–xi, 34–35; W. S. Rossiter, *A Century of Population Growth: From the First to the Twelfth Census of the United States: 1790–1900* (Washington, D.C.: Government Printing Office, 1909; repr., Baltimore: Genealogical Publishing, 1969), 133.

45. The term "de jure discrimination" refers "to all forms of *de jure* discrimination—that is, discrimination 'of right' or by government—and not simply with reference to physical separation based upon race." See Richard A. Paschal, *Jim Crow in North Carolina: The Legislative Program from 1865 to 1920* (Durham, N.C.: Carolina Academic Press, 2021), xv.

46. I refer to Reconstruction with Eric Foner's caveat: "Reconstruction has conveniently been dated from the [Civil] [W]ar's end in 1865 to 1877, when the last southern state came under the control of the white supremacist Democratic party. Lately, scholars have been writing of a 'long Reconstruction' that lasted into the 1880s and even beyond. But whatever its chronological definition, Reconstruction can also be understood as a historical process without a fixed end point—the process by which the United States tried to come to terms with the momentous results of the Civil War, especially the destruction of the institution of slavery. One might almost say that we are still trying to work out the consequences of the abolition of American slavery. In that sense, Reconstruction never ended." See Eric Foner, *The Second Founding: How the Civil War and Reconstruction Remade the Constitution* (New York: Norton, 2019), xx–xxi; see also, e.g., Cody Marrs, "Three Theses on Reconstruction," *American Literary History* 30, no. 3 (Fall 2018): 407–28.

47. See A. E. Keir Nash, "A More Equitable Past? Southern Supreme Courts and the Protection of the Antebellum Negro," *North Carolina Law Review* 48, no. 2 (February 1970): 203; see also A. E. Keir Nash, "Fairness and Formalism in the Trials of Blacks in the State Supreme Courts of the Old South," *Virginia Law Review* 56, no. 1 (February 1970): 67.

48. See Fede, *Homicide Justified*, 6.

49. *Campbell v. The People*, 16 Ill. 17 (1854). A chronological timeline is provided in the book's front matter.

50. O. J. Page, *History of Massac County, Illinois: Life Sketches and Portraits* (Metropolis, Ill., 1900), 76; see *Campbell v. The People*; see also text and notes in chapter 1 at notes 48 to 56.

51. See text and notes in chapter 1 at notes 75 to 86.

52. See *Campbell v. The People*, 18–21. Similar decisions on this issue could not be found in the southern antebellum case law.

53. Compare, e.g., Paul Finkelman, "The Frist Civil Rights Movement: Black Rights in the Age of the Revolution and Chief Taney's Originalism in *Dred Scott*," *Journal of Constitutional Law* 24, no. 3 (June 2022): 720–21 (discussing the 1780 Pennsylvania gradual emancipation law's civil rights provisions), with Mark A. Graber, "Korematsu's Ances-

tors," *Arkansas Law Review* 74, no. 3 (2021): 432 ("No state court opinion issued before the Fourteenth Amendment indicated that a central purpose of any constitutional provision mandating equality was to limit race discriminations, that race discriminations were particularly offensive in light of constitutional commitments to equality, or that race discriminations required a higher degree of judicial scrutiny than other legislative discriminations," but citing *Opinion of Justices*, 44 Me. 521, 575–76 (1857) (Appleton, J., concurring) (free Blacks were citizens with the state constitutional right to vote); see also Christopher W. Schmidt, "Thirteenth Amendment Echoes in Fourteenth Amendment Doctrine," *Hastings Law Journal* 73, no. 3 (April 2022): 723–72 (constitutional jurisprudence can be understood with the equality of rights principle, which, "in its most abstract form," provides that "the strength of the Fourteenth Amendment's nondiscrimination requirement varies in relation to the importance of the sphere of the activity at issue." Ibid., 726. He traces its origin "back to the Reconstruction-era legal debates" [ibid., 727n7], contending that "assumptions about liberty and equality commonly associated with the Thirteenth Amendment" have, in "subtle and often overlooked ways . . . long operated in the Supreme Court's constitutional jurisprudence" [ibid., 725–26]).

54. "Substantive" refers to criminal law rules and doctrines establishing the elements of offenses and available defenses, distinguished from the procedural rules governing the gathering and presenting of evidence at trial. Procedural rules and practices, such as those governing jury qualification and selection leading to all-white male juries, barring Black testimony, or not requiring unanimous jury verdicts, influence the outcomes of cases, even if the substantive law requires formal equality. See, e.g., Thomas O. Main, "The Procedural Foundation of Substantive Law," *Washington University Law Review* 87, no. 4 (January, 2010): 802–41; see also Clint Smith, *How the Word Is Passed: A Reckoning with the History of Slavery Across America* (New York: Little, Brown, 2021), 86–89; Thomas Aiello, *Jim Crow's Last Stand: Nonunanimous Criminal Jury Verdicts in Louisiana* (Baton Rouge: Louisiana State University Press, 2015).

55. See, e.g., James Oakes, "Conflict vs. Racial Consensus in the History of Antislavery Politics," in *Contesting Slavery: The Politics of Bondage and Freedom in the New American Nation*, ed. John Craig Hammond and Matthew Mason (Charlottesville: University of Virginia Press, 2011), 299; see also Foner, *Second Founding*, 8–17; James Oakes, *The Crooked Path to Abolition: Abraham Lincoln and the Antislavery Constitution* (New York: Norton, 2021), xi–xxxii; Martha S. Jones, *Birthright Citizens: A History of Race and Rights in Antebellum America* (New York: Cambridge University Press, 2018), 10–12, 128–46.

56. See, e.g., Foner, *Second Founding*, 13; see also Jones, *Birthright Citizens*, 146–53; Laura F. Edwards, *A Legal History of the Civil War and Reconstruction: A Nation of Rights* (New York: Cambridge University Press, 2015), 120–76; Eric Foner, *Free Soil, Free Labor, Free Men: The Ideology of the Republican Party before the Civil War* (1970; repr., New York: Oxford University Press, 1995), 284–85.

57. See, e.g., Douglas J. Flowe, *Uncontrollable Blackness: African American Men and Criminality in Jim Crow New York* (Chapel Hill: University of North Carolina Press, 2020), 1–57; Jen Manion, *Liberty's Prisoners: Carceral Culture in Early America* (Philadelphia: University of Pennsylvania Press, 2015), 120–52; Reva Siegel, "Why Equal Protection No Longer Protects: The Evolving Forms of Status-Enforcing State Action," *Stanford Law Review* 49, no. 5 (May 1997): 1111–48.

58. See Robert W. Gordon, "Critical Histories," *Stanford Law Review* 36, nos. 1 and 2 (January 1984): 112–13.

59. See Russell Sandberg, *Subversive Legal History: A Manifesto for Legal Education* (New York: Routledge, 2021), 14 (quoting Alan Watson, *Legal Origins and Legal Change* [London: Hambledon Press, 1991], 70–72; Alan Watson, "Legal Change: Sources of Law and Legal Culture," 131 *University of Pennsylvania Law Review* 131, no. 5 [1991]: 1123).

60. See Sandberg, *Subversive Legal History*, 17; see also Russell Sandberg, *A Historical Introduction to English Law: Genesis of the Common Law* (New York: Cambridge University Press, 2023), 7–12; compare Markus D. Dubber, "Histories of Crime and Criminal Justice and the Historical Analysis of Criminal Law," in *The Oxford Handbook of the History of Crime and Criminal Justice*, ed. Paul Knepper and Anja Johansen (Oxford: Oxford University Press, 2016), 597–612 (discussing "the historical analysis of law as critical analysis of law").

61. Not all lynching incidents occurred in the southern states, although the vast majority did. See, e.g., Philip Dray, *A Lynching at Port Jervis: Race and Reckoning in the Gilded Age* (New York: Farrar, Straus and Giroux, 2022); Amy Louise Wood, *Lynching and Spectacle: Witnessing Racial Violence in America, 1890–1940* (Chapel Hill: University of North Carolina Press, 2009); Christopher Waldrep, *The Many Faces of Judge Lynch: Extralegal Violence and Punishment in America* (New York: Palgrave Macmillan, 2002); Ayers, *Vengeance and Justice*, 237–55. A minority of those victimized by lynch mobs also were not Black. See, e.g., Manfred Berg, *Popular Justice: A History of Lynching in America* (Chicago: Ivan R. Dee, 2011), 92, 117–43; Dray, *At the Hands of Persons Unknown*, 130–32; Charles Seguin and Sabrina Nardin, "The Lynching of Italians and the Rise of Antilynching Politics in the United States," *Social Science History* 46, no. 1 (Spring 2022): 65–91.

62. See generally Robert J. Cottrol, *The Long, Lingering Shadow: Slavery, Race, and Law in the American Hemisphere* (Athens: University of Georgia Press, 2013).

63. See John Anthony Scott, "Segregation: A Fundamental Aspect of Southern Race Relations, 1800–1860," *Journal of the Ealy Republic* 4, no. 4 (Winter 1984): 427.

64. See *Civil Rights Cases*, 109 U.S. 3, 3 S. Ct. 18, 27 L. Ed. 835 (1883), 20; see Scott, "Segregation," 427.

65. See, e.g., William M. Carter Jr., "Race, Rights, and the Thirteenth Amendment: Defining the Badges and Incidents of Slavery," *UC Davis Law Review* 40, no. 4 (April 2007): 1311–19.

66. See Matthew Shepard and James Byrd Jr. Hate Crimes Prevention Act, Public Law 111-84, 123 Stat. 2190 (2009), div. E., § 4702 (codified as amended 18 U.S.C. §249(a)).

67. See Matt Mullen, "The Pink Triangle: From Nazi Label to Symbol of Gay Pride," History, June 3, 2019 (updated June 19, 2019), https://www.history.com/news/pink-triangle-nazi-concentration-camps.

68. See Yankah, "Ahmaud Arbery, Reckless Racism," 686–89; see generally Joel Williamson, *After Slavery: The Negro in South Carolina During Reconstruction, 1861–1877* (Chapel Hill: University of North Carolina Press, 1965), 298; see generally George Rutherglen, "The Badges and Incidents of Slavery and the Power of Congress to Enforce the Thirteenth Amendment," in *The Promises of Liberty: The History and Contemporary Relevance of the Thirteenth Amendment*, ed. Alexander Tsesis (New York: Columbia University Press, 2010), 165–67. Appearance or family history are relevant because some

mixed-race people won their freedom in court, at least in part, because of their appearance, while others remained enslaved because of their maternal African ancestry, even though they appeared to be white. See Andrew Fede, *Roadblocks to Freedom: Slavery and Manumission in the United States South* (New Orleans: Quid Pro Books, 2011), 254–68. Some mixed-race people confronted and confounded these racial categories by passing as white or Black. See, e.g., Elizabeth M. Smith-Pryor, *Property Rites: The Rhinelander Trial, Passing, and the Protection of Whiteness* (Chapel Hill: University of North Carolina Press, 2009); Martha A. Sandweiss, *Passing Strange: A Gilded Age Tale of Love and Deception across the Color Line* (New York: Penguin, 2009); Baz Dreisinger, *Near Black: White-to-Black Passing in American Culture* (Amherst: University of Massachusetts Press, 2008); see also Ira Berlin, *Generations in Captivity: A History of African-American Slaves* (Cambridge, Mass.: Harvard University Press, 2003), 66–67.

69. Alfred L. Brophy, "Introducing Applied Legal History," *Law and History Review* 31, no. 1 (February 2013): 233; see Alfred L. Brophy, "Doing Things with Legal History," in Dubber and Tomlins, *Oxford Handbook of Legal History*, 923–40.

70. I thus agree that any attempt to learn "present lessons from history is a risky enterprise. Historians (legal or otherwise) are schooled to avoid the temptations of 'presentism.'" See Daniel Farbman, "Reconstructing Local Government," *Vanderbilt Law Review* 70, no. 2 (March 2017): 482 (citing Hunt, "Against Presentism"). Nevertheless, a careful analysis of the legal sources presented in this book may helpfully inform the necessary national debate about interracial violence. See ibid., 482–83; see also David Armitage, "In Defense of Presentism," in *History and Human Flourishing*, ed. Darren M. McMahon (Oxford: Oxford University Press, 2023), 59–84; Dale, "Spelunking," 317; Daniel Steinmetz-Jenkins, "Introduction: Whose Present? Which History?," *Modern Intellectual History* 1 (2022): 1–12, https://doi.org/10.1017/S1479244322000142; Markus D. Dubber, "New Historical Jurisprudence: Legal History as Critical Analysis of Law," *Critical Analysis of Law* 2, no. 1 (2015): 1–18, https://cal.library.utoronto.ca/index.php/cal/article/view/22512.

71. See "Chapter 31, 39 Congress, Session 1, an Act: To Protect All Persons in the United States in Their Civil Rights, and Furnish a Means of Their Vindication," U.S. Statutes at Large 14, no. Main Section (1866): 27 (codified as amended 42 U.S.C. §§ 1981–1982).

72. See Foner, *Second Founding*, 176.

73. I sketched an outline of these views in Fede, *Homicide Justified*, 223–24, and have accepted the suggestion made by a reviewer to explain my "synthetic analysis." See Jeannine DeLombard, "Review of *Homicide Justified*," *Journal of Southern Studies* 84, no. 3 (August 2018): 723.

74. See Fede, *Homicide Justified*, 224, and, discussing *Jowers*, Fede, *People without Rights*, 172–73. The *Harden* and *Jowers* decisions can be read to exemplify what Mark Tushnet called the failure or inability of most southern judges to "bracket[] slave law off from other areas of law," or the "failed attempt to develop rigid categories" of slavery law and non-slavery law. See Mark V. Tushnet, *The American Law of Slavery 1810–1860: Considerations of Humanity and Interest* (Princeton, N.J.: Princeton University Press, 1981), 8, 40. But Tushnet primarily discussed decisions in which judges reasoned by analogy from non-slavery precedents to create rules and doctrines for slavery law, based on his conceptions of "interest" rather than "humanity," which he stated should govern enslavers. Here the process went in the other direction. See ibid., 37–42; Andrew Fede, "Toward a Solu-

tion of the Slave Law Dilemma: A Critique of Tushnet's American Law of Slavery," *Law and History Review* 2, no. 2 (Fall 1984): 303–11.

75. See Robert Gordon, "Introduction: J. Willard Hurst and the Common Law Tradition in American Historiography," *Law & Society Review* 9, no. 1 (Autumn 1975): 10.

76. See Lawrence M. Friedman, "Legal Culture and Social Development," *Law and Society Review* 4, no. 1 (August 1969): 33. On the studies of the law's impact in society, see generally Friedman, *Impact*.

77. See Gordon, "Introduction," 10.

78. See, e.g., Christopher Tomlins, "What Is Left of the Law and Society Paradigm after Critique? Revisiting Gordon's 'Critical Legal Histories,'" *Law and Social Inquiry* 37, no. 1 (Winter 2012): 164; see also Kunal M. Parker, "Everything Is Contingent: A Comment on Bob Gordon's Taming the Past," *Stanford Law Review* 70, no. 5 (May 2018): 1653–58; Jessica K. Lowe, "Radicalism's Legacy: American Legal History since 1998," *Zeitschrift für Neuere Reichtsgeschicte* 36, no. 3/4 (2014): 288–97; Kunal M. Parker, "The Historiography of Difference," *Law and History Review* 23, no. 3 (Fall 2005): 694–95. For a summary and critique of historicism in legal history, and a materialist alternative based on Walter Benjamin's writings, see Christopher Tomlins, *In the Matter of Nat Turner: A Speculative History* (Princeton, N.J.: Princeton University Press, 2020), 23–24; Christopher Tomlins, "Historicism and Materiality in Legal Theory," in *Law in Theory and History: New Essays on a Neglected Dialogue*, ed. Maksymillian Del Mar and Michael Lobban (Portland, Oreg.: Hart, 2016), 57–83.

79. See John Fabian Witt, "For Bob Gordon," *Stanford Law Review* 70, no. 5 (May 2018): 1683 (citing Gordon, "Critical Histories," 81–87, 103–13).

80. See Cynthia Nicoletti, "Writing the Social History of Legal Doctrine," *Buffalo Law Review* 64, no. 1 (2016): 122 (citing Lowe, "Radicalism's Legacy").

81. See Kelly M. Kennington, *St. Louis Freedom Suits and the Legal Culture of Slavery in Antebellum America* (Athens: University of Georgia Press, 2017), 4 (citing, e.g., Susan Silbey, "Legal Consciousness," in *Oxford Companion to Law*, ed. Peter Cane and Joanne Conaghan [New York: Oxford University Press, 2008], 695–96); see also Friedman, "Legal Culture and Social Development," 33–50.

82. See Sally Engle Merry, *Getting Justice and Getting Even: Legal Consciousness among Working-Class Americans* (Chicago: University of Chicago Press, 1990), 5.

83. Sandberg, *Subversive Legal History*, 99 (discussing the contributions of feminist legal historians); see Roger Cotterrell, "Why Must Legal Ideas Be Interpreted Sociologically?," *Journal of Law and Society* 25, no. 2 (June 1998): 176–77.

84. See Melissa Milewski, *Litigating across the Color Line: Civil Cases between Black and White Southerners from the End of Slavery to Civil Rights* (New York: Oxford University Press, 2018), 17. Milewski's examples of the old school include Thomas Morris, Mark Tushnet, and Judge A. Leon Higginbotham, and her new school includes Ariela Gross, Walter Johnson, Laura Edwards, Dylan Penningroth, Rebecca J. Scott, and Tomiko Brown-Nagin. Ibid., 244n60. She omits this author from her discussion of antebellum enslavement law. Ibid., 20–24.

85. Fede, "Toward a Solution of the Slave Law Dilemma," 319.

86. Ibid.; see Fede, *Roadblocks to Freedom*, v–x; Fede, *People without Rights*, 22–25; see also Sandberg, *Subversive Legal History*, 48–79 (calling for combination of intellectual and social dimensions of legal history); Kermit L. Hall, *The Magic Mirror: Law in Amer-*

ican History (New York: Oxford University Press, 1989), 4 (encouraging study of American law's "internal and external history"). I also have used a comparative approach to study the development of enslavement law over time in different jurisdictions. See Fede, *Homicide Justified*, xi–xiii; Fede, *Roadblocks to Freedom*, iv–vi.

87. See Nicoletti, "Writing the Social History of Legal Doctrine," 139 (quoting Kenneth W. Mack, "Civil Rights History: The Old and the New," *Harvard Law Review* 126, no. 8 [June 2013]: 260, responding to Risa Goluboff, "Lawyers, Law, and the New Civil Rights History," *Harvard Law Review* 126, no. 8 [June 2013]: 2312–35).

88. See Nicoletti, "Writing the Social History of Legal Doctrine," 121; see also Shymkrishna Balganesh, "Forward: The Constraint of Legal Doctrine," *University of Pennsylvania Law Review* 163, no. 7 (June 2015): 1858 (quoting John Dickerson, "Legal Rules: Their Function in the Process of Decision," *University of Pennsylvania Law Review* 79, no. 7 [May 1931]: 835–36). Hendrik Hartog combines these approaches with a doctrinal analysis of one appellate court decision placed within its broader and narrower contexts in Hendrik Hartog, *The Trouble with Minna: A Case of Emancipation in the Antebellum North* (Chapel Hill: University of North Carolina Press, 2018).

89. See Fede, *People without Rights*, 17–27; Fede, "Toward a Solution of the Slave Law Dilemma," 311–18; Jonathan A. Bush, "Free to Enslave: The Foundations of Colonial American Slave Law," *Yale Journal of Law & Humanities* 5, no. 2 (Summer 1993): 417–70; see also Morris, *Southern Slavery and the Law*, 37–57; Alan Watson, *Slave Law in the Americas* (Athens: University of Georgia Press, 1989), 62–82; Lee B. Wilson, *Bonds of Empire: The English Origins of Slave Law in South Carolina and British Plantation America, 1660–1783* (New York: Cambridge University Press, 2021), 3–28; Bradley J. Nicholson, "Legal Borrowing and the Origins of Slave Law in the British Colonies," *American Journal of Legal History* 38, no. 1 (January 1994): 38–54.

90. See John Codman Hurd, *The Law of Freedom and Bondage in the United States* (1858/1862; repr., Boston: Little, Brown, 1968); Thomas R. R. Cobb, *An Inquiry into the Law of Negro Slavery in the United States of America* (Philadelphia: T. & J. W. Johnson and Savannah: W. Thorne Williams, 1858; repr., Athens: University of Georgia Press, 1999); Jacob D. Wheeler, *A Practical Treatise on the Law of Slavery* (New York: Allan Pollock Jr., 1837; repr., New York: Negro University Press, 1968). St. George Tucker included a summary of Virginia's property law on slavery in Appendix Note N of his American edition of William Blackstone's commentaries on the English common law. St. George Tucker, *Blackstone's Commentaries with Notes of Reference, to the Constitution and Laws, of the Federal Government of the United States; and the Commonwealth of Virginia*, vol. 3 (Philadelphia: William Young Birch and Abraham Small, 1803). John Belton O'Neall also published a summary of South Carolina slavery law. John Belton O'Neall, *Negro Law of South Carolina Collected and Digested by John Belton O'Neall* (Columbia: John G. Bowman, 1848), reprinted in *Statutes on Slavery: The Pamphlet Literature*, ed. Paul Finkelman (New York: Garland, 1988), 2:117–72.

91. See Paul Finkelman, "Introduction: Thomas R. R. Cobb and the Law of Slavery," in *Inquiry into the Law of Negro Slavery*, 1.

92. See Cobb, *Inquiry into the Law of Negro Slavery*, 312–17.

93. See text and notes in chapter 7 at notes 74 to 78.

94. See Joseph Story, *Commentaries on the Law of Bailment with Illustrations from the Civil and Foreign Law*, 7th ed., ed. Edmund H. Bennett (Boston: Little, Brown, 1863), 47,

49, 57, 58, 118, 179–80, 189, 284, 318, 335–36, 550–51, 570; Joel Prentiss Bishop, *Commentaries on the Criminal Law*, 2nd ed. (Boston: Little, Brown, 1858), 1:740–45, and passim; Theophilus Parsons, *The Law of Contracts*, vol. 1 (Boston: Little, Brown, 1857), 326–48, and passim; Sir William Oldnall Russell and Charles Sprengel Greaves, *A Treatise on Crimes and Misdemeanors in Two Volumes, Eighth American Edition*, ed. Daniel Davis, Theron Metcalf, and George Sharswood (Philadelphia: T. & J. Johnson, 1857), 1:162–66, 514, 517; Francis Wharton, *A Treatise of the Law of Homicide in the United States* (Philadelphia: Kay & Brothers, 1855), 168–69, 175–76, 288–305; James Kent, *Commentaries on American Law* (New York: O. Halsted, 1827), 2:201–9; see also Justin Simard, "Slavery's Legalisms: Lawyers and the Commercial Routine of Slavery," *Law and History Review* 37, no 2 (May 2019): 583 (citing Joseph Story, *Commentaries on the Law of Bailment with Illustrations from the Civil and Foreign Law* [Cambridge, Mass.: Hilliard and Brown, 1832], § 214, 216).

95. See George M. Stroud, *A Sketch of the Laws Relating to Slavery in the Several States of the United States of America* (2nd ed., 1856; repr., New York: Negro Universities Press, 1968); William Goodell, *The American Slave Code* (1853; repr., New York: Negro Universities Press, 1968); Harriet Beecher Stowe, *The Key to Uncle Tom's Cabin* (Boston: John P. Jewett, 1853; repr., New York: Arno Press and the New York Times, 1968).

96. See Patricia Ewick and Susan S. Silbey, *The Common Place of Law: Stories from Everyday Life* (Chicago: University of Chicago Press, 1998), 33–56. Brian Tamanaha, suggesting one half of this metaphor, attributes to the legal realists and Roberto Unger (and before them the "sociological and historical jurisprudents" beginning with Rudolf von Jhering) the idea "that society oozes through law directly and indirectly through multiple pores—legislative, judicial, executive, administrative, and the daily activities of lawyers, serving the causes of clients." See Brian Tamanaha, *A Realistic Theory of Law* (New York: Cambridge University Press, 2017), 26 (quoting Roberto Mangabeira Unger, *What Should Law Become?* [New York: Verso, 1996], 65, 126–28; Roberto Mangabeira Unger, *Law in Modern Society: Toward a Criticism of Social Theory* [New York: Free Press, 1976], 252, 259). Niklas Luhmann and Gunther Teubner advanced a theory of legal closure analogizing legal change with a biological autopoietic system, which receives extralegal input but transforms this input and reproduces itself as an autonomous communications system. See, generally, Ralf Rogowski, "Law, Autopoiesis in," in *International Encyclopedia of the Social and Behavioral Sciences*, 2nd ed., ed. James D. Wright (Oxford: Amsterdam, 2015), 13:554–56; Roger Cotterrell, "Social Theory and Legal Theory: Contemporary Interactions," *Annual Review of Law and Social Sciences* 17 (2021): 19–20; Hugh Baxter, "Niklas Luhmann's Theory of Autopoietic Legal Systems," *Annual Review of Law and Social Sciences* 9 (2013): 167–84.

97. See Kunal M. Parker, "Writing Legal History Then and Now: A Brief Reflection," *American Journal of Legal History* 56, no. 1 (March 2016): 178 (quoting Duncan Kennedy, "Three Globalizations of Law and Legal Thought: 1850–2000," in *The New Law and Economic Development: A Critical Appraisal*, ed. David Trubek and Alvaro Santos [New York: Cambridge University Press, 2006], 72). I refer to time and place to suggest that we place societies on a continuum from the simple or traditional (status) to the complex or more modern (contract). With this conceptual model we can distinguish the degrees to which the positive law may be more or less reducible to the society in or history of a specific time and place. Fede, *Homicide Justified*, 10–13 (applying concepts from Maine and Weber); see Tamanaha, *Realistic Theory of Law*, 79; Frederick Schauer, "Lawness," *Wash-*

ington *University Law Review* 95, no. 5 (2018): 1144–46. Compare the suggestions that "throughout British plantation America, all law was slave law," Wilson, *Bonds of Empire*, 11, and that law is "not like a circle or a box, with an inside and an outside, but rather a mobius strip or a Klein Bottle, which is a three-dimensional shape with only one side." Charles Barzun, "The Tale of Two Hearts: A Schlegelian Dialectic," *Buffalo Law Review* 69, no. 1 (January 2021): 31n65.

98. See Fede, "Toward a Solution of the Slave Law Dilemma," 319. I subscribe, with the stated caveats, to the "core and conventional understanding" of a "commitment to the existence of an inside and an outside" of the law box in Anglo-American legal history. See Hendrik Hartog, "Four Fragments on Doing Legal History, or Thinking with and against Willard Hurst," *Law and History Review* 39, no. 4 (November 2021): 861 (citing Barzun, "Tale of Two Hearts," 9–42).

99. See Diane Kemker, "Almost Citing Slavery: *Townshend v. Townshend* in Wills & Trusts Casebooks," *University of Pittsburgh Law Review Online* 84 (2023): 1–12; Justin Simard, "The Precedential Weight of Slavery," *New York University Review of Law and Social Change* 47, no. 1 (2023): 167–220; Justin Simard, "Citing Slavery," *Stanford Law Review* 72, no. 1 (January 2020): 92–113; Simard, "Slavery's Legalisms," 584–603; Citing Slavery Project, www.citingslavery.org.

100. See Andrew T. Fede, "Not the Most Insignificant Justice: Reconsidering Justice Gabriel Duvall's Slavery Law Opinions Favoring Liberty," *Journal of Supreme Court History* 42, no. 1 (2017): 1–16; Andrew Fede, "Legal Protection for Slave Buyers in the U.S. South: A Caveat Concerning *Caveat Emptor*," *American Journal of Legal History* 31, no. 4 (October 1987): 322–58; see also David A. Sklansky, "The Neglected Origins of the Hearsay Rule in American Slavery: Recovering *Queen v. Hepburn*," *Supreme Court Review* (forthcoming); Simard, "Citing Slavery," 85–92; Simard, "Slavery's Legalisms," 571–603. For other examples, see, e.g., Michelle A. McKinley, *Fractional Freedoms: Slavery, Intimacy, and Legal Mobilization in Colonial Lima, 1600–1700* (New York: Cambridge University Press, 2016), 203–38; Jenny Bourne Wahl, *The Bondsman's Burden: An Economic Analysis of the Common Law of Southern Slavery* (New York: Cambridge University Press, 1998), 17–19; see also Ariela J. Gross, *What Blood Won't Tell: A History of Race on Trial in America* (Cambridge, Mass.: Harvard University Press, 2008) (discussing how the concept of race arose in enslavement law).

101. See Paul D. Halliday, "Legal History: Taking the Long View," in Dubber and Tomlins, *Oxford Handbook of Legal History*, 330 ("there is no opposition between microhistory and the long view. They require one another"). On the *longue durée* approach, see generally ibid., 323–41; Jo Guldi and David Armitage, *The History Manifesto* (New York: Cambridge University Press, 2014), 1–60, 117–25; Jan de Vries, "Changing the Narrative: The New History That Was and Is to Come," *Journal of Interdisciplinary History* 48, no. 3 (Winter 2018): 313–34; David Armitage and Jo Guldi, "The Return of the *Longue Durée*: An Anglo-American Perspective," *Annales, Histoire, Sciences Sociales* 70, no. 2 (2015): 289–318. On the challenges and possibilities faced by scholars seeking to combine insights derived from the macro/micro and global/local histories, and by the students of the effects of structure and agency and history and the social sciences (to which I would add jurisprudence), see Christian G. De Vito, "History without Scale: The Micro-spatial Perspective," *Past and Present* 242, suppl. 14 (November 2019): 348–72.

102. William H. Newell, "A Theory of Interdisciplinary Studies," *Issues in Integrative Studies* 19 (2001): 4; see Barzun, "Tale of Two Hearts," 36–37. For a critique of contextualization as an "incomplete" interdisciplinary strategy, see Allen F. Repko and Rick Szostak, *Interdisciplinary Research: Process and Theory*, 3rd ed. (Los Angeles: Sage, 2017), 232–33.

103. See Dubber, "Historical Analysis of Law," 160.

104. See Harold J. Berman, "Toward an Integrative Jurisprudence: Politics, Morality, History," *California Law Review* 76, no. 4 (July 1988): 779; see also Jerome Hall, *Theft, Law and Society*, 2nd ed. (New York: Bobbs-Merrill, 1952); iii–xix; Harold J. Berman, *Law and Revolution: The Formation of the Western Legal Tradition* (Cambridge, Mass.: Harvard University Press, 1983), vi–viii, 41–45; Harold J. Berman, "The Historical Foundations of Law," *Emory Law Journal* 13, no. 5 (Special Edition 2005): 13–24.

105. See Hall, *Theft, Law and Society*, xv. Hall thus also called for the use of this approach within jurisprudence to contextualize the generally philosophical work of analytical jurisprudential scholars: "To understand legal positivism and natural law philosophy, one must take account of the political context in which they originated and of their respective policies." See Jerome Hall, "From Legal Theory to Integrative Jurisprudence," *University of Cincinnati Law Review* 33, no. 2 (Spring 1964): 172; see also Dubber, "New Historical Jurisprudence," 3, 6.

106. See, e.g., Repko and Szostak, *Interdisciplinary Research*, 322–46; see also Marietta Auer, "What Is Legal Theory?," *Rechtsgeschichte Legal History* 29 (2021): 30–39 (summarizing and evaluating the views of Hermann Kantrowiscz); Douglas W. Vick, "Interdisciplinarity and the Discipline of Law," *Journal of Law and Society* 31, no. 2 (June 2004): 163–93; Elizabeth Mertz, "Legal Language: Pragmatics, Poetics, and Social Power," *Annual Review of Anthropology* 23 (1994): 435–55.

107. See Tomlins, *In the Matter of Nat Turner*, 23 (quoting Walter Benjamin, "On the Concept of History," in *Walter Benjamin: Selected Writings, Volume 4: 1938–1940*, ed. Howard Eiland and Michael W. Jennings [Cambridge, Mass.: Harvard University Press, 2003], 391 [emphasis added by Tomlins]). For a critique and application of contextualization, see Tomlins, *In the Matter of Nat Turner*, 4–5; see also Kunal M. Parker, "Context in History and Law: A Study of the Late Nineteenth-Century American Jurisprudence of Custom," *Law and History Review* 24, no. 3 (Fall 2006): 517–18.

108. See Tomlins, *In the Matter of Nat Turner*, 19–20 (quoting Walter Benjamin, "Literary History and the Study of Literature," in Eiland and Jennings, *Walter Benjamin: Selected Writings*, 459–65, at 464).

109. See Tomlins, *In the Matter of Nat Turner*, 20 (quoting Walter Benjamin, *The Arcades Project*, trans. Howard Eiland and Kevin McLaughlin [Cambridge, Mass.: Harvard University Press, 1999], 391 [emphasis in Benjamin's original]); see also Armitage, "In Defense of Presentism," 65–66 (citing authors explaining "ideological presentism").

110. See Shadi Bartsch-Zimmer, "Mummy Dearest," review of Jane Draycott, *Cleopatra's Daughter: From Roman Prisoner to African Queen* (New York: Liveright, 2023), *New York Times Book Review* (June 18, 2023): 10.

111. See Fede, *Homicide Justified*, xii (suggesting the need to combine these approaches in legal history and citing as an example Rebecca J. Scott and Jean M. Hebrard, *Freedom Papers: An Atlantic Odyssey in the Age of Emancipation* [Cambridge, Mass.: Harvard University Press, 2012]); Reid, "Beneath the Titans," 673–76 (suggesting how this type of ap-

proach is especially important in the study of enslavement law and its judges). For a collection of some recent "scholarship at the intersection of legal and cultural history," see Patricia Hagler Minter, "Law, Culture, and History: The State of the Field at the Intersections," *American Journal of Legal History* 56, no. 1 (March 2016): 139–49. For an approach to contextualization and not the wider society, see Justin Desautels-Stein, "A Context for Legal History, or, This Is Not Your Father's Contextualism," *American Journal of Legal History* 56, no. 1 (March 2016): 29–40.

112. See Repko and Szostak, *Interdisciplinary Research*, 44–70. For a study explicitly applying this interdisciplinary approach to law, see Marilyn Tayler, "Jewish Marriage as an Expression of Israel's Conflicted Identity," in *Cases in Interdisciplinary Research*, ed. Allen F. Repko, William H. Newell, and Rick Szostak (Thousand Oaks, Calif.: Sage, 2012), 322–46; see also Ian J. Drake, "The Value of an Interdisciplinary Education for Prospective Law Students," *Journal of Interdisciplinary Studies in Education* 2, no. 1 (2013): 8–28. For Jerome Hall's earlier integrative study, see Hall, *Theft, Law and Society*. Other scholars advocating similar approaches combining insights from the analytical and historical/sociological schools of jurisprudence include Brian Tamanaha and Nicola Lacey. See Tamanaha, *Realistic Theory of Law*, 12–37; Nicola Lacey, "Jurisprudence, History, and the Institutional Quality of Law," *Virginia Law Review* 101, no. 4 (June 2015): 919–95.

113. See Dale, "Spelunking," 316 (citing Alfred H. Kelly, "Clio and the Court: An Illicit Love Affair," *Supreme Court Review* 1965 [1965]: 122n13) (defining "law office history" as "the selection of data favorable to the position being advanced without regard to or concern for contradictory data or proper evaluation of the relevance of the data proffered"); see also, e.g., Tomlins, *In the Matter of Nat Turner*, 131–44, 164–67 (discussing how antebellum Virginians used different interpretations of their history in the debates about slavery's origins there and what to do about it in the 1830s); Paul Finkelman, *Supreme Injustice: Slavery and the Nation's Highest Court* (Cambridge, Mass.: Harvard University Press, 2018), 185 (discussing how the "progressives and early New Dealers . . . reimagined" Chief Justice Roger B. Taney's jurisprudence to support their political agenda); Foner, *Second Founding*, xxi–xxix, 159 (discussing the lost cause or Dunning School interpretation of slavery and reconstruction).

114. See Tomlins, *In the Matter of Nat Turner*, 233n25.

115. See Deborah Gray White, *Ar'n't I a Woman? Female Slaves in the Plantation South*, rev. ed. (New York: Norton, 1999), 8; see also Simon P. Newman, *Freedom Seekers: Escaping from Slavery in Restoration London* (London: University of London Press, 2022), xi–xiii; Martha S. Jones, "Owner? Yes. Enslaver? Certainly. Another Chance to Examine the Terms We Use and Why They Matter," *Hard Histories at Hopkins*, July 12, 2022, https://hardhistoriesjhu.substack.com/p/owner-yes-enslaver-certainly?r=3u76o&utm_medium=ios&fbclid=IwAR18X75oSF7FuL_xTnXek2WgNwYNh3PQQWvyHvXugawp9SzuIQNWNOdokb4; P. Gabrielle Foreman et al., "Writing about Slavery / Teaching about Slavery: This Might Help," community-sourced document, https://docs.google.com/document/d/1A4TEdDgYslX-hlKezLodMIM71My3KTNozxRvoIQTOQs/mobilebasic.

116. See Margaret Abruzzo, *Polemical Pain: Slavery, Cruelty, and the Rise of Humanitarianism* (Baltimore: Johns Hopkins University Press, 2011), 14–15; see also Stephanie M. H. Camp, *Closer to Freedom: Enslaved Women and Everyday Resistance in the Plantation South* (Chapel Hill: University of North Carolina Press, 2004), 143n2.

117. See Fede, *Homicide Justified*, xiii; see also Dylan C. Penningroth, *Before the Movement: The Hidden History of Black Civil Rights* (New York: Liveright, 2023), xxvii–xxviii.

118. Jefferson-Jones, "'Driving While Black' as 'Living While Black,'" 2282n1 (quoting Kimberlé Crenshaw, "Mapping the Margins: Intersectionality, Identity Politics, and Violence Against Women of Color," *Stanford Law Review* 43, no. 6 [July 1991]: 1244n6). I will not, however, adopt "the increasingly common practice" of capitalizing "White." See Newman, *Freedom Seekers*, xiii.

119. See, e.g., Camp, *Closer to Freedom*, 1–11; Saidiya Hartman, "Venus in Two Acts," *Small Axe, Number 26* 12, no. 2 (June 2008): 1–14.

120. See Fede, "Toward a Solution of the Slave Law Dilemma," 312–14.

121. See Fede, *Roadblocks to Freedom*, 15–16, 35–36; Fede, *People without Rights*, 19–21, 34; Thomas D. Russell, "A New Image of the Slave Auction: An Empirical Look at the Role of Law in Slave Sales and a Conceptual Reevaluation of the Nature of Slave Property," *Cardozo Law Review* 18, no. 2 (November 1996): 502–4; see also Jeanne L. Schroeder, "Hegel's Slaves, Blackstone's Objects, and Hohfeld's Ghosts: A Comment on Thomas Russell's Imagery of Slave Auctions," *Cardozo Law Review* 18, no. 2 (November 1996): 525–33. Before his untimely death in 1918, Hohfeld began to explain his approach in two principal articles, Wesley N. Hohfeld, "Fundamental Legal Conceptions as Applied in Judicial Reasoning," *Yale Law Journal* 26, no. 8 (June 1917): 710–70 and Wesley N. Hohfeld, "Some Fundamental Legal Conceptions as Applied in Judicial Reasoning," *Yale Law Journal* 16, no. 1 (November 1913): 16–59; see, e.g., Gregory S. Alexander, *Commodity & Property: Competing Visions of Property in American Legal Thought 1776–1970* (Chicago: University of Chicago Press, 1997), 319–23; L. W. Sumner, *The Moral Foundation of Rights* (New York: Oxford University Press, 1987), 18–53; Pierre Schlag, "How to Do things with Hohfeld," *Law and Contemporary Problems* 78, nos. 1–2 (2015): 185–234; Joseph Singer, "The Legal Rights Debate in Analytical Jurisprudence from Bentham to Hohfeld," *Wisconsin Law Review* 1982, no. 6 (1982): 986–95; Max Radin, "A Restatement of Hohfeld," *Harvard Law Review* 51, no. 7 (May 1938): 1141–64; Arthur L. Corbin, "Legal Analysis and Terminology," *Yale Law Journal* 33, no. 5 (March 1924): 501–27; Arthur L. Corbin, "Rights and Duties," *Yale Law Journal* 29, no. 2 (December 1919): 163–73. Throughout this text I use the term "privilege" to mean "legal privilege," the "jural opposite" of "no-right," as defined by Hohfeld, and not Dylan Penningroth's very different use of the word "privilege." See Penningroth, *Before the Movement*, 4–10, 42–49; Hohfeld, "Fundamental Legal Conceptions," 710, 746–47; Hohfeld, "Some Fundamental Legal Conceptions," 16, 30–59. Penningroth emphasizes how enslavers at times granted "privileges" permitting enslaved "people without rights" to "do legal things," based on "widely shared set of understandings about property and contract," although he concedes that enslaved people could not enforce these "privileges" in court, and even when they were permitted to sue for their freedom they confronted laws that created "roadblocks to manumission." See Penningroth, *Before the Movement*, 5, 9, 33; Dylan C. Penningroth, *Joining Places: Slave Neighborhoods in the Old South* (Chapel Hill: University of North Carolina Press, 2003), 5–12. Nevertheless, any "privileges" that enslaved people exercised, like marriage and family relationships, always were subject to "the inhumanity of instant destruction" by enslavers or others, including heirs, creditors, mortgagors, or the state, who elected to enforce their legal rights to terminate any privileges. See Fede, *People without Rights*, 221; Andrew T.

Fede, "Gender in the Law of Slavery in the Antebellum United States," *Cardozo Law Review* 18, no. 2 (November 1996): 414–18.

122. See Laura F. Edwards, "Response to Rebecca Scott's 'Discerning a Dignitary Offense,'" *Law and History Review* 38, no. 3 (August 2020): 574; see generally Hendrik Hartog, "Pigs and Positivism," *Wisconsin Law Review* (1985): 933–35; see also Camp, *Closer to Freedom*, 1–3, 144–45n3; Laura F. Edwards, *The People and Their Peace: Legal Culture and the Transformation of Inequality in the Post-revolutionary South* (Chapel Hill: University of North Carolina Press, 2009), 7–8, 102–3, 117–21, 124–25; John W. Blassingame, *The Slave Community: Plantation Life in the Antebellum South* (New York: Oxford University Press, 1972), 107–8, 112–16. The limits of the agency of enslaved people and their lawyers to influence written enslavement law from the bottom up are illustrated by the freedom and manumission suits and the responses of those at the top who at times further restricted potential legal routes to freedom. See Fede, *Roadblocks to Freedom*, iv.

123. See Bryan A. Garner, *The Elements of Legal Style*, 2nd ed. (New York: Oxford University Press, 2002), 86–89.

CHAPTER 1. The Antebellum Equal Protection
Criminal Justice Road Not Taken

1. See Eric L. Muller, "Judging Thomas Ruffin and the Hindsight Defense," *North Carolina Law Review* 87, no. 3 (March 2009): 769–75; A. E. Keir Nash, "Reason of Slavery: Understanding the Judicial Role in the Peculiar Institution," *Vanderbilt Law Review* 32, no. 1 (January 1979): 218.

2. See Elmer Gertz, "The Black Laws of Illinois," *Journal of the Illinois State Historical Society* 56, no. 3 (Autumn 1963): 463.

3. See "100 Most Valuable Documents at the Illinois State Archives: 28. Campbell v. People, 16 Ill. 17 (1854)," Office of the Illinois Secretary of State, n.d., https://www.cyberdriveillinois.com/departments/archives/online_exhibits/100_documents/1854-cambell-people.html; see also Steven J. Savery, "The Free Negro in Illinois Prior to the Civil War, 1818–1860" (master's thesis, Eastern Illinois University, 1986), 17–35.

4. See Paul Finkelman, "Slavery, the 'More Perfect Union,' and the Prairie State," *Illinois Historical Journal* 80, no. 4 (Winter, 1987): 248.

5. See Paul Finkelman, "Prelude to the Fourteenth Amendment: Black Legal Rights in the Antebellum North," *Rutgers Law Journal* 17, nos. 3–4 (Spring and Summer 1987): 421–43.

6. See Anne Twitty, *Before Dred Scott: Slavery and Legal Culture in the American Confluence, 1787–1857* (New York: Cambridge University Press, 2016), 3–5, 41–43; John Craig Hammond, "Midcontinent Borderlands: Illinois and the Early American Republic, 1774–1854," *Journal of Illinois State Historical Society* 111, no. 1–2 (Spring/Summer 2017): 40–48; see also Stephen Aron, *American Confluence: The Missouri Frontier, from Borderland to Border State* (Bloomington: Indiana University Press, 2006).

7. See Hammond, "Midcontinent Borderlands," 30.

8. Ibid., 47.

9. See Michael Roark, "Little Egypt," in *The American Midwest: An Interpretative Encyclopedia*, ed. Richard Sisson, Christian Zacher, and Andrew Clayton (Bloomington: Indiana University Press, 2007), 171; Hammond, "Midcontinent Borderlands," 36–37, 47–

48; Douglas K. Meyer, "Diffusion of Upland South Folk Housing to the Shawnee Hills of Southern Illinois," *Pioneer America* 7, no. 2 (July 1975): 56.

10. John D. Barnhart, "The Southern Influence in the Formation of Illinois," *Journal of the Illinois State Historical Society* 32, no. 3 (September 1939): 363; see Eric Foner, *Free Soil, Free Labor, Free Men: The Ideology of the Republican Party before the Civil War* (1970; repr., New York: Oxford University Press, 1995), 48–51.

11. See Edward L. Ayers, *Vengeance and Justice: Crime and Punishment in the 19th-Century American South* (New York: Oxford University Press, 1984), 26–27.

12. See Nicole Etcheson, *The Emerging Midwest: Upland Southerners and the Political Culture of the Old Northwest, 1787–1861* (Bloomington: Indiana University Press, 1996), 17–18 (quoting Morris Birkbeck, *Letters from Illinois* [London: Taylor and Hessey, 1818, 97]); see also ibid., 27–39; Nicole Etcheson, "Manliness and the Political Culture of the Old Northwest, 1790–1860," *Journal of the Early Republic* 15, no. 1 (Spring 1995): 59–77.

13. See M. Scott Heerman, *The Alchemy of Slavery: Human Bondage and Emancipation in the Illinois Country, 1730–1865* (Philadelphia: University of Pennsylvania Press, 2018), 17–57; Darel Dexter, *Bondage in Egypt: Slavery in Southern Illinois* (Cape Girardeau: Southeast Missouri State University, 2011), 20–40; N. Dwight Harris, *The History of Negro Servitude in Illinois and of the Slavery Agitation in that State, 1719–1864* (Chicago: A.C. McGlurg, 1904), 1–5; M. Scott Heerman, "Beyond Plantations: Indian and African Slavery in the Illinois Country, 1720–1780," *Slavery & Abolition* 38, no. 3 (September 2017): 489–509; Robert Michael Morissey, "*Le Pays des Illinois* Finds Its Context: The Early History of Illinois in a Continental Perspective," *Journal of Illinois State Historical Society* 111, no. 1–2 (Spring/Summer 2017): 17–19; Carl Ekberg, "Black Slaves in Illinois Country, 1720–1780," *Western Illinois Regional Studies* 11 (1987): 265–77.

14. See Dexter, *Bondage in Egypt*, 41–46; Harris, *History of Negro Servitude in Illinois*, 6–7.

15. See James A. Edstrom, *Avenues of Transformation: Illinois's Path from Territory to State* (Carbondale: Southern Illinois University Press, 2022), 29–33; Heerman, *Alchemy of Slavery*, 58–81; Dexter, *Bondage in Egypt*, 46–57; Harris, *History of Negro Servitude in Illinois*, 7–15; M. Scott Heerman, "In a State of Slavery: Black Servitude in Illinois, 1800–1830," *Early American Studies* 14, no. 1 (Winter 2016): 114–39; Finkelman, "Slavery, the 'More Perfect Union,' and the Prairie State," 250; Gertz, "Black Laws of Illinois," 457–60. For the Northwest Ordinance, article VI, see "An Ordinance for the Government of the Territory of the United States Northwest of the river Ohio," in *The Public Statutes at Large of the United States of America*, ed. Richard Peters (Boston: Charles C. Little and James Brown, 1845), 1:51–53, note a; Paul Finkelman, *Slavery and the Founders: Race and Liberty in the Age of Jefferson*, 2nd ed. (Armonk: M. E. Sharpe, 2001), 32–80; Robert C. Schwemm, "*Strader v. Graham*: Kentucky's Contribution to National Slavery Litigation and the Dred Scott Decision," *Kentucky Law Journal* 97 (2009): 356–57; Paul Finkelman, "Slavery and the Northwest Ordinance: A Study in Ambiguity," *Journal of the Early Republic* 6, no. 4 (Winter 1986): 343–70. On slavery in the Northwest Territory, including Illinois, see, e.g., Christopher P. Lehman, *Slavery in the Upper Mississippi Valley, 1787–1865: A History of Human Bondage in Illinois, Iowa, Minnesota and Wisconsin* (Jefferson, N.C.: McFarland, 2011); Paul Finkelman, "Evading the Ordinance: The Persistence of Bondage in Indiana and Illinois," *Journal of the Early Republic* 9, no. 1 (Spring 1989): 22–40. For the Virginia cession, see Charles Kettleborough, ed., *Constitution Making in Indiana: A*

Source Book of Constitutional Documents with Historical Introduction and Critical Notes (Indianapolis: Indiana Historical Commission, 1916), 1:3–14; Peter Onuf, "Toward Federalism: Virginia, Congress, and the Western Lands," *William and Mary Quarterly* 3rd series, 34, no. 3 (July 1977): 353–74; Merrill Jensen, "The Cession of the Old Northwest," *Mississippi Valley Historical Review* 23, no. 1 (June 1936): 27–48.

16. See Illinois Const., Art. VI, sec. 1 (emphasis added), in *Annotated Statutes of the State of Illinois in Force May 1, 1896*, vol. 1, ed. Merritt Starr and Russell H. Curtis, 2nd ed. (Chicago: Callaghan, 1896), 63; see also John Reda, *From Furs to Farms: The Transformation of the Mississippi Valley, 1762–1825* (DeKalb: Northern Illinois University Press, 2016), 108–13; Harris, *History of Negro Servitude in Illinois*, 18–22; Finkelman, "Slavery, the 'More Perfect Union,' and the Prairie State," 251–52; Gertz, "Black Laws of Illinois," 461.

17. See Illinois Const., Art. VI, sec. 3, in *Annotated Statutes of the State of Illinois*, 63; Edstrom, *Avenues of Transformation*, 29; Heerman, *Alchemy of Slavery*, 82–108; Dexter, *Bondage in Egypt*, 64–134; Harris, *History of Negro Servitude in Illinois*, 7–26; Allison Mileo Gorsuch, "To Indent Oneself: Ownership, Contracts, and Consent in Antebellum Illinois," in *The Legal Understanding of Slavery: From the Historical to the Contemporary*, ed. Jean Allain (Oxford: Oxford University Press, 2012), 135–51; Jerome Meites, "The 1847 Illinois Constitutional Convention and Persons of Color," *Journal of the Illinois State Historical Society* 108, no. 3 and 4 (Fall 2015/Winter 2016): 271–72; Gertz, "Black Laws of Illinois," 458–63. This constitution also permitted, until 1825, the continuation of the annual leasing of slaves from other states at "the salt works near Shawntown." See Meites, "1847 Illinois Constitutional Convention," 272; Thomas Bahde, "'I Would Not Have a White upon the Premises': The Ohio Valley Salt Industry and Slave Hiring in Illinois, 1780–1825," *Ohio Valley History* 15, no. 2 (Summer 2015): 49–69.

18. See John Craig Hammond, "'Uncontrollable Necessity': The Local Politics, Geopolitics, and Sectional Politics of Slavery Expansion," in *Contesting Slavery: The Politics of Bondage and Freedom in the New American Nation*, ed. John Craig Hammond and Matthew Mason (Charlottesville: University of Virginia Press, 2011), 150–51; Robert J. Steinfeld, *The Invention of Free Labor: The Employment Relation in English and American Law and Culture, 1350–1870* (Chapel Hill: University of North Carolina Press, 1991), 142–43.

19. See "An Act respecting free Negroes, Mulattoes, Servants and Slaves," Approved March 30, 1819, in *Laws Passed by the First General Assembly of this State of Illinois at their Second Session, Held at Kaskaskia, 1819* (1819), 354–61; ibid., in J. Nick Perrin, *Perrin's History of Illinois* (Springfield: Illinois State Register, 1906), 158–69; Reda, *From Furs to Farms*, 137–41; Harris, *History of Negro Servitude in Illinois*, 23–24, 50–53; Finkelman, "Slavery, the 'More Perfect Union,' and the Prairie State," 252–53; Gertz, "Black Laws of Illinois," 463–66. The state Supreme Court in 1849 held these provisions regulating fugitive slaves were unconstitutional under the U.S. Constitution's Fugitive Slave Clause. See *Thornton's Case*, 11 Ill. (1 Peck) 332 (1849) (citing *Prigg v. Pennsylvania*, 41 U.S. (16 Pet.) 539 (1842)).

20. See "An Act Regulating the Practice in the Supreme and Circuit Courts of the State, and for Other Purposes, Approved, March 22, 1819," in *Laws Passed by the First General Assembly of this State of Illinois at Their Second Session*, 143. The act defined "mulatto" as anyone with "one fourth part or more of negro blood." Ibid.

21. See Thomas D. Morris, *Southern Slavery and the Law, 1619–1860* (Chapel Hill: University of North Carolina Press, 1996), 229–39; Andrew Fede, *People without Rights: An*

Interpretation of the Fundamentals of the Law of Slavery in the U.S. South (New York: Garland, 1992; repr., New York: Routledge, 2011), 194–95; Daniel Flanigan, *The Criminal Law of Slavery and Freedom 1800–1868* (New York: Garland, 1987), 173–87; Thomas R. R. Cobb, *An Inquiry into the Law of Negro Slavery in the United States of America* (Philadelphia: T. & J. W. Johnson and Savannah: W. Thorne Williams, 1858; repr., Athens: University of Georgia Press, 1999), 230–34; George M. Stroud, *A Sketch of the Laws Relating to Slavery in the Several States of the United States of America* (2nd ed., 1856; repr., New York: Negro Universities Press, 1968), 44–51. This rule was adopted in the other free states, including Indiana, Iowa, and California. Leon F. Litwack, *North of Slavery: The Negro in the Free States, 1790–1860* (Chicago: University of Chicago Press, 1961), 93–94; J. A. C. Grant, "Historical Note Testimonial Exclusion Because of Race: A Chapter in the History of Intolerance in California," *UCLA Law Review* 17, no. 1 (November 1969): 192–201.

22. See Litwack, *North of Slavery*, 93–94. For discussions of the effects of this rule in the unsuccessful prosecution of Baylor Winn for the murder of William Johnson, a wealthy free Black businessperson and slave owner, see Ariela J. Gross, *What Blood Won't Tell: A History of Race on Trial in America* (Cambridge, Mass.: Harvard University Press, 2008), 62; Edwin Adams Davis and William Ransom Hogan, *The Barber of Natchez* (1954; Baton Rouge: Louisiana State University Press, 1973), 262–72; Kimberly Welch, "William Johnson's Hypothesis: A Free Black Man and the Problem of Legal Knowledge in the Antebellum United States South," *Law and History Review* 37, no. 1 (February 2019): 117–24. For a discussion of the unsuccessful prosecution of Eliza Rowand for the murder of an enslaved woman, see Andrew T. Fede, *Homicide Justified: The Legality of Killing Slaves in the United States and the Atlantic World* (Athens: University of Georgia Press, 2017), 1–10.

23. See Finkelman, "Slavery, the 'More Perfect Union,' and the Prairie State," 252; see also Dexter, *Bondage in Egypt*, 180–92; Eugene H. Berwanger, *The Frontier Against Slavery: Western Anti-Negro Prejudice and the Slavery Extension Controversy* (Urbana: University of Illinois Press, 1967), 14–18; Harris, *History of Negro Servitude in Illinois*, 27–49; Suzanne Cooper Guasco, "'To Put into Complete Practice Those Hallowed Principles': Edward Coles and the Crafting of Antislavery Nationalism in Early Nineteenth-Century America," *American Nineteenth Century History* 11, no. 1 (March 2010): 24–27.

24. See *Eells v. People*, 5 Ill. (4 Scam.) 498 (1843), *aff'd sub nom*; *Moore v. People*, 55 U.S. (14 How.) 13, 14 L. Ed. 306 (1852); *Chambers v. People*, 5 Ill. (4 Scam.) 351 (1843). The state's Supreme Court, by a 4–3 vote, held that the indictment need not allege the defendant acted with scienter, or knowledge, of the alleged slave's or servant's status. This was contrary to the Ohio Supreme Court's interpretation of its state's similarly worded statute in *Birney v. State*, 8 Ohio (8 Hammond) 230 (1837). Ibid.

25. See *Revised Statutes of the State of Illinois* (Springfield, Ill.: William Walter, 1845), 387; *Owens v. People*, 13 Ill. 59 (1851); Savery, "Free Negro in Illinois," 18–19; see also, discussing similar limitations considered and either rejected or adopted in other free states, Litwack, *North of Slavery*, 66–74; Finkelman, "Prelude to the Fourteenth Amendment," 435–37. The Supreme Court of Indiana dismissed a constitutional challenge to its statute requiring free Blacks to post bonds when moving to the state. *State v. Cooper*, 5 Blackf. 258 (1839).

26. Darel Dexter, "Free and American: A Study of Eleven Families of Color, Union, Johnson, White, Jackson, Alexander, Saline, Gallatin, Williamson, Franklin, Pope and Bond Counties, Illinois" (last revised September 14, 2002), http://www.freeafrican

americans.com/Illinois.htm. Finkelman also states that the anti-Black laws were not very effective in stopping Black population growth in the Lower Midwest. See Finkelman, "Prelude to the Fourteenth Amendment," 438–39.

27. See Dexter, *Bondage in Egypt*, 15; see also ibid., 434–564; "Little Egypt in the Civil War," *Little Egypt in the Nineteenth Century*, http://littleegyptcivilwar.leadr.msu.edu/understanding-egypt-introduction/understanding-egypt-geography-and-name/. The Chicago City Council's resolutions expressing opposition to the Fugitive Slave Act of 1850 also illustrate these sectional conflicts. See Daniel Farbman, "'An Outrage upon Our Feelings': The Roles of Local Governments in Resistance Movements," *Cardozo Law Review* 42, no. 6 (October 2021): 2134–42.

28. See Etcheson, *Emerging Midwest*, 2–3.

29. Dexter, *Bondage in Egypt*, 133; see Harris, *History of Negro Servitude in Illinois*, 50–67; Meites, "1847 Illinois Constitutional Convention," 277.

30. Meites, "1847 Illinois Constitutional Convention," 282. On the debates and ratification of the 1848 constitution, see Kate Masur, *Until Justice Be Done: America's First Civil Rights Movement, from the Revolution to Reconstruction* (New York: Norton, 2021), 228–30; Berwanger, *Frontier Against Slavery*, 44–46; Meites, "1847 Illinois Constitutional Convention," 277–85. An even more restrictive proposal stating "'no negro or mulatto shall hereafter be permitted to acquire and exercise any civil or political rights, or residence within this state'—was overwhelmingly defeated." Masur, *Until Justice Be Done*, 414n8.

31. See Meites, "1847 Illinois Constitutional Convention," 285; see also Masur, *Until Justice Be Done*, 240–43; Dexter, *Bondage in Egypt*, 381–83; Gary Ecelbarger, *Black Jack Logan: An Extraordinary Life in Peace and War* (Guilford, Conn.: Lyons Press, 2005), 28–30; Berwanger, *Frontier Against Slavery*, 48–49.

32. See Masur, *Until Justice Be Done*, 241 (citing *Moore v. People*, 55 U.S. (14 How.) 13, 14 L. Ed. 306 (1852)). Justice Grier majority included dictum, which is consistent with dictum in *Mayor of New York v. Miln*, 36 U.S. (11 Pet.) 102 (1837), recognizing the states' police power "to protect themselves against the influx either of liberated or fugitive slaves, and to repel from their soil a population likely to become burdensome and injurious, either as paupers or criminals." See *Moore v. People*, 55 U.S., 18 (compare *Edwards v. California*, 314 U.S. 160 (1941) (invalidating law intended to limit migration into California)).

33. See "An Act to Prevent the Immigration of Free Negroes into This State," in *Acts, Resolutions and Memorials Passed at the Regular Session of the Third General Assembly of the State of Iowa* (Iowa City: Palmer and Paul, 1851), 172; "Constitution of Indiana, Article 13, 1851" and "An Act to Enforce the 13th Article of the Constitution. Approved June 18, 1852, Revised Statutes," in Stephen Middleton, *The Black Laws in the Old Northwest: A Documentary History* (Westport, Conn.: Greenwood, 1993), 204–5; Finkelman, "Prelude to the Fourteenth Amendment," 438–41; see also Gerald L. Neuman, "The Lost Century of American Immigration Law (1776–1875)," *Columbia Law Review* 93, no. 8 (December 1993): 1866–67. Oregon's territorial laws of 1844 and 1849, and its 1859 constitution, also included free Black exclusion provisions. See Masur, *Until Justice Be Done*, 264–66; Foner, *Free Soil, Free Labor, Free Men*, 288–91; Finkelman, "Prelude to the Fourteenth Amendment," 437; Quintard Taylor, "Slaves and Free Men: Blacks in Oregon County, 1840–1860," *Oregon Historical Quarterly* 82, no. 2 (Summer 1982): 155–58; "Crafting the Oregon Constitution: Framework for a New State, Oregon State Archives, Transcribed

1857 Oregon Constitution, Article XVIII, Section 4," https://sos.oregon.gov/blue-book/Pages/state-constitution.aspx.

34. See "An Act to Prevent the Immigration of Free Negroes into This State," in *The Statutes of Illinois, Complete to 1865*, ed. Samuel H. Treat, Walter B. Scates, and Robert S. Blackwell (Chicago: E. B. Myers and Chandler, 1866), 2:825–26.

35. See Masur, *Until Justice Be Done*, 2–3; Neuman, "Lost Century of American Immigration Law," 1867–68; see also, e.g., for Virginia, text and notes at notes; for South Carolina, "An ACT to Restrain the Emancipation of Slaves, and to Prevent Free Persons of Color from Entering into This State, and for Other Purposes," in *Statutes at Large of South Carolina*, ed. David J. McCord (Columbia: A. S. Johnston, 1840), 7:459; for North Carolina, *Revised Code of North Carolina, Enacted by the General Assembly at the Session of 1854*, ed. Bartholomew F. Moore and Asa Biggs (Boston: Little, Brown, 1855), 575–76; Warren E. Milteer Jr., *North Carolina's Free People of Color, 1715–1885* (Baton Rouge: Louisiana University Press, 2020), 60–61; for Arkansas, "An Act to Prohibit the Emigration and Settlement of Free Negroes, or Free Persons of Color, into This State," in *Acts Passed at the Fourth Session of the General Assembly of the State of Arkansas* (Little Rock: Eli Colby, 1843), 61–64; see *Pendleton v. State*, 6 Ark. 509 (1846); for Tennessee, "An Act Concerning Free Persons of Colour, and for Other Purposes," in *Public Acts Passed at the Stated Session of the Nineteenth General Assembly of the State of Tennessee, 1831* (Nashville: Republican and Gazette Office, 1832), 121–22; *State v. Claiborne*, 19 Tenn. (Meigs) 331 (1838); for Alabama, John G. Aikin, *A Digest of the Laws of Alabama* (Philadelphia: Alexander Towar, 1833), 396–97.

36. See Masur, *Until Justice Be Done*, 243; see also Dexter, *Bondage in Egypt*, 390–93; Berwanger, *Frontier Against Slavery*, 50–51; Brent M. S. Campney, "'The Peculiar Climate of This Region': The 1854 Cairo Lynching and Historiography of Racist Violence Against Blacks in Illinois," *Journal of the Illinois State Historical Society* 107, no. 2 (Summer 2014): 143–70. For a prosecution under this act during the Civil War, see V. Jacque Voegeli, *Free but Not Equal: The Midwest and the Negro during the Civil War* (Chicago: University of Chicago Press, 1967), 88–89; J. N. Gridley, "A Case under an Illinois Black Law," *Journal of the Illinois State Historical Society* 4, no. 4 (January 2012): 400–425.

37. See Savery, "Free Negro in Illinois," 9.

38. Ibid., 13.

39. See Masur, *Until Justice Be Done*, 244.

40. See ibid., 244–66; see also Ecelbarger, *Black Jack Logan*, 29. Compare Litwack, *North of Slavery*, 74 (noting that Ohio was the only state to repeal its anti-Black immigrations provisions before the Civil War), with, Finkelman, "Prelude to the Fourteenth Amendment," 439, 442 (noting that the Illinois law was ineffective between 1850 and 1860, as the state's free Black population grew by 40 percent, from 5,436 to 7,628).

41. See *Nelson (a mulatto) v. People*, 33 Ill. 390 (1864) (sustaining statute); see also Masur, *Until Justice Be Done*, 299–300; Margaret Garb, *Freedom's Ballot: African American Political Struggles in Chicago from Abolition to the Great Migration* (Chicago: University of Chicago Press, 2014), 39–40; Dexter, *Bondage in Egypt*, 388–90; Harris, *History of Negro Servitude in Illinois*, 236–40; Roger D. Bridges, "Antebellum Struggle for Citizenship," *Journal of the Illinois State Historical Society* 108, nos. 3–4 (Fall 2015/Winter 2016): 296–321; Finkelman, "Prelude to the Fourteenth Amendment," 441–42; Savery, "Free Negro in Illinois," 33–34.

42. See *Campbell v. The People*, 16 Ill. 17 (1854), 18; *Campbell v. People*, Indictment, Illinois State Archives; see also Ecelbarger, *Black Jack Logan*, 33.

43. See George W. May, *History of Massac County* (Galesburg, Ill.: Waggoner, 1955), 74–77.

44. O. J. Page, *History of Massac County, Illinois: Life Sketches and Portraits* (Metropolis, Ill., 1900), 40.

45. See May, *History of Massac County*, 78–89.

46. See ibid., 90.

47. See ibid., 98.

48. See *Campbell v. The People*, 18.

49. See S. A. Buckmaster, "Warden's Report, Illinois Penitentiary," January 1, 1855, in *Reports Made to the Nineteenth General Assembly of the State of Illinois Convened January 1, 1855* (Springfield, Ill.: Lanphier & Walker, 1855), 134.

50. See Sixth Census of the United States, 1840, Williamson, Tennessee, National Archives Microfilm Publication, M704, roll 537, page 162, Ancestry.com; Fifth Census of the United States, 1830, Rutherford, Tennessee, National Archives Microfilm Publication, M19, roll 179, page 345, Ancestry.com; "Free People of Color, Part I (blog)," *From Slaves to Soldiers and Beyond—Williamson County, Tennessee's African American History*, November 3, 2017, http://usctwillcotn.blogspot.com/2017/11/free-people-of-color-part-i.html.

51. See Seventh Census of the United States, 1850, Massac, Illinois, National Archives Microfilm Publication, M432, roll 120, page 221A, Ancestry.com.

52. See Illinois State Census 1855, Illinois State Archives, archive collection number 103.008, roll 21898, line 28, Ancestry.com.

53. See 1860 U.S. Census, population schedule, National Archives Microfilm Publication, M653, roll 120, page 884, Ancestry.com.

54. See Seventh Census of the United States, 1850, Massac, Illinois, National Archives Microfilm Publication, M432, roll 120, page 244B, image 327, Ancestry.com.

55. See ibid.; Kentucky, County Marriage Records, 1783–1965, October 17, 1826, file number 001912849, Ancestry.com (Goodin [sic] Parker and Rosanna [sic] Morgan); Sixth Census of the United States, 1840, Liberty, Casey, Kentucky, National Archives Microfilm Publication, M704, roll 107, page 164, Ancestry.com; Fifth Census of the United States, 1830, Casey Kentucky, National Archives Microfilm Publication, M19, roll 34, Ancestry.com.

56. See Bureau of Land Management, General Land Office Records, U.S. General Land Office Records, 1776–2015, July 1, 1851, Ancestry.com; Illinois, Public Land Purchase Records, 1813–1909, Ancestry.com.

57. See *Franklin County Illinois 1818–1996* (Paducah, Ky.: Turner, 1996), 43; John W. Allen, *Legends and Lore of Southern Illinois* (Carbondale: Southern Illinois University Press, 1963), 30, 250; *Blue Book of the State of Illinois*, ed. James A. Rose (Springfield, Ill.: Phillips Bros., State Printer, 1903); Page, *History of Massac County*, 46, 73; *Journal of the Executive Proceedings of the Senate of the United states of America from December 6, 1850, to August 6, 1861, Inclusive Volume XI* (Washington: Government Printing Office, 1887), 128; *Alton (Ill.) Daily Courier*, April 4, 1859, 2.

58. See Ecelbarger, *Black Jack Logan*, 30; Berwanger, *Frontier Against Slavery*, 49n46.

59. See, for biographies of Logan, Ecelbarger, *Black Jack Logan*; James Pickett Jones, *Black Jack: John A. Logan and Southern Illinois in the Civil War Era* (Tallahassee: Florida

State University Press, 1967); see also Allen, *Legends and Lore of Southern Illinois*, 28–29; General John A. Logan Museum, https://loganmuseum.org/; "A Brief Biography of John A. Logan," John A. Logan College, https://www.jalc.edu/admissions/general-information/a-brief-biography-of-john-a-logan.

60. See "Political Life: How Does an Avid Racist and Author of the Illinois Black Laws Become an Advocate for African American Civil Rights and Education?," General John A. Logan Museum, https://loganmuseum.org/political-life/. On Logan's postwar attitudes on race and support among African Americans, see Ecelbarger, *Black Jack Logan*, 245–47, 294–95, 318–19.

61. See "Reception and Dinner to the Veteran 32d Regiment," *Illinois State Journal* (Springfield), April 27, 1864, 3; Voegeli, *Free but Not Equal*, 179. For what Voegeli calls an "unabashed" statement of the "leading" Republican *Illinois State Journal*'s similar antislavery but derogatory references to Blacks and the state's proposed 1862 constitution's article XVIII, titled "Negroes and Mulattoes," see ibid., 28, quoting "The Nigger and the New Constitution," *Illinois State Journal* (Springfield), March 26, 1862, 2. See also *Page 27 Constitution of the State of Illinois, 1862* [proposed], Illinois Constitution (Illinois State Archives), http://www.idaillinois.org/digital/collections/is/id/319.

62. See *Campbell v. People*, Transcript of Arraignment and Plea and Testimony of G. W. Washburn, Illinois State Archives.

63. See James Campbell Brandon, *History of the Bench and Bar of Butler County Pennsylvania* (Butler County Historical Society, 1968), 62.

64. See James A. McKee, *Twentieth Century History of Butler and Butler County, Pa. and Representative Citizens* (Chicago: Richmond-Arnold, 1909), 248.

65. See Seventh Census of the United States, 1850, Massac, Illinois, National Archives Microfilm Publication, M432, roll 112, page 321B, Ancestry.com; see also "Liston Homer Montgomery," in *A Biographical History with Portraits of the Prominent Men of the Great West* (Chicago: Manhattan, 1894), 127–28; *Chicago Tribune*, September 2, 1883, 6 (death notice for Elizabeth C. Jack, survived by son F. C Taylor and daughter Olive Branch Motherspaw, later Montgomery); see also "Marry Again after Divorce," *Chicago Tribune*, June 9, 1902, 3; "Mrs. Olive B. Montgomery Gets Divorce," *Chicago Tribune*, January 31, 1900, 7; "Montgomery Divorce Suit," *Inter Ocean* (Chicago), December 7, 1899, 5; ibid., April 10, 1899, 6.

66. See Michael E. Bragg and Jon M. Bragg, *Images of America: Metropolis* (Charleston, S.C.: Arcadia, 2010), 7; Page, *History of Massac County*, 76.

67. See Allen, *Legends and Lore of Southern Illinois*, 250; see also Page, *History of Massac County*, 74, 76–77.

68. See "Liston Homer Montgomery," in *Biographical History with Portraits*, 127.

69. See Page, *History of Massac County*, 74, 77; compare "Fatal Affray—Death of J. Jack," *Mound City Weekly Emporium*, Thursday 7 Jan 1858," in Obituaries and Death Notices in Pulaski County, Illinois Newspapers: *The National Emporium* and *Mound City Weekly Emporium* 7 Jan 1858–30 Dec 1858, Mound City, Pulaski County, Ill., transcribed and edited by Darrel Dexter, http://www.rootsweb.ancestry.com/~Pulaski/obits_1858.html; with *The Natchez Weekly Democrat*, January 20, 1858; *Daily Nashville Patriot*, January 11, 1858, 1; *New Albany (Ind.) Ledger*, January 18, 1858, 3; *New Albany (Ind.) Ledger*, January 7, 1858, 3.

70. See Roger L. Steverns, *Prairie Justice: A History of Illinois Courts under Federal, English, and American Law*, ed. John A. Lupton (Carbondale: Southern Illinois University Press, 1959), 59–67; John M. Palmer, *The Bench and Bar of Illinois* (Chicago: Lewis, 1899), 1:39–41; H. W. Howard Knott, "Caton, John Dean," in *Dictionary of American Biography*, ed. Allen Johnson (New York: Charles Scribner's Sons, 1929), 3:575–76; Robert Fergus, *Biographical Sketch of John Dean Caton: Ex-Chief Justice of Illinois* (Chicago: Fergus Printing, 1882), 3–8; "The Third Branch—A Chronicle of the Illinois Supreme Court," http://www.illinoiscourts.gov/supremecourt/JusticeArchive/Bio_Caton.asp.

71. See Knott, "Caton, John Dean," 575.

72. Treat was born in Otsego County, New York. He studied law there and was admitted to the bar. In 1834, he moved to Springfield, Illinois, where, in 1839, he began a forty-eight-year judicial career. See Palmer, *Bench and Bar of Illinois*, 1:34–35; "Samuel Hubbel Treat," Illinois Courts, http://www.illinoiscourts.gov/supremecourt/JusticeArchive/Bio_Treat.asp. Scates was born in Virginia, but he moved with his parents to Kentucky, where he studied law. He later moved to Illinois and started practicing law in 1831. Five years later, he began his judicial career. See Palmer, *Bench and Bar of Illinois*, 1:35–37; "Walter B. Scates," Illinois Courts, http://www.illinoiscourts.gov/supremecourt/JusticeArchive/Bio_Scates.asp.

73. See Edgar F. Raines Jr., "The Ku Klux Klan in Illinois, 1867–1875," *Illinois Historical Journal* 78, no. 1 (Spring 1985): 17–44.

74. See Page, *History of Massac County*, 76; see also *Campbell v. The People*, 18; Allen, *Legends and Lore of Southern Illinois*, 250.

75. See "Old Fashioned House-raising," *Historic Arkansas Museum*, March 1, 2015, https://www.historicarkansas.org/blog/old-fashioned-house-raising; "Barn Raising," *Merriam-Webster*, https://www.merriam-webster.com/dictionary/barn%20raising; "House-Raising," *Merriam-Webster*, https://www.merriam-webster.com/dictionary/house-raising.

76. See *Campbell v. People*, Record of Proceedings, Testimony of Joseph Dupree, Illinois State Archives; Seventh Census of the United States, 1850, Massac, Illinois, National Archives Microfilm Publication, M432, roll 120, page 251B, Ancestry.com.

77. See *Campbell v. The People*, 18.

78. See Page, *History of Massac County*, 76; see also *Campbell v. The People*, 18; Allen, *Legends and Lore of Southern Illinois*, 250.

79. See Seventh Census of the United States, 1850, Massac, Illinois, National Archives Microfilm Publication, M432, roll 120, page 244b, image 327, Ancestry.com; ibid., page 225; ibid., 244b.

80. See *Campbell v. People*, Record of Proceedings, Testimony of James H. Parker and Robert Harris, Illinois State Archives.

81. See ibid., Testimony of Joseph Dupree, Illinois State Archives.

82. See ibid., Testimony of James H. Parker, Illinois State Archives.

83. See ibid., Testimony of Samuel Yandell, Illinois State Archives.

84. See ibid., Proffer of testimony and ruling, Illinois State Archives.

85. See ibid.; *The Statutes of Illinois: An Analytical Digest of the General Laws of the State in Force at the Present time 1818–1868*, ed. Eugene L. Gross (Chicago: E. B. Myers, 1868), 185; *A Compilation of the Statutes of the State of Illinois, of a General Nature, in Force January 1, 1856, Part I*, 362–63; *Sellers v. The People*, 6 Ill. (1 Gil) 183 (1844); see also

Page, *History of Massac County*, 76–77; Buckmaster, "Warden's Report, Illinois Penitentiary," 134.

86. See *Campbell v. People*, Motion for New Trial, Illinois State Archives. A notation in the margin refers to the judge's decision denying the motion. Ibid.

87. See *Campbell v. People*, Bill of Exceptions and Writ of Error, Illinois State Archives.

88. See *Campbell v. People*, Affidavit of John A. Logan, dated November 17, 1854, Illinois State Archives. Jack filed an affidavit opposing Logan's motion. See Affidavit of J. Jack, dated November 17, 1854, Illinois State Archives.

89. *Campbell v. The People*, 18.

90. *A Compilation of the Statutes of the State of Illinois, of a General Nature, in Force January 1, 1856, Part I*, ed. N. H. Purple (Chicago: Keen and Lee, 1856), 362.

91. Ibid., 362–63.

92. Ibid., 363.

93. See *Campbell v. The People*, 18.

94. See Allen, *Legends and Lore of Southern Illinois*, 250–51; Page, *History of Massac County*, 76–77; see also *Wiggins v. People*, 93 U.S. 465, 23 L. Ed. 941 (1876); *Johnson v. State*, 54 Miss. 430, 432 (1877); T. J. Oliver, Annotation, "Admissibility of Evidence of Uncommunicated Threats on Issue of Self-Defense in Prosecution for Homicide," *American Law Reports*, 2nd ed. 98 (New York: Lawyers Co-operative, 1964), 6–185; Note, "Evidence-Admissibility of Uncommunicated Reputation of Deceased in Homicide Cases Where Issue is Self Defense," *Yale Law Journal* 37, no. 8 (June 1921): 1155–56; Note, "Evidence of Threats by Deceased Against Defendant in Support of the Plea of Self-Defence," *Columbia Law Review* 16, no. 1 (January 1916): 57–58; see also Note, "Evidence—Declarations Concerning Intention, Feelings or Bodily Conditions—Admissibility of Uncommunicated Threats in Homicide Case," *Harvard Law Review* 34, no. 6 (April 1921): 675–76.

95. *Campbell v. The People*, 18–19.

96. Ibid., 19.

97. See Richard Singer, "The Resurgence of Mens Rea: II—Honest but Unreasonable Mistake of Fact in Self Defense," *Boston College Law Review* 28, no. 3 (May 1987): 484n148 (citing cases following *Campbell*). Singer notes that this rule established in the *Campbell* decision may be read to be inconsistent with the Illinois homicide statute then and later in effect, "which seems to require absolute necessity." Ibid.; see Gross, *Statutes of Illinois*, 185–86, for the statute in effect when the *Campbell* case was decided. For the more current standard, see, e.g., *People v. Jeffries*, 164 Ill. 2d 104, 646 N.E. 2d 587, 598 (1995) ("After the State establishes the elements of murder . . . , the trier of fact next addresses the issue of lawful justification. In order to instruct the jury on self-defense, the defendant must establish some evidence of each of the following elements: (1) force is threatened against a person; (2) the person threatened is not the aggressor; (3) the danger of harm was imminent; (4) the threatened force was unlawful; (5) he actually and subjectively believed a danger existed which required the use of the force applied; and (6) his beliefs were objectively reasonable [citations and footnote omitted]").

98. *Campbell v. The People*, 19–20. Although Caton does not cite any authority for this principle, it can be found in contemporary legal treatises, including William Oldnall Russell, *A Treatise of Crimes and Misdemeanors in Two Volumes, First American Edition*, ed.

Daniel Davis (Boston: Wells and Lilly, 1824) (citing *King v. Richardson and Greenow*, 1 Leach 387 (1785)).

99. *Campbell v. The People*, 20.

100. See ibid.

101. Ibid., 20–21.

102. See, e.g., *People v. Galloway*, 7 Ill. 2d 527, 536, 131 N.E. 2d 474 (1956) (reversing conviction for sale of heroin); *People v. Crump*, 5 Ill. 2d 251, 125 N.E. 2d 615, 624–25 (1955) (reversing murder conviction); *People v. Kirkendoll*, 415 Ill. 404, 410–11, 114 N.E. 2d 459 (1953) (reversing rape conviction); but see *People v. White*, 48 Ill. App. 3d 907, 914, 363 N.E. 2d 408 (1977) (affirming armed robbery conviction because the trial judge, following Supreme Court IPI Criminal Instruction 1.01, instructed the jury to not "be influenced by race, color, religion or national ancestry").

103. See Page, *History of Massac County*, 77; Buckmaster, "Warden's Report, Illinois Penitentiary," 134.

104. See Gary M. Johnston, "'Truth Somewhere in the Telling': The Legend of the Wigton Massacre," *Pennsylvania Folklife* 43, no. 1 (Autumn 1993): 20.

105. Ibid., 29.

106. Ibid., 29.

107. See *Interesting Trials, Case of Samuel Mohawk, an Indian of the Seneca Tribe, Charged with the Murder of the Wigton Family* (Pittsburgh: Foster, McMillin and Gamble, 1843), 10–11.

108. See ibid., 14.

109. See Johnston, "'Truth Somewhere in the Telling,'" 30.

110. See Charles Clark, "George W. Smith," KansasBogusLegislature.org, http://kansasboguslegislature.org/free/smith_g_w.html.

111. For a study of other foiled or impeded lynching incidents, see E. M. Beck, "Judge Lynch Denied: Combating Mob Violence in the American South, 1877–1950," *Southern Cultures* 21, no. 2 (Summer 2015): 117–39, but see Anthony Gregory, "Policing Jim Crow America: Enforcers' Agency and Structural Transformations," *Law and History Review* 40, no. 1 (February 2022): 102–4 (citing authorities suggesting that, in the Jim Crow South, "law enforcement enabled something akin to a lynching regime").

112. See Charles R. McKirdy, *Lincoln Apostate: The Matson Slave Trial* (Jackson: University Press of Mississippi, 2011), 69–70, 149n96; Harris, *History of Negro Servitude in Illinois*, 110–12.

113. *Somerset v. Stewart*, 98 Eng. Rep. 499, Lofft 1 (1772); see *Hone v. Ammons*, 14 Ill. 29 (1852)(opinion by Caton based on the presumption of freedom affirming the dismissal of suit on a note for the sale of a Black man).

114. See *Willard v. People*, 5 Ill. (4 Scam.) 461 (1843); McKirdy, *Lincoln Apostate*, 71–73; Harris, *History of Negro Servitude in Illinois*, 114.

115. See *Eells v. People*, 5 Ill. (4 Scam.) 498 (1843), *aff'd sub nom. Moore v. People*, 55 U.S. (14 How.) 13, 14 L. Ed. 306 (1852); Harris, *History of Negro Servitude in Illinois*, 112–13.

116. *Jarrot v. Jarrot*, 7 Ill. (2 Gilm.) 1 (1845). See David B. Kopel, "Lyman Trumbull: Author of the Thirteenth Amendment, Author of the Civil Rights Act, and the First Second Amendment Lawyer," *Loyola University Chicago Law Journal* 47, no. 4 (Summer 2016): 1135 (quoting Andrew M. Cooperman, "St. Louis Legal Landmarks," *St. Louis Magazine* [January 20, 2012], https://www.stlmag.com/St-Louis-Legal-Landmarks/).

117. See *Jarrot v. Jarrot*, 2–9; Harris, *History of Negro Servitude in Illinois*, 116–18.

118. See ibid.; Kopel, "Lyman Trumbull," 1125–36.

119. See *Jarrot v. Jarrot*, 3–21; see also Heerman, *Alchemy of Slavery*, 5–6; Harris, *History of Negro Servitude in Illinois*, 116–18; Newton N. Newhouse, "Judicial Decision Making and the End of Slavery in Illinois," *Journal of the Illinois State Historical Society* 98, no. 1–2 (Spring–Summer 2005): 17–21; Finkelman, "Evading the Ordinance," 41–51.

120. See Kopel, "Lyman Trumbull," 1122–27. Trumbull advanced this legislation because he feared that the Court, then dominated by Whigs, would interpret the state constitution to prevent voting by immigrants, who he believed generally supported Democrats. Ibid.

121. See *Jarrot v. Jarrot*, 3–21.

122. Ibid., 21.

123. See "Act Regulating the Practice in the Supreme and Circuit Courts," 143.

124. See Dexter, *Bondage in Egypt*, 386–88; Ecelbarger, *Black Jack Logan*, 28–30; Berwanger, *Frontier Against Slavery*, 48–51; Jones, *Black Jack*, 17–19; Litwack, *North of Slavery*, 93; Harris, *History of Negro Servitude in Illinois*, 235–37; see generally, for the Illinois laws, John Codman Hurd, *The Law of Freedom and Bondage in the United States* (1858/1862; repr., Boston: Little, Brown, 1968), 2:134–37.

125. See Ecelbarger, *Black Jack Logan*, 29 (quoting Arthur C. Cole, *The Era of the Civil War* (Springfield, Ill.: Centennial Commission, 1919), 225).

126. Berwanger, *Frontier Against Slavery*, 49n46 (quoting January 16, 1853, letter from Parrish to Logan, John A. Logan Family Papers, Manuscript Division, Library of Congress).

127. See Foner, *Free Soil, Free Labor, Free Men*, 284 (noting that, in Illinois in the 1840s and 1850s, some opposed the Logan Law, supported the repeal of the Black Laws, assisted fugitive slaves, and "long fought for legal equality for Negroes").

CHAPTER 2. Chief Justice Taylor and
Unequal Criminal Law Protection for Slaves

1. *State v. Tackett*, 8 N.C. (1 Hawks) 210 (1820).

2. See, e.g., A. E. Keir Nash, "Reason of Slavery: Understanding the Judicial Role in the Peculiar Institution," *Vanderbilt Law Review* 32, no. 1 (January 1979): 83.

3. I once again quote the version of the original manuscript cited by Christopher Tomlins in *Freedom Bound: Law, Labor, and Civic Identity in Colonizing English America, 1580–1865* (New York: Cambridge University Press, 2010), 428–29. See Andrew T. Fede, *Homicide Justified: The Legality of Killing Slaves in the United States and the Atlantic World* (Athens: University of Georgia Press, 2017), 42–47. I am grateful to professor Tomlins for his generosity in providing me with a copy of his typescript of the act, portions of which are published as "An Act for the Better Ordering of Negroes," Barbados 1661 (Public Records Office Kew, CO 30/2/16–26, 32–3), in *Slavery: Oxford Readers*, ed. Stanley L. Engerman, Seymour Drescher, and Robert Paquette (New York: Oxford University Press, 2001), 105–13. The manuscript now is available at "Barbados Slave Code," Slavery Law & Power in Early America and the British Empire, https://blog.umd.edu/slaverylawandpower/barbados-slave-code/. Edward Rugemer concurs with Stanley Engerman's equally plausible reading of the original document to refer to Africans as an "uncertain, dan-

gerous *pride* of people," like a pride of lions, which is consistent with the animalization of enslaved people in the thinking of enslavers throughout history. See Edward B. Rugemer, *Slave Law and the Politics of Resistance on the Early Atlantic World* (Cambridge, Mass.: Harvard University Press, 2018), 32–33, 313n50, 314n59–63 (emphasis added). For discussions of this act, see, e.g., ibid., 26–34; Justine Collins, "English Societal Laws as the Origins of the Comprehensive Slave Laws of the British West Indies," in *Common Law, Civil Law, and Colonial Law*, ed. William Eves, John Hudson, Ingrid Ivarsen, and Sarah B. White (New York: Cambridge University Press, 2021), 307–10; Sally E. Hadden, "The Fragmented Laws of Slavery in the Colonial and Revolutionary Eras," in *The Cambridge History of Law in America*, ed. Michael Grossberg and Christopher Tomlins, 3 vols. (New York: Cambridge University Press, 2008), 1:259–63; Jerome S. Handler, "Custom and Law: The Status of Enslaved Africans in Seventeenth-Century Barbados," *Slavery and Abolition* 37, no. 2 (June 2016): 246–47; Paul Finkelman, "The Crime of Color," *Tulane Law Review* 67, no. 6 (June 1993): 2070–77; see also Katherine Gerbner, *Christian Slavery: Conversion and Race in the Protestant Atlantic World* (Philadelphia: University of Pennsylvania Press, 2018), 31–46, 89–90, 193–94 (discussing this and later acts and asserting generally that beliefs in Protestant supremacy were replaced by white supremacy as the moral and legal justification for the enslavement of Africans in the British colonies, including Barbados) and Robert P. Jones, *The Hidden Roots of White Supremacy and the Path to a Shared American Future* (New York: Simon & Schuster, 2023), 14–23 (asserting how the Papal Doctrine of Discovery was used to justify white European Christian supremacist beliefs as well as conquest and enslavement over "all other cultures, religious, and religions").

4. See, e.g., Ely Aaronson, *From Slave Abuse to Hate Crime: The Criminalization of Racial Violence in American History* (New York: Cambridge University Press, 2014), 26–60; James Campbell, *Crime and Punishment in African American History* (New York: Palgrave Macmillan, 2013), 44–48; Thomas D. Morris, *Southern Slavery and the Law, 1619–1860* (Chapel Hill: University of North Carolina Press, 1996), 161–81; Andrew Fede, *People without Rights: An Interpretation of the Fundamentals of the Law of Slavery in the U.S. South* (New York: Garland, 1992; repr., New York: Routledge, 2011), 61–130, 159–80; Daniel Flanigan, *The Criminal Law of Slavery and Freedom 1800–1868* (New York: Garland, 1987), 1–72; George M. Stroud, *A Sketch of the Laws Relating to Slavery in the Several States of the United States of America* (2nd ed., 1856; repr., New York: Negro Universities Press, 1968), 69–95.

5. See Fede, *Homicide Justified*, 11.

6. See ibid., 36.

7. See Francis Wharton, *A Treatise of the Law of Homicide in the United States* (Philadelphia: Kay & Brothers, 1855), 168–69; Sir Michael Foster, *A Report of Some Proceeding of the Commission for the Trial of the Rebels in the Year 1746, in the County of Surry; and Other Crown Cases: To Which Are Added Discourses upon a Few Branches of the Crown Law*, 3rd ed., ed. Michael Dalton (London: W. Clarke & Sons, 1809), 290–97; Edward Hyde East, *A Treatise of the Pleas of the Crown* (Philadelphia: P. Byrne, 1806), 230–46; William Blackstone, *Commentaries on the Laws of England*, 12th ed., ed. Edward Christian (London: A. Strahan and W. Woodfall, 1795), 4:*198–*201.

8. See Fede, *Homicide Justified*, 37; Joel Prentiss Bishop, *Commentaries on the Criminal Law*, 7th ed. (Boston: Little, Brown, 1882), 2:365–66, 371, 383–84; William Oldnall Russell, *A Treatise on Crimes and Indictable Misdemeanors* (London: Joseph Butterworth,

1826), 532–33; William Hawkins, *A Treatise of the Pleas of the Crown; or, A System of the Principal Matters Relating to That Subject Digested under Their Proper Hands* (London: Eliz. Nutt, 1716), 73–74; Michael Dalton, *The Countrey Justice, Conteyning the Practice if the Justices of the Peace of Their Sessions, Gathered for the Better Helpe of Such Justices of the Peace as Have Not Beene Much Conversant in the Studie of the Lawes of This Realme* (London: Societie Stationers, 1618), 216; *Rex v. Grey* (Newgate Sessions 1666), in Courtney Stanhope Kenny, *A Selection of Cases Illustrative of English Criminal Law* (Cambridge: Cambridge University Press, 1901) (affirming blacksmith's murder conviction for killing servant by breaking his skull with an iron bar), 105–6; *State v. Shaw*, 64 S.C. 566, 43 S.E. 14 (1902) (affirming employer's conviction for murdering young boy servant), with annotation in Burdett A. Rich and Henry P. Farnham, *The Lawyers Report Annotated 1903 Extra Annotated Edition of 1913* (Rochester: Lawyers Co-operative Publishing, 1915), 801–5); *State v. Bitman*, 13 Iowa 485 (1862) (sustaining information alleging father cruelly and inhumanly whipped and beat his own three-year-old child); see also Morris, *Southern Slavery and the Law*, 162–63; Lea VanderVelde, "The Last *Legally* Beaten Servant in America: From Compulsion to Coercion in the American Workplace," *Seattle University Law Review* 39, no. 3 (Spring 2016): 727–85.

9. See VanderVelde, "Last *Legally* Beaten Servant in America," 736 (citing Wesley N. Hohfeld, *Fundamental Legal Conceptions as Applied in Judicial Reasoning and Other Legal Essays*, ed. Walter W. Cook [New Haven, Conn.: Yale University Press, 1923]); see also Robert J. Steinfeld, *The Invention of Free Labor: The Employment Relation in English and American Law and Culture, 1350–1870* (Chapel Hill: University of North Carolina Press, 1991), 59, 129–38, 152–53; David Yosifon, "Agent Correction: Chastisement, Wellness, and Personal Ethics," *Florida State University Law Review* 50, no. 3 (Spring 2023): 444–50.

10. See Fede, *Homicide Justified*, 36.

11. See ibid., 37–38.

12. See ibid., 36.

13. See Lawrence M. Friedman, *A History of American Law*, 3rd ed. (New York: Touchstone, 2005), 34; see also George W. Dalzell, *Benefit of Clergy in America and Related Matters* (Winston-Salem, N.C.: John F. Blair, 1955); Jeffrey K. Sawyer, "'Benefit of Clergy' in Maryland and Virginia," *American Journal of Legal History* 33, no. 1 (January 1990): 49–68; Kathryn Preyer, "Crime, the Criminal Law and Reform in Postrevolutionary Virginia," *Law and History Review* 1, no. 1 (Spring 1983): 54n6; Kathryn Preyer, "Penal Measures in the American Colonies: An Overview," *American Journal of Legal History* 26, no. 4 (October 1982): 331–32n93; Thomas A. Green, "The Jury and the English Law of Homicide, 1200–1600," *Michigan Law Review* 74, no. 3 (January 1976): 487–97.

14. See Fede, *Homicide Justified*, 36.

15. See ibid., 100. South Carolina was the last state to amend its homicide laws to make willful slave murder a capital offense. It enacted this reform even after Barbados. See ibid., 97–102, 173–82.

16. See ibid., 102–5.

17. See ibid., 105 (quoting "An Act to Prevent the willful Killing of Slaves," in *The State Records of North Carolina, Laws 1715–1776*, ed. Walter Clark [Goldsboro, N.C.: Nash Brothers, 1904], 23:975–76). See also *State v. Weaver*, 3 N.C. (2 Hayw.) 77 (Sup. Ct. 1798) (extending to hirers the owners' and masters' privilege); Marvin L. Michael Kay and

Lorin Lee Cary, *Slavery in North Carolina, 1748–1775* (Chapel Hill: University of North Carolina Press, 1995), 75–76.

18. See Fede, *Homicide Justified*, 103 (citing "An Act Concerning Servants and Slaves," in *The State Records of North Carolina, Laws 1715–1776*, 23:201–2); see also Deborah A. Rosen, "Slavery, Race, and Outlawry: The Concept of Outlaw in Nineteenth-Century Abolitionist Rhetoric," *American Journal of Legal History* 58, no. 1 (March 2018): 126–56.

19. See *State v. Piver*, 3 N.C. (2 Hayw.) 247 (Sup. Ct. 1799); Fede, *Homicide Justified*, 130–37.

20. "An Act to Punish the Offense of Killing a Slave," in *Laws of the State of North Carolina*, ed. Henry Potter, J. L. Taylor, and Bart Yancey (Raleigh: J. Gales, 1821), chap. 949, 2:1407; "An Act to Punish the Offense of Killing a Slave," in *Laws of the State of North Carolina Enacted in the Year 1817*, chap. 18 (Raleigh: Thomas Henderson, State Printer, 1818), 18–19; see Fede, *Homicide Justified*, 137–38.

21. See Laura F. Edwards, *The People and Their Peace: Legal Culture and the Transformation of Inequality in the Post-revolutionary South* (Chapel Hill: University of North Carolina Press, 2009), 51 (quotation omitted). On the background to creation of the North Carolina Supreme Court, see ibid., 50–53, 208–9, 239.

22. See James A. Wynn Jr., "*State v. Mann*: Judicial Choice or Judicial Duty?," *North Carolina Law Review* 87, no. 3 (March 2009): 992; Martin H. Brinkley, "Supreme Court of North Carolina," NCPedia, https://www.ncpedia.org/supreme-court-north-carolina; Kemp P. Battle, "An Address on the History of the Supreme Court," at 39–43, delivered February 4, 1889, https://ncschs.net/history-of-court/.

23. See Fede, *Homicide Justified*, 137–41; Fede, *People without Rights*, 72–73. This focus on Seawell's contribution is not intended to advance a great person interpretation of legal history. I do, however, agree with Charles Barzun's assertion that, under the common law, one lawyer can argue that the courts should adopt a doctrinal shift, which can reflect and in turn encourage a change in the prevailing legal rules and standards and the legal consciousness of members of the society. See Charles L. Barzun, "The Common Law and Critical Theory," *University of Colorado Law Review* 92, no. 4 (2021): 1232–35; Charles L. Barzun, "Catherine MacKinnon and the Common Law," in Virginia School of Law Public Law and Legal Theory Research Series 4 (Paper No. 2020–69), https://papers.ssrn.com/sol3/papers.cfm?abstract_id=3696540 (discussing Katherine MacKinnon's contribution to the development of sexual harassment doctrine).

24. Marshall De Lancey Haywood, "Henry Seawell," in *Biographical History of North Carolina from Colonial Times to the Present*, ed. Samuel A. Ashe, Stephen B. Weeks, and Charles L. Van Noppen (Greensboro, N.C.: Charles L. Van Noppen, 1905), 2:396.

25. See Henry Seawell, "Seawell, Henry," in *Dictionary of North Carolina Biography*, ed. William S. Powell (Chapel Hill: University of North Carolina Press, 1994), 5:310–11; Haywood, "Henry Seawell," in Ashe, Weeks, and Van Noppen, *Biographical History of North Carolina*, 2:394–97; "Judge Seawell's Resignation," *Carolina Sentinel* (New Bern, N.C.), February 27, 1818, 1; *Carolina Federal Republican* (New Bern, N.C.), December 4, 1813, 2; *Weekly Raleigh (N.C.) Register*, December 13, 1811, 2; ibid., December 6, 1811, 2; ibid., July 12, 1811, 3.

26. See Fifth Census of the United States, 1830, St. Matthews, Wake, North Carolina, National Archives Microfilm Publication, M19, roll 125, page 443, Ancestry.com.

27. See John Hope Franklin, *The Free Negro in North Carolina 1790–1860* (Chapel Hill:

University of North Carolina Press, 1943), 43, 63–64; *Raleigh (N.C.) Register*, January 19, 1827, 2.

28. See *Carolina Advertiser* (Fayetteville, N.C.), January 3, 1827, 1–2.

29. See "An Act to Prevent Free Persons of Colour from Migrating into This State, for the Good Government of Such Persons Resident in the State, and for Other Purposes," in *Acts Passed by the General Assembly of the State of North Carolina at Its Session Commencing on the 25th of December, 1826* (Raleigh, N.C.: Lawrence and Lemay, 1827), 13–16; see also *Revised Code of North Carolina, Enacted by the General Assembly at the Session of 1854*, ed. Bartholomew F. Moore and Asa Biggs (Boston: Little, Brown, 1855), 575–76; Warren E. Milteer Jr., *North Carolina's Free People of Color, 1715–1885* (Baton Rouge: Louisiana University Press, 2020), 60–61.

30. See Franklin, *Free Negro in North Carolina*, 64.

31. See *Proceedings and Debates of the Convention of North-Carolina, Called to Amend the Constitution of the State, Which Assembled at Raleigh, June 4, 1835* (Raleigh, N.C.: J. Gales and Son, 1836), 72–81. The adopted amendment stated, "That no negro, free mulatto, or free person of mixed blood, descended from negro ancestors to the fourth generation inclusive, (though one ancestor of each generation may have been a white person,) shall vote for the members of the Senate or House of Commons." *Journal of the Convention Called by the Freemen of North-Carolina to Amend the Constitution of the State* (Raleigh, N.C.: J. Gales and Son, 1835), 25.

32. See "Constitution of North Carolina: December 18, 1776," Avalon Project, https://avalon.law.yale.edu/18th_century/nc07.asp; John V. Orth and Paul Martin Newby, *The North Carolina State Constitution*, 2nd ed., Oxford Commentaries on the State Constitutions of the United States (New York: Oxford University Press, 2013), 14; Alexander Keyssar, *The Right to Vote: The Contested History of Democracy in the United States*, rev. ed. (New York: Basic Books, 2009), 14 (noting that this was a partial "liberalization" of the colonial property ownership requirement).

33. See Lacy K. Ford, *Deliver Us from Evil: The Slavery Question in the Old South* (New York: Oxford University Press, 2009), 420–22; Franklin, *Free Negro in North Carolina*, 105–20; William Alexander Mabry, *The Negro in North Carolina Politics since Reconstruction* (Durham, N.C.: Duke University Press, 1940; repr., New York: AMS Press, 1970), 3–4.

34. See *Proceedings and Debates of the Convention of North-Carolina*, 71; Ford, *Deliver Us from Evil*, 432.

35. See Milteer, *North Carolina's Free People of Color*, 70–72; Ford, *Deliver Us from Evil*, 428–38.

36. See *Proceedings and Debates of the Convention of North-Carolina*, 355.

37. See ibid., 357–58; see also Orth and Newby, *North Carolina State Constitution*, 14–15; Franklin, *Free Negro in North Carolina*, 114–16; John V. Orth, "North Carolina Constitutional History," *North Carolina Law Review* 70, no. 6 (September 1992): 1771–72.

38. See Fede, *Homicide Justified*, 136–37.

39. See *Hillsborough (N.C.) Recorder*, November 22, 1820, 3.

40. See *Fayetteville (N.C.) Gazette*, November 22, 1820, 2.

41. See Indictment, *State of North Carolina v. Mason Scott*, Superior Court, Wake County, Spring Term 1820, in North Carolina State Archives, Supreme Court, 1800–1909, box 18, case 787.

42. See *State v. Scott*, 8 N.C. (1 Hawks) 24 (1820); "Mason Scott," *Charleston (S.C.)*

Courier, April 19, 1820, 2; "Superior Court," *Raleigh (N.C.) Minerva*, April 14, 1820, 3; see also Fede, *Homicide Justified*, 138–39 (incorrectly stating that Scott's trial began on April 1, 1819). Manly was at the start of his long career in law and politics, which included one term as North Carolina's governor. See Marshall De Lancey Haywood, "Charles Manly," in *Biographical History of North Carolina from Colonial Times to the Present*, ed. Samuel A. Ashe, Stephen B. Weeks, and Charles L. Van Noppen (Greensboro, N.C.: Charles L. Van Noppen, 1907), 4:349–56.

43. *Litchfield Republican* (Litchfield, Ct.), December 11, 1820, 2; see "Murder," *Alexandria (Va.) Gazette*, August 2, 1819, 2.

44. "Execution," *Fayetteville (N.C.) Gazette*, November 22, 1820, 2.

45. See *State v. Scott*, 24–31.

46. See ibid., 32–34; "Execution," *Fayetteville (N.C.) Gazette*, November 22, 1820), 2; "Superior Court," *Raleigh (N.C.) Minerva*, April 14, 1820, 3; see also Fede, *Homicide Justified*, 138–39.

47. See Indictment, *State of North Carolina v. William Tacket*, Superior Court, Wake County, Spring Term 1820, in North Carolina State Archives, Supreme Court, 1800–1909, box 25, case no. 1115.

48. See "The Hotel," *Raleigh (N.C.) Register*, October 18, 1825, 1; "Notice," *Raleigh (N.C.) Register*, September 20, 1825, 4.

49. See "Superior Court," *Raleigh (N.C.) Minerva*, April 14, 1820, 3.

50. See *Charleston (S.C.) Courier*, July 3, 1820, 2; *North Carolina Star* (Raleigh, N.C.), June 30, 1820, 3.

51. See *State v. Tackett*, 8 N.C. (1 Hawks), 210–13; *Weekly Raleigh (N.C.) Register*, October 6, 1820, 3.

52. See Joseph K. L. Reckford, "Daniel, Joseph John," in *Dictionary of North Carolina Biography, Volume 2 D–G* (Chapel Hill: University of North Carolina Press, 1986), 8.

53. See undated affidavit of William Tacket, Superior Court, Wake County, Spring Term 1820, in North Carolina State Archives, Supreme Court, 1800–1909, box 25, case no. 1115.

54. See *State v. Tackett*, 8 N.C. (1 Hawks), 210–13; Indictment, *State of North Carolina v. William Tacket*, Superior Court, Wake County, Spring Term 1820, in North Carolina State Archives, Supreme Court, 1800–1909, box 25, case 1115; see also "Murder!," *Hillsboro Telegraph* (Amherst, N.H.), January 15, 1820, 2; "Murder," *Columbian* (New York, N.Y.), December 30, 1819, 2; "Murder," *Raleigh (N.C.) Minerva*, December 24, 1819, 3; "Murder," *Raleigh (N.C.) Weekly Register*, December 24, 1819, 3.

55. See, e.g., *State v. Samuel*, 19 N.C. (2 Dev. & Bat.) 177, 181–84 (1836); Michael Grossberg, *Governing the Hearth: Law and the Family in Nineteenth-Century America* (Chapel Hill: University of North Carolina Press, 1985), 129–33; Dacia Green, "Ain't I . . . ?: The Dehumanizing Effect of the Regulation of Slave Womanhood and Family Life," *Duke Journal of Gender Law and Policy* 25, no. 2 (Spring 2018): 200–208; Darlene C. Goring, "The History of Slave Marriage in the United States," *John Marshall Law Review* 39 (2006): 306–10, 316; Laura F. Edwards, "'The Marriage Covenant Is at the Foundation of All Our Rights': The Politics of Slave Marriages in North Carolina after Emancipation," *Law and History Review* 14, no. 1 (Spring 1996): 95–96.

56. See "Murder," *Raleigh (N.C.) Minerva*, December 24, 1819, 3.

57. See *State v. Tackett*, 8 N.C. (1 Hawks), 213.

58. Ibid., 213.

59. Ibid, 213–14; see *City of Washington (D.C.) Gazette*, October 19, 1820, 2.

60. See *Spectator* (New York, N.Y.), October 27, 1820; *Hillsborough (N.C.) Recorder*, October 18, 1820, 3; *Weekly Raleigh (N.C.) Register*, October 13, 1820, 3; see also Fede, *Homicide Justified*, 139 (incorrectly stating that Judge Daniel established October 22, 1820, as Scott's initial execution date).

61. See Clairborne T. Smith Jr., "Drew, William (ca. 1770–8 May 1827)," in *Dictionary of North Carolina Biography, Volume 2 D-G*, 104–5.

62. See John W. Moore, *History of North Carolina: From the Earliest Discoveries to the Present* (Raleigh, N.C.: Alfred Williams, 1880), 1:477.

63. *State v. Tackett*, 8 N.C. (1 Hawks), 214.

64. Ibid., 214–15 (emphasis added).

65. Ibid., 215.

66. Ibid., 215.

67. Ibid., 215 (citing East's Cr. L. 234, 236—Fost. 291—4 Bl. Com. 199); see Foster, *Report of Some Proceeding*, 291; East, *Treatise of the Pleas of the Crown*, 234; Blackstone, *Commentaries on the Laws of England*, 4:*199.

68. See ibid., 216–17.

69. See ibid., 217.

70. Ibid., 217–18.

71. Ibid., 218–19. Compare A. E. Keir Nash, "A More Equitable Past? Southern Supreme Courts and the Protection of the Antebellum Negro," *North Carolina Law Review* 48, no 2 (February 1970): 203–11; A. E. Keir Nash, "Fairness and Formalism in the Trials of Blacks in the State Supreme Courts of the Old South," *Virginia Law Review* 56, no. 1 (February 1970): 67–72 (omitting any discussion of the unequal protection doctrine in *Tackett*); see also, discussing this case, Saidiya V. Hartman, *Scenes of Subjection: Terror, Slavery, and Self-Making in Nineteenth-Century America* (New York: Oxford University Press, 1997), 83, 148; Morris, *Southern Slavery and the Law*, 177; William E. Wiethoff, *A Peculiar Humanism: The Judicial Advocacy of Slavery in High Courts of the Old South, 1820–1850* (Athens: University of Georgia Press, 1996), 83–84; Russell K. Osgood, review of *The American Law of Slavery 1810–1860: Considerations of Humanity and Interest*, by Mark Tushnet, *Cornell Law Review* 67, no. 2 (January 1982): 434–38.

72. Compare the textualist approach as exemplified in *Bostock County, Ga. v. Clayton*, 590 U.S. —-, 140 S. Ct. 1731, 1738–54 (2020).

73. *Proceedings and Debates of the Convention of North-Carolina*, 60–62.

74. Ford, *Deliver Us from Evil*, 428; see Franklin, *Free Negro in North Carolina*, 14–19.

75. *State v. Dick, a Slave*, 6 N.C. (2 Mur.) 388 (1818).

76. See ibid., 388–89.

77. *State v. Reed*, 9 N.C. (2 Hawks) 454 (1823).

78. See Indictment, *State of North Carolina v. Thomas Reed*, Superior Court, Hertford County, March Term 1823, in North Carolina State Archives, Supreme Court, 1800–1909, box 50, case no. 1760. *Homicide Justified* apparently first published the facts of the case and Reed's racial identity. Compare Fede, *Homicide Justified*, 142, with, Edwards, *People and Their Peace*, 239; Laura F. Edwards, "The Forgotten Legal World of Thomas Ruffin: The Power of Presentism in the History of Slavery," *North Carolina Law Review* 87, no. 3 (March 2009): 893 (Reed was "a white man convicted of manslaughter for killing a

slave"); Nash, "Fairness and Formalism," 70 (Reed was "a white" who appealed his conviction for "the murder of a black"); compare Steven T. Katz, *The Holocaust and New World Slavery: A Comparative History*, vol. 2 (New York: Cambridge University Press, 2019), 455–57 (acknowledging Reed's race, but stating "that *Tackett* did not decisively or permanently roll back the progress that had been made in the broadening of homicide statutes to include the murder of slaves is convincingly shown by [*State v. Reed*]").

79. See Statement of the case, *State of North Carolina v. Thomas Reed*, Superior Court, Hertford County, March Term 1823, in North Carolina State Archives, Supreme Court, 1800–1909, box 50, case no. 1760.

80. *State v. Reed*, 454.

81. *State v. Boon*, 1 N.C. 103, Tay. 246 (1801).

82. *State v. Reed*, 455; see Fede, *Homicide Justified*, 142. For the opinions in *State v. Boon*, 1 N.C. 103, Tay. 246 (1801), see Fede, *Homicide Justified*, 132–34. On Hogg, see Elizabeth Dortch Dix Keys, "Hogg, Gavin," *NCPedia*, https://www.ncpedia.org/biography/hogg-gavin.

83. See *North-Carolinian* (Fayetteville, N.C.), April 5, 1851, 3; *Wilmington (N.C.) Journal*, April 4, 1851, 2; *Raleigh Register and North-Carolina Gazette*, October 13, 1826, 1; *Raleigh Register and North-Carolina Gazette*, May 5, 1826, 1; Franklin, *Free Negro in North Carolina*, 99–100; see also Milteer, *North Carolina's Free People of Color*, 181 (discussing the 1811 manslaughter conviction of Nancy Robbins, described as "a free person of colour of Indian Extraction," for killing an enslaved man named Allen).

84. *State v. Hale*, 9 N.C. (2 Hawks) 582 (1823).

85. Assault and battery are two different common-law misdemeanors. Battery requires some physical contact resulting in a bodily injury or offensive touching. Assault occurs without physical touching; it is most often defined as an attempted battery or the intentional frightening of another person. See Wayne R. LaFave and Austin W. Scott Jr., *Handbook on Criminal Law* (St. Paul, Minn.: West, 1972), 602–3.

86. See *State v. Hale*, 582. For a similar use of a special verdict in the 1771 North Carolina slave homicide trial of Peter Lord, see Fede, *Homicide Justified*, 104. On the use by trial juries of special verdicts in the late eighteenth- and early nineteenth-century United States, apparently contrary to "a basic truism" that these verdicts "were a device of *judges*, used to take cases away from juries," see Jessica K. Lowe, *Murder in the Shenandoah: Making Law Sovereign in Revolutionary Virginia* (New York: Cambridge University Press, 2019), 7–8 (citing Morton Horwitz, *The Transformation of American Law, 1780–1860* [Cambridge, Mass.: Harvard University Press, 1977]).

87. See John V. Orth, "When Analogy Fails: The Common Law and *State v. Mann*," *North Carolina Law Review* 87, No. 1 (March 2009): 980n8.

88. See *State v. Hale*, 582.

89. Ibid., 582–83.

90. See ibid., 584 (citing from Matthew Hale, *The History of the Pleas of the Crown* [London: E. and R. Nutt and R. Gosling, 1736], 1:455–56).

91. *State v. Hale*, 585.

92. See ibid., 585. Taylor cited a 1783 statute authorizing a single justice of the peace to conduct a summary trial of enslaved people accused of minor offences and to punish them with not more than forty lashes. The legislature found that the otherwise appli-

cable procedure "is found to be attended with delay, great loss of time, and expenses to the owner." See "An act to Amend an Act Passed in the Year of Our Lord, One Thousand Seven Hundred and Forty One, Intitled, An Act Concerning Servants and Slaves," in *Acts of Assembly of the State of North Carolina*, 19, North Carolina Digital Collections, https://digital.ncdcr.gov/digital/collection/p16062coll9/id/263796; Alan D. Watson, "North Carolina Slave Courts, 1715–1785," *North Carolina Historical Review* 60, no. 1 (January 1983): 26–27.

93. See *State v. Hale*, 585.

94. Ibid., 585–86.

95. Ibid., 586–87 (emphasis added); see Fede, *People without Rights*, 103–5. Compare Nash's discussions, which do not mention Taylor and Hall's unequal mitigation and justification doctrine. See Nash, "A More Equitable Past?," 210–11; Nash, "Fairness and Formalism," 71–72.

96. See David Brown, "A Vagabond's Tale: Poor Whites, Herrenvolk Democracy, and the Value of Whiteness in the Late Antebellum South," *Journal of Southern History* 76, no. 4 (November 2013): 806–7. Other writers discussing the social and legal issues arising in poor white and slave fraternization and violence include Jeff Forret, *Race Relations at the Margins: Slaves and Poor Whites in the Antebellum Southern Countryside* (Baton Rouge: Louisiana University Press, 2006), 157–83; Fede, *People without Rights*, 72–77, 100–105, 116–21; James M. Denham, "'A Most Profligate Villain': Poor Whites as Depicted in Antebellum Wanted Proclamations," *Georgia Historical Quarterly* 101, no. 4 (2017): 306; see also, discussing the white elite's attitudes toward the white poor in American history, Nancy Isenberg, *White Trash: The 400-Year Untold History of Class in America* (New York: Viking, 2016), 135–37.

97. *State v. Hale*, 558; see Jenny Bourne Wahl, *The Bondsman's Burden: An Economic Analysis of the Common Law of Southern Slavery* (New York: Cambridge University Press, 1998), 129, 234n32 (noting that Taylor foreshadowed economic theory suggesting "that one purpose of criminal law is to control harmful externalities in circumstances where damage remedies are insufficient, mostly because optimal damages exceed the defendant's wealth"); Fede, *People without Rights*, 72, 85 (noting these economic interests in cases of homicides committed by poor whites and even overseers).

98. *State v. Armfield*, 27 N.C. (5 Ired.) 207 (1844).

99. Ibid., 207–11.

100. Ibid., 211.

101. See Max R. Williams, "Taylor, John Louis," in *The Yale Biographical Dictionary of American Law*, ed. Roger K. Newman (New Haven, Conn.: Yale University Press, 2009), 539.

102. See ibid.; Gertrude S. Carraway, "Taylor, John Louis," in *Dictionary of North Carolina Biography*, ed. William S. Powell (Chapel Hill: University of North Carolina Press, 1996), 6:11–12; Marshall DeLancey Haywood, "John Louis Taylor," in *Biographical History of North Carolina from Colonial Times to the Present*, ed. Samuel A. Ashe (Greensboro, N.C.: Charles L. Van Noppen, 1906), 2:402–6; Walter Clark, "The Supreme Court of North Carolina," *Green Bag* 4 (October 1892): 461–62.

103. *Gobu v. Gobu*, 1 N.C. (Tay.) 188 (Sup. Ct. of Law & Equity 1802).

104. Ibid., 188.

105. See Andrew Fede, *Roadblocks to Freedom: Slavery and Manumission in the United States South* (New Orleans: Quid Pro Books, 2011), 247–85, 372. Scholars have more often cited St. George Tucker's opinion in *Hudgins v. Wrights*, 11 Va. (1 Hen. & M.) 134 (1806) for these race-based presumptions of freedom and bondage. Ibid., 258.

106. See Fede, *People without Rights*, 72–77, 105.

107. See Thomas R. R. Cobb, *An Inquiry into the Law of Negro Slavery in the United States of America* (Philadelphia: T. & J. W. Johnson and Savannah: W. Thorne Williams, 1858; repr., Athens: University of Georgia Press, 1999), 92–95; see also *State v. Cheatwood*, 20 S.C.L. (2 Hill) 459 (Ct. App. L. & Eq. 1834) (affirming conviction for the murder of an enslaved man and interpreting 1821 homicide statute consistent with the common-law definition of murder, but noting that the trial judge's mitigation charge is consistent with *Tackett*); *Fields v. State*, 9 Tenn. (1 Yer.) 156 (1829) (affirming manslaughter conviction but not commenting on mitigation standards); see generally Friedman, *History of American Law*, 162–64; Wahl, *Bondsman's Burden*, 149–51; Morris, *Southern Slavery and the Law*, 171–81; Lawrence M. Friedman, *Crime and Punishment in American History* (New York: Basic Books, 1993), 92–93; Fede, *People without Rights*, 72–77, 167–77; James Oakes, *Slavery and Freedom: An Interpretation of the Old South* (New York: Norton, 1990), 157–66.

108. See Sir William Oldnall Russell and Charles Sprengel Greaves, *A Treatise on Crimes and Misdemeanors in Two Volumes, Eighth American Edition*, ed. Daniel Davis, Theron Metcalf, and George Sharswood (Philadelphia: T. & J. Johnson, 1857), 1:514, 517n1; Wharton, *Treatise of the Law of Homicide*, 168–69, 175–76, 288, 303–5.

109. *Commonwealth v. Lee*, 60 Ky. (3 Met.) 229 (1860).

110. See ibid., 230.

111. See ibid., 230–31.

112. See ibid., 232.

113. See *Oliver v. State*, 39 Miss. 526 (Err. & App. 1860). For discussions of this case, see Fede, *Homicide Justified*, 203–5; Fede, *People without Rights*, 77–80.

114. See *State v. Barfield*, 30 N.C. (8 Ired.) 344 (1848); *State v. Tilly*, 25 N.C. (3 Ired.) 424 (1843); see also, applying this rule, *Evans v. United States*, 277 F. 2d 354 (App. D.C. 1960); "Homicide," *American Jurisprudence*, 2nd ed. (Thompson Reuters, 2019 & Supp. May 2022), 40A: §§ 276–284, 147–60; H. H. Henry, "Admissibility of Evidence as to the Other's Character or Reputation for Turbulence on Question of Self-Defense by One Charged with Assault or Homicide," in *American Law Reports*, 3rd ed. (New York: Lawyers Co-operative, 1965 & Supp. May 2017), 1:571–604; J. T. B. Jr., "Admissibility of Evidence as to the Other's Character or Reputation for Turbulence on Questions of Self-Defense by One Charged with Assault or Homicide," in *American Law Reports Annotated* 64 (Rochester, N.Y.: Lawyers Co-operative, 1929), 1029–47.

115. See *State v. Maner*, 20 S.C.L. (2 Hill) 453 (Ct. App. of Law & Equity 1834).

116. See ibid.; see also, e.g., *Tennent v. Dendy*, 23 S.C.L. (Dud.) 83 (Ct. App. of Law 1837); *Helton v. Caston*, 18 S.C.L. (2 Bail.) 95 (Ct. App. of Law & Equity 1831); *Tate v. O'Neal*, 8 N.C. (1 Hawks) 418 (1821); *State v. Jones*, 1 Del. Cas. 546 (Ct. Common Pleas 1818); *Brown v. May*, 15 Va. (1 Munf.) 288 (1810); *White v. Chambers*, 2 S.C.L. (2 Bay) 70 (Const. Ct. App. 1796); see generally Morris, *Southern Slavery and the Law*, 196–208; Fede, *People without Rights*, 70–72, 100–105, 118, 129n123; Judith K. Schafer, "'Details Are of a Most Revolting Character': Cruelty to Slaves as Seen in Appeals to the Supreme Court of Louisiana," *Chicago-Kent Law Review* 68, no. 3 (1993): 1283–311.

CHAPTER 3. Ruffin and Gaston Extend
Separate and Unequal Protection

1. *State v. Mann*, 13 N.C. (2 Dev.) 263 (1829).

2. *State v. Hoover*, 20 N.C. (4 Dev. & Bat.) 500 (1839).

3. *State v. Will*, 18 N.C. (1 Dev. & Bat.) 121 (1834); *State v. Jarrott*, 23 N.C. (1 Ired.) 76 (1840).

4. See Sally Hadden, "Judging Slavery: Thomas Ruffin and *State v. Mann*," in *Local Matters: Race, Crime, and Justice in the Nineteenth Century South*, ed. Christopher Waldrep and Donald G. Nieman (Athens: University of Georgia Press, 2001), 2.

5. Harriet Beecher Stowe, *The Key to Uncle Tom's Cabin* (Boston: John P. Jewett, 1853; repr., New York: Arno Press and the New York Times, 1968), 147; see, discussing Stowe's writings and Ruffin, Mark V. Tushnet, *Slave Law in the American South: State v. Mann in History and Literature*, Landmark Law Cases and American Society (Lawrence: University Press of Kansas, 2003), 97–137; Alfred L. Brophy, "Thomas Ruffin: Of Moral Philosophy and Monuments," *North Carolina Law Review* 87, no. 3 (March 2009): 800–811.

6. See Roscoe Pound, *The Formative Era of American Law* (Boston: Little, Brown, 1938), 4; see also ibid., 30, 84–85, and Tushnet, *Slave Law in the American South*, 74–75.

7. See Tushnet, *Slave Law in the American South* and the articles in the symposium "Thomas Ruffin and the Perils of Public Homage," *North Carolina Law Review* 87, no. 3 (March 2009): 669–1005. Many other books and articles discuss this decision; see, e.g., Thomas D. Morris, *Southern Slavery and the Law, 1619–1860* (Chapel Hill: University of North Carolina Press, 1996), 188–93; Mark V. Tushnet, *The American Law of Slavery 1810–1860: Considerations of Humanity and Interest* (Princeton, N.J.: Princeton University Press, 1981), 54–65, and my comment on the same in Andrew Fede, *People without Rights: An Interpretation of the Fundamentals of the Law of Slavery in the U.S. South* (New York: Garland, 1992; repr., New York: Routledge, 2011), 126–27n80; Andrew Fede, "Toward a Solution of the Slave Law Dilemma: A Critique of Tushnet's *American Law of Slavery*," *Law and History Review* 2, no. 2 (Fall 1984): 308–11. The versions of my own views on *Mann* and the other authorities relating to nonfatal violence inflicted by masters and hirers are contained in Fede, *People without Rights*, 105–30; Andrew Fede, "Legitimized Violent Slave Abuse in the American South, 1619–1865: A Case Study of Law and Social Change in Six Southern States," *American Journal of Legal History* 29, no. 2 (April 1985): 132–46; Andrew T. Fede, "Gender in the Law of Slavery in the Antebellum United States," *Cardozo Law Review* 18, no. 2 (November 1996): 420–26, from which the following comments are adapted and supplemented.

8. Eric L. Muller, "Judging Thomas Ruffin and the Hindsight Defense," *North Carolina Law Review* 87, no. 3 (March 2009): 761; see ibid., 778–98; see also Hadden, "Judging Slavery," 5–8.

9. See Tushnet, *Slave Law in the American South*, 91–92; Muller, "Judging Thomas Ruffin," 775–77.

10. On Ruffin's biography and his jurisprudence, see, e.g., Tushnet, *Slave Law in the American South*, 75–96; Timothy S. Huebner, *The Southern Judicial Tradition: State Judges and Sectional Distinctiveness, 1790–1890* (Athens: University of Georgia Press, 1999), 130–59; John V. Orth, "Ruffin, Thomas," in *The Yale Biographical Dictionary of American Law*, ed. Roger K. Newman (New Haven, Conn.: Yale University Press, 2009), 471–72; Had-

den, "Judging Slavery," 2–8; Brophy, "Thomas Ruffin," 811–41; Muller, "Judging Thomas Ruffin," 778–98; Timothy C. Meyer, "Slavery Jurisprudence on the Supreme Court of North Carolina, 1828–1858: William Gaston and Thomas Ruffin," *Campbell Law Review* 33, no. 2 (North Carolina 2011): 313–39. On the long history of emancipation in New Jersey, see, e.g., James J. Gigantino II, *The Ragged Road to Abolition: Slavery and Freedom in New Jersey, 1775–1865* (Philadelphia: University of Pennsylvania Press, 2015).

11. See Hadden, "Judging Slavery," 8, 24n46; James A. Wynn Jr., "*State v. Mann*: Judicial Choice or Judicial Duty?," *North Carolina Law Review* 87, no. 3 (March 2009): 992–93; Sally Greene and Eric L. Muller, "Introduction: *State v. Mann* and Thomas Ruffin in History and Memory," *North Carolina Law Review* 87, no. 3 (March 2009): 669; A. E. Keir Nash, "Reason of Slavery: Understanding the Judicial Role in the Peculiar Institution," *Vanderbilt Law Review* 32, no. 1 (January 1979): 119n372.

12. See Tushnet, *Slave Law in the American South*, 72.

13. See Sally Greene, "*State v. Mann* Exhumed," *North Carolina Law Review* 87, no. 3 (March 2009): 714.

14. See ibid., 707–19.

15. Ibid., 719.

16. *State v. Mann*, 263; Greene, "*State v. Mann* Exhumed," 720.

17. Greene, "*State v. Mann* Exhumed," 721–22.

18. Ibid., 723.

19. *State v. Mann*, 263; Greene, "*State v. Mann* Exhumed," 723–27.

20. See Tushnet, *Slave Law in the American South*, 67.

21. See Greene, "*State v. Mann* Exhumed," 729n140.

22. See H. G. Jones, "Saunders, Romulus Mitchell," in *Dictionary of North Carolina Biography*, ed. William S. Powell (Chapel Hill: University of North Carolina Press, 1994), 5:285–86; see also S. A. Ashe, "Romulus Mitchell Saunders," in *Biographical Dictionary of North Carolina*, ed. Samuel A. Ashe, Stephen B. Weeks, and Charles L. Van Noppen (Greensboro, N.C.: Charles L. Van Noppen, 1906), 3:386–93; "Saunders, Romulus Mitchell," in *Biographical Dictionary of the United States*, https://bioguide.congress.gov/search/bio/S000078/.

23. *State v. Mann*, 263–64.

24. See John V. Orth, "When Analogy Fails: The Common Law and *State v. Mann*," *North Carolina Law Review* 87, No. 1 (March 2009): 982; see also William Oldnall Russell, *A Treatise on Crimes and Misdemeanors in Two Volumes, First American Edition*, ed. Daniel Davis (Philadelphia: T. & J. Johnson, 1857), 1:866.

25. On Ruffin's drafts of this opinion, see, e.g., Tushnet, *Slave Law in the American South*, 26–30; Hadden, "Judging Slavery," 9–12.

26. *State v. Mann*, 264.

27. Ibid., 266.

28. Ibid., 267.

29. See Wynn, "*State v. Mann*," 1000 (quoting Fede, "Legitimized Violent Slave Abuse," 139).

30. *State v. Mann*, 266.

31. Ibid., 265.

32. Ibid., 268.

33. *United States v. Brockett*, 24 F. Cas. 1241 (C. C. D.C. 1823) (No. 14,651).

NOTES TO PAGES 66–70   227

34. See Fourth Census of the United States, 1820, Alexandria, District of Columbia, National Archives Microfilm Publication, roll 33, page 202, Ancestry.com; "Out of the Attic: A Place of Learning and a Place of Healing," *Alexandria (Va.) Times*, May 28, 2014, Office of Historic Alexandria, City of Alexandria, https://www.alexandriava.gov/uploadedFiles/historic/info/attic/2014/Attic20140529BrockettSchool601603Queen.pdf.

35. *Republica v. Teischer*, 1 U.S. (1 Dall.) 335, 1 L. Ed. 163 (1788). See *United States v. Brockett*, 1241. On Swann, see *Records of the Columbia Historical Society*, vol. 24, ed. John B. Larner (Washington, D.C., 1922), 68. On Taylor, see "Taylor, William (1788–1846)," *Biographical Directory of the United States Congress 1774-Present*, https://bioguideretro.congress.gov/Home/MemberDetails?memIndex=T000104. For other District of Columbia decisions sustaining prosecutions, not for simple assault and battery, but only if the defendant inflicted "cruel or inhuman" punishment in a public place, to avoid "an annoyance or nuisance to the citizens, whose pleasure or business carry them near the scene of the infliction," see *Hickerson v. United States*, 30 F. Cas. 1087, 1088 (D.C. Cir. 1856) (No. 18,301); *United States v. Lloyd*, 26 F. Cas. 987 (D.C. Cir. 1834) (No. 15,618); *United States v. Butler*, 25 F. Cas. 212 (D.C. Cir. 1806) (No. 14,697); Fede, *People without Rights*, 124n40.

36. See *Commonwealth v. Booth*, 4 Va. (2 Va. Cas.) 394, 394 (1824).

37. See "Preface" and "Brief Sketch of the Courts of this Commonwealth," 2 Va. Cas. iii–xv (1826).

38. See *Commonwealth v. Booth*, 395–96.

39. Ibid., 396.

40. *Commonwealth v. Turner*, 26 Va. (5 Rand) 678 (1827).

41. See Fourth Census of the United States, 1820, Hanover Parish, King George, Virginia, National Archives Microfilm Publication, roll M33, page 126, Ancestry.com; Third Census of the United States, 1810, King George, Virginia, National Archives Microfilm Publication, roll 69, page 219, Ancestry.com; see also *Turner v. South & West Improvement Co.*, 118 Va. 720, 721, 88 S.E. 85, 85 (1916).

42. See *Commonwealth v. Turner*, 67.

43. See Hadden, "Judging Slavery," 15–16, 27n80 (discussing Brockenbrough's relationship with Ruffin and his dissenting opinion in *Turner*). Hadden correctly surmised that I was not aware of the relationship between Ruffin and Brockenbrough when I previously wrote about this decision and *Mann*. Ruffin may have omitted any citation to *Turner* to avoid a public disagreement with his cousin's dissenting opinion. For other discussions of the *Turner* case, see Morris, *Southern Slavery and the Law*, 188–90; A. Leon Higginbotham Jr. and Anne F. Jacobs, "'The Law Only as an Enemy': The Legitimization of Racial Powerlessness through the Colonial and Antebellum Criminal Laws of Virginia," *North Carolina Law Review* 70, no. 4 (April 1992): 1048–56.

44. *Commonwealth v. Turner*, 680.

45. Ibid., 680. For the Virginia cases discussing crimes *contra bonos mores*, see Fede, *People without Rights*, 125n58.

46. See *Commonwealth v. Turner*, 688.

47. Ibid., 688.

48. Ibid., 689 (citing *Republica v. Teischer*, 1 U.S. (1 Dall.) 335, 1 L. Ed. 163 (1788)).

49. Ibid., 690.

50. See Fede, *People without Rights*, 110; Fede, "Gender in the Law of Slavery," 423; Fede, "Legitimized Violent Slave Abuse," 141.

51. See Greene, "*State v. Mann* Exhumed," 735n170 (citing Fede, *People without Rights*, 111).

52. *Commonwealth v. Turner*, 686.

53. *State v. Mann*, 264.

54. See Fede, *People without Rights*, 111; Fede, "Legitimized Violent Slave Abuse," 141 (both quoting Stowe, *Key to Uncle Tom's Cabin*, 233).

55. *State v. Hoover*, 20 N.C. (4 Dev. & Bat.) 500 (1839).

56. See Andrew T. Fede, *Homicide Justified: The Legality of Killing Slaves in the United States and the Atlantic World* (Athens: University of Georgia Press, 2017), 143–46; Fede, *People without Rights*, 95–96n83.

57. See *State v. Hoover*, 503. In the handwritten version of the opinion in the Supreme Court file, the sentence "He must not kill" is an interlineation. See Fede, *Homicide Justified*, 300n89.

58. See chapter 2, note 20.

59. See *State v. Hoover*, 503–4.

60. See Timothy S. Huebner, "The Roots of Fairness: *State v. Caesar* and Slave Justice in Antebellum North Carolina," in Waldrep and Nieman, *Local Matters*, 34–35 (quoting William D. Valentine, *William D. Valentine Diaries*, vol. 14, entry for June 2, 1855); see also ibid., 49n30–31.

61. *State v. Hoover*, 504–5.

62. See Fede, *Homicide Justified*, 142–51 (discussing *Hoover* and other North Carolina homicide prosecutions, including *State v. Robbins*, 48 N.C. (3 Jones) 249 (1855)); see also "Effects of the Late Season-Court Matters," *Daily Dispatch* (Richmond), May 9, 1857, 1 (report of the Wentworth, North Carolina, trial of James Blackwell, an overseer. He was charged with the murder of a slave who died five or six days after a severe whipping. The jury found him guilty of manslaughter and the judge "softened the punishment to a fine of $50, as the negro had been insolent to him, and resisted chastisement").

63. See Mark Tushnet, "*State v. Mann*: Why Ruffin?," *North Carolina Law Review* 87, no. 3 (March 2009): 975–78; Anthony V. Baker, "Slavery and Tushnet and *Mann*, Oh Why? Finding 'Big Law' in Small Places," *Quinnipiac Law Review* 26, no. 3 (2008): 698–701.

64. See Fede, *People without Rights*, 22; Fede, "Legitimized Violent Slave Abuse," 96 (citing Ruffin's *Mann* opinion and Brockenbrough's dissent in *Turner* as examples in which the judges explicitly discussed these interests). Thomas D. Morris offered a similar "multi-factored" analysis of the development of slave law in his 1996 monograph. Morris, *Southern Slavery and the Law*, 9. He stated that the cases and statutes that he studied represented "policy judgments" that judges and legislators made "involved nonlegal matters." These "included concerns that grew out of class relationships among whites, a racist commitment to keep people of color subordinate to whites, market demands and theories of political economy, and even evangelical Christianity." Ibid., 2–3; see Andrew T. Fede, "Review of *Southern Slavery and the Law, 1619–1860*," *American Journal of Legal History* 41, no. 4 (October 1997): 406–7. Mark Tushnet also apparently agrees; he asserts that, as southern judges "defined the precise content of the law of slavery," their decisions "rested on a vision of what the judges thought a well-ordered slave society required." Ruffin's *Mann* opinion was notable, he mused, because Ruffin's "candor, and his talent as a judge, gave his opinion in that case special force." See Tushnet, *Slave Law in the American South*, 18.

65. See Fede, "Legitimized Violent Slave Abuse," 121.
66. See Baker, "Slavery and Tushnet and *Mann*," 706.
67. See generally Fede, *Homicide Justified*, 19–21.
68. See *United States v. Amy*, 24 F. Cas. 792 (C.C.D. Va. 1859) (No. 14,445); Fede, *People without Rights*, 183–99.
69. See Huebner, "Roots of Fairness," 33, 42.
70. *State v. Jarrott*, 23 N.C. (1 Ired.) 76 (1840).
71. See ibid., 81.
72. See Donna J. Spindel, *Crime and Society in North Carolina, 1663–1776* (Baton Rouge: Louisiana State University Press, 1989), 20–25, 112–15, 133–35; George M. Stroud, *A Sketch of the Laws Relating to Slavery in the Several States of the United States of America* (2nd ed., 1856; repr., New York: Negro Universities Press, 1968), 90–91; Huebner, "Roots of Fairness," 30–32; Alan D. Watson, "North Carolina Slave Courts, 1715–1785," *North Carolina Historical Review* 60, no. 1 (January 1983): 24–36; R. H. Taylor, "Humanizing the Slave Code of North Carolina," *North Carolina Historical Review* 2, no. 3 (July 1925): 324–26. South Carolina, Virginia, and Louisiana, in contrast, remained on the other end of the continuum; their statutes continued to grant jurisdiction in slave prosecutions to inferior courts headed by justices of the peace or magistrates. These courts swiftly charged and tried enslaved defendants, who were denied the right to a grand jury hearing on the charges and to an appeal to the state's highest court. Other antebellum southern legislatures over time tended to provide enslaved defendants with a higher level of due process in these criminal prosecutions. This was especially so in capital cases. When the accused slave's life was at risk, his or her interests often converged the owners' interest in his or her property rights in this most valuable enslaved human property. See, e.g., James Campbell, *Crime and Punishment in African American History* (New York: Palgrave Macmillan, 2013), 38–43; James M. Campbell, *Slavery on Trial: Race Class, and Criminal Justice in Antebellum Richmond Virginia* (Gainesville: University Press of Florida, 2007), 76–107; Philip J. Schwarz, *Twice Condemned: Slaves and the Criminal Laws of Virginia, 1705–1865* (Baton Rouge: Louisiana State University Press, 1988), 6–34; Morris, *Southern Slavery and the Law*, 209–48; Fede, *People without Rights*, 159–99; Daniel Flanigan, *The Criminal Law of Slavery and Freedom 1800–1868* (New York: Garland, 1987), 73–188; Thomas R. R. Cobb, *An Inquiry into the Law of Negro Slavery in the United States of America* (Philadelphia: T. & J. W. Johnson and Savannah: W. Thorne Williams, 1858; repr., Athens: University of Georgia Press, 1999), 267–73; Stroud, *Sketch of the Laws Relating to Slavery*, 88–95; Peter Charles Hoffer, "Introduction," in *Criminal Proceedings in Colonial Virginia: [Records of] Fines, Examinations of Criminals, Trials of Slaves, etc., from March 1710 [1711] to [1754] [Richmond County, Virginia] American Legal Records, Volume 10*, ed. Peter Charles Hoffer and William B. Scott (Washington, D.C.: American Historical Association and Athens: University of Georgia Press, 1984), xliv–lii; Tamika Y. Nunley, "Thrice Condemned: Enslaved Women, Violence, and the Practice of Leniency in Antebellum Virginia Courts," *Journal of Southern History* 87, no. 1 (February 2021): 11–12; Judith Kelleher Schafer, "The Long Arm of the Law: Slave Criminals and the Supreme Court in Antebellum Louisiana," *Tulane Law Review* 60, no. 6 (June 1986): 1247–68; Daniel J. Flanigan, "Criminal Procedure in Slave Trials in the Antebellum South," *Journal of Southern History* 40, no. 4 (November 1974): 537–64. For as discussion of how this law evolved in Georgia and Tennessee, see Glenn McNair, *Criminal Injustice: Slaves and Free Blacks in*

Georgia's Criminal Justice System (Charlottesville: University of Virginia Press, 2009), 82–142; H. M. Henry, "The Slave Laws of Tennessee," *Tennessee Historical Magazine* 2, no. 3 (September 1916): 182–85. On the interest convergence theory, see Derrick A. Bell Jr., "*Brown v. Board of Education* and the Interest-Convergence Dilemma," *Harvard Law Review* 93, no. 3 (January 1980): 523.

73. See Spindel, *Crime and Society in North Carolina*, 133–37; Stroud, *Sketch of the Laws Relating to Slavery*, 69–88; see also McNair, *Criminal Injustice*, 36–45, 164–65; Cobb, *Inquiry into the Law of Negro Slavery*, 266–67.

74. See Stroud, *Sketch of the Laws Relating to Slavery*, 86–87.

75. See generally Morris, *Southern Slavery and the Law*, 289–92.

76. *State v. Will*, 18 N.C. (1 Dev. & Bat.) 121 (1834); Alfred L. Brophy, *University, Court, and Slave: Pro-slavery Thought in Southern Colleges and Courts and the Coming of the Civil War* (New York: Oxford University Press, 2016), 208.

77. See Bria Cunningham, "$1,000: The Price of Life and Honor in the 1834 North Carolina Supreme Court Case, State v. Will" (honors thesis, Department of History, University at Albany, State University of New York, May 2013), 7. On Moore, see Memory F. Mitchell, "Moore, Bartholomew Figures," in Powell, *Dictionary of North Carolina Biography*, 4:294–95. On Mordecai, see Jean E. Friedman, *Ways of Wisdom: Moral Education in the Early National Period* (Athens: University of Georgia Press, 2001), 243.

78. See *State v. Will*, 18 N.C. (1 Dev. & Bat.), 121–24. On Donnell, see Gertrude S. Carraway, "John Robert Donnell," in Powell, *Dictionary of North Carolina Biography*, 2:92–93.

79. See *State v. Will*, 18 N.C. (1 Dev. & Bat.), 124–53. On Daniel, see "Daniel, John Reeves Jones (1702–1868)," in *Biographical Directory of the United States Congress 1774–Present*, https://bioguide.congress.gov/search/bio/D000034.

80. See *State v. Will*, 145.

81. See ibid., 139, 149–50.

82. See ibid., 163–72.

83. See ibid., 163.

84. See ibid., 165; see also Patrick S. Brady, "Slavery, Race, and the Criminal Law in Antebellum North Carolina: Reconsideration of the Thomas Ruffin Court," *North Carolina Central Law Journal* 10, no. 2 (April 1979): 251n25.

85. See *State v. Will*, 165–66.

86. See ibid., 171.

87. See ibid., 172.

88. See ibid., 171–72.

89. *State v. Jarrott*, 23 N.C. (1 Ired.) 76 (1840).

90. See *State v. Jarrott*, 76–81; see also Sixth Census of the United States, 1840, Person, North Carolina, National Archives Microfilm Publication, roll 358, page 297, Ancestry.com; Max R. Williams, "Graham, William Alexander," in Powell, *Dictionary of North Carolina Biography*, 2:327–28.

91. See *State v. Jarrott*, 81.

92. Ibid., 82.

93. Ibid., 82–83; see Morris, *Southern Slavery and the Law*, 290–91; Fede, *People without Rights*, 170–71; Barbara A. Jackson, "Called to Duty: Justice William J. Gaston," *North Carolina Law Review* 94, no. 6 (September 2016): 2056–66, 2087–92.

94. See *State v. Jarrott*, 83–84.

95. See ibid., 84 (citing *State v. Hale*, 9 N.C. (2 Hawks) 582, 585 (1823)).

96. See *State v. Jarrott a Slave*, North Carolina State Archives, Minutes of the Superior Court, Orange County, March 1841, March 10, 11, and 12, 1841; *Raleigh (N.C.) Register*, March 16, 1841, 3.

97. See Carl Degler, *The Other South: Southern Dissenters in the Nineteenth Century* (Boston: Northeastern University Press, 1982), 40.

98. See John V. Orth, "Gaston, William," in Newman, *Yale Biographical Dictionary of American Law*, 217.

99. See Brophy, *University, Court, and Slave*, 208.

100. See J. Herman Schauinger, *William Gaston Carolinian* (Milwaukee: Bruce Publishing, 1949), 1–13; G. T., "Hon. William Gaston: Georgetown's First Student," *Georgetown College Journal* 27, no. 5 (February 1899): 198–200; J. Fairfax M'Laughlin, "William Gaston: The First Student of Georgetown College," *American Catholic Historical Society of Philadelphia* 6, no. 3 (September 1899): 225–51; The Price of Georgetown: Gaston Hall, https://storymaps.arcgis.com/stories/dd3964df6f424558af3f65748b560e8.

101. See Gaston Hall (1891), Georgetown University: The Online Tour, https://www.hoyasaxa.com/sports/traditions/gaston.htm.

102. See Brophy, *University, Court, and Slave*, 208; Schauinger, *William Gaston Carolinian*, 13–83, 100–165, 224–25; Timothy S. Huebner, "Gaston, William Joseph, 19 September 1778–23 January 1844)," in *American National Biography* (New York: Oxford University Press, 1999), 8:783; Charles H. Bowman Jr., "Gaston, William, 19, Sept. 1779–23 Jan. 1844," in Powell, *Dictionary of North Carolina Biography*, 2:283–85; R. D. W. Connor, "Gaston, William, Oct. 3, 1820–Jan. 19, 1844)," in *Dictionary of American Biography*, ed. Allen Johnson and Dumas Malone (New York: Charles Scribner's Sons, 1931), 7:180–81; Henry G. Connor, "William Gaston," in *Great American Lawyers*, ed. William Draper Lewis (Philadelphia: John C. Winston, 1907), 3:39–84; Jackson, "Called to Duty," 2056–66; "Gaston, William (1778–1844)," in *Biographical Dictionary of the United States Congress 1774–Present*, https://bioguideretro.congress.gov/Home/MemberDetails?memIndex=G000096.

103. See Huebner, "Gaston, William Joseph," 8:783; Bowman Jr., "Gaston, William, 19, Sept. 1779–23 Jan. 1844," in *American National Biography* (New York: Oxford University Press, 1999), 2:285.

104. See William Gaston to Rev. Joseph Carburry, Georgetown Slavery Archive, http://slaveryarchive.georgetown.edu/files/original/f32482b8422c210f0ac5a056ff8de7e7.jpg. On August 2, 1830, Father Joseph Carberry, the manager of the St. Ingoes plantation, recorded a manumission deed in St. Mary's County Court in Maryland freeing Augustin Linsey, who was described as being "about 25 years, five feet 7 inches high, slender made, yellow complexion, woolly hair, pleasant countenance, rather long face, two scars on his forehead, and many warts on his hands and arms." Ibid., https://slaveryarchive.georgetown.edu/items/show/440; see also Schauinger, *William Gaston Carolinian*; 166; Joseph Herman Schauinger, "William Gaston and the Supreme Court of North Carolina," *North Carolina Historical Review* 21, no. 2 (June 1944): 108.

105. See William Gaston, *Address Delivered before the Dialectic and Philanthropic Societies, at Chapel Hill, N.C., June 20, 1823*, 4th ed. (Raleigh: Seaton Gales, 1849), 20; see also Brophy, *University, Court, and Slave*, 206; Jackson, "Called to Duty," 2061–63; Alfred L. Brophy, "The Nat Turner Trials," *North Carolina Law Review* 91, no. 5 (June 2013): 1070.

106. See *Proceedings and Debates of the Convention of North-Carolina, Called to Amend the Constitution of the State, Which Assembled at Raleigh, June 4, 1835* (Raleigh: J. Gales and Son, 1836), 72–81; Schauinger, *William Gaston Carolinian*, 179–99.

107. See *Proceedings and Debates of the Convention of North-Carolina*, 79.

108. See ibid., 351–52; Schauinger, *William Gaston Carolinian*, 184–85; John Hope Franklin, *The Free Negro in North Carolina 1790–1860* (Chapel Hill: University of North Carolina Press, 1943), 114.

109. *Proceedings and Debates of the Convention of North-Carolina*, 357–58; *Journal of the Convention Called by the Freemen of North-Carolina to Amend the Constitution of the State* (Raleigh: J. Gales and Son, 1835), 74; see Franklin, *Free Negro in North Carolina*, 114–15.

110. See Franklin, *Free Negro in North Carolina*, 114–16. The amendment that was ratified on July 6, 1835, stated, "No free negro, free mulatto, or free person of mixed blood, descended from negro ancestors to the fourth generation inclusive (though one ancestor may have been a white person), shall vote for member of the senate or house of commons." See Franklin, *Free Negro in North Carolina*, 115n279; see generally John V. Orth and Paul Martin Newby, *The North Carolina State Constitution*, 2nd ed., Oxford Commentaries on the State Constitutions of the United States (New York: Oxford University Press, 2013), 14–15; John V. Orth, "North Carolina Constitutional History," *North Carolina Law Review* 70, no. 6 (September 1992): 1771–72.

111. *State v. Will*, 18 N.C. (1 Dev. & Bat.) 121 (1834); see Brophy, *University, Court, and Slave*, 208.

112. See Brady, "Slavery, Race, and the Criminal Law," 251–52.

113. See Schauinger, *William Gaston Carolinian*, 166.

114. See Fede, *People without Rights*, 169 (citing Brady, "Slavery, Race, and the Criminal Law," 251n28); see also Brophy, *University, Court, and Slave*, 208–11; Schauinger, *William Gaston Carolinian*, 166–69; Connor, "William Gaston," in *Great American Lawyers*, 3:68–70; Schauinger, "William Gaston and the Supreme Court of North Carolina," 108–11; George Gordon Battle, "The State of North Carolina v. Negro Will, a Slave of James S. Battle: A Cause Celebre of Ante-Bellum Times," *Virginia Law Review* 6, no. 7 (April 1920): 515–30; John S. Bassett, "The Case of State vs. Will," *Trinity College Historical Papers* 2 (1898): 12–20. For my earlier discussion, see Fede, *People without Rights*, 168–70.

115. See Jackson, "Called to Duty," 2087.

116. See ibid., 2089. For other interpretations of these decisions, see, e.g., Cynthia Lee, *Murder and the Reasonable Man: Passion and Fear in the Criminal Courtroom* (New York: New York University Press, 2003), 58–60; Morris, *Southern Slavery and the Law*, 279–81; James Oakes, *Slavery and Freedom: An Interpretation of the Old South* (New York: Norton, 1990), 159–66; Jackson, "Called to Duty," 2070–83; Meyer, "Slavery Jurisprudence on the Supreme Court of North Carolina," 318–23; Brady, "Slavery, Race, and the Criminal Law," 252–54.

117. See Fede, *People without Rights*, 170–71; see also *State v. Caesar*, 31 N.C. (9 Ired.) 391 (1849) (following Gaston's unequal mitigation holding in *Jarrott*, with Ruffin dissenting, reversing an enslaved man Caesar's conviction for the murder of a white stranger); Huebner, "Roots of Fairness," 29–52; compare Schauinger, *William Gaston Carolinian*, 166 (Gaston "never looked to the advancement of the white race but rather the preservation of society").

118. See Cobb, *Inquiry into the Law of Negro Slavery*, 94–96, 274–76; see also, e.g.,

State v. Austin, 14 Ark. 555 (1854); *Dave v. State*, 22 Ala. 23 (1853); *Nelson v. State*, 29 Tenn. (10 Hum.) 518 (1850); *State v. Jacob*, 22 Tenn. (3 Hum.) 493 (1842); Fede, People without Rights, 167–76.

119. See Katz, *Holocaust and New World Slavery*, 453n53 (suggesting that it is an "open" and "serious question" whether North Carolina "experienced a more lenient development in its slave law"). On homicides of enslaved victims, see Fede, *Homicide Justified*, 105–9, 152–63; Jason Allan Twede, "Going Public: How the Government Assumed the Authority to Prosecute in the Southern United States" (PhD diss., University of North Dakota, May 2016), 154–62.

120. See *State v. Watson*, 287 N.C. 147, 152–54, 214 S.E. 2d 85, 89–90 (1975).

121. Ibid., 287 N.C., 154, 214 S.E. 2d, 90, citing *State v. Benson*, 183 N.C. 795, 799, 111 S.E. 869, 871 (1922) (noting that *Benson* overruled these cases by implication).

122. *The Bluebook* was amended in 2021 to require that citations to cases involving enslaved persons include parenthetical references, either (enslaved party) or (enslaved person at issue). See David J. S. Ziff, "Citation, Slavery, and the Law as Choice: Thoughts on *Bluebook* Rule 10.7.1(d)," *North Carolina Law Review Forum* (2023): 72–104; Justin Simard, "Citing Slavery," *Stanford Law Review* 72, no. 1 (January 2020): 121–22; Bluebook Online, Twenty-First Edition Information, Noteworthy Changes to the 2021 Printing, https://www.legalbluebook.com/preface-to-the-twenty-first-edition.

CHAPTER 4. Justice O'Neall and Unequal Protection for Free Blacks

1. See Joseph A. Ranney, *Bridging Revolutions: The Lives of Chief Justices Richmond Pearson and John Belton O'Neall* (Athens: University of Georgia Press, 2023), 4.

2. See ibid., 4.

3. *State v. Harden*, 29 S.C.L. (2 Speers) 152 (Ct. App. Law 1832).

4. Howell Meadoes Henry, *The Police Control of the Slave in South Carolina* (Emory, 1914; repr., New York: Negro Universities Press, 1968), 181; see ibid., 176–89, for Henry's chapter on South Carolina's free Blacks.

5. Michael P. Johnson and James L. Roark, *Black Masters: A Free Family of Color in the Old South* (New York: Norton, 1984), 48–49.

6. See Ranney, *Bridging Revolutions*, 6–11, 21–24, 30–45, 47–55, 59–60, 69–105, 121–22; Alexander M. Sanders Jr., "O'Neall, John Belton," in *The Yale Biographical Dictionary of American Law*, ed. Roger K. Newman (New Haven, Conn.: Yale University Press, 2009), 411; Alexander M. Sanders Jr., "Judge John Belton O'Neall and Today's McCready's Oath: A Lesson for Today," *Journal of Southern Legal History* 3 (1994): 132–34; A. E. Keir Nash, "Negro Rights, Unionism, and Greatness on the South Carolina Court of Appeals: The Extraordinary Chief Justice John Belton O'Neall," *South Carolina Law Review* 21, no. 1 (1968–1969): 170–72.

7. See "The John Belton O'Neall American Inn of Court," https://inns.innsofcourt.org/for-members/inns/the-john-belton-oneall-american-inn-of-court/.

8. See Sanders, "Judge John Belton O'Neall and Today's McCready's Oath," 134.

9. For example, Joseph Ranney does not refer to O'Neall's *Harden* decision, or his later endorsements of the unequal protection doctrine, in his dual biography of O'Neall and Pearson. See Ranney, *Bridging Revolutions*.

10. See Alan Watson, *Slave Law in the Americas* (Athens: University of Georgia Press,

1989), 67. These facts, which Watson admits were "atypical," suggest that South Carolina might not have been the best colony and state for Watson to use to test his hypothesis on the nature of legal change in what became the U.S. South.

11. See Ira Berlin, *Slaves without Masters: The Free Negro in the Antebellum South* (New York: New Press, 1974), 46–47, 136–37, 397, 399; Donald J. Senese, "The Free Negro and the South Carolina Courts, 1790–1860," *South Carolina Historical Magazine* 68, no. 3 (July 1967): 140.

12. See Andrew T. Fede, *Homicide Justified: The Legality of Killing Slaves in the United States and the Atlantic World* (Athens: University of Georgia Press, 2017), 173–74; see also Matthew Mulcahy, *Hubs of Empire: The Southeastern Lowcountry and British Caribbean, Regional Perspectives in Early America* (Baltimore: Johns Hopkins University Press, 2014), 210–11; Stephanie McCurry, *Masters of Small Worlds: Yeoman Households, Gender Relations, and the Political Culture of the Antebellum South Carolina Low Country* (New York: Oxford University Press, 1995), 33–36, 44–45; Rachel N. Klein, *Unification of a Slave State: The Rise of the Planter Class in the South Carolina Backcountry, 1760–1808* (Chapel Hill: University of North Carolina Press, 1990), 14–15, 150–52, 238–68; Orville Vernon Burton, *In My Father's House Are Many Mansions: Family and Community in Edgefield, South Carolina* (Chapel Hill: University of North Carolina Press, 1985), 15–46.

13. See Marina Wikramanayake, *A World in Shadow: The Free Black in Antebellum South Carolina* (Columbia: University of South Carolina Press, 1973), 22, Appendix A (1)–(3); E. Horace Fitchett, "The Origin and Growth of the Free Negro Population of Charleston, South Carolina," *Journal of Negro History* 26, no. 4 (October 1941): 435; Ulrich Bonnell Phillips, "The Slave Labor Problem in the Charleston District," *Political Science Quarterly* 22, no. 3 (September 1907): 426.

14. See Johnson and Roark, *Black Masters*, 340; Robert L. Harris Jr., "Charleston's Free Afro-American Elite: The Brown Fellowship Society and the Humane Brotherhood," *South Carolina Historical Magazine* 82, no. 4 (October 1981): 303.

15. See Jeff Strickland, *Unequal Freedoms: Ethnicity, Race, and White Supremacy in Civil War-Era Charleston* (Gainesville: University Press of Florida, 2015), 22. The city's free Black population numbers declined between 1830 and 1840 because African Americans moved to an area north of Charleston, which was known as the Neck. The free Black population totals later increased after the Neck was incorporated into the city. See Johnson and Roark, *Black Masters*, 206–7; Wikramanayake, *World in Shadow*, 22; Harris, "Charleston's Free Afro-American Elite," 304.

16. See Peter H. Wood, *Black Majority: Negroes in Colonial South Carolina from 1670 through the Stono Rebellion* (New York: Knopf, 1974), 13; see also Fede, *Homicide Justified*, 98, 284n42; Watson, *Slave Law in the Americas*, 67–70.

17. See Jack P. Greene, "Colonial South Carolina and the Caribbean Connection," *South Carolina Historical Magazine* 88, no. 4 (October 1987): 197; see also Fede, *Homicide Justified*, 41; Mulcahy, *Hubs of Empire*, 84–111. Culture hearth is "defined as an area wherein new basic cultural systems and configurations are developed and nurtured before spreading vigorously outward to alter the character of much larger areas." See D. W. Meinig, *The Shaping of America: A Geographical Perspective on 500 Years of History: Volume I, Atlantic America, 1492–1800* (New Haven, Conn.: Yale University Press, 1986), 52. The colonists in the culture hearths developed "local cultures, including social institutions and ways of manipulating a particular kind of environment." With "appropriate

modifications," the colonists later transferred these cultures and institutions "to other areas in the Anglo-American world." See Greene, "Colonial South Carolina and the Caribbean Connection," 192; see also Meinig, *Shaping of America*, 252; Jack P. Greene, "Early Modern Southeastern North America and the Border Atlantic and American Worlds," *Journal of Southern History* 23, no. 3 (August 2007): 532–33.

18. See James Oliver Horton, *Free People of Color: Inside the African American Community* (Washington, D.C.: Smithsonian Institution Press, 1993), 139–40; Johnson and Roark, *Black Masters*, 53–55; Joel Williamson, *New People: Miscegenation and Mulattoes in the United States* (New York: Free Press, 1980), 18–19, 71–72 (citing *State v. Cantey*, 20 S.C.L. (2 Hill) 614 (1835)); John Belton O'Neall, *Negro Law of South Carolina Collected and Digested by John Belton O'Neall* (Columbia: John G. Bowman, 1848), 5–6, 13, reprinted in *Statutes on Slavery: The Pamphlet Literature*, ed. Paul Finkelman (New York: Garland, 1988), 2:117–72; see also *White v. Tax Collector, Kershaw Dist.*, 37 S.C.L. (3 Rich.) 136 (Ct. App. 1846); *State v. Davis*, 18 S.C.L. (2 Bail.) 558 (Ct. App. of Law & Eq. 1831); Frank W. Sweet, *Legal History of the Color Line: The Rise and Triumph of the One-Drop Rule* (Palm Coast, Fla.: Backintyme, 2005), 181–93, 396–401, 403–6; but see text and note at note 24.

19. See Carl N. Degler, *Neither Black nor White: Slavery and Race Relations in Brazil and the United States* (New York: Macmillan, 1971), 178; see also ibid., 226–45. Degler explained that this escape hatch, which he stated was in existence in Brazil and not the United States, permitted "the recognition of a special place for mixed bloods." See ibid., 245. For the Jamaica statute, see ibid., 240; Winthrop D. Jordan, "American Chiaroscuro: The Status and Definition of Mulattoes in the British Colonies," *William & Mary Quarterly* 19, no. 2 (April 1962): 198; see also Samuel J. Hurwitz and Edith F. Hurwitz, "A Token of Freedom: Private Bill Legislation for Free Negroes in Eighteenth-Century Jamaica," *William & Mary Quarterly* 24, no. 3 (July 1967): 423–31; see also, e.g., discussing this concept, Robert J. Cottrol, *The Long, Lingering Shadow: Slavery, Race, and Law in the American Hemisphere* (Athens: University of Georgia Press, 2013), 159; Andrew Fede, *Roadblocks to Freedom: Slavery and Manumission in the United States South* (New Orleans: Quid Pro Books, 2011), 40; Julissa Reynoso, "Race, Censuses, and Attempts at Racial Democracy," *Columbia Journal of Transnational Law* 39, no. 2 (2001): 545; Tanya Kateri Hernandez, "'Multiracial' Discourse: Racial Classifications in an Era of Color-Blind Jurisprudence," *Maryland Law Review* 57, no. 1 (1998): 122.

20. *State v. Cantey*, 615–16.

21. See Ariela Gross, "Litigating Whiteness: Trials of Racial Determination in the Nineteenth Century South," *Yale Law Journal* 108, no. 1 (October 1998): 162–64; see also D. Wendy Greene, "Determining the (In)determinate: Race in Brazil and the United States," *Michigan Journal of Race and Law* 14, no. 2 (Spring 2009): 175.

22. See, discussing the white elite's attitudes toward the white poor in American history, Nancy Isenberg, *White Trash: The 400-Year Untold History of Class in America* (New York: Viking, 2016), 135–37.

23. See A Carolinian, *A Refutation of the Calumnies Circulated Against the Southern and Western States* (Charleston: A. E. Miller, 1822), 85.

24. See "An Act for the Better Governing and Regulating White Servants, and to Repeal a Former Act Entitled 'An Act for the Better Governing and Regulating of White Servants,'" in Thomas Cooper, *The Statutes at Large of South Carolina* (Columbia, S.C.:

A. S. Johnston, 1838), 3:629; "An Act for the Better Governing and Regulating White Servants," in Cooper, *Statutes at Large of South Carolina*, 20; "An Additional and Explanatory Act to an Act Entituled, An Act to Keep Inviolate and Preserve the freedom of Elections, and to Appoint Who Shall Be Deemed and Adjudged Capable of Choosing or Being Chosen Members of the Commons House of Assembly: Duely Ratified in Open Assembly the Fifteenth Day of December, 1776," in Cooper, *Statutes at Large of South Carolina*, 2–4; Williamson, *New People*, 17; Wood, *Black Majority*, 102–3; John Codman Hurd, *The Law of Freedom and Bondage in the United States* (1858/1862; repr., Boston: Little, Brown, 1968), 1:301–2.

25. See "An ACT for the Better Ordering and Governing Negroes and Other Slaves," in David J. McCord, ed., *Statutes at Large of South Carolina* (Columbia: A. S. Johnston, 1840), 7:384; see also Edward R. Rugemer, *Slave Law and the Politics of Resistance in the Early Atlantic World* (Cambridge, Mass.: Harvard University Press, 2018), 103.

26. Sally E. Hadden, *Slave Patrols: Law and Violence in Virginia and the Carolinas* (Cambridge, Mass.: Harvard University Press, 2001), 19. Hadden explains how the South Carolina provisions differed from those that preceded them on Barbados. Ibid., 19–24. On the influence of slave patrols on modern policing, see Amna A. Akbar, "An Abolitionist Horizon for (Police) Reform," *California Law Review* 108, no. 6 (December 2020): 1811–13; K. B. Turner, David Giacopassi, and Margaret Vandiver, "Ignoring the Past: Coverage of Slavery and Slave Patrols in Criminal Justice Texts," *Journal of Criminal Justice Education* 17, no. 1 (April 2006): 181–95.

27. See Elizabeth Dale, *Criminal Justice in the United States, 1789–1939* (New York: Cambridge University Press, 2011), 36–37; see also Amrita Chakrabarti Myers, *Forging Freedom: Black Women and the Pursuit of Liberty in Antebellum Charleston* (Chapel Hill: University of North Carolina Press, 2011), 21–32, 26; Hadden, *Slave Patrols*, 84; Robert N. Rosen, *A Short History of Charleston*, 2nd ed. (Columbia: University of South Carolina Press, 1992), 67–70, 75–77; Frederic Cople Jaher, *The Urban Establishment: Upper Strata in Boston, New York, Charleston, Chicago, and Los Angeles* (Urbana: University of Illinois Press, 1982), 317–451; Stephanie E. Yuhl, "Hidden in Plain Sight: Centering the Domestic Slave Trade in American Public History," *Journal of Southern History* 73, no. 3 (August 2013): 593–624.

28. See Fede, *Homicide Justified*, 173–82.

29. See "An ACT for the Better Ordering and Governing Negroes and Other Slaves," in McCord, *Statutes at Large of South Carolina*, 7:373–74; "An ACT for the Better Ordering and Governing Negroes and Slaves," in McCord, *Statutes at Large of South Carolina*, 7:354–55, "An ACT for the Better Ordering of Slaves," in McCord, *Statutes at Large of South Carolina*, 7:345–46; Christopher Tomlins, *Freedom Bound: Law, Labor, and Civic Identity in Colonizing English America, 1580–1865* (New York: Cambridge University Press, 2010), 437–46; see also Rugemer, *Slave Law*, 64–103.

30. See Lee B. Wilson, *Bonds of Empire: The English Origins of Slave Law in South Carolina and British Plantation America, 1660–1783* (New York: Cambridge University Press, 2021), 40; Tomlins, *Freedom Bound*, 428–30.

31. See "An ACT for the Better Ordering and Governing Negroes and Slaves," in McCord, *Statutes at Large of South Carolina*, 7:343; see also Watson, *Slave Law in the Americas*, 68–69 (noting the similarities between this provision and a section in the 1688 Barbados slave code).

32. See "An ACT for the Better Ordering and Governing Negroes and Other Slaves," in McCord, *Statutes at Large of South Carolina*, 7:390–91. For the 1712 law, which criminalized this violence against "any christian or white person," see "An ACT for the Better Ordering and Governing Negroes and Slaves," in McCord, *Statutes at Large of South Carolina*, 7:358–59.

33. Tomlins, *Freedom Bound*, 446–47.

34. See ibid., 449; see also Rugemer, *Slave Law*, 103–19; Watson, *Slave Law in the Americas*, 82.

35. See "An Act for the Better Ordering and Governing Negroes and Other Slaves in This Province," in McCord, *Statutes at Large of South Carolina*, 7:400–401.

36. Ibid., 402; see *State v. Scott*, 17 S.C.L. (1 Bail.) 294, 296–97 (Ct. of App. Law and Eq. 1829); Wikramanayake, *World in Shadow*, 63–65; O'Neall, *Negro Law of South Carolina*, 6, 33–36 (also noting that Charleston's procedures were "better" than elsewhere in the state); see also Fede, *Homicide Justified*, 3–4; Bruce Eelman, *Entrepreneurs in the Southern Upcountry: Commercial Culture in Spartanburg, South Carolina, 1845–1880* (Athens: University of Georgia Press, 2008), 92–98; Robert Olwell, *Masters, Slaves, and Subjects: The Culture of Power in the South Carolina Low Country, 1740–1790* (Ithaca, N.Y.: Cornell University Press, 1998), 63, 71–101; Thomas D. Morris, *Southern Slavery and the Law, 1619–1860* (Chapel Hill: University of North Carolina Press, 1996), 212, 216–17, 219–20, 222; Michael Stephen Hindus, *Prison and Plantation: Crime, Justice, and Authority in Massachusetts and South Carolina, 1767–1878* (Chapel Hill: University of North Carolina Press, 1980), 129–61; A. Leon Higginbotham Jr., *In the Matter of Color: Race and the American Legal Process: The Colonial Period* (New York: Oxford University Press, 1978), 179–81; Henry, *Police Control of the Slave*, 58–65; Michael Hindus, "Black Justice under White Law: Criminal Prosecutions of Blacks in Antebellum South Carolina," *Journal of American History* 63, no. 3 (December 1976): 576–79; Terry W. Lipscomb and Theresa Jacobs, "The Magistrate and Freeholders Court," *South Carolina Historical Magazine* 77, no. 1 (January 1976): 62–63; Daniel J. Flanigan, "Criminal Procedure in Slave Trials in the Antebellum South," *Journal of Southern History* 40, no. 4 (November 1974): 540–45; see also *State ex rel. Fanning v. Mayor of Charleston*, 46 S.C.L. (12 Rich.) 480 (Ct. App. 1860) (holding this statutory procedure did not prevent prosecutions for violations of municipal ordinances in Charleston's Police Court, also called the Mayor's Court, under procedures established by city ordinance); Strickland, *Unequal Freedoms*, 104–5; Richard C. Wade, *Slavery in the Cities: The South 1820–1860* (New York: Oxford University Press, 1964), 102–6.

37. See generally Daniel J. Sharfstein, "Crossing the Color Line: Racial Migration and the One Drop Rule, 1600–1860," *Minnesota Law Review* 91, no. 3 (February 2007): 637–40.

38. See Morris, *Southern Slavery and the Law*, 215–19. The Virginia and Louisiana legislators adopted similar criminal procedural models for slave prosecutions and trials. See Philip J. Schwarz, *Twice Condemned: Slaves and the Criminal Laws of Virginia, 1705–1865* (Baton Rouge: Louisiana State University Press, 1988), 17–34. For discussions of the three antebellum models for criminal procedures in slave prosecutions and trials, see Morris, *Southern Slavery and the Law*, 209–28; Andrew Fede, *People without Rights: An Interpretation of the Fundamentals of the Law of Slavery in the U.S. South* (New York: Garland, 1992; repr., New York: Routledge, 2011), 181–99; Alan D. Watson, "North Carolina Slave Courts, 1715–1785," *North Carolina Historical Review* 60, no. 1 (January 1983): 24–36.

39. See, e.g., Morris, *Southern Slavery and the Law*, 229–39; Fede, *People without Rights*, 194–95; Daniel Flanigan, *The Criminal Law of Slavery and Freedom 1800–1868* (New York: Garland, 1987), 173–87; Wikramanayake, *World in Shadow*, 52–53; Thomas R. R. Cobb, *An Inquiry into the Law of Negro Slavery in the United States of America* (Philadelphia: T. & J. W. Johnson and Savannah: W. Thorne Williams, 1858; repr., Athens: University of Georgia Press, 1999), 230–34; George M. Stroud, *A Sketch of the Laws Relating to Slavery in the Several States of the United States of America* (2nd ed., 1856; repr., New York: Negro Universities Press, 1968), 44–52; O'Neall, *Negro Law of South Carolina*, 13–14; Senese, "Free Negro and the South Carolina Courts," 150–52; see also *Jones v. Jones*, 46 S.C.L. (12 Rich.) 116 (Ct. App. 1859); *Groning v. Devana*, 18 S.C.L. (2 Bail.) 192 (Ct. App. of Law & Eq. 1831); *White v. Helmes*, 12 S.C.L. (1 McCord) 430 (Const. Ct. App. 1821).

40. See, e.g., *State v. Nathan, the slave of Gabriel South*, 38 S.C.L. (4 Rich.) 513 (Court of Appeals of Law 1851); *State v. Ridgell*, 18 S.C.L. (2 Bail.) 560 (Court of Appeals of Law and Equity 1832); *Ex parte, Jesse Brown*, 18 S.C.L. (2 Bail.) 323 (Court of Appeals of Law and Equity 1832); *Kinloch v. Harvey*, 16 S.C.L. (Harp.) 508 (Court of Appeals of Law and Equity 1830); see also *Ex parte Boylston*, 33 S.C.L. (2 Strob.) 41 (Court of Appeals of Law 1847); *State v. Whyte*, 11 S.C.L (2 Nott & McC.) 174 (Court of Appeals of Law 1840); *State v. Toomer*, 25 S.C.L (Chev.) 106 (Constitutional Court of Appeals of Law 1819); O'Neall, *Negro Law of South Carolina*, 6, 34–35; Flanigan, "Criminal Procedure in Slave Trials," 540–44.

41. See *Kinloch v. Harvey*, 16 S.C.L. (Harp.), 511–12.

42. See "An Act Abolishing Certain Punishments and Amending the Law for the Trial of Slaves and Free Persons of Color," in McCord, *Statutes at Large of South Carolina*, 6:489–90; Morris, *Southern Slavery and the Law*, 226–27; O'Neall, *Negro Law of South Carolina*, 34. The legislature refers to this law in an 1839 law, "An Act Concerning the Office and Duties of Magistrates," in David J. McCord, ed. *The Statutes at Large of South Carolina Volume XI Containing the Acts from 1838 Exclusive* (Columbia, S.C.: Republican Printing Company, 1873), 26. It appears that Morris refers to this 1839 act instead of the 1833 act. See Morris, *Southern Slavery and the Law*, 226.

43. *State v. Nicholas, slave of William Kelly*, 33 S.C.L. (2 Strob.) 278, 292 (Court of Appeals of Law 1848); see Hindus, *Prison and Plantation*, 131, 150–6; Henry, *Police Control of the Slave*, 58–65; Hindus, "Black Justice under White Law," 591–95.

44. See *State v. Friday, a slave of David Lopez*, 38 S.C.L. (4 Rich.) 291 (Court of Appeals of Law 1851) (denying the defendant's right to appeal an order denying a new trial motion). The court had previously held that the state cannot appeal orders granting defendants' new trial motions under this statute. See *State v. Nicholas, slave of William Kelly*, 33 S.C.L. (2 Strob.), 292. Daniel Flannigan cites several cases in which Court of Appeals judges attempted to convince the other judges to agree to review motions *en banc*. "Predictably, few judges doubted their own wisdom enough to seek the advice of their fellow justices." Flanigan, "Criminal Procedure in Slave Trials," 542.

45. See *Ex parte Boylston*, 33 S.C.L. (2 Strob.), 42–46 (affirming enslaved defendant Jim's conviction on charge of "insolent language and action," with O'Neall dissenting); *State v. Porter*, 5 S.C.L. (3 Brev.) 175 (Const. Court of Appeals 1815) (free Black defendant, Amey Lapier, charged with slandering and insulting a white woman, Mrs. Thomas; evidence allegedly proved that she committed barratry and an assault).

46. See Henry, *Police Control of the Slave*, 176–89.

47. Johnson and Roark, *Black Masters*, 48; see Sharfstein, "Crossing the Color Line, 1600–1860," 636–40.

48. See, e.g., Berlin, *Slaves without Masters*, 183, 316–40; Arthur F. Howington, *What Sayeth the Law: The Treatment of Slaves and Free Blacks in the State and Local Courts of Tennessee* (New York: Garland, 1986), 217–46; John Hope Franklin, *The Free Negro in North Carolina 1790–1860* (Chapel Hill: University of North Carolina Press, 1943), 58–100; Stroud, *Sketch of the Laws Relating to Slavery*, 88–95; Wilbert E. Moore, "Slave Law and Social Structure," *Journal of Negro History* 26, no. 2 (April 1941): 180–84; see also Strickland, *Unequal Freedoms*, 80 (citing prosecutions of free Blacks).

49. See "An ACT to Inflict Capital Punishment on Slaves and Free Persons of Color Who May Commit a Certain Offence," in *Acts of the General Assembly of the State of South Carolina Passed in December, 1843* (Columbia, S.C.: A. H. Pemberton, 1844), 258.

50. See *State ex rel. Fanning v. Mayor of Charleston*, 46 S.C.L. (12 Rich.) 480, 480–81 (Ct. App. 1860) (denying motion to reverse convictions of "free persons of color" under Charleston's anti-gambling ordinance). An 1834 South Carolina law, like the antebellum law in other southern states, later prohibited whites from gambling with "any free negro or person of color or slave." See "An Act to Amend the Laws in Relation to Slaves and Free Persons of Color," in McCord, *Statutes at Large of South Carolina*, 7:469–70; *State v. Laney*, 38 S.C.L. (3 Rich.) 193 (Court of Appeals 1850); *State v. Nates*, 21 S.C.L. (3 Hill) 200 (Court of Appeals 1836); Robert M. Jarvis, "Slave Gambling in the Antebellum South," *Florida A&M University Law Review* 13, no. 2 (Spring 2018): 173–76. On the laws prohibiting gambling by slaves and evidence of prosecutions, see Jeff Forret, *Race Relations at the Margins: Slaves and Poor Whites in the Antebellum Southern Countryside* (Baton Rouge: Louisiana University Press, 2006), 56–61; Jarvis, "Slave Gambling in the Antebellum South," 167–81.

51. See "An ACT to Restrain the Emancipation of Slaves, and to Prevent Free Persons of Color from Entering into This State, and for Other Purposes," in McCord, *Statutes at Large of South Carolina*, 7:459.

52. Ibid., 7:459–60; see Wikramanayake, *World in Shadow*, 55–56. On the evolution of South Carolina's laws, and the laws of the other colonies and states, regulating and prohibiting manumission, see Fede, *Roadblocks to Freedom*, 87–138. The fifth section may have been enacted in response to *Pepoon v. Clarke*, 8 S.C.L. (1 Mill Const.) 137 (Constitutional Ct. of App. 1817) (affirming judgment for guardian of free young woman of color who was illegally enslaved by the defendant as a child after being brought into the state from Baltimore); see also *Wellborn v. Little*, 10 S.C.L. (1 Mill Const.) 263 (Const. Ct. App. 1818); *State v. Greenwood*, 8 S.C.L. (1 Nott. & Mc.) 263 (Const. Ct. App. 1817).

53. On the Vesey matter, see, e.g., Lacy K. Ford, *Deliver Us from Evil: The Slavery Question in the Old South* (New York: Oxford University Press, 2009), 205–96; Edlie L. Wong, *Neither Fugitive nor Free: Atlantic Slavery, Freedom Suits, and the Legal Culture of Travel* (New York: New York University Press, 2009), 183–94; Wikramanayake, *World in Shadow*, 133–53; Michael P. Johnson, "Denmark Vesey and His Co-conspirators," *William and Mary Quarterly*, 3rd ser., 58, no. 4 (October 2001): 915–76; and the articles in "Forum: The Making of a Slave Conspiracy, Part 2," *William and Mary Quarterly*, 3rd ser., 59, no. 1 (January 2002): 135–202.

54. See "Memorial of the Citizens of Charleston in the Senate and House of Representatives of the State of South Carolina [Charleston, 1822]," in *Plantation and Frontier Documents: 1649–1863*, ed. Ulrich B. Phillips (Cleveland: Arthur Clark, 1909), 2:103–16; see also Phillips, "Slave Labor Problem in the Charleston District," 429–33. On race-based laws regulating the permitted clothing of African Americans, including South Carolina's laws, see Richard Ford Thompson, *Dress Codes: How Laws of Fashion Made History* (New York: Simon & Schuster, 2021), 157–67; Shane White and Graham White, "Slave Clothing and African-American Culture in the Eighteenth and Nineteenth Centuries," *Past and Present* 148, no. 1 (August 1995): 149–86.

55. Phillips quoted the petition at length in his 1907 article, but did not even mention the 1822 statute. In contrast, he declared, "The fright of 1822 soon passed; no important changes in the general system were instituted; and the previous conditions of life and industry were in the main restored." See Phillips, "Slave Labor Problem in the Charleston District," 433.

56. See "An ACT for the Better Regulation and Government of Free Negroes and Persons of Color, and for Other Proposes," in McCord, *Statutes at Large of South Carolina*, 7:461–62; see also Kate Masur, *Until Justice Be Done: America's First Civil Rights Movement, from the Revolution to Reconstruction* (New York: Norton, 2021), 119–51; Michael A. Schoeppner, *Moral Contagion: Black Atlantic Sailors, Citizenship, and Diplomacy in Antebellum America* (New York: Cambridge University Press, 2019), 1–30; Wong, *Neither Fugitive nor Free*, 183–239; William M. Wiecek, *The Sources of Antislavery Constitutionalism in America 1760–1848* (Ithaca, N.Y.: Cornell University Press, 1977), 128–42; Michael A. Schoeppner, "Peculiar Quarantines: The Seamen Acts and Regulatory Authority in the Antebellum South," *Law and History Review* 31, no. 3 (August 2013): 559–86; Michael A. Schoeppner, "Status across Borders: Roger Taney, Black British Subjects, and a Diplomatic Antecedent to the Dred Scott Decision," *Journal of American History* 100, no. 1 (June 2013): 46–67.

57. See Berlin, *Slaves without Masters*, 137, 403; Harris, "Charleston's Free Afro-American Elite," 302–3.

58. Wikramanayake, *World in Shadow*, 45–46.

59. Ibid., 169; see Jeff Strickland, *All for Liberty: The Charleston Workhouse Slave Rebellion of 1849* (New York: Cambridge University Press, 2022), 178–79.

60. See Emily West, *Family or Freedom: People of Color in the Antebellum South* (Lexington: University Press of Kentucky, 2012), 41–42; Bernard E. Powers Jr., *Black Charlestonians: A Social History, 1822–1885* (Fayetteville: University of Arkansas Press, 1994), 63–65; Wikramanayake, *World in Shadow*, 169–70; Eric William Rose, "The Charleston 'School of Slavery': Race, Religion, and Community in the Capital of Southern Civilization" (PhD diss., George Mason University, 2014), 195–97.

61. See Strickland, *Unequal Freedoms*, 43–44; see also Powers, *Black Charlestonians*, 41–47; Johnson and Roark, *Black Masters*, 54–62; Berlin, *Slaves without Masters*, 215–44; Wikramanayake, *World in Shadow*, 103–6; Phillips, "Slave Labor Problem in the Charleston District," 434–35.

62. See David O. Stowell, "The Free Black Population of Columbia South Carolina in 1860: A Snapshot of Occupation and Personal Wealth," *South Carolina Historical Magazine* 104, no. 1 (January 2003): 6–24; see generally Ira Berlin and Herbert G. Gutman,

"Natives and Immigrants, Free Men and Slaves: Urban Workingmen in the Antebellum South," *American Historical Review* 88, no. 5 (December 1983): 1175–1200.

63. See Powers, *Black Charlestonians*, 47–48; Loren Schweninger, *Black Property Owners in the South 1790–1915* (Urbana: University of Illinois Press, 1990), 61–142; Johnson and Roark, *Black Masters*, 62–64; Berlin, *Slaves without Masters*, 244–49; Wikramanayake, *World in Shadow*, 106–9.

64. See Larry Koger, *Black Slaveowners: Free Black Slavemasters in South Carolina, 1790–1860* (Jefferson, N.C.: McFarland, 1985), 18–30; see also Powers, *Black Charlestonians*, 48–50; Johnson and Roark, *Black Masters*, 63–64; Phillips, "Slave Labor Problem in the Charleston District," 434. On the scholarly debate about whether the majority of free Blacks enslaved people out of benevolent or profit motives, see, e.g., Ira Berlin, *Generations of Captivity: A History of African-American Slaves* (Cambridge, Mass.: Belknap, 2003), 37–38, 138–39, 144–45; Ira Berlin, *Many Thousands Gone: The First Two Centuries of Slavery in North America* (Cambridge, Mass.: Harvard University Press, 1998), 30–32; Schweninger, *Black Property Owners in the South*, 15, 22–28, 100–109; Eugene D. Genovese, *Roll, Jordan, Roll: The World the Slaves Made* (New York: Vintage, 1976), 406–8; Kenneth M. Stampp, *The Peculiar Institution: Slavery in the Ante-Bellum South* (New York: Vintage, 1956), 194–95; Ellen D. Katz, "African-American Freedom in Antebellum Cumberland County, Virginia," *Chicago-Kent Law Review* 70, no. 3 (1995): 962–64; Philip J. Schwarz, "Emancipators, Protectors, and Anomalies: Free Black Slaveowners in Virginia," *Virginia Magazine of History & Biography* 95, no. 3 (July 1987): 317–38; David L. Lightner and Alexander M. Ragan, "Were African American Slaveholders Benevolent or Exploitative? A Quantitative Analysis," *Journal of Southern History* 71, no. 3 (August 2005): 535–58; Carter G. Woodson, "Free Negro Owners of Slaves in the United States in 1830," *Journal of Negro History* 9, no. 1 (January 1924): 48–85. Some southern court decisions and statutes eventually banned Black slave ownership because of racist public policy notions. See *Ewell v. Tidwell*, 20 Ark. 136 (1859); *Davis v. Evans*, 18 Mo. 249 (1853); *Tindal v. Hudson*, 2 Del. (2 Harr.) 441 (1838); Morris, *Southern Slavery and the Law*, 30–31.

65. See Stowell, "Free Black Population of Columbia," 18–24; see also Powers, *Black Charlestonians*, 58–62.

66. See Wikramanayake, *World in Shadow*, 108–12; see also Johnson and Roark, *Black Masters*, 58–64.

67. See Harris, "Charleston's Free Afro-American Elite," 304–5; see also Wikramanayake, *World in Shadow*, 47–70; Ira Berlin, "Time, Space, and the Evolution of Afro-American Society on British Mainland North America," *American Historical Review* 85, no. 1 (February 1980): 63–64; Ira Berlin, "The Structure of the Free Negro Caste in the Antebellum United States," *Journal of Social History* 9, no. 3 (Spring 1976): 309–14.

68. See David W. Dangerfield, "Just Beyond the Reach of Servitude: Free Black Farmers in the Antebellum South Carolina Upcountry," *American Nineteenth Century History* 22, no. 1 (April 2021): 27–47; David W. Dangerfield, "Turning the Earth: Free Black Yeomanry in the Antebellum South Carolina Lowcountry," *Agricultural History* 89, no. 2 (Spring 2015): 200–224; see also David W. Dangerfield, "Hard Rows to Hoe: Free Black Farmers in Antebellum South Carolina" (PhD diss., University of South Carolina, September 2014).

69. See Dangerfield, "Turning the Earth," 220n4 (citing Kirt von Daacke, *Freedom Has*

a Face: Race, Identity, and Community in Jefferson's Virginia [Charlottesville: University of Virginia Press, 2012], 4–5); see also Dangerfield, "Just Beyond the Reach of Servitude," 29–30, 40.

70. See Dangerfield, "Turning the Earth," 216–19; Dangerfield, "Hard Rows to Hoe," 149–54. Dangerfield also discusses the successful 1859 prosecution for riot of Pringle, Henry, and Morgan Jackson. They were among the mixed-race people who were deemed to be white under South Carolina law. But they nevertheless were convicted after protesting the effort to seat them between Blacks and whites in the Appii Free Methodist Church. See ibid.; *Charleston (S.C.) Courier*, October 31, 1859, 3; *Charleston (S.C.) Mercury*, May 2, 1859, 2.

71. A. E. Keir Nash first used the term "extraordinary" to describe O'Neall's jurisprudence, but he offered another interpretation. See Nash, "Negro Rights," 141–90.

72. See *State v. Crank*, 18 S.C.L. (2 Bail.) 66, 66–70 (Ct. of Appeals of Law & Equity 1831).

73. See *State v. Crank*, 75 (emphasis added); see also *Charleston (S.C.) Mercury*, March 15, 1831, 2; *Charleston (S.C.) Mercury*, February 8, 1831, 2.

74. See *State v. Harden*, 152. On Judge Earle, see William E. Wiethoff, *A Peculiar Humanism: The Judicial Advocacy of Slavery in High Courts of the Old South, 1820–1850* (Athens: University of Georgia Press, 1996), 55; John Belton O'Neall, "Baylies John Earle," in *Biographical Sketches of the Bench and Bar of South Carolina* (Charleston, S.C.: S. G. Courtenay, 1859), 1:195–97.

75. See "United States Census, 1830," database with images, *FamilySearch* (https://familysearch.org/ark:/61903/1:1:XH5S-F9Y), T Archer, Chester South Carolina, United States; citing 308, NRA microfilm publication M19, (Washington D.C.: National Archives and Records Administration, n.d.), roll 169; FHL microfilm 22, 503; ibid., 352.

76. See, e.g., Ford, *Deliver Us from Evil*, 460–65; Charles Edward Morris, "Panic and Reprisal: Reaction in North Carolina to the Nat Turner Insurrection, 1831," *North Carolina Historical Review* 62, no. 1 (January 1985): 29–52; see also Wikramanayake, *World in Shadow*, 166–68.

77. See *State v. Harden*, 152.

78. Ibid., 152–53.

79. See ibid., 153.

80. See ibid., 154.

81. Ibid., 154–55.

82. Ibid., 155. Nash, unlike Ranney, discusses the *Harden* decision, but he omits O'Neall's description of the unequal protection doctrine. See Nash, "Negro Rights," 170–71.

83. *State v. Harden*, 155–56; see Fede, *Roadblocks to Freedom*, 182–89 (discussing this doctrine's demise in the later antebellum years in the South).

84. *State v. Harden*, 156.

85. John Fauchereaud Grimké, *The South-Carolina Justice of the Peace*, 3rd ed. (New York: T. & J. Swords, 1810), 22 (citing William Hawkins, *A Treatise of the Pleas of the Crown; or, A System of the Principal Matters Relating to That Subject Digested under Their Proper Hands* [London: Eliz. Nutt, 1716], 134).

86. Ibid., 23 (citing *State v. Wood*, 1 S.C.L. (1 Bay) 351 (Courts of Common Pleas and General Sessions of the Peace of South Carolina 1794), but only for the ruling also reported that an assault will justify only a proportional beating in response).

87. Ibid., 23 (citing William Salkeld, *Reports of Cases Adjudged in the Court of King's Bench*, vol. 3 [Dublin: James Moore, 1791], 46).

88. Ibid., 23 (citing Hawkins, *Treatise of the Pleas of the Crown*, 130).

89. See John Bouvier, *A Law Dictionary, Adapted to the Constitution and Laws of the United States of America* (Philadelphia: T. & W. J. Johnson, 1839), 122–23. On the debate about the husbands' common-law assault and battery immunity, see, e.g., Laura Edwards, "'The Peace,' Domestic Violence, and Firearms in the New Republic," *Fordham Urban Law Journal* 51, no. 1 (2023): 1–23; Henry Ansgar Kelly, "*Rule of Thumb* and the Folklaw of the Husband's Stick," *Journal of Legal Education* 44, no. 3 (September 1994): 341–65.

90. See Johnson and Roark, *Black Masters*, 48–49.

91. Judge Earle later instructed a jury consistent with this unequal mitigation doctrine in *State v. Cheatwood*, 20 S.C.L. (2 Hill) 459 (Ct. App. L. & Eq. 1834) (affirming defendant's conviction for murder of another person's slave); see Fede, *Homicide Justified*, 182; Fede, *People without Rights*, 76–77; Henry, *Police Control of the Slave*, 70; G. W. Featherstonhaugh, *Excursion through the Slave States* (London: John Murray, 1844), 2:346–47; Bertram Wyatt-Brown, "Barn Burning and Other Snopesian Crimes: Class and Justice in the Old South," in *Class, Conflict and Consensus: Antebellum Southern Community Studies*, ed. Orville Vernon Burton and Robert C. McMath (Westport, Conn.: Greenwood, 1982), 198.

92. *State v. Hill*, 29 S.C.L. (2 Speers) 151 (Ct. App. Law 1843).

93. Ibid., 151–57.

94. See Jasper M. Cureton, "Coming of Age: The South Carolina Court of Appeals" (South Carolina Judicial Department, South Carolina Court of Appeals), https://www.sccourts.org/appeals/history.cfm.

95. *State v. Hill*, 158–59.

96. See ibid., 160–61. For the 1800 act and the later acts further restricting and eventually prohibiting manumission in South Carolina, see Fede, *Roadblocks to Freedom*, 97–98, 104; O'Neall, *Negro Law of South Carolina*, 10–12.

97. *State v. Maner*, 20 S.C.L. (2 Hill) 453 (Ct. App. of Law & Equity 1834).

98. See ibid., 453–54.

99. Ibid., 454 (citation omitted).

100. See *State v. Maner*, 454.

101. Ibid., 454 (quoting "An ACT for the Better Ordering and Governing Negroes and Other Slave in the Province," in McCord, *Statutes at Large of South Carolina*, 7:411).

102. *State v. Maner*, 454–55.

103. "An ACT for the Better Ordering and Governing Negroes and Other Slave in the Province," in McCord, *Statutes at Large of South Carolina*, 7:399.

104. See *State v. Quintana*, 308 Wis. 2d 615, 628, 748 N.W. 2d 447, 453 (2008) (quoting Blackstone, *Commentaries on the Laws of England*, 4:*207 (emphasis in opinion in Blackstone omitted)); Wayne R. LaFave and Austin W. Scott Jr., *Handbook on Criminal Law* (St. Paul, Minn.: West, 1972), 614–17; see also Fede, *People without Rights*, 102, 108, 114–15.

105. See Fede, *People without Rights*, 99–130 (advancing this interpretation of this and other slave state laws prohibiting "cruel or unusual" slave punishments); see also Alexander A. Reinert, "Reconceptualizing the Eighth Amendment: Slaves, Prisoners, and 'Cruel and Unusual' Punishment," *North Carolina Law Review* 94, no. 3 (March 2016): 834–54.

106. *State v. Mann*, 13 N.C. (2 Dev. & Bat.) 263 (1829).

107. *Commonwealth v. Turner*, 26 Va. (5 Rand.) 678 (1827). See Fede, *People without Rights*, 105–30; Andrew T. Fede, "Gender in the Law of Slavery in the Antebellum United States," *Cardozo Law Review* 18, no. 2 (November 1996): 420–24.

108. For a different interpretation of *Maner*, see Ranney, *Bridging Revolutions*, 59.

109. *Tennent v. Dendy*, 23 S.C.L. (Dud.) 83 (Ct. App. of Law 1837).

110. Ibid., 84–85.

111. Ibid., 86–87.

112. See "Slave Laws—Letter from Judge O'Neall," *New-York Tribune*, August 15, 1853, 6. The letter is dated July 23, 1853. O'Neall sent with it a copy of his enslavement law treatise.

113. "AN ACT to Make the Unlawful Whipping or Beating of a Slave an Indictable Offence," in *Acts of the General Assembly of the State of South Carolina* (Columbia, S.C.: A. H. Pemberton, 1842), 155. In the same term, the legislature adopted an act that included provisions prohibiting the manumission of South Carolina slaves, even out of the state, as well as the practice of holding slaves in "nominal servitude." See "AN ACT to Prevent the Emancipation of Slaves, and for Other Purposes," in *Acts of the General Assembly of the State of South Carolina*, 154–55; Fede, *Roadblocks to Freedom*, 104, 235–38.

114. See Ranney, *Bridging Revolutions*, 59–60; Fede, *People without Rights*, 103; see also *State v. Harlan*, 39 S.C.L. (5 Rich.) 470 (Ct. of App. of Law 1852) (affirming conviction under the 1841 act, O'Neall was the trial judge). An 1858 act later imposed fines and prison terms on slave owners or other persons "having the care, management, or control of any slave" who inflicted "any cruel or unusual punishment." This act, however, did not "prevent the owner or person having charge of any slave, from inflicting on such slave such punishment as may be necessary for the good governance of the same." See "An ACT to Alter and Amend the 37th Section of an Act, Entitled 'An ACT for the Better Ordering and Governing Negroes and Other Slaves in This Province, Passed the Tenth Day of May, in the Year of Our Lord One Thousand Seven Hundred and Forty,'" in John Codman Hurd, *The Law of Freedom and Bondage in the United States* (1858/1862; repr., Boston: Little, Brown, 1968), 2:100; Fede, *Homicide Justified*, 191; Fede, *People without Rights*, 127n82. On these cruel or unusual punishment statutes, see ibid., 111–16, 126–29.

115. See Ranney, *Bridging Revolutions*, 6–11.

116. See ibid., 21–22.

117. *State ex rel. McCready v. Hunt*, 20 S.C.L. (2 Hill) 1 (Ct. of App. 1834). On this case and the controversy over nullification, the oath, and the courts, see, e.g., Ranney, *Bridging Revolutions*, 30–39; Laura F. Edwards, *The People and Their Peace: Legal Culture and the Transformation of Inequality in the Post-revolutionary South* (Chapel Hill: University of North Carolina Press, 2009), 266–71; William W. Freehling, *Prelude to Civil War: The Nullification Controversy in South Carolina 1816–1836* (New York: Oxford University Press, 1965), 316–21; Nash, "Negro Rights," 145–66.

118. See Ranney, *Bridging Revolutions*, 23–24, 30–39.

119. See ibid., 45–48; see also, on O'Neall's biography, Sanders, "O'Neall, John Belton," in Newman, *Yale Biographical Dictionary of American Law*, 410–11; Thomas D. Morris, "O'Neall, John Belton," in *American National Biography*, ed. John A. Garraty and Mark C. Carnes (New York: Oxford University Press, 1999), 4; Julius W. Pratt, "O'Neall, John Belton," in *Dictionary of American Biography*, ed. Dumas Malone (New York: Charles Scribner's Sons, 1934), 14:42–43; Sanders, "Judge John Belton O'Neall and Today's McCready's Oath," 127–35; Roberta V. H. Copp, "O'Neall, John Belton," in *South Carolina En-*

cyclopedia, http://www.scencyclopedia.org/sce/entries/oneall-john-belton/. For a contemporary tribute, see "Tribute to Chief Justice John Belton O'Neall," *Charleston (S.C.) Mercury*, February 17, 1864, 2. For a summary of the history of South Carolina's appellate courts, see Cureton, "Coming of Age."

120. See *Carmille v. Carmille's Adm'r*, 27 S.C.L. (2 McMul.) 454, 470 (S.C. Err. 1842); see also Fede, *Roadblocks to Freedom*, 372–75 (discussing this case).

121. O'Neall, *Negro Law of South Carolina*, 1–56.

122. Ibid., 12.

123. See Finkelman, *Statutes on Slavery*, 173–76, for the report. For analysis of the report and the public debate it caused, see Ranney, *Bridging Revolutions*, 71–76; Hindus, *Prison and Plantation*, 132–33; and Nash, "Negro Rights," 177–87.

124. Bernie D. Jones, *Fathers of Conscience: Mixed-Race Inheritance in the Antebellum South* (Athens: University of Georgia Press, 2009), 146; see also Edwards, *People and Their Peace*, 34–35 (including O'Neall among the antebellum legal reformers).

125. See O'Neall, *Negro Law of South Carolina*, 12.

126. See ibid., 13.

127. *State v. Young*, 41 S.C.L. (7 Rich.) 1 (Ct. App. of Law 1853).

128. See ibid., 1.

129. See Russell K. Robinson, "Unequal Protection," *Sandford Law Review* 68, no. 1 (January 2016): 151–232.

130. *The State v. Jose Fuentes*, 5 La. Ann. 427 (Supreme Court 1850).

131. Ibid., 427.

132. See "Refused New Trial," *Daily Delta* (New Orleans), May 8, 1849, 3.

133. *The State v. Jose Fuentes*, 428.

134. Ibid., 428–29; see William Blackstone, *Commentaries on the Laws of England*, ed. Edward Christian, 12th ed. (London: A. Strahan and W. Woodfall, 1795), 4:*198–*201.

135. *The Louisiana Digest* (New Orleans: Benjamin Levy, 1841), 1:220.

136. See, discussing the statute and cases in which it was enforced, Judith Kelleher Schafer, *Becoming Free, Remaining Free: Manumission and Enslavement in New Orleans, 1846–1862* (Baton Rouge: Louisiana State University Press, 2003), 97–99; chapter 6, notes 23–28.

137. See Nash, "Negro Rights," 172; see also Arnold Edmund Keir Nash, "Negro Rights and Judicial Behavior in the Old South" (PhD diss., Harvard University, September 1967).

138. *State v. Harden*, 155.

139. *State v. Nathan*, 39 S.C. L. (5 Rich.) 219 (Ct. of App. 1851).

140. See Sanders, "O'Neall, John Belton," in Newman, *Yale Biographical Dictionary of American Law*, 411; see also Sanders, "Judge John Belton O'Neall and Today's McCready's Oath," 132.

141. See W. Caleb McDaniel, "The Case of John L. Brown: Sex, Slavery, and the Trials of a Transatlantic Abolitionist Campaign," *American Nineteenth Century History* 14, no. 2 (2013): 151.

142. See ibid., 143–48.

143. *State v. Brown*, 29 S.C.L. (Speers) 129 (Ct. of App. of Law 1843).

144. See McDaniel, "Case of John L. Brown," 143.

145. See ibid., 145–46.

146. *Edgefield (S.C.) Advertiser*, May 8, 1844, 2.

147. *Edgefield (S.C.) Advertiser*, August 14, 1844, 2.
148. Ibid.
149. See McDaniel, "Case of John L. Brown," 146.
150. Harriet Beecher Stowe, *The Key to Uncle Tom's Cabin* (Boston: John P. Jewett, 1853; repr., New York: Arno Press and the New York Times, 1968).
151. See "Slave Laws—Letter from Judge O'Neall," *New-York Tribune*, August 15, 1853, 6; see also Ranney, *Bridging Revolutions*, 71–72; Fede, *Homicide Justified*, 1–6, 191 (discussing O'Neall's defense in that letter of Eliza Rowand's murder trial and acquittal, as well as his own actions as the trial judge).
152. See George Fitzhugh, *Sociology for the South, Or the Failure of Free Society* (Richmond: A. Morris, 1854), 27–28; see, generally, e.g., Fede, *Roadblocks to Freedom*, 109–14.
153. See O'Neall, *Negro Law of South Carolina*, 35. Others, including three governors, condemned the magistrates and freeholders courts, see Flanigan, *Criminal Law of Slavery and Freedom*, 94–96.
154. See Hindus, *Prison and Plantation*, 158; Hindus, "Black Justice under White Law," 596–97; "An Act to Provide Compensation to Owners of Slaves Executed," in David J. McCord, ed., *Statutes at Large of South Carolina* (Columbia, S.C.: Republican Printing, 1873), 11:285–86.
155. See Gary B. Mills, *The Forgotten People: Cane River's Creoles of Color*, rev. ed., ed. Elizabeth Shown Mills (1977; Baton Rouge: Louisiana State University Press, 2013), 218.
156. See Ranney, *Bridging Revolutions*, 2.
157. See *Carmille v. Carmille's Adm'r*, 27 S.C.L. (2 McMul.), 470; see also Ranney, *Bridging Revolutions*, 59–60.
158. See *State v. Harden*, 29 S.C.L. (2 Speers), 155.

CHAPTER 5. Justice Pearson and Unequal Protection for Free Blacks

1. *State v. Jowers*, 33 N.C. (11 Ired. Law) 555 (1850).
2. *State v. Davis*, 52 N.C. (7 Jones Law) 52 (1859).
3. See John Hope Franklin, *The Free Negro in North Carolina 1790–1860* (Chapel Hill: University of North Carolina Press, 1943), 93.
4. *State v. Manuel*, 20 N.C. (3 & 4 Dev. & Bat.) 20 (1838).
5. See Daniel Flanigan, *The Criminal Law of Slavery and Freedom 1800–1868* (New York: Garland, 1987), 209, and compare A. E. Keir Nash, "A More Equitable Past? Southern Supreme Courts and the Protection of the Antebellum Negro," *North Carolina Law Review* 48, no. 2 (February 1970): 223–27.
6. Joseph A. Ranney, *Bridging Revolutions: The Lives of Chief Justices Richmond Pearson and John Belton O'Neall* (Athens: University of Georgia Press, 2023), 139; see ibid., 195. On Pearson's post–Civil War career, see ibid., 125–204.
7. See Warren Eugene Milteer Jr., *North Carolina's Free People of Color, 1715–1885* (Baton Rouge: Louisiana University Press, 2020), 5–8; Ira Berlin, *Slaves without Masters: The Free Negro in the Antebellum South* (New York: New Press, 1974), 46–47, 136, 397, 399; Franklin, *Free Negro in North Carolina*, 14–19; Richard C. Rohrs, "*State v. Edmund, a Slave* (1833): Perceptions of the Legal Status of Slaves and Free Blacks in Antebellum North Carolina," *North Carolina Historical Review* 95, no. 1 (January 2018): 30–31. Milteer refers to "free people of color" instead of "free Blacks," noting that this phrase has a more

fluid meaning and is accurate in view of the number of mixed-race people among the state's population. See Milteer, *North Carolina's Free People of Color*, 9–11.

8. See Franklin, *Free Negro in North Carolina*, 19–57.

9. See Milteer, *North Carolina's Free People of Color*, 105.

10. See ibid., 105–60; Franklin, *Free Negro in North Carolina*, 121–50.

11. See Milteer, *North Carolina's Free People of Color*, 41–47, 160–70; Franklin, *Free Negro in North Carolina*, 150–62, 227–37; Rohrs, "State v. Edmund, a Slave," 32–40.

12. See Milteer, *North Carolina's Free People of Color*, 47.

13. "An Act Concerning Servants & Slaves," in *The State Records of North Carolina, Laws 1715–1776*, ed. Walter Clark (Goldsboro, N.C.: Nash Brothers, 1904), 23:64–65; see Milteer, *North Carolina's Free People of Color*, 33.

14. "Act Relating to the Biennial & Other Assemblys & Regulating Elections & Members," in Clark, *State Records of North Carolina, Laws 1715–1776*, 23:12–13; see Franklin, *Free Negro in North Carolina*, 105; William Alexander Mabry, *The Negro in North Carolina Politics since Reconstruction* (Durham, N.C.: Duke University Press, 1940; repr., New York: AMS Press, 1970), 3.

15. "An Act for an Additional Tax on All Free Negroes, Mulattoes, Mustees, and Such Persons, Male and Female, as Now Are, or Hereafter Shall Be, Intermarried with Any Such Persons, Resident in This Government," in Clark, *State Records of North Carolina, Laws 1715–1776*, 23:106–7; see Milteer, *North Carolina's Free People of Color*, 34.

16. "An Act, for Establishing the Supreme Courts of Justice, Oyer and Terminer, and General Gaol Delivery of North Carolina," in *The State Records of North Carolina*, ed. Walter Clark (Goldsboro, N.C.: Nash Brothers, 1906), 25:283; see Milteer, *North Carolina's Free People of Color*, 35–36; Franklin, *Free Negro in North Carolina*, 82–86.

17. "An Act Declaring the Punishment of Persons of Colour, in Certain Cases," in *Acts Passed by the General Assembly of the State of North Carolina, At Its Session, Commencing on the 17th of November, 1823* (Raleigh, N.C.: J. Gales R & Sons, 1824), 42.

18. See Franklin, *Free Negro in North Carolina*, 98; see also, discussing prosecutions under this act, ibid., 98–99.

19. See ibid., 64–74; Rohrs, "State v. Edmund, a Slave," 30–32.

20. See *Acts Passed by the General Assembly of the State of North Carolina at the Session of 1830–31* (Raleigh, N.C.: Lawrence and Lemay, 1831), 9–18.

21. "An Act to Amend the Several Laws Now in Force in This State Regulating Quarantine," in *Acts Passed by the General Assembly of the State of North Carolina at the Session of 1830–31*, 29–30; see Rohrs, "State v. Edmund, a Slave," 29–30.

22. See Milteer, *North Carolina's Free People of Color*, 70–73; Franklin, *Free Negro in North Carolina*, 91–120.

23. See John Hope Franklin, "The Enslavement of Free Negroes in North Carolina," *Journal of Negro History* 29, no. 4 (October 1944): 404; see also Milteer, *North Carolina's Free People of Color*, 171–93.

24. Franklin, "Enslavement of Free Negroes in North Carolina," 405.

25. Ibid., 406–14; see Emily West, *Family or Freedom: People of Color in the Antebellum South* (Lexington: University Press of Kentucky, 2012), 48.

26. See Ted Maris-Wolf, *Family Bonds: Free Blacks and Re-enslavement Law in Antebellum Virginia* (Chapel Hill: University of North Carolina Press, 2015), 102–5; West, *Family or Freedom*, 23–48; Andrew Fede, *Roadblocks to Freedom: Slavery and Manumis-*

sion in the United States South (New Orleans: Quid Pro Books, 2011), 114–17; Judith Kelleher Schafer, *Becoming Free, Remaining Free: Manumission and Enslavement in New Orleans, 1846–1862* (Baton Rouge: Louisiana State University Press, 2003), 150–61; Thomas D. Morris, *Southern Slavery and the Law, 1619–1860* (Chapel Hill: University of North Carolina Press, 1996), 32–36: Emily West, "Free People of Color, Expulsion, and Enslavement in the Antebellum South," in *Creating Citizenship in the Nineteenth Century South*, ed. William A. Link, David Brown, Brian Ward, and Martyn Bone (Gainesville: University Press of Florida, 2013), 64–83.

27. Franklin, "Enslavement of Free Negroes in North Carolina," 414; see West, *Family or Freedom*, 116–18, 133–36, 143–44; Franklin, "Enslavement of Free Negroes in North Carolina," 414–28 (discussing these petitions and their relevance).

28. See Milteer, *North Carolina's Free People of Color*, 47 (citing Berlin, *Slaves without Masters*, 123).

29. See Milteer, *North Carolina's Free People of Color*, 14 (citing Melvin Patrick Ely, *Israel on the Appomattox: A Southern Experiment in Black Freedom from the 1790s through the Civil War* (New York: Knopf, 2004)); see also ibid., 47. For a summary of the historiography on North Carolina free African Americans, see ibid., 11–14; see also Kirt von Daacke, *Freedom Has a Face: Race, Identity, and Community in Jefferson's Virginia* (Charlottesville: University of Virginia Press, 2012).

30. See Richard C. Rohrs, "The Free Black Experience in Antebellum Wilmington, North Carolina: Refining Generalizations about Race Relations," *Journal of Southern History* 78, no. 3 (August 2012): 620.

31. See ibid., 615–38. Wilmington's free Blacks' relative prosperity continued after the Civil War, but it was shattered by the 1898 massacre and coup d'état, which the city's Democrats perpetrated to restore the antebellum white supremacist domination. See, e.g., David Zucchino, *Wilmington's Lie: The Murderous Coup of 1898 and the Rise of White Supremacy* (New York: Atlantic Monthly Press, 2020); Sandra L. Rierson and Melanie H. Schwimmer, "The Wilmington Massacre and Coup of 1898 and the Search for Restorative Justice," *Elon Law Journal* 14, no. 1 (2022): 118–45.

32. See Franklin, *Free Negro in North Carolina*, 163–225.

33. *State v. Manuel*, 20 N.C. (3 & 4 Dev. & Bat.) 20 (1838).

34. See "An Act to Provide for the Collection of Fines Imposed upon Free Negroes or Free Persons of Colour," in *Acts passed by the General Assembly of the State of North Carolina at the Session of 1831–32* (Raleigh, N.C.: Lawrence and Lemay, 1832), 10–11; *State v. Manuel*, 21; Franklin, *Free Negro in North Carolina*, 89.

35. See Franklin, *Free Negro in North Carolina*, 88–89; see also Laura F. Edwards, "Response to Rebecca Scott's 'Discerning a Dignitary Offense,'" *Law and History Review* 38, no. 3 (August 2020): 576–80 (discussing trend from specific local to general laws).

36. *State v. Manuel*, 37.

37. *The Constitution of North Carolina, Adopted December 17, 1776, and Amendments Thereto* (Raleigh, N.C.: J. Gales and Son, 1835), 3; see John V. Orth, "The Emoluments Clause of the North Carolina Constitution," https://www.sog.unc.edu/sites/www.sog.unc.edu/files/course_materials/ORTH%20-%20emoluments_script.pdf.

38. *State v. Manuel*, 37.

39. For discussions of antebellum Black citizenship, see, e.g., *Scott v. Sandford*, 60 U.S.

(19 How.) 393, 15 L. Ed. 691 (1857); *Bryan v. Walton*, 14 Ga. 185 (1853); *Mayor, etc. of Memphis v. Winfield*, 27 Tenn. 707 (1848); *Pendleton v. State*, 6 Ark. 509 (1846); *State v. Cooper*, 5 Blackf. 258 (1839); *State v. Clairborne*, 19 Tenn. (1 Meigs) 331 (1838); *Aldridge v. Commonwealth*, 4 Va. (2 Va. Cas.) 447 (1824); *Amy v. Smith*, 11 Ky. (1 Litt.) 326 (1822); *Costin v. Washington*, 6 F. Cas. 612 (C.C.D.C. 1821) (No. 3,266); Mark A. Graber, *Dred Scott and the Problem of Constitutional Evil* (New York: Cambridge University Press, 2006), 46–57; Mark A. Graber, "Korematsu's Ancestors," *Arkansas Law Review* 74, no. 3 (2021): 429–39; Ryan C. Williams, "Originalism and the Other Desegregation Decision," *Virginia Law Review* 99, no. 3 (May 2013): 511–20. For other interpretations of *Manuel*, see Milteer, *North Carolina's Free People of Color*, 80–81; Franklin, *Free Negro in North Carolina*, 89–90; Barbara A. Jackson, "Called to Duty: Justice William J. Gaston," *North Carolina Law Review* 94, no. 6 (September 2016): 2083–87; Joseph Herman Schauinger, "William Gaston and the Supreme Court of North Carolina," *North Carolina Historical Review* 21, no. 2 (June 1944): 111–12. This holding in *Manuel* is not inconsistent with *State v. Edmund, a Slave*, 15 N.C. (4 Dev.) 340 (1833), which held that a free Black slave owner could be a "citizen" protected by a statute prohibiting persons enabling slaves to escape, as illustrated by an 1861 act that declared that free Blacks could no longer "buy, purchase, or hire slaves." See "An Act to Prevent Free Negroes from Hiring or Having the Control of Slaves," in *Public Laws of the State of North Carolina Passed by the General Assembly, at its Session of 1860-61* (Raleigh, N.C.: John Spellman, 1861), 69; compare Rohrs, "*State v. Edmund, a Slave*," 32–46.

40. See "An Act Concerning the Collection of Fines and Costs from Free Negroes and Free Persons of Colour," in *Laws of the State of North Carolina, Passed by the General Assembly, at the Session of 1840-41* (Raleigh, N.C.: W. B. Gales, 1841), 61; Franklin, *Free Negro in North Carolina*, 90.

41. See Antwain K. Hunter, "'A Nuisance Requiring Correction': Firearm Laws, Black Mobility, and White Property in Antebellum Eastern North Carolina," *North Carolina Historical Review* 93, no. 4 (October 2016): 397.

42. See "An Act to Prevent Free Persons of Colour from Carrying Fire-arms," in *Laws of the State of North Carolina, Passed by the General Assembly, at the Session of 1840-41*, 61–62; Hunter, "'A Nuisance Requiring Correction,'" 397–99.

43. See Hunter, "'A Nuisance Requiring Correction,'" 397n35.

44. *State v. Newsom*, 27 N.C. (5 Ired.) 250 (1844).

45. Ibid., 250–55.

46. Ibid., 254–55; see Milteer, *North Carolina's Free People of Color*, 80–82 (discussing *Manuel*, *Newsom*, and later cases).

47. *State v. Lane*, 30 N.C. (8 Ired.) 256 (1848).

48. See ibid., 256.

49. See ibid., 257.

50. See ibid., 257–58; compare *State v. Harris*, 51 N.C. (6 Jones) 448 (1859) (affirming Harris's conviction for carrying a shotgun off his property, when the County Court limited his license to carrying a gun on his own land); Hunter, "'A Nuisance Requiring Correction,'" 399–400.

51. See Rohrs, "*State v. Edmund, a Slave*," 43 (quoting "An Act to Amend Chapter 107, Section 66, of the Revised Code, Relating to Free Negroes Having Arms," in *Public Laws of the State of North Carolina Passed by the General Assembly, at its Session of 1860-61*, 68).

52. *State v. Jowers*, 33 N.C. (11 Ired. Law) 555 (1850); see *Raleigh (N.C.) Register and North-Carolina Gazette*, October 18, 1842, 3.

53. See *State v. Jowers*, 555; Indictment, *The State v. Atlas Jowers*, North Carolina State Archives, Supreme Court, 1800–1909, case no. 6717.

54. See, e.g., *In re May*, 357 N.C. 423, 425–28, 584 S.E. 2d 271, 273–75 (2003); *State v. Huntly*, 25 N.C. (3 Ired.) 418, 420–22 (1843).

55. *State v. Jowers*, 555; *The State v. Atlas Jowers*, North Carolina State Archives, Supreme Court, 1800–1909, case no. 6717.

56. See Seventh Census of the United States, 1850, Wadesboro, Anson, North Carolina, National Archives Microfilm Publication, roll M432_619, page 163B, image 330, Ancestry.com; ibid., Slave Schedules, Ancestry.com; Bill Cecil-Fronsman, *Common Whites: Class and Culture in Antebellum North Carolina* (Lexington: University Press of Kentucky, 1992), 78.

57. See Sixth Census of the United States, 1840, Anson, North Carolina, National Archives Microfilm Publication, roll 354, page 97, Ancestry.com; Fifth Census of the United States, 1830, Anson, North Carolina, National Archives Microfilm Publication, M 19, roll 118, page 58, Ancestry.com.

58. *State v. Jowers*, 555–56; *The State v. Atlas Jowers*, North Carolina State Archives, Supreme Court, 1800–1909, case no. 6717.

59. See *State v. Jowers*, 556; Memory F. Mitchell, "Moore, Bartholomew Figures," in *Dictionary of North Carolina Biography*, ed. William S. Powell (Chapel Hill: University of North Carolina Press, 1991), 4:294–95. But Moore also authored the state's post–Civil War Black Code. See Ranney, *Bridging Revolutions*, 137–38.

60. *State v. Jowers*, 556. A. E. Keir Nash interpreted Pearson's reference to a "majority" of the court to mean that "one member dissented silently—almost certainly Frederick Nash rather than Thomas Ruffin." A. E. Keir Nash, "A More Equitable Past? Southern Supreme Courts and the Protection of the Antebellum Negro," *North Carolina Law Review* 48, no. 2 (February 1970): 223n107; see Ranney, *Bridging Revolutions*, 65, 221n17. The official case report does not include a dissenting opinion, nor does it note a dissent without an opinion. The Supreme Court's file also does not include a dissenting opinion.

61. *State v. Jowers*, 556.

62. Ibid., 556.

63. Ibid., 556; see William E. Wiethoff, *A Peculiar Humanism: The Judicial Advocacy of Slavery in High Courts of the Old South, 1820–1850* (Athens: University of Georgia Press, 1996), 94.

64. See Franklin, *Free Negro in North Carolina*, 92 (quoting *Raleigh Register*, October 26, 1842); see also "Mob Law Rebuked," *North Carolina Standard* (Raleigh, N.C.), October 26, 1842, 3; "Disgraceful Outrage," *Raleigh (N.C.) Register and North Carolina Gazette*, October 8, 1842, 3; Milteer, *North Carolina's Free People of Color*, 99–100.

65. *State v. Davis*, 52 N.C. (7 Jones Law) 52 (1859).

66. See W. Conrad Gass, "Battle, William Horn," in Powell, *Dictionary of North Carolina Biography*, 1:118.

67. *State v. Davis*, 52; North Carolina State Archives, Supreme Court, 1800–1909, Indictment, *State v. Lawrence Davis*, case no. 7705; *State v. Lawrence Davis*, North Carolina State Archives, Minutes of the Superior Courts, 1807–1966, Craven County, Fall Term 1859.

68. See H. G. Jones, "Saunders, Romulus Mitchell," in Powell, *Dictionary of North Carolina Biography*, 5:285–86.

69. *State v. Davis*, 52–53; *State v. Lawrence Davis*, North Carolina State Archives, Supreme Court, 1800–1909, case no. 7705. On the statutes and court decisions imposing and enforcing discriminatory free Black taxation requirements, see Christopher J. Bryant, "Without Representation, No Taxation: Free Blacks, Taxes, and Tax Exemptions between the Revolutionary and Civil Wars," *Michigan Journal of Race and Law* 21, no. 1 (Fall 2015): 91–123.

70. Martin Reidinger, "McRae, Duncan Kirkland," in Powell, *Dictionary of North Carolina Biography*, 4:189–90; see North Carolina State Archives, Supreme Court, 1800–1909, *State v. Lawrence Davis*, case no. 7705.

71. *State v. Davis*, 52–53; *State v. Lawrence Davis*, North Carolina State Archives, Supreme Court, 1800–1909, case no. 7705.

72. *State v. Davis*, 53.

73. Ibid., 53–54.

74. *State v. Caesar*, 31 N.C. (9 Ired.) 391 (1849).

75. *State v. Davis*, 54.

76. Ibid., 54–55.

77. See generally Scott A. Keller, "Qualified and Absolute Immunity at Common Law," *Stanford Law Review* 73, no. 6 (June 2021): 1361–62 (quoting *Kendall v. Stokes*, 44 U.S. (3 How.) 87, 87n2 (1845)); see also James E. Pfander, "Zones of Discretion at Common Law," *Northwestern University Law Review Colloquy* (2021) (quoting *Wilkes v. Dinsman*, 48 U.S. (7 How.) 89, 130 (1849)), https://scholarlycommons.law.northwestern.edu/nulr_online/315/.

78. *State v. Norman*, 53 N.C. (8 Jones) 220 (1860).

79. *State v. Manuel*, 20 N.C. (3 & 4 Dev. & Bat.) 20 (1838).

80. *State v. Fisher*, 52 N.C. (6 Jones) 478 (1859).

81. See ibid., 478.

82. See ibid., 478–79.

83. See Lawrence M. Friedman, *Crime without Punishment: Aspects of the History of Homicide* (Cambridge, Mass.: Harvard University Press, 2018), 20–28 (quotation at 21); Hendrik Hartog, "Lawyering, Husband's Rights, and 'the Unwritten Law' in Nineteenth-Century America," *Journal of American History* 84, no. 1 (June 1997): 67–96.

84. See *State v. Fisher*, 479–80; see also Hartog, "Lawyering, Husband's Rights, and 'the Unwritten Law,'" 69 (citing Joel Prentiss Bishop, *Commentaries on the Criminal Law*, 7th ed. [Boston: Little, Brown, 1882], 2:400–401).

85. See *State v. Fisher*, 481–84.

86. See *State v. Norman*, 220–21. The special verdict found that Fisher had "been convicted of larceny, in the County Court of Washington, and by the Court was ordered to be sold for the fine imposed, to cover the costs, and [he] was so sold for five years to one Peacock." During this statutory term of involuntary servitude or apprenticeship, "Fisher was taken up on the charge of killing one Hussell, who was found dead in his yard." Norman then "gave [Fisher] five licks to make him show where the gun was, with which he killed Hussell. Peacock was present when Fisher was whipped, and gave his consent to it, and said it ought to be done." Ibid., 220–21.

87. See ibid., 221. On Manly, see William C. Fields, "Manly, Matthias Evans," in Powell, *Dictionary of North Carolina Biography*, 4:211.

88. See *State v. Norman*, 221–22.

89. Ibid., 222.

90. See Franklin, *Free Negro in North Carolina*, 93 (quoting Gaston's opinion in *State v. Bennett*, 20 N.C. (3 & 4 Dev. & Bat.) 43, 49 (1838)).

91. *Moore v. Dempsey*, 261 U.S. 86 (1923); *Brown v. Mississippi*, 297 U.S. 278 (1936).

92. See A. E. Keir Nash, "Fairness and Formalism in the Trials of Blacks in the State Supreme Courts of the Old South," *Virginia Law Review* 56, no. 1 (February 1970): 64–65; see also Nash, "A More Equitable Past?" 223 (discussing *Jowers*) and 226–27 (discussing the *Davis*).

93. Nash, "Fairness and Formalism," 66.

94. See Nash, "A More Equitable Past?" 200.

95. See Nash, "Fairness and Formalism," 65 (citing Ulrich Bonnell Phillips, *The Course of the South to Secession: An Interpretation by Ulrich Bonnell Phillips*, ed. E. Merton Coulter [New York: D. Appleton-Century, 1939], 151–65, reprinting Ulrich B. Phillips, "The Central Theme in Southern History," *American Historical Review* 34, no. 1 [October 1928]: 30–43).

96. See Nash, "Fairness and Formalism," 65. Nash fails to note Pearson's unequal mitigation language in *Davis* and that the arrest was based on the racially discriminatory tax ordinance. Ibid., 65–66; see also, discussing Nash's interpretation, Flanigan, *Criminal Law of Slavery and Freedom*, 105–6, 494–96.

97. See Patrick S. Brady, "Slavery, Race, and the Criminal Law in Antebellum North Carolina: Reconsideration of the Thomas Ruffin Court," *North Carolina Central Law Journal* 10, no. 2 (April 1979): 258.

98. See Michael Stephen Hindus, *Prison and Plantation: Crime, Justice, and Authority in Massachusetts and South Carolina, 1767–1878* (Chapel Hill: University of North Carolina Press, 1980), 131n3; Michael Hindus, "Black Justice under White Law: Criminal Prosecutions of Blacks in Antebellum South Carolina," *Journal of American History* 63, no. 3 (December 1976): 576n4; see also A. E. Keir Nash, "Reason of Slavery: Understanding the Judicial Role in the Peculiar Institution," *Vanderbilt Law Review* 32, no. 1 (January 1979): 70.

99. See Reuel E. Schiller, "Conflicting Obligations: Slave Law and the Late Antebellum North Carolina Supreme Court," *Virginia Law Review* 78 (August 1992): 1224, 1227.

100. See Joseph A. Ranney, *In the Wake of Slavery: Civil War, Civil Rights, and the Reconstruction of Southern Law* (Westport, Conn.: Praeger, 2006), 19; see also Ranney, *Bridging Revolutions*, 3–5, 63–67, 195–204.

101. See Ranney, *Bridging Revolutions*, 4.

102. See Milteer, *North Carolina's Free People of Color*, 83. Milteer refers to Pearson's *Jowers* decision in a footnote to his discussion of *Davis* as evidence of Pearson's belief in free Black inequality. See ibid., 245n88.

103. *Scott v. Sandford*, 60 U.S. (19 How.), 407.

104. See Milteer, *North Carolina's Free People of Color*, 84.

105. Wilson Angley, *Richmond M. Pearson and the Richmond Hill Law School* (Raleigh: North Carolina Department of Cultural Resources, 1978), 29.

106. See Cody Marrs, *Nineteenth-Century American Literature and the Long Civil War* (New York: Cambridge University Press, 2015), 3.

107. See Ranney, *Bridging Revolutions*, 12–15, 24–29; Ranney, *In the Wake of Slavery*, 19; Memory F. Mitchell, "Pearson, Richmond," in Powell, *Dictionary of North Carolina Biography*, 5:49–51; Robert P. Dick, "Richmond M. Pearson," in *Biographical History of North Carolina from Colonial Times to the Present*, ed. Samuel A. Ashe (Greensboro, N.C.: Charles L. Van Noppen, 1906), 5:295–309; Albert Coates, "The Story of the Law School at the University of North Carolina," *North Carolina Law Review* 47, special issue (October 1968): 8–10.

108. See Ranney, *Bridging Revolutions*, 46–47; Angley, *Richmond M. Pearson and the Richmond Hill Law School*, 28–29.

109. See Wiethoff, *Peculiar Humanism*, 94; see also Ranney, *In the Wake of Slavery*, 18–19; Mitchell, "Pearson, Richmond," 50–51.

110. See Wiethoff, *Peculiar Humanism*, 94, quoting "Letter—An Appeal to Calm Judgment of North Carolinians," July 20, 1868, 3, North Carolina Collection (Wilson Library), University of North Carolina. On antebellum free Black voting in North Carolina, see, e.g., Franklin, *Free Negro in North Carolina*, 105–6, 110–20.

111. *Howard v. Howard*, 51 N.C. (6 Jones) 235 (1858).

112. See ibid., 236; see also Andrew Fede, *People without Rights: An Interpretation of the Fundamentals of the Law of Slavery in the U.S. South* (New York: Garland, 1992; repr., New York: Routledge, 2011), 10, 222; Laura F. Edwards, "'The Marriage Covenant is at the Foundation of all Our Rights,' The Politics of Slave Marriages in North Carolina after Emancipation," *Law and History Review* 14, no. 1 (Spring 1996): 95–96; see also H. Robert Baker, "At Least Some Rights the White Man Was Bound to Respect: *Bland v. Beverly* and a Contract for Freedom in the Age of Slavery," *Cardozo Journal of Equal Rights and Social Justice* 25, no. 3 (Spring 2019): 409–34.

113. *Lea v. Brown*, 58 N.C. (5 Jones Eq.) 379 (1860).

114. See ibid., 381.

115. Ibid., 381–82; see *Love v. Brindle*, 52 N.C. (7 Jones) 560 (1860); *White v. Cline*, 52 N.C. (7 Jones) 174 (1859); *Barker v. Swain*, 57 N.C. (4 Jones Eq.) 560 (1858); *Waddill v. Martin*, 38 N.C. (3 Ired. Eq.) 562 (1845); see generally Fede, *People without Rights*, 20–22; William Goodell, *The American Slave Code* (1853; repr., New York: Negro Universities Press, 1968), 89–104; George M. Stroud, *A Sketch of the Laws Relating to Slavery in the Several States of the United States of America* (2nd ed., 1856; repr., New York: Negro Universities Press, 1968), 29–33.

116. *State v. Caesar*, 31 N.C. (9 Ired.) 391 (1849).

117. See ibid., 405–6. For differing interpretations of this decision, see, e.g., Ranney, *Bridging Revolutions*, 63–65, 24–29; Morris, *Southern Slavery and the Law*, 291–92; Fede, *People without Rights*, 171–72; Mark V. Tushnet, *The American Law of Slavery 1810–1860: Considerations of Humanity and Interest* (Princeton, N.J.: Princeton University Press, 1981), 115–20; Thomas R. R. Cobb, *An Inquiry Into the Law of Negro Slavery in the United States of America* (Philadelphia: T. & J. W. Johnson and Savannah: W. Thorne Williams, 1858; repr., Athens: University of Georgia Press, 1999), 272752; Timothy S. Huebner, "The Roots of Fairness: *State v. Caesar* and Slave Justice in Antebellum North Carolina," in *Local Matters: Race, Crime, and Justice in the Nineteenth Century South*, ed. Christopher Waldrep and Donald G. Nieman (Athens: University of Georgia Press, 2001), 29–52; Ernest James Clark Jr., "Aspects of the North Carolina Slave Code, 1715–1860," *North Carolina Historical Review* 39, no. 2 (April 1962): 158–62.

118. See *State v. George*, 50 N.C. (5 Jones) 233 (1858); *State v. Jim*, 48 N.C. (3 Jones) 348 (1856); Fede, *People without Rights*, 187–89, 191–92.
119. See Flanigan, *Criminal Law of Slavery and Freedom*, 213.
120. *State v. Haithcock*, 33 N.C. (11 Ired.) 32 (1850).
121. See ibid., 32–33. For the state's bastardy laws, see *Revised Code of North Carolina, Enacted by the General Assembly at the Session of 1854*, ed. Bartholomew F. Moore and Asa Biggs (Boston: Little, Brown, 1855), 107–9; and for discriminatory provisions referring to free Blacks, see ibid., 339, 579.
122. See "Violent Death," *Wilmington (N.C.) Advertiser*, February 1, 1839, 3.
123. See "Murder. State vs. Nicholas C. Robinson," *Wilmington (N.C.) Advertiser*, May 3, 1839, 3.
124. See text and notes at chapter 3, notes 1–56.
125. See *Copeland v. Parker*, 25 N.C. (3 Ired.) 513, 513–14 (1843).
126. See ibid., 514–15.
127. Cecil-Fronsman, *Common Whites*, 76. The discussion of this case is derived from Andrew T. Fede, *Homicide Justified: The Legality of Killing Slaves in the United States and the Atlantic World* (Athens: University of Georgia Press, 2017), 149.
128. "Killing a Slave," *Pennsylvania Freeman* (Philadelphia), March 25, 1847, 3.
129. See ibid.; see also Cecil-Fronsman, *Common Whites*, 76.
130. "Trial for Murder," *Raleigh (N.C.) Star and North Carolina Gazette*, March 24, 1847, 3; see "Killing a Slave," *Boston Liberator*, August 20, 1847, 134; "Trial for Murder," *Raleigh (N.C.) Star and North Carolina Gazette*, March 24, 1847, 3.
131. *State v. Bennett*, 20 N.C. (3 & 4 Dev. & Bat.) 43 (1838).
132. See ibid., 43–49.
133. Ibid., 51; see Dionne R. Gonder-Stanley, "Facing a Legislative Straight Jacket at the 21st Century: North Carolina Courts and the Prayer for Judgment Continued," *North Carolina Central Law Review* 40, no. 1 (2017): 32–91.
134. See *Weekly Raleigh (N.C.) Register*, December 9, 1857, 3.
135. *Campbell v. The People*, 16 Ill. 17 (1854).
136. Christopher Waldrep, *Roots of Disorder: Race and Criminal Justice in the American South, 1817–80* (Urbana: University of Illinois Press, 1998), 51; see Christopher Waldrep, *Jury Discrimination: The Supreme Court, Public Opinion, and a Grassroots Fight for Racial Equality in Mississippi* (Athens: University of Georgia Press, 2010), 214; Christopher Waldrep, "Substituting Law for the Lash: Emancipation and Legal Formalism in a Mississippi County," *Journal of American History* 82, no. 4 (March 1996): 1433.
137. See Fede, *People without Rights*, 181–87.
138. See Ely, *Israel on the Appomattox*, 249.
139. See Fede, *People without Rights*, 181–82; Flanigan, *Criminal Law of Slavery and Freedom*, 104–6; Jason A. Gillmer, "Poor Whites, Benevolent Masters, and the Ideologies of Slavery: The Local Trial of a Slave Accused of Rape," *North Carolina Law Review* 85, no. 2 (January 2007): 523–27.
140. See James Campbell, *Crime and Punishment in African American History* (New York: Palgrave Macmillan, 2013), 46–48; Morris, *Southern Slavery and the Law*, 266–72, 286–88; Fede, *People without Rights*, 195–97; Flanigan, *Criminal Law of Slavery and Freedom*, 143–44; Arthur F. Howington, *What Sayeth the Law: The Treatment of Slaves and Free Blacks in the State and Local Courts of Tennessee* (New York: Garland, 1986), 217; Al-

fred L. Brophy, "The Nat Turner Trials," *North Carolina Law Review* 91, no. 5 (June 2013): 1871–80; Christopher Morris, "An Event in Community Organization: The Mississippi Slave Insurrection Scare of 1835," *Journal of Social History* 22, no. 1 (Autumn 1988): 93–111; see, e.g., *Polk & Wilson Co. v. Fanchier*, 38 Tenn. (1 Head) 336 (1858) (slave owner sued lynch mob members who killed slave who was accused of rape).

141. See Campbell, *Crime and Punishment*, 55–59; Neil R. McMillen, *Dark Journey: Black Mississippians in the Age of Jim Crow* (Urbana: University of Illinois Press, 1989), 223; Flanigan, *Criminal Law of Slavery and Freedom*, 139–41; Berlin, *Slaves without Masters*, 336–40.

142. See Derrick A. Bell Jr., "*Brown v. Board of Education* and the Interest-Convergence Dilemma," *Harvard Law Review* 93, no. 3 (January 1980): 523; see also Dylan C. Penningroth, *Before the Movement: The Hidden History of Black Civil Rights* (New York: Liveright, 2023), xxii (suggesting a similar convergence was advanced by civil suits filed by Blacks "because life's ordinary business could not go on if whites could not make contracts and convey property to Black people").

143. See Walter Johnson, "On Agency," *Journal of Social History* 37, no. 1 (Fall 2003): 115–16 (suggesting need for new approaches to issues of enslaved humanity, agency, and resistance).

144. See Kimberly M. Welch, *Black Litigants in the Antebellum American South* (Chapel Hill: University of North Carolina Press, 2018), 5–21, 81 (discussing free and enslaved Black antebellum litigation, and how Blacks "took advantage of the tensions between whites' interests in upholding and enacting white supremacy and their dedication to private property").

145. See Berlin, *Slaves without Masters*, 338–39.

146. Kimberly Welch, "William Johnson's Hypothesis: A Free Black Man and the Problem of Legal Knowledge in the Antebellum United States South," *Law and History Review* 37, no. 1 (February 2019): 28; see Melissa Milewski, *Litigating across the Color Line: Civil Cases between Black and White Southerners from the End of Slavery to Civil Rights* (New York: Oxford University Press, 2018), 22; Welch, *Black Litigants in the Antebellum American South*, 60–112; Kimberly Welch, "Arteries of Capital: William Johnson and the Practice of Black Money Lending in the Antebellum U.S. South," *Slavery and Abolition* 41, no. 2 (June 2020): 304–26.

147. See Laura F. Edwards, *The People and Their Peace: Legal Culture and the Transformation of Inequality in the Post-revolutionary South* (Chapel Hill: University of North Carolina Press, 2009), 34.

148. Ibid., 94, quoting John Haywood, *The Duty and Office of Justices of the Peace, Sheriffs, Coroners, Constables, etc. According to the Laws of the State of North Carolina* (Raleigh, N.C.: J. Gales and W. Boylan, 1808), 191.

149. Edwards, *People and Their Peace*, 4.

150. See ibid., 30, 34, 43, 220–21.

151. See, for other analysis, Lee B. Wilson, *Bonds of Empire: The English Origins of Slave Law in South Carolina and British Plantation America, 1660–1783* (New York: Cambridge University Press, 2021), 264; Jessica K. Lowe, *Murder in the Shenandoah: Making Law Sovereign in Revolutionary Virginia* (New York: Cambridge University Press, 2019), 183–88; Jessica K. Lowe, "A Separate Peace? The Politics of Localized Law in the Post-Revolutionary Era," *Law and Social Inquiry* 36, no. 3 (Summer 2011): 788–817.

152. See, e.g., on the debate about whether and when common-law judges make new law, Richard H. Fallon Jr. and Daniel J. Meltzer, "New Law, Non-Retroactivity, and Constitutional Remedies," *Harvard Law Review* 104, no. 8 (June 1991): 1758–64; Note, "Prospective Overruling and Retroactive Application in the Federal Courts," *Yale Law Journal* 71, no. 5 (April 1962): 907–51.

CHAPTER 6. The Louisiana and Virginia Statutes Criminalizing Insolence

1. See Thomas R. R. Cobb, *An Inquiry into the Law of Negro Slavery in the United States of America* (Philadelphia: T. & J. W. Johnson and Savannah: W. Thorne Williams, 1858; repr., Athens: University of Georgia Press, 1999), 273; George M. Stroud, *A Sketch of the Laws Relating to Slavery in the Several States of the United States of America* (2nd ed., 1856; repr., New York: Negro Universities Press, 1968), 68–69 (discussing the two legal approaches to insolence by enslaved people).

2. See A. Leon Higginbotham Jr., *In the Matter of Color: Race and the American Legal Process: The Colonial Period* (New York: Oxford University Press, 1978), 19–60; see also, e.g., Paul Finkelman, "The Crime of Color," *Tulane Law Review* 67, no. 6 (June 1993): 2070–112. Compare, arguing that South Carolina's slave law became the principal model for the Deep South territories and states, Lee B. Wilson, *Bonds of Empire: The English Origins of Slave Law in South Carolina and British Plantation America, 1660–1783* (New York: Cambridge University Press, 2021), 68 (quoting Sally E. Hadden, "The Fragmented Laws of Slavery in the Colonial and Revolutionary Eras," in *The Cambridge History of Law in America*, ed. Michael Grossberg and Christopher Tomlins, 3 vols. [New York: Cambridge University Press, 2008], 1:281–82). For a comparison of race and law in Virginia, Louisiana, and Cuba, see Alejandro de la Fuente and Ariela J. Gross, *Becoming Free, Becoming Black: Race, Freedom, and Law in Cuba, Virginia, and Louisiana* (New York: Cambridge University Press, 2020).

3. See John Henderson Russell, *The Free Negro in Virginia, 1619–1865* (Baltimore: Johns Hopkins University Press, 1913), 88–122; A. Leon Higginbotham Jr. and Greer C. Bosworth, "'Rather Than the Free': Free Blacks in Colonial and Antebellum Virginia," *Harvard Civil Rights–Civil Liberties Law Review* 26, no. 1 (Winter 1991): 17–66.

4. See Vernon Valentine Palmer, *Through the Codes Darkly: Slave Law and the Civil Law in Louisiana* (Clark, N.J.: Lawbook Exchange, 2012), 141–62; Thomas N. Ingersoll, *Mammon and Manon in Early New Orleans: The First Slave Society in the Deep South, 1718–1819* (Knoxville: University of Tennessee Press, 1999), xxi–xxii; Judith Kelleher Schafer, *Slavery, the Civil Law, and the Supreme Court of Louisiana* (Baton Rouge: Louisiana State University Press, 1994), 1–10; Hans W. Baade, "The Law of Slavery in Spanish Luisiana, 1769–1803," in *Louisiana Legal Heritage*, ed. Edward F. Haas (Pensacola, Fla.: Perdido Bay Press for the Louisiana State Museum, 1983), 43–86; Vernon Valentine Palmer, "The Strange Science of Codifying Slavery—Moreau Lislet and the Louisiana Digest of 1808," *Tulane European & Civil Law Forum* 24 (2009): 83–113; Hans W. Baade, "The Bifurcated Romanist Tradition of Slavery in Louisiana," *Tulane Law Review* 70, no. 6 (May 1996): 1481–99; Thomas N. Ingersoll, "Slave Codes and Judicial Practice in New Orleans, 1718–1897," *Law and History Review* 13, no. 1 (Spring 1995): 23–62; see also Shael Herman, "The

Contributions of Roman Law to the Jurisprudence of Antebellum Louisiana," *Louisiana Law Review* 56, no. 2 (1995–1996): 257–315.

5. See Jenifer M. Spear, *Race, Sex, and Social Order in Early New Orleans* (Baltimore: Johns Hopkins University Press, 2009), 9, 53; Ingersoll, *Mammon and Manon*, 35–92; Joe Gray Taylor, *Negro Slavery in Louisiana* (Baton Rouge: Louisiana Historical Association, 1963), 3–20, 21; see also Joe Gray Taylor, *Louisiana: A Bicentennial History* (New York: Norton, 1976), 57–86.

6. See Spear, *Race, Sex, and Social Order in Early New Orleans*, 19–20, 54–59; Clayton E. Jewett and John O. Allen, *Slavery in the South: A State-by-State History* (Westport, Conn.: Greenwood, 2004), 122–23; Peter Kolchin, *American Slavery 1619–1877*, rev. ed. (New York: Hill & Wang, 2003), 254, 256.

7. See Palmer, "Strange Science of Codifying Slavery," 98–99.

8. See ibid., 100; see also Ingersoll, *Mammon and Manon*, 321–23.

9. See Andrew T. Fede, *Homicide Justified: The Legality of Killing Slaves in the United States and the Atlantic World* (Athens: University of Georgia Press, 2017), 25–27; Andrew Fede, *Roadblocks to Freedom: Slavery and Manumission in the United States South* (New Orleans: Quid Pro Books, 2011), 260–61; Ingersoll, *Mammon and Manon*, 233–34.

10. "French Crown, the Code Noir 1685," in *Slavery, Freedom, and the Law in the Atlantic World: A Brief History with Documents*, Bedford Series in History and Culture, ed. Sue Peabody and Keila Grinberg (Boston: Bedford/St. Martin's, 2007), 31; see Fede, *Homicide Justified*, 43; Ingersoll, *Mammon and Manon*, 134–35.

11. Spear, *Race, Sex, and Social Order in Early New Orleans*, 53; Ingersoll, *Mammon and Manon*, 135–40; see also de la Fuente and Gross, *Becoming Free, Becoming Black*, 34–35; Thomas N. Ingersoll, "Free Blacks in a Slave Society: New Orleans, 1718–1812," *William and Mary Quarterly* 48, no. 2 (April 1991): 176–77.

12. See Palmer, "Strange Science of Codifying Slavery," 90–101, quotation at 97; see also de la Fuente and Gross, *Becoming Free, Becoming Black*, 19–21; Ingersoll, *Mammon and Manon*, 234–39, 321–26.

13. See Heloise H. Cruzat, "Records of the Superior Council of Louisiana XLVII," *Louisiana Historical Quarterly* 13, no. 3 (July 1930): 506.

14. See Henry P. Dart, "A Criminal Trial before the Superior Council of Louisiana, May, 1747," *Louisiana Historical Quarterly* 13, no. 3 (July 1930): 375–83.

15. See de la Fuente and Gross, *Becoming Free, Becoming Black*, 35; Charles Gayarre, *History of Louisiana: The French Dominion* (New Orleans: Armand Hawkins, 1885) 2:54–55, 361–67. On Rigaud, see Donald J. Lemieux, "Pierre François de Rigaud, Marquis de Vaudreuil, Colonial Governor, 1743–1753," in *The Louisiana Governors: From Iberville to Edwards*, ed. Joseph G. Dawson III (Baton Rouge: Louisiana State University Press, 1990), 29–32.

16. "Regulation of Police," in Gayarre, *History of Louisiana*, 366.

17. Ibid., 365; see Ingersoll, "Free Blacks in a Slave Society," 178–79.

18. See *A New Digest of the Statute Laws of the State of Louisiana*, ed. Henry A. Bullard and Thomas Curry (New Orleans: E. Johns, 1842), 1:57; *The Louisiana Digest* (New Orleans: Benjamin Levy, 1841), 1:220; Stroud, *Sketch of the Laws Relating to Slavery*, 68–69. On the Louisiana Civil Code, see generally Alan Watson, *Legal Transplants: An Approach to Comparative Law*, 2nd ed. (Athens: University of Georgia Press, 1993), 103–4.

19. See Palmer, "Strange Science of Codifying Slavery," 98.

20. See ibid., 100; see also Ingersoll, "Free Blacks in a Slave Society," 189 ("the increasing numbers of free blacks provoked whites to discriminate against them whenever possible").

21. See Palmer, "Strange Science of Codifying Slavery," 90–101; see also *State v. Judge of the Commercial Court*, 15 La. 192 (1840); de la Fuente and Gross, *Becoming Free, Becoming Black*, 34–35, 126; Fede, *Roadblocks to Freedom*, 100–101; James E. Wainwright, "William Claiborne and New Orleans's Battalion of Color, 1803–1815: Race and the Limits of Federal Power in the Early Republic," *Louisiana History* 57, no. 1 (Winter 2016): 27–28; Gwendoline Alphonso, "Public & Private Order: Race, Morality, and the Antebellum Courts of Louisiana, 1830–1860," *Journal of Southern Legal History* 23 (2015): 123–25; Gerald L. Neuman, "The Lost Century of American Immigration Law (1776–1875)," *Columbia Law Review* 93, no. 8 (December 1993): 1868; Ingersoll, "Free Blacks in a Slave Society," 189–200.

22. See Emily West, *Family or Freedom: People of Color in the Antebellum South* (Lexington: University Press of Kentucky, 2012), 39.

23. See Judith Kelleher Schafer, *Becoming Free, Remaining Free: Manumission and Enslavement in New Orleans, 1846–1862* (Baton Rouge: Louisiana State University Press, 2003), 97–98.

24. See ibid., 98n1 (citing State v. Black, f.w.c., no. 1095, June 11, 1847 and State v. Charles, f.m.c., nos. 1159, 1302, June 28 and July 8, 1847); see also *Bore v. Bush*, 6 Mart. (n.s.) 1 (1827) (remanding false imprisonment action for trial against justice of the peace and constable who arrested and apparently tried free Black plaintiff for violating statute; holding that plaintiff was entitled to a jury trial).

25. Schafer, *Becoming Free, Remaining Free*, 98; see Ingersoll, *Mammon and Manon*, 327.

26. "Insulting White Persons," *Daily Picayune* (New Orleans), October 29, 1852, 2; see Schafer, *Becoming Free, Remaining Free*, 98.

27. "Abusing White People," *New Orleans Daily Crescent*, September 8, 1855, 3.

28. "Police Matters," *Daily Picayune* (New Orleans), September 13, 1855, 2; see Schafer, *Becoming Free, Remaining Free*, 98n1.

29. See Ellen Eslinger, "Free Black Residency in Two Antebellum Virginia Counties: How the Laws Functioned," *Journal of Southern History* 79, no. 2 (May 2013): 265.

30. See Ira Berlin, *Slaves without Masters: The Free Negro in the Antebellum South* (New York: New Press, 1974), 46–47, 136, 396–99; Russell, *Free Negro in Virginia*, 9–15. On the manumission law, see "An Act to Authorize the Manumission of Slaves," in *Statutes at Large of Virginia*, ed. William W. Hening (Richmond: George Cochran, 1819–1823), 11:39–40; Fede, *Roadblocks to Freedom*, 90–92.

31. See "An ACT to Prevent the Migration of Free Negroes and Mulattoes into This Commonwealth," in Samuel Shepherd, *The Statutes at Large of Virginia, from October Session 1792, to December Session 1806, Inclusive* (Richmond: Samuel Shepherd), 1:239; "An ACT for Regulating the Police of Towns in This Commonwealth, and to Restrain the Practice of Negroes Going at Large," in ibid., 1:238; Russell, *Free Negro in Virginia*, 63–64, 101, 107; Eslinger, "Free Black Residency," 266–70.

32. See "An ACT to Amend the Several Laws Concerning Slaves," in Shepherd, *The Statutes at Large of Virginia, from October Session 1792, to December Session 1806*, 3:252;

Ted Maris-Wolf, *Family Bonds: Free Blacks and Re-enslavement Law in Antebellum Virginia* (Chapel Hill: University of North Carolina Press, 2015), 27–62; Fede, *Roadblocks to Freedom*, 92–93; Russell, *Free Negro in Virginia*, 70–79, 101, 107; Eslinger, "Free Black Residency," 270–98; see also, for later constitutional and statutory provisions, *Code of Virginia, Second Edition, Including Legislation to the Year 1860* (Richmond: Ritchie, Dunnavant, 1860), 46, 519–22, 810.

33. See "An Act for Arming of Persons," in Hening, *Statutes at Large of Virginia*, 1:226; Paul Finkelman, *The Law of Freedom and Bondage: A Casebook* (New York: Oceana, 1986), 14.

34. Paul Finkelman, "Slavery in the United States: Persons or Property?," in *The Legal Understanding of Slavery: From the Historical to the Contemporary*, ed. Jean Allain (Oxford: Oxford University Press, 2012), 108; see de la Fuente and Gross, *Becoming Free, Becoming Black*, 29. Other scholars interpret that act to, without exception, prohibit "Africans from carrying guns." See Carol Anderson, *The Second: Race and Guns in a Fatally Unequal America* (New York: Bloomsbury, 2021), 12 (citing Joyce Tang, "Enslaved African Rebellions in Virginia," *Journal of Black Studies* 27, no. 5 [May 1997]: 600).

35. See "An Act Directing the Trial of Slaves, Committing Capital Crimes; and for the More Effectual Punishing Conspiracies and Insurrections of Them; and for the Better Government of Negros, Mulattos, and Indians, Bond or Free," in Hening, *Statutes at Large of Virginia*, 4:131; see also Higginbotham and Bosworth, "'Rather Than the Free,'" 27–28; Finkelman, "Crime of Color," 2092–93. For similar laws, see "An ACT Concerning Free Negroes and Mulattoes," in *A Collection of All Such Acts of the General Assembly of Virginia* (Richmond: Samuel Pleasants Jr., 1808), 2:108–9 (adopted February 4, 1806); "An Act to Reduce to One, the Several Acts Concerning Slaves, Free Negroes, and Mulattoes," in Shepherd, *The Statutes at Large of Virginia, from October Session 1792, to December Session 1806*, 1:122–23 (adopted December 17, 1792).

36. See "An ACT to Amend an Act Entitled, 'An Act Reducing into One the Several Acts Concerning Slaves, Free Negroes and Mulattoes, and for Other Purposes,'" in *Supplement to the Revised Code of the Laws of Virginia* (Richmond: Samuel Shepherd, 1833), 246–47. For other antebellum state discriminatory gun control laws, see Anderson, *The Second*, 70–71; Patrick J. Charles, "Racist History and the Second Amendment: A Critical Commentary," *Cardozo Law Review* 43, no. 4 (April 2022): 1245–52; Robert J. Cottrol and Raymond T. Diamond, "The Second Amendment: Toward an Afro-Americanist Reconsideration," *Georgetown Law Journal* 80, no. 2 (December 1991): 335–38.

37. See Anderson, *The Second*, 12–13 (quoting de la Fuente and Gross, *Becoming Free, Becoming Black*, 74).

38. See "An Act Directing the Trial of Slaves," in Hening, *Statutes at Large of Virginia*, 4:133–34.

39. See "An Act Farther to Amend the Penal Laws of This Commonwealth," in *Acts Passed at a General Assembly of the Commonwealth of Virginia* (Richmond: Thomas Ritchie, 1823), 35–36; *Aldridge v. The Commonwealth*, 4 Va. (2 Va. Cas.) 447, 447–50 (General Court 1824); Daniel Flanigan, *The Criminal Law of Slavery and Freedom 1800–1868* (New York: Garland, 1987), 200–203.

40. See, e.g., "An Act to Amend an Act, Entitled 'An Act Reducing into One the Several Acts Concerning Slaves, Free Negroes and Mulattoes, and for Other Purposes,'" in

Supplement to the Revised Code of the Laws of the Virginia, 248; Philip J. Schwarz, *Twice Condemned: Slaves and the Criminal Laws of Virginia, 1705–1865* (Baton Rouge: Louisiana State University Press, 1988), 318; Russell, *Free Negro in Virginia*, 103–5.

41. See "An Act for Preventing Negroes Insurrections," in Hening, *Statutes at Large of Virginia*, 2:481.

42. See generally Gregory Ablavsky, "Making Indians 'White': The Judicial Abolition of Native Slavery in Revolutionary Virginia and Its Racial Legacy," *University of Pennsylvania Law Review* 159, no. 5 (April 2011): 1457–1531. Other scholars construe the phrase "negroes or other slaves" to apply to any Black person, whether enslaved or free, which is the wording used in the 1705 act discussed next. See Anderson, *The Second*, 12; de la Fuente and Gross, *Becoming Free, Becoming Black*, 31.

43. See Higginbotham, *In the Matter of Color*, 39; see also Cottrol and Diamond, "Second Amendment," 325. The act's other prohibitions are as follows: "It shall not be lawfull for any negroe or other slave to carry or arme himselfe with any club, staffe, gunn, sword or any other weapon of defence or offence, nor to go or depart from of his masters ground without a certificate from his master, mistris or overseer, and such permission not to be granted but upon perticuler and necessary occasions; and every negroe or slave soe offending not haveing a certificate as aforesaid shalbe sent to the next constable, who is hereby enjoyned and required to give the said negroe twenty lashes on his bare back well layd on, and soe sent home to his said master, mistris or overseer"; and "if any negroe or other slave shall absent himselfe from his masters service and lye hidand lurking in obscure places, comitting injuries to the inhabitants, and shall resist any person or persons that shalby any lawfull authority be imployed to apprehend and take the said negroe, that then in case of such resistance, it shalbe lawfull for such person or persons to kill the said negroe or slave soe lying out and resisting, and that this law be once every six months published at the respective county courts and parish churches within this colony." See "An Act for Preventing Negroes Insurrections," in Hening, *Statutes at Large of Virginia*, 2:481.

44. See "An Act Concerning Servants and Slaves," in Hening, *Statutes at Large of Virginia*, 3:459 (emphasis added); see also Finkelman, "Crime of Color," 2092–93.

45. See Finkelman, "Crime of Color," 2091.

46. See Andrew Fede, *People without Rights: An Interpretation of the Fundamentals of the Law of Slavery in the U.S. South* (New York: Garland, 1992; repr., New York: Routledge, 2011), 100.

47. See "An Act Concerning Servants and Slaves," 3:459.

48. See *Ely v. Thompson*, 10 Ky. (3 A. K. Marsh.) 70, 75 (1820) (citing William Littell, ed., *The Statute Law of Kentucky* [Frankfort, Ky.: Johnson and Pleasants, 1810], 2:116).

49. See "An Act to Reduce into One, the Several Acts Concerning Slaves, Free Negroes and Mulattoes," in *A Collection of All Such Acts of the General Assembly of Virginia* (Richmond: Samuel Pleasants Jr. and Henry Pace, 1803), 188; see also Fede, *People without Rights*, 174–75; Schwarz, *Twice Condemned*, 240–41; A. Leon Higginbotham Jr. and Anne F. Jacobs, "'The Law Only as an Enemy': The Legitimization of Racial Powerlessness through the Colonial and Antebellum Criminal Laws of Virginia," *North Carolina Law Review* 70, no. 4 (April 1992): 1029.

50. See Fede, *Homicide Justified*, 113–14. For a discussion of other cases evidencing violent acts of enslaved people in Virginia and the reactions of the whites, see Christopher

H. Bouton, *Setting Slavery's Limits: Physical Confrontations in Antebellum Virginia, 1801–1860* (Lanham, Md.: Lexington Books, 2020).

51. See "Daring Negro," *Daily Dispatch* (Richmond), April 16, 1857, 1; "Laid Over," *Daily Dispatch* (Richmond), April 15, 1857, 1. For the prosecution, conviction, and commutation of the death sentence of Jordan Hatcher, an enslaved man hired out to work in a Richmond tobacco factory, for the murder of an overseer, see Bouton, *Setting Slavery's Limits*, 139–46; William A. Link, "The Jordan Hatcher Case: Politics and 'A Spirit of Insubordination' in Antebellum Virginia," *Journal of Southern History* 64, no. 4 (November 1998): 615–48. On the Hustings Court, see, quoting William M. Robinson Jr., *Justice in Grey: A History of the Judicial System of the Confederate States of America* (Cambridge, Mass.: Harvard University Press, 1941), 76–77, Courts, Civil War Richmond, https://www.civilwarrichmond.com/courts: "The hustings court of Richmond, spiritual offspring of the hustings court of London, was held not exceeding six days a month by the mayor, recorder, and aldermen, or any four of them, and twenty days by the judge of the court of hustings, who was elected for a term of eight years. In addition to the monthly courts, quarterly sessions were held in February, May, August, and November, at which grand juries attended. The hustings' jurisdiction, at law, in chancery, and in criminal causes, was almost as extensive as a circuit court's and furthermore included probate matters, fiduciaries, bastardies, registration of free negroes, and police cases. Decisions made by the aldermanic bench on city ordinances were subject to revision by the judge of hustings and on general questions by the Circuit Court for the City of Richmond; but appeals from the decisions of the judge lay to the district court or to the Supreme Court of Appeals in the same manner as from a circuit court." In Virginia's cities, including Richmond, the Hustings Court also "handled cases of violent crime and served the same function as the oyer and terminer courts." Bouton, *Setting Slavery's Limits*, 140.

52. See, generally on the code's adoption, Christopher Michael Curtis, *Jefferson's Freeholders and the Politics of Ownership in the Old Dominion* (New York: Cambridge University Press, 2012), 196n6; William E. Ross, "History of Virginian Codification," *Virginia Law Register* 11, no. 2 (June 1905): 93; see also W. Hamilton Bryson, ed., *Virginia Law Books: Essays and Bibliographies* (Philadelphia: American Philosophical Society, 2000), 18. For Leigh's pro-slavery views, see Lacy K. Ford, *Deliver Us from Evil: The Slavery Question in the Old South* (New York: Oxford University Press, 2009), 378–80.

53. See B. W. Leigh, ed., *The Revised Code of the Laws of Virginia* (Richmond: Thomas Ritchie, 1819), 1:426–27.

54. See "An Act to Reduce into One the Several Acts Concerning Slaves, Free Negroes, and Mulattoes," in *Code of Mississippi, from 1798 to 1848*, ed. A. Hutchinson (Jackson, Miss.: Price and Fall, 1848), 517; and *A Manual or Digest of the Statute Law of the State of Florida*, ed. Leslie A. Thompson (Boston: Charles C. Little and James Brown, 1848), 540; "An Act Relating to Crimes and Misdemeanors Committed by Slaves, Free Negroes, and Mulattoes," in *Compilation of the Public Acts of the Legislative Council of the Territory of Florida, Passed Prior to 1840*, ed. John P. Duval (Tallahassee: Samuel S. Sibley, 1839), 220; see also Thomas D. Morris, *Southern Slavery and the Law, 1619–1860* (Chapel Hill: University of North Carolina Press, 1996), 297.

55. See "An Act to Reduce into One the Several Acts Concerning Crimes and Punishments and Proceedings in Criminal Cases," in *Acts of the General Assembly of Virginia, Passed at the Session Commencing December 6, 1847, and Ending April 5, 1848* (Richmond:

Samuel Shepherd, 1848), 125–26; see also Higginbotham and Jacobs, "'Law Only as an Enemy,'" 1029.

56. See *Code of Virginia, Second Edition, Including Legislation to the Year 1860* (Richmond: Ritchie, Dunnavant, 1860), 816–17; *The Code of Virginia* (Richmond: William F. Ritchie, 1849), 754; see also Ross, "History of Virginian Codification," 94–97.

57. On enslavement as punishment for a crime, see "An ACT Authorizing the Sale of Free Negroes into Slavery Who Are Sentenced to Receive Certain Punishments and Imprisonment," in *Acts of the General Assembly of Virginia Passed in 1859-60* (Richmond: William F. Ritchie, 1860), 163–64; Schwarz, *Twice Condemned*, 318; Kenneth M. Stampp, *The Peculiar Institution: Slavery in the Ante-Bellum South* (New York: Vintage, 1956), 216–17; and, for the self-enslavement laws, see "An ACT for the Voluntary Enslavement of Free Negroes, without Compensation to the Commonwealth," in *Acts of the General Assembly of Virginia Passed in 1861* (Richmond: William F. Ritchie, 1861), 52–53; "An Act Providing for the Voluntary Enslavement of the Free Negroes of the Commonwealth," in *Acts of the General Assembly of Virginia Passed in 1855-6* (Richmond: William F. Ritchie, 1856), 37–38; Maris-Wolf, *Family Bonds*, 102–5, 173–79; West, *Family or Freedom*, 45–46; Fede, *Roadblocks to Freedom*, 114–17; Morris, *Southern Slavery and the Law*, 32–36; Russell, *Free Negro in Virginia*, 108–9.

58. See "Hand Party," *Daily Dispatch* (Richmond), September 29, 1854, 2.

59. See "Northern Ebo [sic] with Southern Stripes," *Daily Dispatch* (Richmond), April 14, 1857, 1.

60. See, e.g., "Impudent Gang," *Daily Dispatch* (Richmond), August 1, 1860, 1 (four free Black men sentenced to whippings for "using provoking and insolent language to Jeremiah Ahern"); "Impudence Punished," *Daily Dispatch* (Richmond), April 6, 1860, 1 (Isaac Gaines, a free Black man, sentenced to whipping "for using insolent and provoking language to Mr. James Belcher"); "Insolence," *Daily Dispatch* (Richmond), March 31, 1857, 1 (Julia Fortune, "a free negress," sentenced to "punishment" for "using insolent and provoking language to Sarah Howell, a white woman"); "Insolent," *Daily Dispatch* (Richmond), April 1, 1856, 1 (Henry Gentry, a free Black man, sentenced to "fifteen stripes . . . for using insolent and provoking language to John Miller"); "Impudence Punished," *Daily Dispatch* (Richmond), December 18, 1854, 2 (Lucinda Barker, a free Black woman sentenced to "stripes" for "using insulting, provoking, and abusive language" to "Clara Green, an old white woman").

61. See, e.g., "Insolent," *Daily Dispatch* (Richmond), June 8, 1859, 1 (charge against "Mary Jones a free negress" for "using insolent and provoking language to H. F. Timberlake" was withdrawn "on the prisoner's promising not to repeat it"); "Frivolous Complaint," *Daily Dispatch* (Richmond), May 30, 1854, 2 (charge against "a very bad free negro named Alexander Jackson" was dismissed based on conflicting testimony, "and the prisoner, bad as he is known to be, was at once discharged").

62. See Ervin L. Jordan Jr., *Black Confederates and Afro-Yankees in Civil War Virginia* (Charlottesville: University of Virginia Press, 1995), 168.

63. See Joshua D. Rothman, *Notorious in the Neighborhood: Sex and Families across the Color Line in Virginia, 1787–1861* (Chapel Hill: University of North Carolina Press, 2003), 95.

64. See ibid., 92–115; see also Midori Takagi, *Rearing Wolves to Our Own Destruction: Slavery in Richmond, Virginia, 1782–1865* (Charlottesville: University of Virginia Press,

1999), 16–21; Shane White, "'Bring on Da Noise, Bering on Da Funk': The Sounds of Slavery in Richmond Virginia in the 1850s," *Arts: The Journal of the Sydney University Arts Association* 26 (2004): 32–33; John T. O'Brien, "Factory, Church, and Community: Blacks in Antebellum Richmond," *Journal of Southern History* 44, no. 4 (November 1978): 511–15.

65. See Rothman, *Notorious in the Neighborhood*, 100.

66. See ibid., 101.

67. See ibid., 273n20.

68. See ibid., 101.

69. See ibid., 274n21.

70. See Suzanne Lebsock, *The Free Women of Petersburg: Status and Culture in a Southern Town 1784–1860* (New York: Norton, 1984), 11.

71. See ibid., 93.

72. See "Using Abusive Language," *Daily Express* (Petersburg, Va.), December 4, 1856, 2. Lebsock also notes that the local court records confirm that, on January 24, 1853, "a free black woman who had been sentenced to ten lashes for insulting a white had the sentence reversed on appeal." See Lebsock, *Free Women of Petersburg*, 281n112.

73. See Rothman, *Notorious in the Neighborhood*, 116; Dean Hoffmeyer, "The History of the Richmond Times-Dispatch," *Richmond Times-Dispatch*, February 5, 2014, https://richmond.com/the-history-of-the-richmond-times-dispatch/article_5d7412c0-8f5f-11e3-a538-0017a43b2370.html#:~:text=The%20Richmond%20Times%2DDispatch%20traces,association%20with%20the%20Bryan%20family.

74. See Rothman, *Notorious in the Neighborhood*, 113.

75. See ibid., 113–18. On Mayo, see ibid., 118, 277–78n67; "Joseph C. Mayo," *Encyclopedia Virginia*, https://encyclopediavirginia.org/1813hpr-661bae1b9c85a61/. Mayo was mayor from 1853 until the surrender of Richmond on April 3, 1865. He was again the mayor from April 7, 1866, until March 15, 1870. Ibid.

76. See Rothman, *Notorious in the Neighborhood*, 119–22; Richard C. Wade, *Slavery in the Cities: The South 1820–1860* (New York: Oxford University Press, 1964), 106–9; see also *Charters and Ordinances of the City of Richmond* (Richmond: Ellyson's Steam Presses, 1859), 192–200; "To Owners and Hirers of Slaves," *Daily Dispatch* (Richmond), December 22, 1852, 2; "Local Matters," *Daily Dispatch* (Richmond), March 23, 1853, 2; "Local Matters: City Council," *Daily Dispatch* (Richmond), September 23, 1852, 2.

77. See *Charters and Ordinances of the City of Richmond*, 198.

78. Rothman, *Notorious in the Neighborhood*, 120.

79. See Wade, *Slavery in the Cities*, 106.

80. See Rothman, *Notorious in the Neighborhood*, 118–29.

81. "Punished," *Daily Dispatch* (Richmond), February 27, 1856, 4.

82. "Insolent," *Daily Dispatch* (Richmond), October 5, 1856, 1.

83. "Striped," *Daily Dispatch* (Richmond), November 25, 1857, 1.

84. "Failed to Appear," *Daily Dispatch* (Richmond), January 18, 1858, 1.

85. See "Caught at Last," *Daily Dispatch* (Richmond), January 25, 1858, 1; "Not Forthcoming," *Daily Dispatch* (Richmond), January 16, 1858, 1.

86. See Wade, *Slavery in the Cities*, 108; "To Owners and Hirers of Slaves," *Daily Dispatch* (Richmond), December 22, 1852, 2; "Local Matters," *Daily Dispatch* (Richmond), March 23, 1853, 2; "Local Matters: City Council," *Daily Dispatch* (Richmond), September 23, 1852, 2; see also, discussing sidewalk usage and regulation, Nicholas Blomley,

Sidewalks and the Regulation of Public Flow (New York: Routledge, 2011), 71; Anastasia Loukaitou-Sideris and Renia Ehrenfeucht, *Sidewalks: and Negotiation over Public Space* (Cambridge, Mass.: MIT Press, 2009), 87.

87. See *Charters and Ordinances of the City of Richmond*, 196. For a similar provision in an 1860 ordinance enacted in Petersburg, see Lebsock, *Free Women of Petersburg*, 94.

88. See Berlin, *Slaves without Masters*, 317.

89. See William J. Novak, *The People's Welfare: Law and Regulation in Nineteenth-Century America* (Chapel Hill: University of North Carolina Press, 1996), 148.

90. See, e.g., "Nuisances," *Daily Dispatch* (Richmond), September 27, 1859, 1; "Hard Job," *Daily Dispatch* (Richmond), January 2, 1857, 1; "The Hirers of Negroes," *Daily Dispatch* (Richmond), December 30, 1856, 1; "Clear the Sidewalks," *Daily Dispatch* (Richmond), December 16, 1856, 1; *Daily Dispatch* (Richmond), January 2, 1856, 4; "Hiring Time," *Daily Dispatch* (Richmond), January 1, 1856, 1.

91. See, e.g., "Getting High," *Daily Dispatch* (Richmond), October 7, 1856, 1.

92. "Protecting Ladies," *Daily Dispatch* (Richmond), May 25, 1859, 1.

93. "Warning to Negroes," *Daily Dispatch* (Richmond), September 24, 1857, 1.

94. See, e.g., "Local Matters," *Daily Dispatch* (Richmond), January 24, 1860, 1.

95. See "Not Enforced," *Daily Dispatch* (Richmond), November 17, 1857, 1.

96. See "Local Matters," *Daily Dispatch* (Richmond), January 24, 1860, 1.

97. *Commonwealth v. Howard*, 38 Va. (11 Leigh) 631 (1841).

98. Ibid., 631.

99. See "An Act to Provide the More Effectual Punishment of Certain Offences," in *Acts of the General Assembly of the Commonwealth of Virginia* (Richmond: Thomas Ritchie, 1823), 36–37; see also *Code of Virginia* (Richmond: Thomas Ritchie, 1823), 732.

100. See *Commonwealth v. Howard*, 631 (citing *Commonwealth v. Percavil*, 31 Va. (4 Leigh) 686 (1834)); see also *Commonwealth v. Israel*, 31 Va. (4 Leigh) 675 (1834) (applying statute to a case involving a horse); Fede, *People without Rights*, 100–102; Higginbotham and Jacobs, "'Law Only as an Enemy,'" 1053–54; Andrew Fede, "Legitimized Violent Slave Abuse in the American South, 1619-1865: A Case Study of Law and Social Change in Six Southern States," *American Journal of Legal History* 29, no. 2 (April 1985): 128–29.

101. See "Heard and Disposed Of," *Daily Dispatch* (Richmond), May 28, 1857, 1.

102. See "That Ordinance," *Daily Dispatch* (Richmond), December 13, 1856, 1.

103. See "Not Enforced," *Daily Dispatch* (Richmond), May 23, 1859, 1.

104. See Wade, *Slavery in the Cities*, 182. For other southern municipal ordinances, see Berlin, *Slaves without Masters*, 317–23.

105. Berlin, *Slaves without Masters*, 319–20.

106. See "Local Matters," *Daily Dispatch* (Richmond), September 12, 1856, 1; Rothman, *Notorious in the Neighborhood*, 121–22.

107. See "Vile Nest," *Daily Dispatch* (Richmond), February 16, 1858, 1; see also Berlin, *Slaves without Masters*, 338. William Novak discusses the racial justification of the regulation of the sale of alcohol to enslaved and free Blacks. See Novak, *People's Welfare*, 161–62.

108. See Markus Dirk Dubber, *The Police Power: Patriarchy and the Foundations of American Government* (New York: Columbia University Press, 2005). Scholars of literature and culture have found this book to be helpful. See, e.g., Sal Nicolazzo, *Vagrant Figures: Law, Literature, and the Origins of the Police* (New Haven, Conn.: Yale University

Press, 2020), 1–40, 202–36; Bryan Wagner, *Disturbing the Peace: Black Culture and the Police Power after Slavery* (Cambridge, Mass.: Harvard University Press, 2009), 1–24, 37–42, 71–75, 138–41.

109. See Dubber, *Police Power*, xi–xvi.
110. See ibid., 51–53, 130–38.
111. See ibid., 61–62; see also ibid., 41, 231n192.
112. I acknowledge an anonymous reader's suggestion that the police concept provides a "potentially fruitful connection." See report on file with author. For a critique of Dubber's interpretation, see Christopher Tomlins, "To Improve the State and Condition of Man: The Power to Police and the History of American Governance," *Buffalo Law Review* 53, no. 4 (Fall 2005): 1215–71.

CHAPTER 7. The Differing Texas and Georgia Legislative Responses to Insolence

1. See Randolph B. Campbell, *An Empire for Slavery: The Peculiar Institution in Texas, 1821–1865* (Baton Rouge: Louisiana State University Press, 1989), 1–9; see also Annette Gordon-Reed, *On Juneteenth* (New York: Liveright, 2021), 19.
2. Gordon-Reed, *On Juneteenth*, 22–23.
3. See ibid., 23.
4. See Bryan Burrough, Chris Tomlinson, and Jason Stanford, *Forget the Alamo: The Rise and Fall of an American Myth* (New York: Penguin, 2021), 1–28; Andrew J. Torget, *Seeds of Empire: Cotton, Slavery, and the Transformation of the Texas Borderlands, 1800–1850* (Chapel Hill: University of North Carolina Press, 2015), 1–176, 270–71; Campbell, *Empire for Slavery*, 10–34; George R. Woolfolk, "Cotton Capitalism and Slave Labor in Texas," *Southwestern Social Science Quarterly* 37, no. 1 (June 1956): 43–52.
5. See Torget, *Seeds of Empire*, 177–254.
6. See Randolph B. Campbell, "Introduction. Human Chattels: The Laws of Slavery in Texas," in *The Laws of Slavery in Texas*, ed. Randolph B. Campbell (Austin: University of Texas Press, 2010), 3; see generally Campbell, *Empire for Slavery*, 15–49; John Codman Hurd, *The Law of Freedom and Bondage in the United States* (1858/1862; repr., Boston: Little, Brown, 1968), 2:193; see also, discussing legal transplanting or legal borrowing, Alan Watson, *Legal Transplants: An Approach to Comparative Law*, 2nd ed. (Athens: University of Georgia Press, 1993), 21–121; Alan Watson, *Slave Law in the Americas* (Athens: University of Georgia Press, 1989), 125–33; Christopher Tomlins, "Transplants and Timing: Passages in the Creation of an Anglo-American Law of Slavery," *Theoretical Inquiries in Law* 10, no. 2 (July 2009): 389–422; David B. Schorr, "Horizontal and Vertical Influences in Colonial Legal Transplantation: Water-by Laws in British Palestine," *American Journal of Legal History* 61, no. 3 (September 2021): 308–31; Bradley J. Nicholson, "Legal Borrowing and the Origins of Slave Law in the British Colonies," *American Journal of Legal History* 38, no. 1 (January 1994): 38–54.
7. See Andrew T. Fede, *Homicide Justified: The Legality of Killing Slaves in the United States and the Atlantic World* (Athens: University of Georgia Press, 2017), 219–20; Campbell, *Empire for Slavery*, 56–59; Ira Berlin, *Slaves without Masters: The Free Negro in the Antebellum South* (New York: New Press, 1974), 136, 396–99; Cecil Harper Jr., "Slavery

without Cotton: Hunt County Texas, 1846–1864," *Southwest Historical Quarterly* 88 (April 1985): 387–405; see generally Alwyn Barr, *Black Texans: A History of African Americans in Texas, 1528–1995*, 2nd ed. (Norman: University of Oklahoma Press, 1996).

8. See Torget, *Seeds of Empire*, 166–71.

9. See Jason A. Gillmer, *Slavery and Freedom in Texas: Stories from the Courtroom, 1821–1871* (Athens: University of Georgia Press, 2017), 104–5 (quoting "Constitution of the Republic of Texas of 1836," in *The Laws of Texas 1822–1897*, ed. H. P. N. Gammel [Austin, Tex.: Gammel, 1898], 1:1069, 1079).

10. See Gillmer, *Slavery and Freedom in Texas*, 106 (quoting "Joint Resolution for the relief of Free Persons of Color, June 5, 1837," in *Laws of Texas 1822–1897*, 1:1292); see also John E. Fisher, "The Legal Status of Free Blacks in Texas, 1836–1861," *Texas Southern Law Review* 4, no. 3 (Summer 1977): 346–56.

11. See Gillmer, *Slavery and Freedom in Texas*, 105.

12. See "An Act to Provide for the Punishment of Crimes and Misdemeanors Committed by Slaves and Free Persons, Dec, 14, 1837," in *Laws of Texas 1822–1897*, 1:1386. Gillmer discusses the prosecution and conviction of Sam Ashworth, who was sentenced "to thirty lashes on his bare back" for challenging a white man to a duel; see Gillmer, *Slavery and Freedom in Texas*, 123–24; "Disturbances in Orange County," *Galveston (Tex.) Weekly News*, July 15, 1856, 2.

13. See Gillmer, *Slavery and Freedom in Texas*, 106.

14. See ibid., 109–18; Torget, *Seeds of Empire*, 234; Harold Schoen, "The Free Negro in the Republic of Texas: The Extent of Discrimination and Its Effects," in Campbell, *Laws of Slavery in Texas*, 118–33; Andrew Forest Muir, "The Free Negro in Harris County Texas," *Southwestern Historical Quarterly* 46, no. 3 (January 1943): 216–35; see also *State v. Asbury*, 26 Tex. 82 (1861) (affirming dismissal of untimely prosecution of defendant for aiding and bringing "a free person of color" into the state).

15. See Andrew Fede, *Roadblocks to Freedom: Slavery and Manumission in the United States South* (New Orleans: Quid Pro Books, 2011), 114–17.

16. See ibid., 105.

17. See Kenneth M. Stampp, *The Peculiar Institution: Slavery in the Ante-Bellum South* (New York: Vintage, 1956), 216.

18. See "Free Negroes—The Necessity of Reducing Them in Slavery," *State Gazette* (Austin, Tex.), September 12, 1857, 2.

19. See *Chandler v. State*, 2 Tex. 305, 309 (1847); see also, citing *Chandler*, *State v. Stephenson*, 20 Tex. 151, 152 (1857); *Nix v. State*, 13 Tex. 575, 578–79 (1855).

20. For a different interpretation of these decisions, see A. E. Keir Nash, "The Texas Supreme Court and Trial Rights of Blacks, 1845–1860," *Journal of American History* 58, no. 3 (December 1971): 625.

21. See James Willie, "[Preface]," *The Penal Code of the State of Texas* (Galveston: News Office, 1857), n.p., *Texas State Law Library*, http://www.lrl.state.tx.us/scanned/statutes_and_codes/Penal_Code.pdf; *The Code of Criminal Procedure of the State of Texas* (Galveston: News Office, 1857), *Texas State Law Library*, https://lrl.texas.gov/scanned/statutes_and_codes/code_of_criminal_procedure.pdf; "The Codes of 1856," *Texas State Law Library*, http://www.lrl.state.tx.us/collections/oldcodes.cfm.

22. See James D. Lynch, *The Bench and the Bar of Texas* (St. Louis: Nixon-Jones Print-

ing, 1885), 208–10; see also A. E. Wilkinson, "Edward Livingston and the Penal Code," *Texas Law Review* 1, no. 1 (December, 1922): 38n13.

23. See Wilkinson, "Edward Livingston and the Penal Code," 38n13.

24. See ibid., 41.

25. See *The Texas Senate, Volume II Republic to Civil War, 1836–1861*, ed. Patsy McDonald Spaw (College Station: Texas A&M Press, 1990), 274.

26. See *Texas Penal Code*, 7; Muir, "Free Negro in Harris County Texas," 214–16. This percentage of "blood" later was reduced to one-eighth. See ibid., 215n3.

27. See *Texas Penal Code*, 7, 157–58.

28. See Muir, "Free Negro in Harris County Texas," 215–16.

29. See *Texas Penal Code*, 159; compare "An Act to Provide for the Punishment of Crimes and Misdemeanors Committed by Slaves and Free Persons," in *Laws of Texas 1822–1897*, 1:1386.

30. See *Texas Penal Code*, 160.

31. See ibid., 93.

32. See ibid., 160; see also ibid., 134 ("Insulting language or gestures from a slave to a free white person will justify reasonable chastisement, whether such person has lawful control over the slave or not").

33. See ibid., 158.

34. See ibid., 159; see also Fede, *Homicide Justified*, 221–22 (discussing the provisions regulating the masters' right to kill people they enslaved).

35. See *Texas Penal Code*, 159.

36. See "An Act Supplementary to and Amendatory of an Act to Adopt and Establish a Penal Code for the State of Texas, approved 28th August, 1856," in Gammel, *Laws of Texas 1822–1897*, 4:1059.

37. See text and notes at notes 66–72.

38. *Texas Penal Code*, 161; see Campbell, *Empire for Slavery*, 144–45. This exception enacted the prosecution's argument that the South Carolina appellate court rejected in *State v. Cheatwood*, 20 S.C.L. (2 Hill) 459 (Ct. App. L. & Eq. 1834) (affirming murder conviction and trial judge's charge when white defendant killed another person's slave after gambling with Blacks, which the prosecutor stated "placed himself on a footing of equality with the slave").

39. *Texas Penal Code*, 161.

40. See ibid., 12.

41. See ibid., 157.

42. See ibid., 164. An 1858 act modified these discriminatory punishments for enslaved persons to be death or whipping, and for free persons of color to be death, whipping, and labor upon any public works of a county. See *Digest of the General Statute Laws of the State of Texas*, 561, 563 (citing Act of February 12, 1858).

43. Compare Nash, "Texas Supreme Court and Trial Rights of Blacks," 642.

44. See Watson W. Jennison, *Cultivating Race: The Expansion of Slavery in Georgia, 1750–1860* (Lexington: University Press of Kentucky, 2012), 11.

45. See ibid., 7.

46. See ibid., 11–18 (quotation at 11); Christopher Leslie Brown, *Moral Capital: Foundations of British Abolitionism* (Chapel Hill: University of North Carolina Press, 2006),

78–85; Betty Wood, *Slavery in Colonial Georgia, 1730–1775* (Athens: University of Georgia Press, 1984), 1–23; Douglas C. Wilms, "The Development of Rice Culture in 18th Century Georgia," *Southeastern Geographer* 12, no. 1 (May 1972): 45–57.

47. See Fede, *Homicide Justified*, 105–9; Glenn McNair, *Criminal Injustice: Slaves and Free Blacks in Georgia's Criminal Justice System* (Charlottesville: University of Virginia Press, 2009), 37; A. Leon Higginbotham Jr., *In the Matter of Color: Race and the American Legal Process: The Colonial Period* (New York: Oxford University Press, 1978), 216–53; see generally Paul M. Pressly, *On the Rim of the Caribbean: Colonial Georgia and the British Atlantic World* (Athens: University of Georgia Press, 2013), 11–31; Jennison, *Cultivating Race*, 18–40; Wood, *Slavery in Colonial Georgia*, 24–87; Ralph Betts Flanders, *Plantation Slavery in Georgia* (Chapel Hill: University of North Carolina Press, 1933), 3–22; Betty Wood, "'Until He Shall Be Dead, Dead, Dead': The Judicial Treatment of Slaves in Eighteenth Century," *Georgia Historical Quarterly* 71, no. 3 (Fall 1987): 377–98.

48. See W. McDowell Rogers, "Free Negro Legislation in Georgia before 1865," *Georgia Historical Quarterly* 16, no. 1 (March 1932): 27.

49. See Berlin, *Slaves without Masters*, 46, 136, 397, 399.

50. See Fede, *Roadblocks to Freedom*, 95, 98, 104; David J. Grindle, "Manumission: The Weak Link in Georgia's Law of Slavery," *Mercer Law Review* 41, no. 2 (Winter 1990): 704–5.

51. "An Act to Prohibit the Post-mortem Manumission of Slaves," in *Acts of the General Assembly of the State of Georgia, 1859* (Milledgeville, Ga.: Boughton, Nisbet and Barnes, 1860), 68; see Fede, *Roadblocks to Freedom*, 104; Grindle, "Manumission," 714.

52. See Rogers, "Free Negro Legislation in Georgia before 1865," 27–30.

53. See "An Act to Allow All Slaves and Free Persons of Color, Who May Leave This State in the Service of Any Person in, or Connected with the Military Service, to Return to the State of Georgia," in *Acts of the General Assembly of the State of Georgia, 1861* (Milledgeville, Ga.: Boughton, Nisbet and Barnes, 1862), 71–72; "An Act to Prevent Free Persons of Color, Commonly Known as Free Negroes, from Being Brought or Coming to the State of Georgia," in *Acts of the General Assembly of the State of Georgia, 1859*, 68–69; Rogers, "Free Negro Legislation in Georgia before 1865," 37.

54. See *Bryan v. Walton*, 14 Ga. 185, 202 (1853); see also "An Act Concerning Free Persons of Colour, Their Guardians, and Coloured Preachers," in *Acts of the General Assembly of the State of Georgia, 1833* (n.p.: Polhill and Fort, 1834), 227–28. On Lumpkin, see Alfred L. Brophy, *University, Court, and Slave: Pro-slavery Thought in Southern Colleges and Courts and the Coming of the Civil War* (New York: Oxford University Press, 2016), 212–22; Paul DeForest Hicks, *Joseph Henry Lumpkin: Georgia's First Chief Justice* (Athens: University of Georgia Press, 2002); Timothy S. Huebner, *The Southern Judicial Tradition: State Judges and Sectional Distinctiveness, 1790–1890* (Athens: University of Georgia Press, 1999), 70–98; Watson Jennison, "Rewriting the Free Negro Past: Joseph Lumpkin, Pro-slavery Ideology, and Citizenship in Antebellum Georgia," in *Creating Citizenship in the Nineteenth Century South*, ed. William A. Link, David Brown, Brian Ward, and Martyn Bone (Gainesville: University Press of Florida, 2013), 41–63; John Phillip Reid, "Lessons of Lumpkin: A Review of Recent Literature on Law, Comity, and the Impending Crisis," *William and Mary Law Review* 23, no. 4 (Summer 1982): 571–624; Mason W. Stephenson and D. Grier Stephenson, "'To Protect and Defend': Joseph Henry Lumpkin, the Supreme Court of Georgia and Slavery," *Emory Law Journal* 25, no. 3 (Summer 1976): 579–608.

55. *Bryan v. Walton*, 202–3.

56. See "An Act to Prohibit Colored Mechanics and Masons, Being Slaves or Free Persons of Color Being Mechanics or Masons, from Making Contracts for the Erection of Buildings, or for the Repair of Buildings, and Declaring the White Person or Persons Directly or Indirectly Contracting with or Employing Them as Well as the Master Employer, Manager or Agent for Said Slave, or Guardian of Said Free Person of Color, Authorizing or Permitting the Same, Guilty of a Misdemeanor, and Prescribing Punishment for Violating This Act," in Howell Cobb, *A Compilation of the Penal Code of the State of Georgia* (Macon, Ga.: Joseph M. Boardman, 1850), 49; "An Act to Be Entitled An Act to Prohibit the Employment of Slaves and Free Persons of Colour from Compounding or Dispensing of Medicines in Druggists and Apothecaries' Stores, and to Compel Druggists and Apothecaries to Keep Arsenic and Other Dangerous Poisons under Lock and Key, Etc.," in *Acts of the General Assembly of the State of Georgia, 1835* (Milledgeville, Ga.: John A. Cuthbert, 1836), 268–69; Rogers, "Free Negro Legislation in Georgia before 1865," 30–31; see also Ralph B. Flanders, "The Free Negro in Ante-Bellum Georgia," *North Carolina Historical Review* 9, no. 3 (July 1932): 260–62 (discussing discriminatory municipal ordinances regulating free Blacks).

57. See "An Act to Be Entitled An Act, Supplementary to, and More Effectually to Enforce an Act, Entitled an Act, Prescribing the Mode of Manumiting Slaves in This State, to Prevent the Future Migration of Free Persons of Color Thereto; to Regulate Such Free Persons of Color, as Now Reside Therein, and for Other Purposes," in Lucius Q. C. Lamar, *A Compilation of the Laws of the State of Georgia, 1810–1819* (Augusta, Ga.: T.S. Hannon, 1821), 815; Rogers, "Free Negro Legislation in Georgia before 1865," 31.

58. See "An Act to Alter and Amend an Act Entitled an Act, Supplementary to, and More Effectually to Enforce an Act, Entitled an Act, Prescribing the Mode of Manumiting Slaves in This State, to Prevent the Future Migration of Free Persons of Color Thereto; to Regulate Such Free Persons of Color, as Now Reside Therein, and for Other Purposes, Passed the 19th December, 1818," in *Acts of the State of Georgia, 1819* (Milledgeville, Ga.: Cmak and Hines, 1819), 42; Rogers, "Free Negro Legislation in Georgia before 1865," 31.

59. See "An Act to Define and Punish Vagrancy in Free Persons of Color," in *Acts of the General Assembly of the State of Georgia, 1859*, 69–70; Rogers, "Free Negro Legislation in Georgia before 1865," 34.

60. See *William, (a Slave) v. the State*, 18 Ga. 356, 359–60 (1855); McNair, *Criminal Injustice*, 82–105; Rogers, "Free Negro Legislation in Georgia before 1865," 33–34.

61. "An Act to Point Out the Mode of Trial of Offences Committed by Free Persons of Color, Approved Nov. 23, 1815," in Howell Cobb, *A Compilation of the General and Public Statutes of the State of Georgia* (New York: Edward O. Jenkins, 1859), 607; see also "An Act for the Trial and Punishment of Slaves and Free Persons of Color,—Approved Dec. 19, 1816," in Cobb, *Compilation of the General and Public Statutes*, 610–11.

62. See Wood, "'Until He Shall Be Dead, Dead, Dead,'" 380. An 1811 statute modified these procedures, but it continued to require that all criminal trials of enslaved Blacks be held in the inferior Justice of the Peace Courts. "An Act to Establish a Tribunal for the Trial of Slaves within This State," in Lamar, *Compilation of the Laws of the State of Georgia*, 797–800.

63. "An Act to Provide for the Trial by the Superior Courts of This State of Any Slave

or Slaves or Free Person of Color Charged with Any Capital Offence Against the Laws of This State," in *Acts of the State of Georgia, 1849–50* (Milledgeville, Ga.: Richard M. Orme, 1850), 372–73; see Flanders, "Free Negro in Ante-Bellum Georgia," 260.

64. See *Bryan v. Walton*, 202.

65. Jennison, *Cultivating Race*, 84 (quoting "An Act to Manumit and Exempt from Certain Penalties, Silvia, and Her Son David, Now the Property of Joseph Gabriel Posner," in *Acts of the General Assembly of the State of Georgia: Passed at Louisville in January and February, 1799* (Louisville, Ga.: Elisha H. Waldo, 1799), 148–49); see Michael Thurmond, *Freedom: Georgia's Antislavery Heritage, 1733–1865* (Atlanta: Longstreet Press, 2003), 129; Victoria Logue and Frank Logue, *Touring the Backroads of North and South Georgia* (Winston-Salem, N.C.: John F. Blair, 1997), 262; Yulssus Lynn Holmes, *Those Glorious Days: A History of Louisville as Georgia's Capital, 1796–1807* (Macon, Ga.: Mercer University Press, 1996), 102–9; Jennison, "Rewriting the Free Negro Past," 50–51.

66. Legislation creating the Georgia Supreme Court was not enacted until 1845. See Huebner, *Southern Judicial Tradition*, 72.

67. *Jim v. State*, 15 Ga. 535 (1854).

68. Ibid., 544; see Andrew Fede, *People without Rights: An Interpretation of the Fundamentals of the Law of Slavery in the U.S. South* (New York: Garland, 1992; repr., New York: Routledge, 2011), 173. On Starnes and for another view on the case, see Brophy, *University, Court, and Slave*, 222–26.

69. *John v. State*, 16 Ga. 200 (1854).

70. Ibid., 203; see Fede, *People without Rights*, 173.

71. See Thomas R. R. Cobb, *An Inquiry into the Law of Negro Slavery in the United States of America* (Philadelphia: T. & J. W. Johnson and Savannah: W. Thorne Williams, 1858; repr., Athens: University of Georgia Press, 1999), 95.

72. See R. H. Clark, T. R. R. Cobb, and D. Irwin, *The Code of the State of Georgia* (Atlanta: John H. Seals, 1861).

73. See William B. McCash, *Thomas R. R. Cobb: The Making of a Southern Nationalist* (Macon, Ga.: Mercer University Press, 1983), 59–60 (quoting "An Act to Provide for the Codification of the Laws of Georgia," in *Acts of the General Assembly of the State of Georgia, 1858* (Columbus, Ga.: Tennent Lomax, 1858), 95–96); see also Jefferson James Davis, "The Georgia Code of 1863: America's First Comprehensive Code," *Journal of Southern Legal History* 4 (1995–1996): 13. For the background to the authorizing act, see McCash, *Thomas R. R. Cobb*, 56–60; Erwin C. Surrency, "The Georgia Code of 1863 and Its Place in the Codification Movement," *Journal of Southern Legal History* 11 (2003): 81–89; Davis, "Georgia Code of 1863," 1–13; William B. McCash, "Thomas Cobb and the Codification of Georgia Law," *Georgia Historical Quarterly* 62, no. 1 (Spring 1978): 9–17; Richard H. Clark, "The History of the First Georgia Code," in *Report of the Seventh Annual Meeting of the Georgia Bar Association* (Atlanta: Franklin Publishing House, 1890), 150–51. For the 1852 Alabama Code, see John J. Ormond, Arthur P. Bagby, and George Goldthwaite, *The Code of Alabama* (Montgomery: Brittan and DeWolf, State Printers, 1852).

74. See McCash, *Thomas R. R. Cobb*, 64–65. On Cobb's military career and death, see ibid., 237–317.

75. See Paul Finkelman, "Introduction: Thomas R. R. Cobb and the Law of Slavery," in *Inquiry into the Law of Negro Slavery*, 2–3.

76. See Cobb, *Inquiry into the Law of Negro Slavery*; Thomas R. R. Cobb, *A Digest of the Statute Laws of Georgia* (Athens: Christy, Kelsea, and Burke, 1851). At the end of the last section of the enslavement law treatise, Cobb asserts that he concluded his "view of the negro slave *as a person*, and we shall hereafter consider of those rules of law to which *as property* he is subject. In that investigation we shall find that his nature as a man, and his consequent power of volition and locomotion, introduce important variations in those rules which regulate property in general." He added a "Note" stating, "This branch of the subject will be considered in another volume." Cobb, *Inquiry into the Law of Negro Slavery*, 317; see McCash, *Thomas R. R. Cobb*, 157 (noting that Cobb "had begun collecting material for his new volume").

77. See Finkelman, "Introduction," 7. On the drafting, contents, and lasting significance of the treatise, see ibid., 6–20; see also Paul Finkelman, "Thomas R. R. Cobb and the Negro Law of Slavery," *Roger Williams University Law Review* 5, no. 1 (Fall 1999): 75–115 (discussing Cobb's biography, his treatise, and the treatise's influence).

78. See Finkelman, "Introduction," 4–6. For more on Cobb, see McCash, *Thomas R. R. Cobb* and Paul Finkelman, "Introduction: Thomas R. R. Cobb and the Law of Slavery," in *Inquiry into the Law of Negro Slavery*, 1–20; Matthew Bailey and Steven Nash, "Thomas R. R. Cobb," *New Georgia Encyclopedia*, last modified March 11, 2020, https://www.georgiaencyclopedia.org/articles/history-archaeology/thomas-r-r-cobb-1823-1862/.

79. See Clark, Cobb, and Irwin, *Code of the State of Georgia*, 3.

80. See ibid., 320.

81. Ibid., 321.

82. See ibid., 920–21.

83. See ibid., 921–22.

84. See ibid. New Jersey courts were the first in the United States to liberally issue writs of certiorari to supervise and review the proceedings of inferior statutory tribunals, governmental agencies, and municipal corporations "not proceeding according to the course of the common law, for the correction of jurisdictional excesses and errors of law revealed by the record." See *Fisher v. Twp. of Bedminster*, 5 N.J. 534, 539–40, 76 A. 2d 673, 675–76 (1950); see generally James E. Pfander and Jacob P. Wentzel, "The Common Law Origins of *Ex parte Young*," *Stanford Law Review* 72, no. 5 (May 2020): 1311–24.

85. See Clark, Cobb, and Irwin, *Code of the State of Georgia*, 202–3. The code defines "felony" as an offense for which an offender "shall be liable by law to be punished as if he, she, or they, had perpetrated the offence." Ibid., 316.

86. See, explaining how the common-law citizen's arrest doctrine changed over the centuries as the nonlegal context changed, Jerome Hall, "Legal and Social Aspects of Arrest without a Warrant," *Harvard Law Review* 49, no. 4 (February 1936): 566–92; see also Roger M. Stevens, "A Legacy of Slavery: The Citizen's Arrest Laws of Georgia and South Carolina," *South Carolina Law Review* 72, no. 4 (Summer 2021): 1021–22; Chad Flanders, Raina Brooks, Jack Compton, and Lyz Riley, "The Puzzling Persistence of Citizen's Arrest Laws and the Need to Revisit Them," *Howard Law Journal* 64, no. 1 (Fall 2020): 161–237; Ira P. Robbins, "Vilifying the Vigilante: A Narrowed Scope of Citizen's Arrest," *Cornell Journal of Law and Public Policy* 25, no. 3 (Spring 2016): 557–600; Wilbur R. Miller, "A State within 'The States': Private Policing and Delegation of Power in America," *Crime,*

History & Societies 17, no. 2 (2013): 125–35; Alvin Stauber, "Citizen's Arrest: Rights and Responsibilities," *Midwest Law Review* 18 (Winter 2002): 31–38; Note, "The Law of Citizen's Arrest," *Columbia Law Review* 65, no. 3 (March 1965): 502–13.

87. See Stevens, "Legacy of Slavery," 1025–26.

88. See McCash, *Thomas R. R. Cobb*, 65–66 (quoting Linton Stephens to Alexander Stephens, January 4, 1863, Stephens Correspondence, University of North Carolina Library).

89. Clark, Cobb, and Irwin, *Code of the State of Georgia*, 320–21; see Jennison, "Rewriting the Free Negro Past," 58–59; Flanders, "Free Negro in Ante-Bellum Georgia," 259–60.

90. Clark, Cobb, and Irwin, *Code of the State of Georgia*, 919; see Fede, *People without Rights*, 174; Stephenson and Stephenson, "'To Protect and Defend,'" 595.

91. See Clark, Cobb, and Irwin, *Code of the State of Georgia*, 919.

92. See ibid.; Fede, *People without Rights*, 174; Stephenson and Stephenson, "'To Protect and Defend,'" 595.

93. See McNair, *Criminal Injustice*, 120–42; Huebner, *Southern Judicial Tradition*, 72.

94. See Jennison, "Rewriting the Free Negro Past," 59.

95. *Bryan v. Walton*, 205–6.

96. See McCash, *Thomas R. R. Cobb*, 156.

97. See Richard C. Wade, *Slavery in the Cities: The South 1820–1860* (New York: Oxford University Press, 1964), 182.

CONCLUSION. A Violent Badge of Slavery

1. *State v. Harden*, 29 S.C.L. (2 Speers) 152, 155 (Ct. App. Law 1832); *State v. Jowers*, 33 N.C. (11 Ired. Law) 555 (1850).

2. See *State v. Harden*, 155.

3. See James Kent, *Commentaries on American Law*, 2nd ed. (New York: O. Halsted, 1832), 2:258na. This treatise later cited O'Neall's opinions in *Harden* and *State v. Hill*, 29 S.C.L. (2 Speers) 151 (Ct. App. Law 1843). See James Kent, *Commentaries on American Law*, 10th ed. (Boston: Little, Brown, 1860), 2:299na.

4. See, generally, e.g., on the proslavery argument, the introduction and selections in Paul Finkelman, ed., *Defending Slavery: Proslavery Thought in the Old South: A Brief History with Documents*, 2nd ed. Bedford Series in History and Culture, ed. Paul Finkelman (Boston: Bedford/St. Martin's, 2020); Andrew Fede, *Roadblocks to Freedom: Slavery and Manumission in the United States South* (New Orleans: Quid Pro Books, 2011), 109–14.

5. See, e.g., Lea VanderVelde, "The Last *Legally* Beaten Servant in America: From Compulsion to Coercion in the American Workplace," *Seattle University Law Review* 39, no. 3 (Spring 2016): 727–85; Reva B. Siegel, "'The Rule of Love': Wife Beating as Prerogative and Privacy," *Yale Law Journal* 105, no. 8 (June 1996): 2117–207; text and note at chapter 1, note 9.

6. *Campbell v. The People*, 16 Ill. 17 (1854).

7. See *Plessy v. Ferguson*, 163 U.S. 537, 559, 16 S. Ct. 1138 (1896) (Harlan, J., dissenting).

8. See Daniel Kiel, "No Caste Here? Toward a Structural Critique of American Education," *Penn State Law Review* 119, no. 3 (Winter 2015): 612.

9. See ibid., 612.
10. See *Plessy v. Ferguson*, 556.
11. See ibid., 551.
12. See Rebecca J. Scott, "Public Rights, Social Equality, and the Conceptual Roots of the *Plessy* Challenge," *Michigan Law Review* 106, no. 5 (March 2008): 803–4 (mandated racial segregation accurately perceived as "an act of intentional humiliation"); see also Rebecca J. Scott, "Discerning a Dignitary Offense: The Concept of Equal 'Public Rights' during Reconstruction," *Law and History Review* 38, no. 3 (August 2020): 519–53.
13. See *United States v. Nelson*, 277 F. 3d 164, 189–90 (2d Cir.) (sustaining hate crimes provisions of the Civil Rights Act of 1968 under the Thirteenth Amendment and citing Andrew Fede, "Legitimized Violent Slave Abuse in the American South, 1619–1865: A Case Study of Law and Social Change in Six Southern States," *American Journal of Legal History* 29, no. 2 [April 1985]: 95), *cert.* denied, *Nelson v. United States*, 537 U.S. 835, 123 S. Ct. 145, 154 L. Ed. 2d 54 (2002); *United States v. Beebe*, 807 F. Supp. 2d 1045, 1052 (D. N.M. 2011) (sustaining Matthew Shepard and James Byrd Jr. Hate Crimes Prevention Act under the Thirteenth Amendment and citing Fede, "Legitimized Violent Slave Abuse," 132, 141–42), *aff'd*, *United States v. Hatch*, 722 F. 3d 1193 (10th Cir. 2013), *cert.* denied, 572 U.S. 1018, 134 S. Ct. 1538, 188 L. Ed. 2d 561 (2014).
14. See Ira Berlin, *Slaves without Masters: The Free Negro in the Antebellum South* (New York: New Press, 1974), 338 (for the quotations and citations to the decisions); see generally ibid., 183, 316–40. Berlin included Delaware, the District of Columbia, Kentucky, Maryland, Missouri, North Carolina, Tennessee, and Virginia in the Upper South, and Alabama, Arkansas, Florida, Georgia, Louisiana, Mississippi, South Carolina, and Texas in the Lower South. Ibid.; see Kenneth M. Stampp, *The Peculiar Institution: Slavery in the Ante-Bellum South* (New York: Vintage, 1956), 210, 215–17.
15. See, e.g., Dylan C. Penningroth, *Before the Movement: The Hidden History of Black Civil Rights* (New York: Liveright, 2023), xxii, 27–51; Warren E. Milteer Jr., *North Carolina's Free People of Color, 1715–1885* (Baton Rouge: Louisiana University Press, 2020), 11–14; Kirt von Daacke, *Freedom Has a Face: Race, Identity, and Community in Jefferson's Virginia* (Charlottesville: University of Virginia Press, 2012), 1–5 (citing Melvin Patrick Ely, *Israel on the Appomattox: A Southern Experiment in Black Freedom from the 1790s through the Civil War* [New York: Knopf, 2004]); see also Richard C. Rohrs, "The Free Black Experience in Antebellum Wilmington, North Carolina: Refining Generalizations about Race Relations," *Journal of Southern History* 78, no. 3 (August 2012): 620 ("lax" enforcement of harsh laws permitted some southern free Blacks to achieve a measure of economic prosperity in business, as skilled or semiskilled laborers, and as slave owners).
16. See John Hope Franklin, *The Free Negro in North Carolina 1790–1860* (Chapel Hill: University of North Carolina Press, 1943), 163–225.
17. W. Fitzhugh Brundage, "Introduction," in *The Folly of Jim Crow: Rethinking the Segregated South*, ed. Stephanie Cole and Natalie J. Ring (Arlington: University of Texas, 2012), 5; see John Anthony Scott, "Segregation: A Fundamental Aspect of Southern Race Relations, 1800–1860," *Journal of the Ealy Republic* 4, no. 4 (Winter 1984): 421–26.
18. See C. Vann Woodward, *The Strange Career of Jim Crow: A Commemorative Edition* (New York: Oxford University Press, 2002), 3–109; C. Vann Woodward, *Origins of the Old South, 1877–1913* (Baton Rouge, Louisiana State University Press, 1951), 210–12,

355–57; see also Barbara Young Welke, *Recasting American Liberty: Gender, Race, Law, and the Railroad Revolution, 1865–1920* (New York: Cambridge University Press, 2001), 306–7.

19. See Joel Williamson, *After Slavery: The Negro in South Carolina During Reconstruction, 1861–1877* (Chapel Hill: University of North Carolina Press, 1965), 298; see also Howard N. Rabinowitz, *Race Relations in the Urban South, 1865–1890* (New York: Oxford University Press, 1978), 329–39; Roger A. Fischer, *The Segregation Struggle in Louisiana, 1862–1877* (Urbana: University of Illinois Press, 1974), 3–5; Williamson, *After Slavery*, 240–99; Howard N. Rabinowitz, "Segregation and Reconstruction," in *Race Ethnicity, and Urbanization: Selected Essays* (Columbia: University of Missouri Press, 1994), 42–58; Howard N. Rabinowitz, "More Than the Woodward Thesis: Assessing *The Strange Career of Jim Crow*," *Journal of American History* 75, no. 3 (December 1988): 842–56; Scott, "Segregation," 426–41.

20. See Ulrich B. Phillips, "The Central Theme in Southern History," *American Historical Review* 34, no. 1 (October 1928): 31. For the Phillips interpretation of slavery, see, e.g., Ulrich B. Phillips, *American Negro Slavery: A Survey of the Supply, Employment and Control of Negro Labor as Determined by the Plantation Regime* (New York: D. Appleton, 1918). For commentary on Phillips, see John David Smith, *An Old Creed for the New South: Proslavery Ideology and Histography, 1865–1918* (Westport, Conn.: Greenwood, 1985), 239–83; John David Smith, "The Construction of Ulrich Bonnell Phillips's Interpretation of Slavery," *American Studies Journal* 45 (Summer 2000): 4–17; John David Smith, "The Historiographic Rise, Fall, and Resurrection of Ulrich Bonnell Phillips," *Georgia Historical Quarterly* 65, no. 2 (Summer 1981): 138–53, and the essays in *Ulrich Bonnell Phillips: A Southern Historian and His Critics*, ed. John C. Inscoe and John David Smith (New York: Greenwood, 1990).

21. William A. Dunning, "The Undoing of Reconstruction," *Atlantic Monthly* 88 (October 1901): 449; see generally William Archibald Dunning, *Reconstruction, Political and Economic 1865–1877* (New York: Harper and Brothers, 1907). For commentary on the Dunning School critique of Reconstruction, see the seminal chapter 17 in W. E. Burghardt Du Bois, *Black Reconstruction: An Essay toward a History of the Part Which Black Folk Played in the Attempt to Reconstruct Democracy in America, 1860–1880* (New York: Harcourt, Brace, 1935), 711–29, and the essays in *The Dunning School: Historians, Race, and the Meaning of Reconstruction*, ed. John David Smith and J. Vincent Lowery (Lexington: University Press of Kentucky, 2013).

22. See George M. Fredrickson, *White Supremacy: A Comparative Study in American and South African History* (New York: Oxford University Press, 1981), 58–70; Pierre L. Van den Berghe, *Race and Racism: A Comparative Perspective* (New York: Wiley, 1967), 17–18; see also Robert J. Cottrol, "Law, Politics and Race in Urban America: Towards a New Synthesis," *Rutgers Law Journal* 17, nos. 3 & 4 (Spring and Summer, 1987): 310.

23. See Edmund S. Morgan, *American Slavery American Freedom: The Ordeal of Colonial Virginia* (New York: Norton, 1975), 381; see also Nikole Hannah-Jones, "Democracy," in *The 1619 Project*, ed. Nikole Hannah-Jones, Caitlin Roper, and Jake Silverstein (New York: One World, 2021), 19 ("Slavery was not a necessary ingredient for the founders' belief in Republican equality, Morgan writes, but in Virginia and other Southern colonies, it proved to be *the* ingredient").

24. See Barbara J. Fields, "Origins of the New South and the Negro Question," *Jour-

nal of Southern History 67, no. 4 (November 2001): 815 (quoting Woodward, *Origins of the Old South*, 328).

25. See Woodward, *Strange Career of Jim Crow*, 4–10; see also Richard A. Paschal, *Jim Crow in North Carolina: The Legislative Program from 1865 to 1920* (Durham, N.C.: Carolina Academic Press, 2021), 43–55; Benjamin H. Pollak, "'A New Ethnology': The Legal Expansion of Whiteness under Early Jim Crow," *Law and History Review* 39, no. 2 (August 2021): 513–38 (discussing how the definitions of white and Black changed in the early years of Jim Crow legislation, while the purpose to degrade those labeled as Black remained constant); John K. Bardes, "Redefining Vagrancy: Policing Freedom and Disorder in Reconstruction New Orleans, 1862–1868," *Journal of Southern History* 84, no. 1 (February 2018): 69–112 (discussing how vagrancy law was redefined and redeployed as southern society evolved). Most of the northern free states and territories also made either immediate or gradual transitions from societies with slaves to free societies; in New Jersey, for example, the transition was still underway when the Civil War broke out in 1861. See Hendrik Hartog, *The Trouble with Minna: A Case of Emancipation in the Antebellum North* (Chapel Hill: University of North Carolina Press, 2018), 5–7; James J. Gigantino II, *The Ragged Road to Abolition: Slavery and Freedom in New Jersey, 1775–1865* (Philadelphia: University of Pennsylvania Press, 2015); see generally Manisha Sinha, *The Slave's Cause: A History of Abolition* (New Haven, Conn.: Yale University Press, 2016); Patrick Rael, *Eighty-Eight Years: The Long Death of Slavery in the United States* (Athens: University of Georgia Press, 2015); Ira Berlin, *The Long Emancipation: The Demise of Slavery in the United States* (Cambridge, Mass.: Harvard University Press, 2015); Arthur Zilversmit, *The First Emancipation: The Abolition of Slavery in the North* (Chicago: University of Chicago Press, 1967).

26. See Quincy Ewing, "The Heart of the Race Problem," *Atlantic Monthly* 103 (March 1901): 396 (quoted in Fields, "Origins of the New South," 813). Reva Siegel thus explained this pattern of legal change: "Status regimes are not static, but dynamic—revitalized from time to time as they are reshaped by diverse political forces and draw on evolving social norms." See Siegel, "'The Rule of Love,'" 2175.

27. See, e.g., Margaret A. Burnham, *By Hands Known: Jim Crow's Legal Executioners* (New York: Norton, 2022); Ely Aaronson, *From Slave Abuse to Hate Crime: The Criminalization of Racial Violence in American History* (New York: Cambridge University Press, 2014), 90–98; Manfred Berg, *Popular Justice: A History of Lynching in America* (Chicago: Ivan R. Dee, 2011), 69–116; see also Ibram X. Kendi, *Stamped from the Beginning: The Definitive History of Racist Ideas in America* (New York: Bold Type Books, 2016), 9–11 (suggesting that racial discrimination based on economic self-interest caused racist ideas, which in turn caused ignorance and hate).

28. See Leon F. Litwack, "Jim Crow Blues," *OAH Magazine of History* 18, no. 2 (January 2004): 9.

29. See Leon F. Litwack, *Trouble in the Mind: Black Southerners in the Age of Jim Crow* (New York: Knopf, 1998), 200–201; see also Leon F. Litwack, *Been in the Storm So Long: The Aftermath of Slavery* (New York: Random House, 1979), 265, 366–71.

30. See Keith S. Hébert, *Cornerstone of the Confederacy: Alexander Stephens and the Speech That Defined the Lost Cause* (Knoxville: University of Tennessee Press, 2021), 1, 223. On the Cornerstone Speech and its significance, see ibid., especially 39–65, 219–30. According to Litwack, the Jim Crow era's "most intense years were between 1890 and the

first Great Migration in the 1910s, but the seeds had been planted in the forceable overthrow of Reconstruction in the 1870s." Litwack, "Jim Crow Blues," 7. This book suggests instead that these seeds were planted in the antebellum era, and that the Jim Crow era extended further, until the separate but equal doctrine was held to be unconstitutional, beginning with the Supreme Court's decision in *Brown v. Board of Education*, 347 U.S. 483 (1954). On the origins of the term "Jim Crow," see Paschal, *Jim Crow in North Carolina*, xv–xx; Litwack, "Jim Crow Blues," 7.

31. See James Oakes, "Conflict vs. Racial Consensus in the History of Antislavery Politics," in *Contesting Slavery: The Politics of Bondage and Freedom in the New American Nation*, ed. John Craig Hammond and Matthew Mason (Charlottesville: University of Virginia Press, 2011), 299; see generally, e.g., Paul D. Escott, *The Worst Passions of Human Nature: White Supremacy in the Civil War North* (Charlottesville: University of Virginia Press, 2020), 1–7, 165–79; Woodward, *Strange Career of Jim Crow*, 11–65; Leon F. Litwack, *North of Slavery: The Negro in the Free States, 1790–1860* (Chicago: University of Chicago Press, 1961), 277–79; C. Vann Woodward, "Seeds of Failure in Racial Race Policy," *Proceedings of the American Philosophical Society* 110, no. 4 (February 18, 1966): 1–9; see also Charles W. Mills, *The Racial Contract* (Ithaca, N.Y.: Cornell University Press, 1997), 1 ("White supremacy is the unnamed political system that has made the modern world what it is today").

32. See Oakes, "Conflict vs. Racial Consensus," 299; see also Kate Masur, *Until Justice Be Done: America's First Civil Rights Movement, from the Revolution to Reconstruction* (New York: Norton, 2021), 365–72; Paul J. Polgar, *Bearers of Equality: America's First Abolition Movement* (Chapel Hill: University of North Carolina Press, 2019), 1–21; Martha S. Jones, *Birthright Citizens: A History of Race and Rights in Antebellum America* (New York: Cambridge University Press, 2018), 10–12, 128–46; Timothy S. Huebner, *Liberty and Union: The Civil War and American Constitutionalism* (Lawrence: University of Kansas Press, 2016), 3–136; Eric Foner, *Free Soil, Free Labor, Free Men: The Ideology of the Republican Party before the Civil War* (1970; repr., New York: Oxford University Press, 1995), 261–300; Oakes, "Conflict vs. Racial Consensus," 291–304; Paul Finkelman, "Rehearsal for Reconstruction: Antebellum Origins of the Fourteenth Amendment," in *The Facts of Reconstruction: Essays in Honor of John Hope Franklin*, ed. Eric Anderson and Alfred A. Moss Jr. (Baton Rouge: Louisianian State University Press, 1991), 1–27; Paul J. Polgar, "A Clash of Principles: The Frist Federal Debate over Slavery and Race, 1790," *Federal History* 14 (2022): 15–37; Paul Finkelman, "The Frist Civil Rights Movement: Black Rights in the Age of the Revolution and Chief Taney's Originalism in *Dred Scott*," *Journal of Constitutional Law* 24, no. 3 (June 2022): 677–728; Paul Finkelman, "Prelude to the Fourteenth Amendment: Black Legal Rights in the Antebellum North," *Rutgers Law Journal* 17, nos. 3–4 (Spring and Summer 1987): 415–82; see also Van Gosse, *The First Reconstruction: Black Politics in America from the Revolution to the Civil War* (Chapel Hill: University of North Carolina Press, 2021) (discussing antebellum Black voting and political action in northern states).

33. See Edward J. Larson, *American Inheritance: Liberty and Slavery in the Birth of a Nation 1765–1795* (New York: Norton, 2023), 268; see also James Oakes, *The Crooked Path to Abolition: Abraham Lincoln and the Antislavery Constitution* (New York: Norton, 2021), xi–xxxii; David W. Blight, "The Two Constitutions," *New York Review of Books* 70, no.

10 (June 8, 2023): 30–35 (discussing the antebellum pro-slavery and antislavery constitutional interpretations).

34. See Kendi, *Stamped from the Beginning*, 286–88; Dunning, "Undoing of Reconstruction," 437–49. For Woodrow Wilson's interpretation of Reconstruction, see Woodrow Wilson, "The Reconstruction of the Southern States," *Atlantic Monthly* 87 (January 1901): 11.

35. See U.S. Constitution, amend. 13, sec. 1 and sec. 2. The abolition decreed in section 1 of the amendment does not apply, however, to a person who was "duly convicted" of committing a "crime." For different interpretations of this exception, see, e.g., Peter Wallenstein, "Slavery under the Thirteenth Amendment: Race and the Law of Crime and Punishment in the Post–Civil War South," *Louisiana Law Review* 77, no. 1 (Fall 2016): 1–20; Andrea C. Armstrong, "Slavery Revisited in Penal Plantation Labor," *Seattle University Law Review* 35, no. 3 (Spring 2012): 869–910.

36. See Douglas R. Egerton, *The Wars of Reconstruction: The Brief, Violent History of America's Most Progressive Era* (New York: Bloomsbury Press, 2014), 176–77; Scott, "Segregation," 426. For a discussion of the political context and debates in the adoption process, see Michael Vorenberg, *Final Freedom: The Civil War, the Abolition of Slavery, and the Thirteenth Amendment* (New York: Cambridge University Press, 2001).

37. See Litwack, *Been in the Storm So Long*, 251–67, 361–86; see also Giuliana Perrone, *Nothing More Than Freedom: The Failure of Abolition in American Law* (New York: Cambridge University Press, 2023), 1–5; Du Bois, *Black Reconstruction*, 166–80.

38. See Perrone, *Nothing More Than Freedom*, 165–68; Masur, *Until Justice Be Done*, 309–11; Christopher W. Schmidt, *Civil Rights in America: A History* (New York: Cambridge University Press, 2020), 15–18; Joseph A. Ranney, *A Legal History of Mississippi: Race, Class, and the Struggle for Opportunity* (Jackson: University Press of Mississippi, 2019), 86–88; Egerton, *Wars of Reconstruction*, 178–82; Joseph A. Ranney, *In the Wake of Slavery: Civil War, Civil Rights, and the Reconstruction of Southern Law* (Westport, Conn.: Praeger, 2006), 43–63; Christopher Waldrep, *Roots of Disorder: Race and Criminal Justice in the American South, 1817–80* (Urbana: University of Illinois Press, 1998), 104–19; Daniel A. Novak, *The Wheel of Servitude: Black Forced Labor after Slavery* (Lexington: University Press of Kansas, 1978), 1–8; Williamson, *After Slavery*, 72–79; see also, e.g., "An Act Concerning Negroes and Persons of Color or of Mixed Blood," in *Public Laws of the State of North-Carolina, Passed by the General Assembly, at the Session of 1865–66, and 1861–62–63 and 1864* (Raleigh, N.C.: Robert W. Best, 1866), 99–105.

39. "Chapter 31, 39 Congress, Session 1, an Act: To Protect All Persons in the United States in Their Civil Rights, and Furnish a Means of Their Vindication," U.S. Statutes at Large 14, no. Main Section (1866): 27 (codified as amended 42 U.S.C. §§ 1981–1982); see, e.g., Masur, *Until Justice Be Done*, 311–30; Schmidt, *Civil Rights in America*, 25–30, and the essays in *The Greatest and the Grandest Act: The Civil Rights Act of 1866 from Reconstruction to Today*, ed. Christian G. Samito (Carbondale: Southern Illinois University Press, 2018).

40. See John Rawls, *A Theory of Justice* (Cambridge, Mass.: Harvard University Press, 1971), 60, 302; see also Randy E. Barnett and Evan D. Bernick, *The Original Meaning of the Fourteenth Amendment: Its Letter and Spirit* (Cambridge, Mass.: Belknap, 2021), 117–55; George Rutherglen, *Civil Rights in the Shadow of Slavery: The Constitution, Common*

Law, and the Civil Rights Act of 1866 (New York: Oxford University Press, 2013), 56–57; Earl M. Maltz, *Civil Rights, the Constitution, and Congress, 1863–1869* (Lawrence: University Press of Kansas, 1990), 67–70 (discussing the addition of the phrase "as is enjoyed by white citizens"). George Rutherglen notes that the Black Codes' drafters also used white rights as the benchmark for all citizens, but with exceptions diluting the very rights that they purportedly guaranteed. See Rutherglen, *Civil Rights in the Shadow of Slavery*, 46–49; see also Harold M. Hyman and William M. Wiecek, *Equal Justice Under Law: Constitutional Development, 1835–1875* (New York: Harper & Row, 1982), 319–24.

41. See Michael J. Klarman, "The Racial Origins of Modern Criminal Procedure," *Michigan Law Review* 99, no. 1 (October 2000): 48; see also Andres Resendez, *The Other Slavery: The Uncovered Story of Indian Enslavement in America* (New York: Houghton Mifflin Harcourt, 2016), 4, 295–314 (defining "the other slavery" to include slave-like relationships after Spain's 1542 abolition of Native American slavery, when officials failed to enact or enforce laws against slavery's badges and incidents).

42. See David A. Hall, "Ten Years Fighting Hate," *University of Miami Race and Social Justice Law Review* 10, no. 2 (April 2020): 79–92; Margalynne J. Armstrong, "Are We Nearing the End of Impunity for Taking Black Lives?," *Santa Clara Law Review* 56, no. 4 (2016): 749–50; but see Charles H. Jones Jr., "An Argument for Federal Protection Against Racially Motivated Crimes: 18 U.S.C. § 241 and the Thirteenth Amendment," *Harvard Civil Rights–Civil Liberties Law Review* 21, no. 2 (Summer 1986): 690–737 (suggesting a broader interpretation of the then-current federal criminal civil rights laws).

43. See, e.g., Gloria J. Browne, *Race, Law, and American Society: 1607 to Present*, 2nd ed. (New York: Routledge, 2013), 70–73; Philip Dray, *At the Hands of Persons Unknown: The Lynching of Black America* (New York: Random House, 2002), 258–73; Armstrong, "Are We Nearing the End of Impunity for Taking Black Lives?," 739–49.

44. See Emmett Till Antilynching Act, Public Law 117-107, 136 Stat. 1125 (2022) (codified as amended 18 U.S.C. § 241(a)(5) and (6)); Jamelle Bouie, "This Is Why It Took More Than 100 Years to Get an Anti-Lynching Bill," *New York Times*, April 1, 2022, https://www.nytimes.com/2022/04/01/opinion/anti-lynching-bill-biden.html?searchResultPosition=2; Orlando Mayorquin, "Biden Signed the Emmett Till Antilynching Act. Who Killed Emmett Till and What Happened to Him," *USA Today*, March 29, 2022, https://www.usatoday.com/story/news/politics/2022/03/29/who-is-emmett-till-civil-rights/7203642001/; Meagan Flynn, "A Black Lawmaker's Anti-lynching Bill Failed 120 Years Ago. Now, the House May Finally Act," *Washington Post*, February 21, 2020, http://www.washingtonpost.com/nation/2020/02/21/house-may-finally-act-after-anti-lynching-bill-failed-120-years-ago/. Manfred Berg suggests that "the murder of Emmett Till was an act of personal revenge tolerated by the community, but it lacked the key characteristics of popular justice," which is what distinguished lynchings. See Berg, *Popular Justice*, 174.

45. See generally, e.g., Michele Goodwin, "The Thirteenth Amendment: Modern Slavery, Capitalism, and Mass Incarceration," *Cornell Law Review* 104, no. 4 (May 2019): 899–990; James Gray Pope, "Section 1 of the Thirteenth Amendment and the Badges and Incidents of Slavery," *UCLA Law Review* 65, no. 2 (March 2018): 426–87; Darrell A. H. Miller, "The Thirteenth Amendment and the Regulation of Custom," *Columbia Law Review* 112, no. 7 (November 2012): 1811–54; Lea VanderVelde, "The Thirteenth Amendment of Our Aspirations," *University of Toledo Law Review* 38, no. 3 (Spring 2007): 855–82; Lauren Kares, "The Unlucky Thirteenth: A Constitutional Amendment in Search of a Doctrine,"

Cornell Law Review 80, no. 2 (1994–1995): 372–412; see also Arthur Kinoy, "The Constitutional Right of Negro Freedom," *Rutgers Law Review* 21, no. 3 (1967): 408–10 (contrasting Justice Taney's pro-slavery jurisprudence in *Scott v. Sandford*, 60 U.S. (19 How.) 393 (1856) defining enslaver constitutional rights with the post-reconstruction court's failure to define the nature of the rights guaranteed by the Civil War Amendments).

46. *United States v. Cruickshank*, 92 U.S. 542, 23 L. Ed. 588 (1875); *Hodges v. United States*, 203 U.S. 1, 27 S. Ct. 6, 51 L. Ed. 65 (1906). See Pamela S. Karlan, "Contracting the Thirteenth Amendment: *Hodges v. United States*," *Boston University Law Review* 85, no. 3 (June 2005): 783–809; see also Pamela Brandwein, *Rethinking the Judicial Settlement of Reconstruction* (New York: Cambridge University Press, 2011), 18–20, 184–205; John Montoya, "Defying Congressional Intent: Justices Miller and Bradley Alter the Course of Reconstruction," *Columbia Journal of Race and Law* 10, no. 2 (May 2020): 83–138; James Gray Pope, "Snubbed Landmark: Why *United States v. Cruikshank* (1876) Belongs at the Heart of the American Constitutional Cannon," *Harvard Civil Rights–Civil Liberties Law Review* 49, no. 2 (Summer 2014): 385–447; David E. Bernstein, "Thoughts on *Hodges v. United States*," *Boston University Law Review* 85, no. 3 (June 2005): 811–19.

47. See George Rutherglen, "The Thirteenth Amendment in Legal Theory," *Cornell Law Review Online* 104 (September 2019): 170; see also Carol Anderson, *The Second: Race and Guns in a Fatally Unequal America* (New York: Bloomsbury, 2021), 84–125.

48. See *Civil Rights Cases*, 109 U.S. 3, 20, 3 S. Ct. 18, 27 L. Ed. 835 (1883); see also Peter Nicolas, "Reconstruction," *U.C. Irvine Law Review* 10, no. 3 (March 2020): 943–46.

49. See, e.g., Aaronson, *From Slave Abuse to Hate Crime*, 61–90; R. Owen Williams, "The Civil Rights Act of 1866 at the Supreme Court," in Samito, *Greatest and the Grandest Act*, 163–87; Aaron Astor, "The Civil Rights Act of 1866 in Kentucky and Missouri," in Samito, *Greatest and the Grandest Act*, 112–36; Pope, "Section 1 of the Thirteenth Amendment and the Badges and Incidents of Slavery," 452–57; Jennifer Mason McAward, "Defining the Badges and Incidents of Slavery," *University of Pennsylvania Journal of Constitutional Law* 14, no. 3 (February 2012): 582–90; George Rutherglen, "The Improbable History of Section 1981: Clio Still Bemused and Confused," *Supreme Court Review* 2003 (2003): 322–30; Kares, "Unlucky Thirteenth," 375–78; Douglas L. Corbet, "Liberating the Thirteenth Amendment," *Harvard Civil Rights–Civil Liberties Law Review* 30, no. 1 (Winter 1995): 1–56; Robert D. Goldstein, "*Blyew*: Variations on a Jurisdictional Theme," *Stanford Law Review* 41, no. 3 (February 1989): 469–566; Jones, "An Argument for Federal Protection Against Racially Motivated Crimes," 707–10, 720–28; see also Burnham, *By Hands Known*, 165–98. Michael Vorenberg also noted, "The Court's narrow reading of the Thirteenth Amendment was coupled with an evisceration of the Fourteenth Amendment." Vorenberg, *Final Freedom*, 241.

50. *Jones v. Alfred H. Mayer Co.*, 392 U.S. 409, 88 S. Ct. 2186, 20 L. Ed.2d 1189 (1968), 438–44; ibid., 444–48 (Douglas, J., dissenting); see George Rutherglen, "The Badges and Incidents of Slavery and the Power of Congress to Enforce the Thirteenth Amendment," in *The Promises of Liberty: The History and Contemporary Relevance of the Thirteenth Amendment*, ed. Alexander Tsesis (New York: Columbia University Press, 2010), 163–64; Larry J. Pittman, "The Thirteenth Amendment and Equal Protection: A Structural Interpretation to 'Free' the Amendment," *William and Mary Journal of Race, Gender, and Social Justice* 27, no. 2 (Winter 2021): 461–76; Pope, "Section 1 of the Thirteenth Amendment and the Badges and Incidents of Slavery," 457–63; McAward, "Defining the Badges and

Incidents of Slavery," 592–621; Kares, "Unlucky Thirteenth," 378–79; Jones, "An Argument for Federal Protection Against Racially Motivated Crimes," 728–36; Arthur Kinoy, "*Jones v. Alfred H. Mayer Co.*: A Historic Step Forward," *Vanderbilt Law Review* 22, no. 3 (April 1969): 475–83; see also Dawinder S. Sidhu, "Threshold Liberty," *Cardozo Law Review* 37, no. 2 (December 2015): 508–21.

51. An Act to Prescribe Penalties for Certain Acts of Violence or Intimidation, and for Other Purposes, Public Law 90-84, 82 Stat. 73 (1969) (codified as amended 18 U.S.C. §245); see Matthew Trout, "Federalizing Hate: Constitutional and Practical Limitations to the Matthew Shepard and James Byrd Jr. Hate Crimes Prevention Act of 2009," *American Criminal Law Review* 52, no. 2 (Winter 2015): 136–37.

52. See 18 U.S.C. § 245(b).

53. See *United States v. Allen*, 341 F. 3d 870, 883–85 (9th Cir. 2003), *cert.* denied, *Flom v. United States*, 541 U.S. 975, 124 S. Ct. 1876, 158 L. Ed. 2d 471 (2004); *United States v. Nelson*, 277 F. 3d, 175–99; *United States v. Bledsoe*, 728 F. 2d 1094, 1096–98 (8th Cir. 1983), *cert.* denied, *Bledsoe v. United States*, 469 U.S. 838, 105 S. Ct. 136, 83 L. Ed. 2d 76 (1984).

54. See Aaronson, *From Slave Abuse to Hate Crime*, 165–83; Browne, *Race, Law, and American Society*, 72–73; Hall, "Ten Years Fighting Hate," 85–89; Jennifer Mason McAward, "The Thirteenth Amendment, Human Trafficking, and Hate Crimes," *Seattle University Law Review* 39, no. 3 (Spring 2016): 834–39; Meredith Boram, "The Matthew Shepard and James Byrd Jr. Hate Crimes Prevention Act: A Criminal Law Perspective," *University of Baltimore Law Review* 45, no. 2 (Spring 2016): 343–46.

55. See Matthew Shepard and James Byrd Jr. Hate Crimes Prevention Act, Public Law 111-84, 123 Stat. 2190 (2009), div. E., § 4702 (codified as amended 18 U.S.C. §249(a)); Hall, "Ten Years Fighting Hate," 79–92.

56. See *United States v. Hatch*, 722 F. 3d, 1200.

57. See Matthew Shepard and James Byrd Jr. Hate Crimes Prevention Act, Public Law 111-84, 123 Stat. 2190 (2009), div. E., § 4702 (7).

58. See, e.g., *United States v. Diggins*, 36 F. 4th 302, 307–17 (1st Cir.), *cert.* denied, —- U.S. —-, 143 S. Ct. 383 (2022); *United States v. Roof*, 10 F. 4th 314, 390–95 (4th Cir. 2021), *cert.* denied, —- U.S. —-, 143 S. Ct. 303 (2022); *United States v. Metcalf*, 881 F. 3d 641, 644–46 (8th Cir.), *cert.* denied, —- U.S. —-, 139 S. Ct. 412 (2018); *United States v. Cannon*, 750 F. 3d 492, 497–505 (5th Cir.), *cert.* denied, 574 U.S. 1029, 135 S. Ct. 709, 190 L. Ed. 2d 445 (2014); *United States v. Hatch*, 722 F. 3d, 1200–1206; *United States v. Maybee*, 687 F. 3d 1026, 1030–31 (8th Cir.), *cert.* denied, 568 U.S. 991, 133 S. Ct. 566, 184 L. Ed. 2d 362 (2012); *United States v. Bowers*, 495 F. Supp. 3d 362, 364–70 (W.D. Pa. 2020); *United States v. Henry*, 60 F. Supp. 3d 1126, 1127–32 (D. Id. 2014); Hall, "Ten Years Fighting Hate," 92–97.

59. See *United States v. Hatch*, 722 F. 3d, 1206; see also *United States v. Cannon*, 750 F. 3d, 502; (quoting *United States v. Hatch*, 722 F. 3d, 1206); Joseph W. Mark, "*United States v. Hatch*: The Significance of the Thirteenth Amendment in Contemporary American Jurisprudence," *Denver University Law Review* 91, no. 3 (2014): 693–713.

60. McAward, "Defining the Badges and Incidents of Slavery," 575; see George M. Stroud, *A Sketch of the Laws Relating to Slavery in the Several States of the United States of America* (2nd ed., 1856; repr., New York: Negro Universities Press, 1968), 9–43; Rutherglen, "Badges and Incidents of Slavery," 164–65; McAward, "Defining the Badges and Incidents of Slavery," 570–75.

61. McAward, "Defining the Badges and Incidents of Slavery," 605n235 (citing Jennifer Mason McAward, "The Scope of Congress's Thirteenth Amendment Enforcement Power after *City of Boerne v. Flores*," *Washington University Law Review* 88, no. 1 (2010): 130–46). McAward proposes that the Supreme Court overrule *Jones*, but she rejects the first approach rejecting the badges and incidents doctrine, which she attributes to David Currie. See McAward, "Defining the Badges and Incidents of Slavery," 564 (citing David P. Currie, *The Constitution in the Supreme Court: The Frist Hundred Years 1789-1888* (Chicago: University of Chicago Press, 1985), 400–401); see also David R. Upham, "The Understanding of 'Neither Slavery nor Involuntary Servitude Shall Exist' before the Thirteenth Amendment," *Georgetown Journal of Law and Public Policy* 15, no. 1 (Winter 2017): 169–71; David P. Currie, "The Reconstruction Congress," *University of Chicago Law Review* 75, no. 1 (Winter 2008): 394–99; David P. Currie, "The Civil War Congress," *University of Chicago Law Review* 73, no. 4 (Fall 2006): 1175–76.

62. See McAward, "Defining the Badges and Incidents of Slavery," 575; see generally Rutherglen, "Badges and Incidents of Slavery," 165–66; McAward, "Defining the Badges and Incidents of Slavery," 575–82.

63. See Nicholas Serafin, "Redefining the Badges of Slavery," *University of Richmond Law Review* 56, no. 4 (Spring 2022): 1295–1309.

64. See McAward, "Defining the Badges and Incidents of Slavery," 628. She also asserted this definition: "public or widespread private conduct that targets a group on the basis of race or previous condition of servitude, that mimics the law of slavery, and that poses a substantial risk that the members of the targeted population will be returned to de facto slavery or otherwise denied the ability to participate in the basic transactions of civil society." Ibid., 606.

65. See *United States v. Cannon*, 750 F. 3d, 500–506; ibid., 509–14 (Elrod, J., specially concurring); *United States v. Hatch*, 722 F. 3d, 1201–5; Hall, "Ten Years Fighting Hate," 92–97; McAward, "Thirteenth Amendment, Human Trafficking, and Hate Crimes," 829–45; Sidhu, "Threshold Liberty," 521–32; Mark, "*United States v. Hatch*," 705–7, 711–13; McAward, "Defining the Badges and Incidents of Slavery," 621–29; Jennifer Mason McAward, "*McCulloch* and the Thirteenth Amendment," *Columbia Law Review* 112, no. 7 (November 2012): 1784–1810 (citing McAward, "Scope of Congress's Thirteenth Amendment Enforcement Power," 81, 115–16).

66. *City of Boerne v. Flores*, 521 U.S. 507, 117 S. Ct. 2157, 138 L. Ed. 2d 624 (1997); see *Shelby County v. Holder*, 570 U.S. 529, 133 S. Ct. 2612, 186 L. Ed. 2d 651 (2013) (invalidating the Voting Rights Act's section 5 pre-clearance requirement). See McAward, "Defining the Badges and Incidents of Slavery," 564n15, 565–66, 568n35, 606, 610, 624; McAward, "Scope of Congress's Thirteenth Amendment Enforcement Power," 145–46; see also Michael W. McConnell, "Institutions and Interpretation: A Critique of *City of Boerne v. Flores*," *Harvard Law Review* 111, no. 1 (November 1997): 153–96.

67. See Scott, "Segregation," 427; *Civil Rights Cases*, 109 U.S., 24; see also, e.g., discussing Bradley's evolving views, Barnett and Bernick, *Original Meaning of the Fourteenth Amendment*, xiii–xviii, 171–82, 348–50; Brandwein, *Rethinking the Judicial Settlement of Reconstruction*, 103–4; John Anthony Scott, "Justice Bradley's Evolving Concept of the Fourteenth Amendment from the Slaughterhouse Cases to the Civil Rights Cases," *Rutgers Law Review* 25, no. 4 (Summer 1971): 552–69.

68. See *Civil Rights Cases*, 109 U.S., 34 (Harlan, J., dissenting) ("My brethren admit that [the Amendment] established and decreed universal *civil freedom* throughout the United States. But did the freedom thus established involve nothing more than exemption from actual slavery? Was nothing more intended than to forbid one man from owning another as property?"); see also Perrone, *Nothing More Than Freedom*, 158–74. For discussions of sales law and enslavement, see Andrew Fede, "Legal Protection for Slave Buyers in the U.S. South: A Caveat Concerning *Caveat Emptor*," *American Journal of Legal History* 31, no. 4 (October 1987): 322–58; Judith K. Schafer, "'Guaranteed Against the Vices and Maladies Prescribed by Law': Consumer Protection, the Law of Slave States, and the Supreme Court in Antebellum Louisiana," *American Journal of Legal History* 31, no. 4 (October 1987): 306–21.

69. See Serafin, "Redefining the Badges of Slavery," 1331, 1335.

70. See Kares, "Unlucky Thirteenth," 372; see also Amir Paz-Fuchs, "Badges of Modern Slavery," *Modern Law Review* 79, no. 5 (September 2016): 757–85. This response could be grounded in the Thirteenth and Fourteenth Amendments' different texts and historical contexts. See, e.g., *United States v. Diggins*, 36 F. 4th, 312–17; Michael A. Lawrence, "Falling Short of the Promise of the Thirteenth Amendment: Time for a Change," *ConLawNOW* 12, no. 2 (2021): 143–55; George Rutherglen, "State Action, Private Action, and the Thirteenth Amendment," *Virginia Law Review* 94, no. 6 (October 2008): 1367–1406; Alexander Tsesis, "Furthering American Freedom: Civil Rights and the Thirteenth Amendment," *Boston College Law Review* 45, no. 2 (March 2004): 361–68.

71. See William M. Carter Jr., "Race, Rights, and the Thirteenth Amendment: Defining the Badges and Incidents of Slavery," *UC Davis Law Review* 40, no. 4 (April 2007): 1367–68; see generally Jamal Greene, "Thirteenth Amendment Optimism," *Columbia Law Review* 112, no. 7 (November 2012): 1765 (expressing concerns about the consequences of what he calls Thirteenth Amendment optimism, but stating that the amendment "suggests an affirmative right on the part of African-Americans, at a minimum, to be free from the race-based intimidation characteristic of the antebellum south, even if that intimidation is accomplished (as it often was then) through speech").

72. The other elements are the slave's "natal alienation," which is defined as the absence of "all 'rights' or claims of birth," and the slave's dishonored condition. See Orlando Patterson, *Slavery and Social Death: A Comparative Study* (Cambridge, Mass.: Harvard University Press, 1982), 1–14, 17–101; see also Orlando Patterson, *Freedom: Freedom in the Making of Western Culture* (New York: Basic Books, 1991), 347–62; David Brion Davis, *Inhuman Bondage: The Rise and Fall of Slavery in the New World* (New York: Oxford University Press, 2006), 27–47; M. L. Bush, *Servitude in Modern Times* (Cambridge: Polity, 2000), 12–17; Moses I. Finley, *Ancient Slavery and Modern Ideology*, expanded ed., ed. Brent D. Shaw (Princeton, N.J.: Markus Wiener, 1998), 145; Robin Blackburn, "Slave Exploitation and the Elementary Structures of Enslavement," in *Serfdom and Slavery: Studies in Legal Bondage*, ed. M. L. Bush (New York: Longman, 1996), 158–80; Claude Meillassoux, *The Anthropology of Slavery: The Womb of Iron and Gold*, trans. Alide Dasnois (Chicago: University of Chicago Press, 1991), 9–12, 33–40; 99–175; M. I. Finley, "Slavery," in *International Encyclopedia of the Social Sciences*, ed. David L. Stills (New York: Macmillan, 1968), 14:307–9. For a critique of Patterson's approach, see Vincent Brown, "Social Death and Political Life in the Study of Slavery," *American Historical Review* 114, no. 5

(December 2009): 1231–49; see also Daragh Grant, "'Civilizing' the Colonial Subject: The Co-evolution of State and Slavery in South Carolina, 1670-1739," *Comparative Studies in Society and History* 57, no. 3 (July 2015): 608n16 (suggesting use of the term "civic death" to distinguish the slaves' legal status from their social status in practice).

73. See Barbara Perry, *In the Name of Hate: Understanding Hate Crimes* (New York: Routledge, 2001), 3 (quoted in Serafin, "Redefining the Badges of Slavery," 1331).

74. See ibid., 5.

75. See ibid., 10.

76. See Serafin, "Redefining the Badges of Slavery," 1331 (quoting Aaronson, *From Slave Abuse to Hate Crime*, 97).

77. See generally Eric Foner, *The Second Founding: How the Civil War and Reconstruction Remade the Constitution* (New York: Norton, 2019), 8–17; Laura F. Edwards, *A Legal History of the Civil War and Reconstruction: A Nation of Rights* (New York: Cambridge University Press, 2015), 153–56, 166–67; Aaronson, *From Slave Abuse to Hate Crime*, 90–98; John Hope Franklin and Alfred A. Moss Jr., *From Slavery to Freedom: A History of Negro Americans*, 6th ed. (New York: McGraw Hill, 1988), 201–38; David Brown, "A Vagabond's Tale: Poor Whites, Herrenvolk Democracy, and the Value of Whiteness in the Late Antebellum South," *Journal of Southern History* 76, no. 4 (November 2013): 799–840; Mark Grimsley, "Wars for the American South: The First and Second Reconstructions Considered as Insurgencies," *Civil War History* 58, no. 1 (March 2012): 6–36.

78. See Jeff Strickland, "The Civil Rights Act of 1866 in South Carolina," in Samito, *Greatest and the Grandest Act*, 137–62.

79. See *United States v. Cannon*, 750 F. 3d, 502; see also Jones, "An Argument for Federal Protection Against Racially Motivated Crimes," 734–35.

80. See Daniel Farbman, "Redemption Localism," *North Carolina Law Review* 100, no. 5 (June 2022): 1537 (quoting Thaddeus Stevens, "Reconstruction: Hon. Thaddeus Stevens on the Great Topic of the Hour, an Address Delivered to the Citizens of Lancaster, Sept. 6, 1865," *New York Times*, September 10, 1865, 2); Serafin, "Redefining the Badges of Slavery," 1330–37.

81. See Du Bois, *Black Reconstruction*, 189.

82. See Foner, *Second Founding*, 129.

83. See Scott, "Segregation," 427; see generally Perrone, *Nothing More Than Freedom*, 5–8.

84. See generally, e.g., Kathleen M. Brown, *Undoing Slavery: Bodies, Race, and Rights in the Age of Abolition* (Philadelphia: University of Pennsylvania Press, 2023); Perrone, *Nothing More Than Freedom*, 198–202.

85. See generally Perrone, *Nothing More Than Freedom*, 280–84; Allen C. Guelzo, *Reconstruction: A Concise History* (New York: Oxford University Press, 2018), 115–30; Foner, *Second Founding*, 209–16; Farbman, "Redemption Localism," 1538–51; Cynthia Nicoletti, "William Trescot, Pardon Broker," *Journal of the Civil War Era* 11, no. 4 (December 2021): 478–506; Lisset Marie Pino and John Fabian Witt, "The Fourteenth Amendment as an Ending: Constitutional Beginnings and the Demise of the War Power," *Journal of the Civil War Era* 10, no. 1 (March 2020): 5–28; Cody Marrs, "Three Theses on Reconstruction," *American Literary History* 30, no. 3 (Fall 2018): 409–14; Daniel Farbman, "Reconstructing Local Government," *Vanderbilt Law Review* 70, no. 2 (March 2017): 435–82.

86. See James Dobbins, Michele A. Poole, Austin Long, and Benjamin Runkle, *After the War: Nation-Building from FDR to George W. Bush* (Santa Monica, Calif.: RAND Corporation, 2008), 11–35; Gunter Bischof, "The Post–World War II Allied Occupation of Austria: What Can We Learn about It for Iraq in Successful Nation Building?," *Journal of Austrian-American History* 4 (2020): 60–72.

87. See, e.g., Michael A. Lawrence, "The Thirteenth Amendment as Basis for Racial Truth and Reconciliation," *Arizona Law Review* 62, no. 3 (2020): 637–82; Michael A. Lawrence, "Racial Justice Demands Truth and Reconciliation," *University of Pittsburgh Law Review* 80, no. 1 (Fall 2018): 69–136.

88. See *Georgia Code Annotated*, secs. 17-4-60 and -61; *Graham v. State*, 143 Ga. 440, 85 S.E. 328 (1915); Marty Johnson, "Kemp Signs Bill Repealing Citizen's Arrest Law after Ahmaud Arbery Shooting," *The Hill*, May 10, 2021, https://thehill.com/homenews/state-watch/552737-kemp-signs-bill-repealing-citizens-arrest-law-after-ahmaud-arbery/; Jeff Amy, "Gov. Kemp Signs Bill Repealing Georgia's 1863 Citizen's Arrest Law," *News4Jax*, May 10, 2021, https://www.news4jax.com/news/georgia/2021/05/10/gov-kemp-signs-bill-repealing-georgias-1863-citizens-arrest-law/; see also Frances Robles, "The Citizen's Arrest Law Cited in Arbery's Killing Dates Back to the Civil War," *New York Times*, May 13, 2020, https://www.nytimes.com/article/ahmaud-arbery-citizen-arrest-law-georgia.html.

89. See Aaronson, *From Slave Abuse to Hate Crime*, 198–200 (suggesting that hate crime laws be combined with changes in the "structural social conditions" out of which these crimes occur).

90. See Foner, *Second Founding*, xx; see also Lawrence, "Falling Short of the Promise of the Thirteenth Amendment," 146–47. The post–Civil War revival of the separate and unequal criminalization of free Black conduct was another persistent badge of slavery. Although the positive law could no longer explicitly impose crimes and punishments based on perceptions of race, the same effect was achieved under ostensibly race-neutral laws, including those prohibiting vagrancy and insolence, which were disproportionally enforced against Blacks. See, e.g., Clint Smith, *How the Word Is Passed: A Reckoning with the History of Slavery Across America* (New York: Little, Brown, 2021), 87; Daniel Thoennessen, "'An Act Authorizing Sterilization of Persons Convicted of Murder, Rape, Chicken Stealing . . .': Southern Chicken Theft Laws as an Expression of Racialised Political Violence," in *Food for Thought: Nourishment, Culture, Meaning*, ed. Simona Stano and Amy Bently (Cham: Springer, 2022), 91–100; see also Dennis Childs, *Slaves of the State: Black Incarceration from the Chain Gang to the Penitentiary* (Minneapolis: University of Minnesota Press, 2015); Michelle Alexander, *The New Jim Crow: Mass Incarceration in an Age of Colorblindness* (New York: New Press, 2010); Douglas A. Blackmon, *Slavery by Another Name: The Re-enslavement of Black Americans from the Civil War to World War II* (New York: Anchor Books, 2008); David M. Oshinsky, *"Worse Than Slavery": Parchman Farm and the Ordeal of Jim Crow Justice* (New York: Free Press, 1996).

INDEX

abolitionists, 82, 108–10, 184–85
Abrahams, Nancy, 151–52
Abruzzo, Margaret, 17
Adams, Elizabeth F., 153
adultery, 127–28
affrays, 3, 28, 32–33, 118, 121, 211n69
Alabama Code, 169, 173
ameliorationists, 85, 104, 105, 110–12
Angley, Wilson, 131
applied legal history, 10
Arbery, Ahmaud, 1–3, 185, 188n4, 188nn11–13, 190n18, 284n88
Archer, Tom, 4, 95–96, 98–99, 112
Ashworth, Sam, 266n12
assault, battery and, 222n85, 227n35
assembly, freedom of, 154
Ayers, Edward, 4, 20

badges and incidents of slavery, 7, 9–10, 176, 181–83, 185, 281n61, 281n64
Bailey, John L., 64, 119
Bailey, Samuel, 45
Baker, Anthony V., 74
Baker, D. B., 133
Barbados: Carolinian migrants from, 86–87; slave codes of, 40, 88, 215n3
Barnhart, John, 20
Bartsch-Zimmer, Shadi, 16
Barzun, Charles L., 218n23
battery, assault and, 222n85, 227n35
Battle, James S., 75
Battle, William H., 4, 121, 124, 127–28, 137
Baxter, Richard, 75
Bell, Derrick, 138
Benjamin, Walter, 16, 197n78
Bennett, John H., 136
Berlin, Ira, 154, 157, 176
Birkbeck, Morris, 20–21
"Black, running/living/driving while," 188nn11–13, 203n118
Black Codes, 6, 141–44, 179, 184, 278n40

Black Laws (Ill.), 20, 21, 24, 25, 37–38
Blackstone, William, 50, 102, 107, 198n90
Blackwell, James, 228n62
Bond, Benjamin, 23
Booth, William, 67
Bouvier, John, 99
Bowser, Judah, 99–100
Bradley, Joseph, 9, 181, 183
Brady, Patrick, 81
Brander, Athele, 152
Brazil, 87, 94
Brockenbrough, William, 68–70, 228n64
Brockett, Robert, Sr., 66
Brooks, Thomas, 154
Brophy, Alfred, 10, 80
Brown, Albert, 148
Brown, Henry Billings, 176
Brown, John L., 108–9
Brown v. Board of Education (1954), 276n30
Brown v. Mississippi, 129
Browne, Thomas C., 37
Bryan, James W., 135–36
Bryan, William, 10, 184
Bryant, James, 136
Burton, Hutchins G., 44
Byrd, James, Jr., 9–10, 181, 195n66

Calhoun, John C., 65, 110
Campbell, Decator, 7–8, 10, 19, 24–26, 38, 175
Campbell v. The People, 7–8, 10–11, 25, 137, 175; Caton on, 213n98; evaluation of, 34–38; participants in, 24–28; Singer on, 213n97; trials of, 28–34
Carburry, Joseph, 80, 231n104
Caton, John Dean, 8, 28, 29, 31–37 passim, 213n98
certiorari, writ of, 171, 271n84
Charles, Maurice, 144
Chatham, Thomas, 77

286 INDEX

citizen arrest law, 2–3, 171, 190n18, 271n86, 284n88
City of Boerne v. Flores, 183
Civil Rights Act (1866), 10, 179–80, 181, 183, 184
Civil Rights Act (1875), 180–81
Civil Rights Act (1968), 181
Clark, Richard H., 169
clergy, benefit of, 42, 46
Cobb, Howell, 169
Cobb, Thomas R. R., 3, 13, 60, 82, 110, 169–72
Commonwealth v. Howard (Va.), 155–56
Commonwealth v. Lee (Ky.), 60
Commonwealth v. Turner (Va.), 68, 70, 102
contextualization, 15, 201n102, 201n107, 202n111
Cooke, John R., 45
Cooper-Jones, Wanda, 2
Copeland, James W., 83
Copeland, Martha, 134
Cornerstone Speech, 178, 275n30
Coventry Act (1670), 102
Crank, Thomas, 94–95
Crowder, Mrs. Jacob, 152
Curry, Benjamin, 136

Dade, William, 68–71
Dale, Elizabeth, 6–7, 88, 202n113
Dangerfield, David, 94
Daniel, John R. J., 76
Daniel, Joseph J., 47, 48, 50–54; on Hale trial, 56; on Mann trial, 64
Davis, John, 45
Davis, Lawrence, 124–25
Degler, Carl, 79, 87
"degraded caste," free Blacks as, 192n42; Kent on, 174–75; Nash on, 120; O'Neall on, 97–98, 108, 112; Pearson on, 122; Savery on, 24
Dendy, Charles, 102–3
DeSaussure, Wilmot G., 105
Dew, Thomas R., 110
Dexter, Darel, 22
Dick, John M., 72, 77–79, 128
Dickenson, N. B., 156
discontinuity thesis, 183

discrimination, de jure, 112–18 passim, 137, 165, 177, 184, 193n45. *See also* unequal protection rule
Dixon, Wright T., Jr., 83
Donnell, John Robert, 76
Douglass, Bob, 3–5, 121
Drew, William, 48–50, 65
Dryden, John, 49
Du Bois, W. E. B., 184–85
Dubber, Markus Dirk, 6, 158
Dunning, William A., 177, 179, 274n21

Earle, Baylis J., 95, 96
East, Edward, 50, 54
Eaves, N. R., 96
education, female, 85
Edwards, Laura, 43, 139–40
Elrod, Jennifer Walker, 183
Ely, Melvin P., 117, 138, 176
emancipation. *See* Thirteenth Amendment
Engerman, Stanley, 215n3
enslaved persons: enslaver privileges of, 203n121; homicide of, 42, 49, 109; manumission of, 88; marriage among, 47–48; masters' relations with, 4, 65–66, 73, 76; Native American, 21, 89; nonfatal violence to, 55–59, 65–66, 101–2; runaway, 22, 42, 109; violence to whites by, 74–76, 172
enslavement, 108; amelioration of, 85, 104, 105, 110–12; antebellum, 3–14, 110, 141; "benefits" of, 110; common law of, 40–43, 54; definition of, 182; elements of, 184, 282n72; Gaston on, 80–81; language of, 17–18; law box of, 6, 11–12; "voluntary," 21, 116–17, 144, 149, 262n57
equal protection rule, 8, 108. *See also* unequal protection rule
Escott, Paul D., 178
Eslinger, Ellen, 145
Etcheson, Nicole, 20
Ex parte Boylston, 5–6

Fells, Esther, 152
Fenn, Robert, 67
Ferris, Mary Ann, 152

Finkelman, Paul, 13, 20, 146, 170, 178
Fischer, Roger A., 177
Fisher, Richard, 126–29, 251n86
Fitzhugh, George, 110
Flanigan, Daniel, 133, 146
Floyd, George, 3
Foner, Eric, 178, 193n46
Foster, Michael, 50
Fourteenth Amendment, 108, 183, 194n53, 277n40
Franklin, John Hope, 4; on free Blacks, 44, 113, 114, 116–17; on mob violence, 123; on Pearson, 129
Frazier, David, 156
Fredrickson, George M., 177
free Blacks, 94–104, 246n7; associations of, 94; demographics of, 86, 93–94, 114, 142, 145; enslavement of, 262n57; as enslavers, 93; Georgia Code on, 170, 172; gun control laws for, 119–20, 143, 146; Louisiana Code and, 143–44; lynchings of, 2, 9, 35, 180; migrant, 86–87, 91–92, 94; natural rights of, 97, 125; as slave owners, 117; stereotypes of, 117–18; testimony of, 90, 115; unequal protection for, 84–85, 94–106; violence against whites by, 89, 102, 124–29; violence by whites against, 96–102, 120–23, 138–40, 143, 172–73; Virginia Codes and, 145; voting rights of, 45, 53, 81, 88, 115, 146. *See also* "degraded caste"
French slave codes, 142
Freyfoyle, Christian, 151
Friedman, Lawrence M., 11, 42
Fuentes, Jose, 106–7
Fulcher, Mary, 151

gambling laws, 91, 116
Gaston, William J., 6, 45, 174; career of, 80; on "mere words" rule, 75; Pearson and, 113–14; on racial castes, 117; on slavery, 80–81; on unequal protection rule, 39, 62–63, 74–83, 118–19; on voting rights, 81
Georgia Code, 6, 13–14, 141, 165–73
Gerbner, Katherine, 216n3
Gertz, Elmer, 20

Gillmer, Jason A., 266n12
Glynn, Anthony G., 46
Gobu v. Gobu, 60
Goings, Jane, 154
Goode, Trueman, 55
Goodell, William, 82
Gordon, Robert, 8–9, 11, 12
Graham, William A., 77
Greene, Sally, 64
Grimké, John Fauchereaud, 98–99
Gross, Ariela, 87
gun control laws, 119–20, 143, 146, 260n43

Hadden, Sally, 63, 88, 227n43
Haithcock, Williamson, 133
Haitian Revolution, 142
Hale, Matthew, 56–59
Hall, Jerome, 202n112
Hall, John, 43, 55, 56, 58
Hamilton, Letty, 151–52
Hammond, James Henry, 110
Hammond, John Craig, 20
Harden, Charles, 10, 95–96, 112, 184, 196n74
Harlan, John Marshall, 175–76
Harper, William, 87, 98, 104, 110
Harris, Edward, 43
Harris, Robert L., 94
Hart, Edward H., 124
Hartog, Hendrik, 198n88
Hassell, Elijah, 126
Hatcher, Jordan, 261n51
hate crimes: definition of, 183; legislation on, 3, 10, 176, 179–81, 190n18, 284n89; punishment for, 188nn11–13; Thirteenth Amendment and, 187n3, 273n13
Haywood, John, 139
Henderson, Leonard, 43, 46, 70
Henry, Howell Meadoes, 85
Higginbotham, A. Leon, 141, 147
Hill, Polly, 152
Hill, William, 99, 100
Hindus, Michael, 130
Hodges v. United States, 180
Hogg, Gavin, 55
Hohfeld, Wesley N., 17, 41
Holmes, George Frederick, 110

Holmes, Owen, 133
homicide: classes of, 31, 41; common law of, 40–43, 54; enslavers' liability in, 62, 71–72; manslaughter versus, 76–78, 95, 107, 127; mitigation of, 12, 75, 76, 175
housing discrimination, 181
Howard v. Howard, 132
Huebner, Timothy, 72, 178
Hughes, Henry, 110
Hughes, Jack, 77
Hunt, Louis, 55
hustings court, 261n51

Illinois, 19–24; Black Laws of, 20, 21, 24, 25, 37–38, 116, 175; constitutions of, 23, 37
Indiana, 20
insolence, 50–55, 98, 142–45, 158, 175; definitions of, 5, 85; Drew on, 50; free Blacks and, 81, 84, 106, 112, 172–73; Georgia Code on, 170–71; Louisiana Code on, 143–44; O'Neall on, 191n36; punishment of, 147, 149–50; Richmond ordinances against, 153; Tackett trial and, 48; J. L. Taylor on, 51; Virginia Codes on, 147–50
instrumentalist theories, 14
interdisciplinary legal history, 15–16, 201n102, 202n112
Irwin, David, 169

Jack, Jedediah, 27–28, 30–31, 35, 37–38
Jackson, Barbara, 82
Jamaica, 86, 87
James, Clinton, 157–58
Jarrot v. Jarrot, 36, 79
Jefferson-Jones, Jamila, 17
Jenkins, William A., 124
Jennison, Watson, 172
Jim Crow laws, 6, 129, 177; de jure discrimination and, 193n45; Litwack on, 178, 275n30; Milewski on, 12; origins of, 183, 184
Johnson, Andrew, 131
Johnson, David, 98, 99, 104
Johnson, Mark, 106
Johnson, Michael, 85

Jones, Allen, 123
Jones, Martha, 178
Jones v. Alred H. Mayer Co., 181, 183
Jordan, Ervin, 150
Jowers, Atlas, 3–5, 10, 121, 184, 196n74

Kemp, Brian, 190n18, 284n88
Kent, James, 174–75

Lacey, Nicola, 202n112
Lane, Ephraim, 120
Larson, Edward J., 178
law box, 6, 11–12
"law office history," 202n113
Lea v. Brown, 132
Lebsock, Suzanne, 152
legal consciousness, 12; Nicoletti on, 13; J. L. Taylor on, 52
legal culture, 12
Leigh, Benjamin Watkins, 149
Lemoine, Charles, 143
Lewis, Mary, 153
Linsey, Augustin, 231n104
literacy prohibition, 92
Litwack, Leon, 178, 275n30
Lockwood, Samuel D., 37
Logan, John A., 23–27 passim
longue durée, 15, 200n101
Louisiana: demographics of, 142; history of, 142–43
Louisiana Code, 6, 107, 141–45, 158
Lovejoy, Owen, 36
Luhmann, Niklas, 199n96
Lumpkin, Joseph Henry, 39–40, 82, 170, 171
lynchings, 2, 9, 35, 180, 195n61, 278n44

Maner, Jonathan, 100–101
Manly, Charles, 46
Manly, Matthias Evans, 128–29
Mann, John, 64, 66, 68, 124, 228n64
Mansfield, Lord, 36
manslaughter, 31, 41; homicide versus, 76–78, 95, 107, 127; penalties for, 42; slave, 49
Manuel, William, 117–18
manumission, 100; approval of, 91; deed of, 96, 100, 231n104; implied, 98

marriage, 47; among enslaved persons, 47–48, 132; interracial, 45, 87, 88, 115, 116
Marrs, Cody, 131
Marshall, Frederick S., 46
Martin, François-Xavier, 80
Mason-Dixon line, 20
master-slave relations, 4, 65–66, 73, 76. *See also* enslaved persons
Masur, Kate, 23–24, 178
Maxfield, Mary, 153
May, George W., 25
mayhem, 102
Mayo, Joseph C., 148, 152, 154–56, 157–58
McAward, Jennifer Mason, 182–83, 281n61, 281n64
McCash, William, 172
McDaniel, W. Caleb, 108, 110
McMichael, Gregory, 1–2, 184, 185, 188n4, 188nn11–13
McMichael, Travis, 1–2, 184, 185, 188n4, 188nn11–13
McRae, Duncan Kirkland, 124
"mere words" rule, 41, 84, 151; Battle on, 4; Caton on, 31; Dixon on, 83; Drew on, 50; Gaston on, 75; O'Neall on, 98, 103, 106, 112; Preston on, 107, 122–23; J. L. Taylor on, 52
Merrick, Othello, 133–34
Merry, Sally Engle, 12
migrants, free Black, 86–87, 91–92, 94
Milewski, Melissa, 12, 197n84
Mills, Benjamin, 148
Mills, Gary B., 111
Milteer, Warren, 114–15, 117, 131, 246n7, 252n102
Mississippi Black Code, 179
mixed-race people. *See* mulattoes
Mohawk, Samuel, 35–36
Moore, Bartholomew Figures, 75, 76, 121–22
Moore v. Dempsey, 129
Mordecai, George Washington, 75, 76
Morgan, Edmund S., 177
Morris, Thomas D., 228n64
mulattoes, 23, 45, 195n68, 246n7; gun control laws for, 146; legal rights of, 105–6;
one-drop rule and, 87, 89, 170; in South Carolina, 87–92; unequal treatment of, 87–88, 94; in Virginia, 146–49; voting rights of, 115, 146
Muller, Eric, 63
murder. *See* homicide
Murray, William, 36

Nash, A. E. Keir, 7, 107–8, 129–30, 250n60
Nash, Frederick, 5, 119; *Caesar* case and, 132–33; *Jowers* case and, 121
Nat Turner insurrection (1831), 96, 146–47
Native Americans, 35, 146; enslaved, 21, 89, 277n41; gun control laws for, 146; mixed-race children of, 115; testimony of, 115
natural rights, 97, 125
Negro Law of South Carolina (O'Neall), 105–6, 111
Negro Seamen Act (1822), 92, 116
Newsom, Elijah, 119
Nicoletti, Cynthia, 13
Norman, Nehemiah, 126–29
Northwest Ordinance (1787), 21, 37
Novak, William, 154, 264n107
nullification debate, 104, 105, 131

Oakes, James, 178
O'Neall, John Belton, 4–6, 84–86; career of, 104–5; on insolence, 81, 191n36; on "mere words" rule, 98, 103, 106, 112; as moderate jurist, 104–11, 137; *Negro Law of South Carolina*, 105–6, 111; on nullification, 104, 105; on unequal protection rule, 84–85, 94–106, 110–12, 174; on white supremacy, 85, 113, 122–23
one-drop rule, 87, 89, 170
Oregon, 20
Orth, John, 56, 79–80

Page, O. J., 28, 34
Palmer, Vernon Valentine, 144
Panic of 1819, 150
Parker, Goodwin, 8, 10, 19, 24–25, 184; family of, 26; as white supremacist, 28–29

Parker, John F., 134–35
Parker, Kunal, 14
Parker, Richard E., 67–68
Parrish, William K., 26, 30
Patterson, Orlando, 184
Paxton, John: on Scott trial, 46; on Tackett trial, 47
Pearson, Richmond Mumford, 4–6; on extrajudicial violence, 123, 129; Gaston and, 113–14; on interracial violence, 39–40, 113–14, 120–29; on *Jowers* case, 174, 252n102; legacy of, 129–37; on "mere words" rule, 107, 122–23; on nullification, 131; on unequal protection rule, 79, 84, 113–14, 174, 175
Penningroth, Dylan C., 203n121
People v. Jeffries (Ill.), 213n97
Perry, Barbara, 184
Peters, Belvard J., 60–61
Phillips, Ulrich Bonnell, 130, 177, 179, 274n20
Plessy v. Ferguson, 175–76
Polgar, Paul, 178
police power, 158
Polk, James K., 65
Post, Elizabeth, 136
Pound, Roscoe, 63
Preston, Isaac, 106–7
privilege, definition of, 203n121
procedural versus substantive rules, 194n54
prohibition, writ of, 90
prostitution, 144

Ranney, Joseph, 84, 130, 192n38
rape: North Carolina law on, 54, 115; South Carolina law on, 91, 108; Texas law on, 161, 164
Rawls, John, 180
Read, William M., 148
Reconstruction: definition of, 193n46; W. Wilson on, 277n34
Reed, Thomas, 54
Religious Freedom Restoration Act, 183
Respublica v. Teischer, 67
Richmond ordinances, 6, 150–58
Roark, James, 85, 99

Robinson, Nicholas C., 133–34
Rohrs, Richard C., 117
Rothman, Joshua, 150, 151, 152, 153, 157
Rowlett, Frances Ann, 153
Ruffin, Thomas, 81, 83, 102, 227n43, 228n64; career of, 63–64; *Jowers* case and, 121; legacy of, 63; on master-slave relation, 65–66; on *State v. Mann*, 62–73
Ruffin, William, 47
Rugemer, Edward, 215n3
Rutherglen, George, 278n40

Sandberg, Russell, 9, 12
Sanders, Alexander, 108
sartorial laws, 92, 132
Saunders, Romulus, 124–25, 126, 127
Savery, Steven J., 24
Scates, Walter B., 28, 37
Schafer, Judith, 144
Schauinger, Herman, 81–82
Schiller, Reuel E., 130
Scott, John Anthony, 183
Scott, Mason, 43; prison escape by, 47; trial of, 45–46, 48
Scott v. Sandford (1856), 131, 279n45
Seabrook, Whitemarsh Benjamin, 93
Seawell, Harry: career of, 43–45; J. L. Taylor and, 49–55, 60, 61, 74; on white supremacists, 49–50
Second Amendment, 260n43
self-defense, 31, 41, 125, 147, 171
self-enslavement, 21, 116–17, 144, 149, 262n57
separate but equal doctrine, 175–76. *See also* unequal protection rule
sex workers, 144
sexual assault. *See* rape
Shepard, Matthew, 9–10, 181, 195n66
Siegel, Reva, 275n26
Singer, Richard, 213n97
slave rebellions, 92, 260n43; Stono, 89; Nat Turner, 96, 96
slavery. *See* enslavement
Small, Josiah, 64
socialism, 110
Somerset v. Stewart, 36

INDEX 291

South Carolina: demographics of, 86, 91, 93–94; slave codes of, 88, 105, 256n2
"Southern law," 190n20
Spanish slave codes, 142, 277n41
"special verdicts," 222n86
Spencer, Joseph, 24
State ex rel. McCready v. Hunt (S.C.), 104
State v. Armfield (N.C.), 59
State v. Asbury (Texas), 266n14
State v. Bennett (N.C.), 136
State v. Bill, a Slave (N.C.), 5
State v. Boon (N.C.), 55
State v. Caesar (N.C.), 125, 132–33, 139
State v. Cantey (S.C.), 87–88
State v. Cheatwood (S.C.), 267n38
State v. Davis (N.C.), 124–25, 129, 130, 131, 139
State v. Dick, a Slave (N.C.), 54
State v. Fisher (N.C.), 126–28
State v. Haithcock (N.C.), 133
State v. Hale (N.C.), 55–60, 62, 65, 79, 82–83, 101; *Mann* case and, 70, 73
State v. Hall (N.C.), 70
State v. Harden (S.C.), 4, 6, 14, 84–85, 94, 96; effect of, 140, 174, 196n74; *Hill* case and, 99–100; Mills on, 111; *Young* case and, 106
State v. Hill (S.C.), 99–100, 103; *Young* case and, 106
State v. Hoover (N.C.), 62, 71–74
State v. Jarrott (N.C.), 63, 77, 82, 137
State v. Jose Fuentes (La.), 106–7
State v. Jowers (N.C.), 3–4, 6, 14, 84, 196n74; Pearson on, 121, 125, 126, 129, 130, 140
State v. Lane (N.C.), 120
State v. Maner (S.C.), 100–101, 102, 104
State v. Mann (N.C.), 62–66, 102, 124, 134, 228n64; appeal of, 65; background of, 64, 66; evaluation of, 66–72, 77, 83; *Hale* case and, 70, 73
State v. Manuel (N.C.), 113, 117–18, 126
State v. Nathan (S.C.), 108
State v. Newsom (N.C.), 119
State v. Norman (N.C.), 126–29, 251n86
State v. Reed (N.C.), 54
State v. Tackett (N.C.), 3, 39, 40, 43–62; Gaston's extension of, 75–79; *Hale* case and, 70; *Mann* case and, 65–66, 71, 73, 78
State v. Will (N.C.), 63, 75–76, 81, 82, 122
State v. Young (S.C.), 106
states' rights, 65
Stephens, Alexander H., 178; Cornerstone Speech of, 178, 275n30
Stephens, Linton, 171
Stevens, Thaddeus, 184
Stewart, Potter, 181
Stono slave rebellion (1739), 89
Stowe, Harriet Beecher, 63, 110
Stowell, David O., 93
Strange, Robert, 133
Strickland, Jeff, 86, 93
Stroud, George, 75, 82
substantive versus procedural rules, 194n54
subversive legal history, 9
Swann, Thomas, 67

Tackett, William, 43, 46–51, 78
Tallmadge, James, 21
Tamanaha, Brian, 199n96, 202n112
Taney, Roger B., 74, 131, 202n113
Tate, Joseph, 151, 152
Taylor, Breonna, 3
Taylor, John Louis, 3, 6, 62, 80, 174; on common law, 99; on insolence, 51; on legal consciousness, 52; on "mere words" rule, 52; on nonfatal violence, 55–59; Seawell and, 43–55, 60, 61, 74; on unequal protection rule, 39, 40, 59–61, 97
Taylor, William, 67
temperance movement, 85, 105
Tennent v. Dendy, 102–3
Teubner, Gunther, 199n96
Texas Code, 141, 159–65, 172–73
Thirteenth Amendment, 9, 108, 179–83, 277n35; Harlan on, 282n68; hate crimes and, 187n3, 273n13
Thompson, Thomas, 5
Till, Emmett, 2–3, 180, 278n44
Tomlins, Christopher, 11–12, 15–16, 89, 197n78, 215n3

"totalized contingency," 11–12
Treat, Samuel H., 28, 212n72
Trotter, Thomas, 77
Troy, Alexander, 56
Trumbull, Lyman, 36–37, 215n120
Tucker, St. George, 198n90
Tucker, Thomas, 152
Turner, Nat, 96, 146–47
Turner, Richard, 68, 228n64
Tushnet, Mark V., 63, 64, 196n74, 228n64
Tyree, Lucy, 153

underground railroad, 157–58
unequal protection rule, 40, 59–61, 91, 110–12; civil rights laws and, 180; T. R. R. Cobb on, 170–71; de jure, 8, 112, 174, 184; expansion of, 62–63; Gaston on, 39, 62–63, 74–83, 118–19; Litwack on, 178; O'Neall on, 84–85, 94–106, 110–12; Pearson on, 79, 84, 113–14, 120–29; T. Ruffin on, 62–73, 81, 83; J. L. Taylor on, 39, 40, 59–61, 97. *See also* discrimination, de jure
Unger, Roberto, 199n96
United States v. Cruickshank (1875), 180, 279n46
Upshur, Abel P., 155–56

VanderVelde, Lea, 41
Vermont, 44
Vesey, Denmark, 92
Virginia Codes, 6, 117, 141, 144, 145–58
von Daacke, Kirt, 94
von Jhering, Rudolf, 199n96

Vorenberg, Michael, 279n49
voting rights, 45, 88, 115, 146; J. J. Daniel on, 53; Gaston on, 81; Pearson on, 131–32

Wade, Richard, 153, 156–57, 173, 177
Waldrep, Christopher, 137
Walker, David, 116
Wardlaw, David L., 5–6
Watson, Alan, 9
Westbrook, Ira, 135–36
White, Deborah Gray, 17
white privilege, 84, 112, 156, 175; racial categories and, 87–88
white supremacists, 17, 123, 137, 175, 185, 192n42; Democratic Party and, 178; Georgia Code and, 172; Harper on, 87–88; O'Neall on, 85, 113, 122–23; G. Parker as, 28–29; Seawell on, 49–50; J. L. Taylor on, 52
white trash, 87, 88, 178
Wigton, James, 35–36
Wikramanayake, Marina, 93–94
Williamson, Joel, 177
Wilson, Jesse, 45
Wilson, William C., 37
Wilson, Woodrow, 179, 277n34
Wood, Lisa Godbey, 2, 189nn12–13
Wood, Peter, 86
Woodward, C. Vann, 177, 178, 183

Young, Allen, 106
Young, Richard M., 37

Milton Keynes UK
Ingram Content Group UK Ltd.
UKHW041847230924
448765UK00006B/90

9 780820 366296